George Henry

When London burned

A story of restoration times and the great fire

George Henry

When London burned

A story of restoration times and the great fire

ISBN/EAN: 9783744749305

Printed in Europe, USA, Canada, Australia, Japan

Cover: Foto ©ninafisch / pixelio.de

More available books at **www.hansebooks.com**

WHEN LONDON BURNED

A STORY OF

RESTORATION TIMES AND THE GREAT FIRE

BY

G. A. HENTY

Author of "Beric the Briton", "By Pike and Dyke", "One of the 28th", "The Lion of St. Mark",
"In the Reign of Terror", "The Dash for Khartoum", &c.

WITH TWELVE PAGE ILLUSTRATIONS BY J. FINNEMORE

LONDON
BLACKIE & SON, LIMITED, 50 OLD BAILEY, E.C.
GLASGOW AND DUBLIN
1895

PREFACE.

We are accustomed to regard the Reign of Charles II. as one of the most inglorious periods of English History; but this was far from being the case. It is true that the extravagance and profligacy of the Court were carried to a point unknown before or since, forming,—by the indignation they excited among the people at large,—the main cause of the overthrow of the House of Stuart. But, on the other hand, the nation made extraordinary advances in commerce and wealth, while the valour of our sailors was as conspicuous under the Dukes of York and Albemarle, Prince Rupert and the Earl of Sandwich, as it had been under Blake himself, and their victories resulted in transferring the commercial as well as the naval supremacy of Holland to this country. In spite of the cruel blows inflicted on the well-being of the country, alike by the extravagance of the Court, the badness of the Government, the Great Plague, and the destruction of London by fire, an extraordinary extension of our trade occurred during the reign of Charles II. Such a period, therefore, although its brilliancy was marred by dark shadows, cannot be considered as an inglorious epoch. It was ennobled by the bravery of our sailors, by the fearlessness with which the coalition of France with Holland was faced, and by the spirit of enterprise with which our merchants and traders seized the opportunity, and, in spite of national misfortunes, raised England in the course of a few years to the rank of the greatest commercial power in the world.

G. A. HENTY.

CONTENTS.

Chap.		Page
I.	Fatherless,	11
II.	A Change for the Better,	34
III.	A Thief Somewhere,	51
IV.	Captured,	69
V.	Kidnapped,	87
VI.	A Narrow Escape,	106
VII.	Saved from a Villain,	124
VIII.	The Captain's Yarn,	141
IX.	The Fire in the Savoy,	161
X.	How John Wilkes fought the Dutch,	169
XI.	Prince Rupert,	179
XII.	New Friends,	196
XIII.	The Battle of Lowestoft,	213
XIV.	Honourable Scars,	230
XV.	The Plague,	248
XVI.	Father and Son,	266
XVII.	Smitten Down,	284
XVIII.	A Stroke of Good Fortune,	302
XIX.	Taking Possession,	319
XX.	The Fight off Dunkirk,	335
XXI.	London in Flames,	351
XXII.	After the Fire,	369

ILLUSTRATIONS.

	Page
"With great rapidity the flames spread from house to house,"............*Frontis.*	358
"Don't cry, lad; you will get on better without me,"	25
"This is my Prince of Scriveners, Mary,".......	35
"Robert Ashford, knife in hand, attacked John Wilkes with fury,".................	76
"Cyril sat up and drank off the contents of the pannikin,"	94
"For Heaven's sake, sir, do not cause trouble,"....	122
"Take her down quick, John, there are three others,".	166
"Cyril raised the King's hands to his lips,"......	185
"A Dutch man-of-war ran alongside and fired a broadside,"..................	230
"For the last time: Will you sign the deed?"....	274
"Welcome back to your own again, Sir Cyril!"....	322
"What news, James?" the king asked eagerly,.....	346

WHEN LONDON BURNED.

CHAPTER I.

FATHERLESS.

LAD stood looking out of the dormer window in a scantily furnished attic in the high-pitched roof of a house in Holborn, in September 1664. Numbers of persons were traversing the street below, many of them going out through the bars, fifty yards away, into the fields beyond, where some sports were being held that morning, while country people were coming in with their baskets from the villages of Highgate and Hampstead, Tyburn and Bayswater. But the lad noted nothing that was going on; his eyes were filled with tears, and his thoughts were in the little room behind him; for here, coffined in readiness for burial, lay the body of his father.

Sir Aubrey Shenstone had not been a good father in any sense of the word. He had not been harsh or cruel, but he had altogether neglected his son. Beyond the virtues of loyalty and courage, he possessed few others. He had fought, as a young man, for Charles, and even among the Cavaliers who rode behind Prince Rupert was noted for reckless bravery. When, on the fatal field of Worcester, the last hopes of the Royalists were crushed, he had effected his escape to France and taken up his abode at Dunkirk. His estates had been forfeited; and after spending the proceeds of his wife's jewels and those he had carried about with him in case fortune went against the cause for which he fought, he sank lower and lower, and had for years lived on the scanty pension allowed by Louis to the King and his adherents.

Sir Aubrey had been one of the wild, reckless spirits whose conduct did much towards setting the people of England against the cause of Charles. He gambled and drank, interlarded his conversation with oaths, and despised as well as hated the Puritans against whom he fought. Misfortune did not improve him; he still drank when he had money to do so, gambled for small sums in low taverns with men of his own kind, and quarrelled and fought on the smallest provocation. Had it not been for his son he would have taken service in the army of some foreign Power; but he could not take the child about with him, nor could he leave it behind.

Sir Aubrey was not altogether without good points. He would divide his last crown with a comrade poorer than himself. In the worst of times he was as cheerful as when money was plentiful, making a joke of his necessities and keeping a brave face to the world.

Wholly neglected by his father, who spent the greater portion of his time abroad, Cyril would have fared badly indeed had it not been for the kindness of Lady Parton, the wife of a Cavalier of very different type to Sir Aubrey. He had been an intimate friend of Lord Falkland, and, like that nobleman, had drawn his sword with the greatest reluctance, and only when he saw that Parliament was bent upon overthrowing the other two estates in the realm and constituting itself the sole authority in England. After the execution of Charles he had retired to France, and did not take part in the later risings, but lived a secluded life with his wife and children. The eldest of these was of the same age as Cyril; and as the latter's mother had been a neighbour of hers before marriage, Lady Parton promised her, on her death-bed, to look after the child, a promise that she faithfully kept.

Sir John Parton had always been adverse to the association of his boy with the son of Sir Aubrey Shenstone; but he had reluctantly yielded to his wife's wishes, and Cyril passed the greater portion of his time at their house, sharing the lessons Harry received from an English clergyman who had been expelled from his living by the fanatics of Parliament. He was a good and pious man, as well as an excellent scholar, and under his teaching, aided by the gentle precepts of Lady Parton, and the strict but kindly rule of her husband, Cyril received a training of a far better kind than he would ever have been likely to obtain had he been brought up in his father's house near Norfolk. Sir Aubrey exclaimed sometimes that the boy was growing up a little Puritan, and had he taken more interest in his welfare would undoubtedly have withdrawn him from the healthy influences that were benefiting him so greatly; but, with the usual acuteness of children, Cyril soon learnt that any allusion to his studies or his life at Sir John Parton's was disagreeable to his father, and therefore seldom spoke of them.

Sir Aubrey was never, even when under the influence of his potations, unkind to Cyril. The boy bore a strong likeness to his mother, whom his father had, in his rough way, really loved passionately. He seldom spoke even a harsh word to him, and although he occasionally expressed his disapproval of the teaching he was receiving, was at heart not sorry to see the boy growing up so different from himself; and Cyril, in spite of his father's faults, loved him. When Sir Aubrey came back with unsteady step, late at night, and threw himself on his pallet, Cyril would say to himself, "Poor father! How different he would have been had it not been for his misfortunes! He is to be pitied rather than blamed!" And so, as years went on, in spite of the difference between their natures, there had grown up a sort of fellowship between the two; and of an evening sometimes, when his father's purse was so low that he could not indulge in his usual stoup of wine at the tavern, they would sit together while Sir Aubrey talked of his fights and adventures.

"As to the estates, Cyril," he said one day, "I don't know that Cromwell and his Roundheads have done you much harm. I should have run through them, lad—I should have diced them away years ago—and I am not sure but that their forfeiture has been a benefit to you. If the King ever gets his own, you may come to the estates; while, if I had had the handling of them, the usurers would have had such a grip on them that you would never have had a penny of the income."

"It doesn't matter, father," the boy replied. "I mean to be a soldier some day, as you have been, and I shall take service with some of the Protestant Princes of Germany; or, if I can't do that, I shall be able to work my way somehow."

"What can you work at, lad?" his father said, contemptuously.

"I don't know yet, father; but I shall find some work to do."

Sir Aubrey was about to burst into a tirade against work, but he checked himself. If Cyril never came into the estates he would have to earn his living somehow.

"All right, my boy. But do you stick to your idea of earning your living by your sword; it is a gentleman's profession, and I would rather see you eating dry bread as a soldier of fortune than prospering in some vile trading business."

Cyril never argued with his father, and he simply nodded an assent and then asked some question that turned Sir Aubrey's thoughts on other matters.

The news that Monk had declared for the King, and that Charles would speedily return to take his place on his father's throne, caused great excitement among the Cavaliers scattered over the Continent; and as soon as the matter was settled, all prepared to return to England, in the full belief that their evil days were over, and that they would speedily be restored to their former estates, with honours and rewards for their many sacrifices.

"I must leave you behind for a short time, Cyril," his father said to the boy, when he came in one afternoon. "I must be in London before the King arrives there, to join in his welcome home, and for the moment I cannot take you; I shall be busy from morning till night. Of course, in the pressure of things at first it will be impossible for the King to do everything at once, and it may be a few weeks before all these Roundheads can be turned out of the snug nests they have made for themselves, and the rightful owners come to their own again. As I have no friends in London, I should have nowhere to bestow you, until I can take you down with me to Norfolk to present you to our tenants, and you would be grievously in my way; but as soon as things are settled I will write to you or come over myself to fetch you. In the meantime I must think over where I had best place you. It will not matter for so short a time, but I would that you should be as comfortable as possible. Think it over yourself, and let me know if you have any wishes in the matter. Sir John Parton leaves at the end of the week, and ere another fortnight there will be scarce another Englishman left at Dunkirk."

"Don't you think you can take me with you, father?"

"Impossible," Sir Aubrey said shortly. "Lodgings will be at a great price in London, for the city will be full of people from all parts coming up to welcome the King home. I can bestow myself in a garret anywhere, but I could not leave you there all day. Besides, I shall have to get more fitting clothes, and shall have many expenses. You are at home here, and will not feel it dull for the short time you have to remain behind."

Cyril said no more, but went up, with a heavy heart, for his last day's lessons at the Partons'. Young as he was, he was accustomed to think for himself, for it was but little guidance he received from his father; and after his studies were over he laid the case before his master, Mr. Felton, and asked if he could advise him. Mr. Felton was himself in high spirits, and was hoping to be speedily reinstated in his living. He looked grave when Cyril told his story.

"I think it is a pity that your father, Sir Aubrey, does not take you over with him, for it will assuredly take longer to bring all these matters into order than he seems to think. However, that is his affair. I should think he could not do better for you than place you with the people where I lodge. You know them, and they are a worthy couple; the husband is, as you know, a fisherman, and you and Harry Parton have often been out with him in his boat, so it would not be like going among strangers. Continue your studies. I should be sorry to think that you were forgetting all that you have learnt. I will take you this afternoon, if you like, to my friend, the Curé of St. Ursula. Although we differ on religion we are good friends, and should you need advice on any matters he will give it to you, and may be of use in arranging for a passage for you to England, should your father not be able himself to come and fetch you."

Sir Aubrey at once assented to the plan when Cyril mentioned it to him, and a week later sailed for England; Cyril moving, with his few belongings, to the house of Jean Baudoin, who was the owner and master of one of the largest fishing-boats in Dunkirk. Sir Aubrey had paid for his board and lodgings for two months.

"I expect to be over to fetch you long before that, Cyril," he had said, "but it is as well to be on the safe side. Here are four crowns, which will furnish you with ample pocket-money. And I have arranged with your fencing-master for you to have lessons regularly, as before; it will not do for you to neglect so important an accomplishment, for which, as he tells me, you show great aptitude."

The two months passed. Cyril had received but one letter

from his father. Although it expressed hopes of his speedy restoration to his estates, Cyril could see, by its tone, that his father was far from satisfied with the progress he had made in the matter. Madame Baudoin was a good and pious woman, and was very kind to the forlorn English boy; but when a fortnight over the two months had passed, Cyril could see that the fisherman was becoming anxious. Regularly, on his return from the fishing, he inquired if letters had arrived, and seemed much put out when he heard that there was no news. One day, when Cyril was in the garden that surrounded the cottage, he heard him say to his wife,—

"Well, I will say nothing about it until after the next voyage, and then if we don't hear, the boy must do something for his living. I can take him in the boat with me; he can earn his victuals in that way. If he won't do that, I shall wash my hands of him altogether, and he must shift for himself. I believe his father has left him with us for good. We were wrong in taking him only on the recommendation of Mr. Felton. I have been inquiring about his father, and hear little good of him."

Cyril, as soon as the fisherman had gone, stole up to his little room. He was but twelve years old, and he threw himself down on his bed and cried bitterly. Then a thought struck him; he went to his box, and took out from it a sealed parcel; on it was written, "To my son. This parcel is only to be opened should you find yourself in great need, Your Loving Mother." He remembered how she had placed it in his hands a few hours before her death, and had said to him,—

"Put this away, Cyril. I charge you let no one see it. Do not speak of it to any one—not even to your father. Keep it as a sacred gift, and do not open it unless you are in sore need. It is for you, and you alone. It is the sole thing that I have to leave you; use it with discretion. I fear that hard times will come upon you."

Cyril felt that his need could hardly be sorer than it was

now, and without hesitation he broke the seals, and opened the packet. He found first a letter directed to himself. It began,—

"My Darling Cyril,—I trust that it will be many years before you open this parcel and read these words. I have left the enclosed as a parting gift to you. I know not how long this exile may last, or whether you will ever be able to return to England. But whether you do or not, it may well be that the time will arrive when you may find yourself in sore need. Your father has been a loving husband to me, and will, I am sure, do what he can for you; but he is not provident in his habits, and may not, after he is left alone, be as careful in his expenditure as I have tried to be. I fear then that the time will come when you will be in need of money, possibly even in want of the necessaries of life. All my other trinkets I have given to him; but the one enclosed, which belonged to my mother, I leave to you. It is worth a good deal of money, and this it is my desire that you shall spend upon yourself. Use it wisely, my son. If, when you open this, you are of age to enter the service of a foreign Prince, as is, I know, the intention of your father, it will provide you with a suitable outfit. If, as is possible, you may lose your father by death or otherwise while you are still young, spend it on your education, which is the best of all heritages. Should your father be alive when you open this, I pray you not to inform him of it. The money, in his hands, would last but a short time, and might, I fear, be wasted. Think not that I am speaking or thinking hardly of him. All men, even the best, have their faults, and his is a carelessness as to money matters, and a certain recklessness concerning them; therefore, I pray you to keep it secret from him, though I do not say that you should not use the money for your common good, if it be needful; only, in that case, I beg you will not inform him as to what money you have in your possession, but use it carefully and prudently for the household wants, and make it last as long as may be. My good friend, Lady Parton, if still near you, will doubtless aid you in disposing of the jewels to the best advantage. God bless you, my son! This is the only secret I ever had from your father, but for your good I have hidden this one thing from him, and I pray that this deceit, which is practised for your advantage, may be forgiven me.

"YOUR LOVING MOTHER."

It was some time before Cyril opened the parcel; it contained a jewel-box in which was a necklace of pearls. After some consideration he took this to the Curé of St. Ursula, and, giving him his mother's letter to read, asked him for his advice as to its disposal.

"Your mother was a thoughtful and pious woman," the good priest said, after he had read the letter, "and has acted wisely in your behalf. The need she foresaw might come, has arisen, and you are surely justified in using her gift. I will dispose of this trinket for you; it is doubtless of considerable value. If it should be that your father speedily sends for you, you ought to lay aside the money for some future necessity. If he does not come for some time, as may well be—for, from the news that comes from England, it is like to be many months before affairs are settled—then draw from it only such amounts as are needed for your living and education. Study hard, my son, for so will you best be fulfilling the intentions of your mother. If you like, I will keep the money in my hands, serving it out to you as you need it; and in order that you may keep the matter a secret, I will myself go to Baudoin, and tell him that he need not be disquieted as to the cost of your maintenance, for that I have money in hand with which to discharge your expenses, so long as you may remain with him."

The next day the Curé informed Cyril that he had disposed of the necklace for fifty louis. Upon this sum Cyril lived for two years.

Things had gone very hardly with Sir Aubrey Shenstone. The King had a difficult course to steer. To have evicted all those who had obtained possession of the forfeited estates of the Cavaliers' would have been to excite a deep feeling of resentment among the Nonconformists. In vain Sir Aubrey pressed his claims, in season and out of season. He had no powerful friends to aid him; his conduct had alienated the men who could have assisted him, and, like so many other Cavaliers who had fought and suffered for Charles I., Sir Aubrey Shenstone found himself left altogether in the cold. For a time he was able to keep up a fair appearance, as he obtained loans from Prince Rupert and other Royalists whom he had known in the old days, and who had been more fortunate than himself; but the money so obtained lasted but a short time, and it was not long before he was again in dire straits.

Cyril had from the first but little hope that his father would recover his estates. He had, shortly before his father left France, heard a conversation between Sir John Parton and a gentleman who was in the inner circle of Charles's advisers. The latter had said,—

"One of the King's great difficulties will be to satisfy the exiles. Undoubtedly, could he consult his own inclinations only, he would on his return at once reinstate all those who have suffered in their estates from their loyalty to his father and himself. But this will be impossible. It was absolutely necessary for him, in his proclamation at Breda, to promise an amnesty for all offences, liberty of conscience and an oblivion as to the past, and he specially says that all questions of grants, sales and purchases of land, and titles, shall be referred to Parliament. The Nonconformists are at present in a majority, and although it seems that all parties are willing to welcome the King back, you may be sure that no Parliament will consent to anything like a general disturbance of the possessors of estates formerly owned by Royalists. In a vast number of cases, the persons to whom such grants were made disposed of them by sale to others, and it would be as hard on them to be ousted as it is upon the original proprietors to be kept out of their possession. Truly it is a most difficult position, and one that will have to be approached with great judgment, the more so since most of those to whom the lands were granted were generals, officers, and soldiers of the Parliament, and Monk would naturally oppose any steps to the detriment of his old comrades.

"I fear there will be much bitter disappointment among the exiles, and that the King will be charged with ingratitude by those who think that he has only to sign an order for their reinstatement, whereas Charles will have himself a most difficult course to steer, and will have to govern himself most circumspectly, so as to give offence to none of the governing parties. As to his granting estates, or dispossessing their holders, he will have no more power to do so than you or I. Doubtless some of the exiles will be restored to their estates; but I fear that the great bulk are doomed to disappointment. At any rate, for a time no extensive changes can be made, though it may be that in the distance, when the temper of the nation at large is better understood, the King will be able to do something for those who suffered in the cause.

"It was all very well for Cromwell, who leant solely on the Army, to dispense with a Parliament, and to govern far more autocratically than James or Charles even dreamt of doing; but the Army that supported Cromwell would certainly not support Charles. It is composed for the most part of stern fanatics, and will be the first to oppose any attempt of the King to override the law. No doubt it will ere long be disbanded; but you will see that Parliament will then recover the authority of which Cromwell deprived it; and Charles is a far wiser man than his father, and will never set himself against the feeling of the country. Certainly, anything like a general reinstatement of the men who have been for the last ten years haunting the taverns of the Continent is out of the question; they would speedily create such a revulsion of public opinion as might bring about another rebellion. Hyde, staunch Royalist as he is, would never suffer the King to make so grievous an error; nor do I think for a moment that Charles, who is shrewd and politic, and above all things a lover of ease and quiet, would think of bringing such a nest of hornets about his ears."

When, after his return to England, it became evident that Sir Aubrey had but small chance of reinstatement in his lands, his former friends began to close their purses and to refuse to grant further loans, and he was presently reduced to straits as severe as those he had suffered during his exile. The good spirits that had borne him up so long failed now, and he grew morose and petulant. His loyalty to the King was unshaken; Charles had several times granted him audiences, and had assured him that, did it rest with him, justice should be at once dealt to him, but that he was practically powerless in the matter, and the knight's resentment was concentrated upon Hyde, now Lord Clarendon, and the rest of the King's advisers. He wrote but seldom to Cyril; he had no wish to have the boy with him until he could take him down with him in triumph to Norfolk, and show him to the tenants as his heir. Living from hand to mouth as he did, he worried but little as to how Cyril was getting on.

"The lad has fallen on his feet somehow," he said, "and he is better where he is than he would be with me. I suppose when he wants money he will write and say so, though where I should get any to send to him I know not. Anyhow, I need not worry about him at present."

Cyril, indeed, had written to him soon after the sale of the necklace, telling him that he need not distress himself about his condition, for that he had obtained sufficient money for his present necessities from the sale of a small trinket his mother had given him before her death, and that when this was spent he should doubtless find some means of earning his living until he could rejoin him. His father never inquired into the matter, though he made a casual reference to it in his next letter, saying that he was glad Cyril had obtained some money, as it would, at the moment, have been inconvenient to him to send any over.

Cyril worked assiduously at the school that had been recommended to him by the Curé, and at the end of two years he had still twenty louis left. He had several conversations with his adviser as to the best way of earning his living.

"I do not wish to spend any more, Father," he said, "and would fain keep this for some future necessity."

The Curé agreed with him as to this, and, learning from his master that he was extremely quick at figures and wrote an excellent hand, he obtained a place for him with one of the principal traders of the town. He was to receive no salary for a year, but was to learn book-keeping and accounts. Although but fourteen, the boy was so intelligent and zealous that his employer told the Curé that he found him of real service, and that he was able to entrust some of his books entirely to his charge.

Six months after entering his service, however, Cyril received a letter from his father, saying that he believed his affairs were on the point of settlement, and therefore wished him to come over in the first ship sailing. He enclosed an order on a house at Dunkirk for fifty francs, to pay his passage. His employer parted with him with regret, and the kind Curé bade him farewell in terms of real affection, for he had come to take a great interest in him.

"At any rate, Cyril," he said, "your time here has not been wasted, and your mother's gift has been turned to as much advantage as even she can have hoped that it would be. Should your father's hopes be again disappointed, and fresh delays arise, you may, with the practice you have had, be able to earn your living in London. There must be there, as in France, many persons in trade who have had but little education, and you may be able to obtain employment in keeping the books of such people, who are, I believe, more common in England than here. Here are the sixteen louis that still remain; put them aside, Cyril, and use them only for urgent necessity."

Cyril, on arriving in London, was heartily welcomed by his father, who had, for the moment, high hopes of recovering his estates. These, however, soon faded, and although Sir Aubrey would not allow it, even to himself, no chance remained of those Royalists, who had, like him, parted with their estates for trifling sums, to be spent in the King's service, ever regaining possession of them.

It was not long before Cyril perceived that unless he himself obtained work of some sort they would soon be face to face with actual starvation. He said nothing to his father, but started out one morning on a round of visits among the smaller class of shopkeepers, offering to make up their books and write out their bills and accounts for a small remuneration. As he had a frank and pleasant face, and his foreign bringing up had given him an ease and politeness of manner rare among English lads of the day, it was not long before he obtained several clients. To some of the smaller class of traders he went only for an hour or two, once a week, while others required their bills and accounts to be made out daily. The pay was very small, but it sufficed to keep absolute want from the door. When he told his father of the arrangements he had made, Sir Aubrey at first raged and stormed; but he had come, during the last year or two, to recognise the good sense and strong will of his son, and although he never verbally acquiesced in what he considered a degradation, he offered no actual opposition to a plan that at least enabled them to live, and furnished him occasionally with a few groats with which he could visit a tavern.

So things had gone on for more than a year. Cyril was now sixteen, and his punctuality, and the neatness of his work, had been so appreciated by the tradesmen who first employed him, that his time was now fully occupied, and that at rates more remunerative than those he had at first obtained. He kept the state of his resources to himself, and had no difficulty in doing this, as his father never alluded to the subject of his

"DON'T CRY, LAD; YOU WILL GET ON BETTER WITHOUT ME."

work. Cyril knew that, did he hand over to him all the money he made, it would be wasted in drink or at cards; consequently, he kept the table furnished as modestly as at first, and regularly placed after dinner on the corner of the mantel a few coins, which his father as regularly dropped into his pocket.

A few days before the story opens, Sir Aubrey had, late one evening, been carried upstairs, mortally wounded in a brawl; he only recovered consciousness a few minutes before his death.

"You have been a good lad, Cyril," he said faintly, as he feebly pressed the boy's hand; "far better than I deserve to have had. Don't cry, lad; you will get on better without me, and things are just as well as they are. I hope you will come to your estates some day; you will make a better master than I should ever have done. I hope that in time you will carry out your plan of entering some foreign service; there is no chance here. I don't want you to settle down as a city scrivener. Still, do as you like, lad, and unless your wishes go with mine, think no further of service."

"I would rather be a soldier, father. I only undertook this work because I could see nothing else."

"That is right, my boy, that is right. I know you won't forget that you come of a race of gentlemen."

He spoke but little after that. A few broken words came from his lips that showed that his thoughts had gone back to old times. "Boot and saddle," he murmured. "That is right. Now we are ready for them. Down with the prick-eared knaves! God and King Charles!" These were the last words he spoke.

Cyril had done all that was necessary. He had laid by more than half his earnings for the last eight or nine months. One of his clients, an undertaker, had made all the necessary preparations for the funeral, and in a few hours his father would be borne to his last resting-place. As he stood at the open window he thought sadly over the past, and of his father's wasted life. Had it not been for the war he might have lived and died a country gentleman. It was the war, with its wild excitements, that had ruined him. What was there for him to do in a foreign country, without resource or employment, having no love for reading, but to waste his life as he had done? Had his wife lived it might have been different. Cyril had still a vivid remembrance of his mother, and though his father had but seldom spoken to him of her, he knew that he had loved her, and that, had she lived, he would never have given way to drink as he had done of late years.

To his father's faults he could not be blind; but they stood for nothing now. He had been his only friend, and of late they had been drawn closer to each other in their loneliness; and although scarce a word of endearment had passed between them, he knew that his father had cared for him more than was apparent in his manner.

A few hours later, Sir Aubrey Shenstone was laid to rest in a little graveyard outside the city walls. Cyril was the only mourner; and when it was over, instead of going back to his lonely room, he turned away and wandered far out through the fields towards Hampstead, and then sat himself down to think what he had best do. Another three or four years must pass before he could try to get service abroad. When the time came he should find Sir John Parton, and beg him to procure for him some letter of introduction to the many British gentlemen serving abroad. He had not seen him since he came to England. His father had met him, but had quarrelled with him upon Sir John declining to interest himself actively to push his claims, and had forbidden Cyril to go near those who had been so kind to him.

The boy had felt it greatly at first, but he came, after a time, to see that it was best so. It seemed to him that he had fallen altogether out of their station in life when the hope of his father's recovering his estates vanished, and although he was sure of a kindly reception from Lady Parton, he shrank from going there in his present position. They had done so much for him already, that the thought that his visit might seem to them a sort of petition for further benefits was intolerable to him.

For the present, the question in his mind was whether he should continue at his present work, which at any rate sufficed to keep him, or should seek other employment. He would greatly have preferred some life of action,—something that would fit him better to bear the fatigues and hardships of war, —but he saw no prospect of obtaining any such position.

"I should be a fool to throw up what I have," he said to himself at last. "I will stick to it anyhow until some opportunity offers; but the sooner I leave it the better. It was bad enough before; it will be worse now. If I had but a friend or two it would not be so hard; but to have no one to speak to, and no one to think about, when work is done, will be lonely indeed."

At any rate, he determined to change his room as soon as possible. It mattered little where he went so that it was a change. He thought over various tradesmen for whom he worked. Some of them might have an attic, he cared not how small, that they might let him have in lieu of paying him for his work. Even if they never spoke to him, it would be better to be in a house where he knew something of those downstairs, than to lodge in one where he was an utter stranger to all. He had gone round to the shops where he worked, on the day after his father's death, to explain that he could not come again until after the funeral, and he resolved that next morning he would ask each in turn whether he could obtain a lodging with them.

The sun was already setting when he rose from the bank on which he had seated himself, and returned to the city. The room did not feel so lonely to him as it would have done had he not been accustomed to spending the evenings alone. He took out his little hoard and counted it. After paying the expenses of the funeral there would still remain sufficient to keep him for three or four months should he fall ill, or, from any cause, lose his work. He had one good suit of clothes that had been bought on his return to England,—when his father thought that they would assuredly be going down almost immediately to take possession of the old Hall,—and the rest were all in fair condition.

The next day he began his work again; he had two visits to pay of an hour each, and one of two hours, and the spare time between these he filled up by calling at two or three other shops to make up for the arrears of work during the last few days.

The last place he had to visit was that at which he had the longest task to perform. It was at a ship-chandler's in Tower Street, a large and dingy house, the lower portion being filled with canvas, cordage, barrels of pitch and tar, candles, oil, and matters of all sorts needed by ship-masters, including many cannon of different sizes, piles of balls, anchors, and other heavy work, all of which were stowed away in a yard behind it. The owner of this store was a one-armed man. His father had kept it before him, but he himself, after working there long enough to become a citizen and a member of the Ironmongers' Guild, had quarrelled with his father and had taken to the sea. For twenty years he had voyaged to many lands, principally in ships trading in the Levant, and had passed through a great many adventures, including several fights with the Moorish corsairs. In the last voyage he took, he had had his arm shot off by a ball from a Greek pirate among the Islands. He had long before made up his differences with his father, but had resisted the latter's entreaties that he should give up the sea and settle down at the shop; on his return after this unfortunate voyage he told him that he had come home to stay.

"I shall be able to help about the stores after a while," he said, "but I shall never be the man I was on board ship. It will be hard work to take to measuring out canvas and to weighing iron, after a free life on the sea, but I don't so much mind now I have had my share of adventures; though

I dare say I should have gone on for a few more years if that rascally ball had not carried away my arm. I don't know but that it is best as it is, for the older I got the harder I should find it to fall into new ways and to settle down here."

"Anyhow, I am glad you are back, David," his father said. "You are forty-five, and though I don't say it would not have been better if you had remained here from the first, you have learnt many things you would not have learnt here. You know just the sort of things that masters of ships require, and what canvas and cables and cordage will suit their wants. Besides, customers like to talk with men of their own way of thinking, and sailors more, I think, than other men. You know, too, most of the captains who sail up the Mediterranean, and may be able to bring fresh custom into the shop. Therefore, do not think that you will be of no use to me. As to your wife and child, there is plenty of room for them as well as for you, and it will be better for them here, with you always at hand, than it would be for them to remain over at Rotherhithe and only to see you after the shutters are up."

Eight years later Captain Dave, as he was always called, became sole owner of the house and business. A year after he did so he was lamenting to a friend the trouble that he had with his accounts.

"My father always kept that part of the business in his own hands," he said, "and I find it a mighty heavy burden. Beyond checking a bill of lading, or reading the marks on the bales and boxes, I never had occasion to read or write for twenty years, and there has not been much more of it for the last fifteen; and although I was a smart scholar enough in my young days, my fingers are stiff with hauling at ropes and using the marling-spike, and my eyes are not so clear as they used to be, and it is no slight toil and labour to me to make up an account for goods sold. John Wilkes, my head shopman, is a handy fellow; he was my boatswain in the *Kate*, and I took him on when we found that the man who had been my father's right hand for twenty years had been cheating him all along. We got on well enough as long as I could give all my time in the shop; but he is no good with the pen—all he can do is to enter receipts and sales.

"He has a man under him, who helps him in measuring out the right length of canvas and cables or for weighing a chain or an anchor, and knows enough to put down the figures; but that is all. Then there are the two smiths and the two apprentices; they don't count in the matter. Robert Ashford, the eldest apprentice, could do the work, but I have no fancy for him; he does not look one straight in the face as one who is honest and above board should do. I shall have to keep a clerk, and I know what it will be—he will be setting me right, and I shall not feel my own master; he will be out of place in my crew altogether. I never liked pursers; most of them are rogues. Still, I suppose it must come to that."

"I have a boy come in to write my bills and to make up my accounts, who would be just the lad for you, Captain Dave. He is the son of a broken-down Cavalier, but he is a steady, honest young fellow, and I fancy his pen keeps his father, who is a roystering blade, and spends most of his time at the taverns. The boy comes to me for an hour, twice a week; he writes as good a hand as any clerk and can reckon as quickly, and I pay him but a groat a week, which was all he asked."

"Tell him to come to me, then. I should want him every day, if he could manage it, and it would be the very thing for me."

"I am sure you would like him the other said; "he is a good-looking young fellow and his face speaks for him without any recommendation. I was afraid at first that he would not do for me; I thought there was too much of the gentleman about him. He has good manners, and a gentle sort of way. He has been living in France all his life, and though he has never said anything about his family—indeed he talks but little, he just comes in and does his work and goes away—I fancy his father was one of King Charles's men and of good blood."

"Well, that doesn't sound so well," the sailor said, "but anyhow I should like to have a look at him."

"He comes to me to-morrow at eleven and goes at twelve," the man said, "and I will send him round to you when he has done."

Cyril had gone round the next morning to the ships' store.

"So you are the lad that works for my neighbour Anderson?" Captain Dave said, as he surveyed him closely. "I like your looks, lad, but I doubt whether we shall get on together. I am an old sailor, you know, and I am quick of speech and don't stop to choose my words, so if you are quick to take offence it would be of no use your coming to me."

"I don't think I am likely to take offence," Cyril said quietly; "and if we don't get on well together, sir, you will only have to tell me that you don't want me any longer; but I trust you will not have often the occasion to use hard words, for at any rate I will do my best to please you."

"You can't say more, lad. Well, let us have a taste of your quality. Come in here," and he led him into a little room partitioned off from the shop. "There, you see," and he opened a book, "is the account of the sales and orders yesterday; the ready-money sales have got to be entered in that ledger with the red cover; the sales where no money passed have to be entered to the various customers or ships in the ledger. I have made out a list—here it is—of twelve accounts that have to be drawn out from that ledger and sent in to customers. You will find some of them are of somewhat long standing, for I have been putting off that job. Sit you down here. When you have done one or two of them I will have a look at your work, and if that is satisfactory we will have a talk as to what hours you have got disengaged, and what days in the week will suit you best."

It was two hours before Captain Dave came in again. Cyril had just finished the work; some of the accounts were long ones, and the writing was so crabbed that it took him some time to decipher it.

"Well, how are you getting on, lad?" the Captain asked.

"I have this moment finished the last account."

"What! Do you mean to say that you have done them all. Why, it would have taken me all my evenings for a week. Now, hand me the books; it is best to do things ship-shape."

He first compared the list of the sales with the entries, and then Cyril handed him the twelve accounts he had drawn up. Captain David did not speak until he had finished looking through them.

"I would not have believed all that work could have been done in two hours," he said, getting up from his chair. "Orderly and well written, and without a blot. The King's secretary could not have done better! Well, now you have seen the list of sales for a day, and I take it that be about the average, so if you come three times a week you will always have two days' sales to enter in the ledger. There are a lot of other books my father used to keep, but I have never had time to bother myself about them, and as I have got on very well so far, I do not see any occasion for you to do so, for my part it seems to me that all these books are only invented by clerks to give themselves something to do to fill up their time. Of course, there won't be accounts to send out every day. Do you think with two hours, three times a week, you could keep things straight?"

"I should certainly think so, sir, but I can hardly say until I try, because it seems to me that there must be a great many items, and I can't say how long it will take entering all the goods received under their proper headings; but if the books are thoroughly made up now, I should think I could keep them all going."

"That they are not," Captain David said ruefully; "they are all horribly in arrears. I took charge of them myself three years ago, and though I spend three hours every evening worrying over them, they get further and further in arrears. Look at those files over there," and he pointed to three long wires, on each of which was strung a large bundle of papers; " I am afraid you will have to enter them all up before you can get matters into ship-shape order. The daily sale book is the only one that has been kept up regularly."

"But these accounts I have made up, sir? Probably in those files there are many other goods supplied to the same people."

"Of course there are, lad, though I did not think of it before. Well, we must wait, then, until you can make up the arrears a bit, though I really want to get some money in."

"Well, sir, I might write at the bottom of each bill "Account made up to," and then put in the date of the latest entry charged."

"That would do capitally, lad—I did not think of that. I see you will be of great use to me. I can buy and sell, for I know the value of the goods I deal in; but as to accounts, they are altogether out of my way. And now, lad, what do you charge?"

"I charge a groat for two hours' work, sir; but if I came to you three times a week, I would do it for a little less."

"No, lad, I don't want to beat you down; indeed, I don't think you charge enough. However, let us say, to begin with, three groats a week."

This had been six weeks before Sir Aubrey Shenstone's death; and in the interval Cyril had gradually wiped off all the arrears, and had all the books in order up to date, to the astonishment of his employer.

CHAPTER II.

A CHANGE FOR THE BETTER.

"I AM glad to see you again, lad," Captain David said, when Cyril entered his shop. "I have been thinking of the news you gave me last week, and the mistress and I have been talking it over. Where are you lodging?"

"I have been lodging until now in Holborn," Cyril replied; "but I am going to move."

"Yes; that is what we thought you would be doing. It is always better to make a change after a loss. I don't want to interfere in your business, lad, but have you any friends you are thinking of going to?"

"No, sir; I do not know a soul in London save those I work for."

"That is bad, lad—very bad. I was talking it over with my wife, and I said that maybe you were lonely. I am sure, lad, you are one of the right sort. I don't mean only in your work, for as for that I would back you against any scrivener in London, but I mean about yourself. It don't need half an eye to see that you have not been brought up to this sort of thing, though you have taken to it so kindly, but there is not one in a thousand boys of your age who would have settled down to work and made their way without a friend to help them as you have done; it shows that there is right good stuff in you. There, I am so long getting under weigh that I shall never get into port if I don't steer a straight course. Now, my ideas and my wife's come to this: if you have got no friends you will have to take a lodging somewhere among strangers, and then it would be one of two things—you would either stop at home and mope by yourself, or you would go out, and maybe get into bad company. If I had not come across you I should have had to employ a clerk, and he would either have lived here with us or I should have had to pay him enough to keep house for himself. Now in fact you

"THIS IS MY PRINCE OF SCRIVENERS, MARY."

are a clerk; for though you are only here for six hours a week—you do all the work there is to do, and no clerk could do more. Well, we have got an attic upstairs which is not used, and if you like to come here and live with us, my wife and I will make you heartily welcome."

"Thank you, indeed," Cyril said warmly. "It is of all things what I should like; but of course I should wish to pay you for my board. I can afford to do so if you will employ me for the same hours as at present."

"No, I would not have that, lad; but if you like we can reckon your board against what I now pay you. We feed John Wilkes and the two apprentices, and one mouth extra will make but little difference. I don't want it to be a matter of obligation, so we will put your board against the work you do for me. I shall consider that we are making a good bargain."

"It is your pleasure to say so, sir; but I cannot tell you what a load your kind offer takes off my mind. The future has seemed very dark to me."

"Very well. That matter is settled, then. Come upstairs with me and I will present you to my wife and daughter; they have heard me speak of you so often that they will be glad to see you. In the first place, though, I must ask you your name. Since you first signed articles and entered the crew I have never thought of asking you."

"My name is Cyril, sir—Cyril Shenstone."

His employer nodded and at once led the way upstairs. A motherly looking woman rose from the seat where she was sitting at work, as they entered the living-room.

"This is my Prince of Scriveners, Mary, the lad I have often spoken to you about. His name is Cyril; he has accepted the proposal we talked over last night, and is going to become one of the crew on board our ship."

"I am glad to see you," she said to Cyril, holding out her hand to him. "I have not met you before, but I feel very grateful to you Till you came, my husband was bothered nearly out of his wits; he used to sit here worrying over his books, and writing from the time the shop closed till the hour for bed, and Nellie and I dared not to say as much as a word. Now we see no more of his books, and he is able to go out for a walk in the fields with us as he used to do before."

"It is very kind of you to say so, Mistress," Cyril said earnestly; "but it is I, on the contrary, who am deeply grateful to you for the offer Captain Dave has been good enough to make me. You cannot tell the pleasure it has given me, for you cannot understand how lonely and friendless I have been feeling. Believe me, I will strive to give you as little trouble as possible, and to conform myself in all ways to your wishes."

At this moment Nellie Dowsett came into the room. She was a pretty girl some eighteen years of age.

"This is Cyril, your father's assistant, Nellie," her mother said.

"You are welcome, Master Cyril. I have been wanting to see you. Father has been praising you up to the skies so often that I have had quite a curiosity to see what you could be like."

"Your father is altogether too good, Mistress Nellie, and makes far more of my poor ability than it deserves."

"And is he going to live with us, mother?" Nellie asked.

"Yes, child; he has accepted your father's offer."

Nellie clapped her hands.

"That is good," she said. "I shall expect you to escort me out sometimes, Cyril. Father always wants me to go down to the wharf to look at the ships or to go into the fields; but I want to go sometimes to see the fashions, and there is no one to take me, for John Wilkes always goes off to smoke a pipe with some sailor or other, and the apprentices are stupid and have nothing to say for themselves; and besides, one can't walk alongside a boy in an apprentice cap."

"I shall be very happy to, Mistress, when my work is done, though I fear that I shall make but a poor escort, for indeed I have had no practice whatever in the esquiring of dames."

"I am sure you will do very well," Nellie said, nodding approvingly. "Is it true that you have been in France? Father said he was told so."

"Yes; I have lived almost all my life in France."

"And do you speak French?"

"Yes; I speak it as well as English."

"It must have been very hard to learn?"

"Not at all. It came to me naturally, just as English did."

"You must not keep him any longer now, Nellie; he has other appointments to keep, and when he has done that, to go and pack up his things and see that they are brought here by a porter. He can answer some more of your questions when he comes here this evening."

Cyril returned to Holborn with a lighter heart than he had felt for a long time. His preparations for the move took him but a short time, and two hours later he was installed in a little attic in the ship-chandler's house. He spent half-an-hour in unpacking his things, and then heard a stentorian shout from below,—

"Masthead, ahoy! Supper's waiting."

Supposing that this hail was intended for himself, he at once went downstairs. The table was laid. Mistress Dowsett took her seat at the head; her husband sat on one side of her, and Nellie on the other. John Wilkes sat next to his master, and beyond him the elder of the two apprentices. A seat was left between Nellie and the other apprentice for Cyril.

"Now our crew is complete, John," Captain Dave said. "We have been wanting a supercargo badly."

"Ay, ay, Captain Dave, there is no doubt we have been short-handed in that respect; but things have been more ship-shape lately."

"That is so, John. I can make a shift to keep the vessel on her course, but when it comes to writing up the log, and keeping the reckoning, I make but a poor hand at it. It was getting to be as bad as that voyage of the *Jane* in the Levant, when the supercargo had got himself stabbed at Lemnos"

"I mind it, Captain—I mind it well. And what a trouble there was with the owners when we got back again!"

"Yes, yes," the Captain said; "it was worse work than having a brush with a Barbary corsair. I shall never forget that day. When I went to the office to report, the three owners were all in.

"'Well, Captain Dave, back from your voyage?' said the littlest of the three. 'Made a good voyage, I hope?'

"First-rate, says I, except that the supercargo got killed at Lemnos by one of them rascally Greeks.

"'Dear, dear,' said another of them—he was a prim, sanctimonious sort—'Has our brother Jenkins left us?'

"I don't know about his leaving us, says I, but we left him sure enough in a burying-place there.

"'And how did you manage without him?'

"I made as good a shift as I could, I said. I have sold all the cargo, and I have brought back a freight of six tons of Turkey figs, and four hundred boxes of currants. And these two bags hold the difference.

"'Have you brought the books with you, Captain?'

"Never a book, said I. I have had to navigate the ship and to look after the crew, and do the best I could at each port. The books are on board, made out up to the day before the supercargo was killed, three months ago; but I have never had time to make an entry since.

"They looked at each other like owls for a minute or two, and then they all began to talk at once. How had I sold the goods? had I charged the prices mentioned in the invoice? what percentage had I put on for profit? and a lot of other things. I waited until they were all out of breath, and then I said I had not bothered about invoices. I knew pretty well the prices such things cost in England. I clapped on so much more for the expenses of the voyage and a fair profit. I could tell them what I had paid for the figs and the currants, and for some bags of Smyrna sponges I had bought, but as to the prices I had charged, it was too much to expect that I could carry them in my head. All I knew was I had paid for the things I had bought, I had paid all the port dues and other charges, I had advanced the men one-fourth of their wages each month, and I had brought them back the balance.

"Such a hubbub you never heard. One would have thought they would have gone raving mad. The sanctimonious partner was the worst of the lot. He threatened me with the Lord Mayor and the Aldermen, and went on till I thought he would have had a fit.

"Look here, says I, at last, I'll tell you what I will do. You tell me what the cargo cost you altogether, and put on so much for the hire of the ship. I will pay you for them and settle up with the crew, and take the cargo and sell it. That is a fair offer. And I advise you to keep civil tongues in your heads, or I will knock them off and take my chance before the Lord Mayor for assault and battery.

"With that I took off my coat and laid it on a bench. I reckon they saw that I was in earnest, and they just sat as mum as mice. Then the little man said, in a quieter sort of voice,—

"'You are too hasty, Captain Dowsett. We know you to be an honest man and a good sailor, and had no suspicion that you would wrong us; but no merchant in the City of London could hear that his business had been conducted in such a way as you have carried it through without for a time losing countenance. Let us talk the matter over reasonably and quietly.'

"That is just what I am wanting, I said; and if there hasn't been reason and quiet it is from no fault of mine.

"'Well, please to put your coat on again, Captain, and let us see how matters stand!'

"Then they took their ink-horns and pens, and, on finding out what I had paid for the figs and other matters, they reckoned them up; then they put down what I said was due to the sailors and the mate and myself; then they got out some books, and for an hour they were busy reckoning up figures; then they opened the bags and counted up the gold we had brought home. Well, when they had done, you would hardly have known them for the same men. First of all, they went through all their calculations again to be sure they had made no mistake about them; then they laid down their pens, and the sanctimonious man mopped the perspiration from his face, and the others smiled at each other. Then the biggest of the three, who had scarcely spoken before, said,—

"'Well, Captain Dowsett, I must own that my partners were a little hasty. The result of our calculations is that the voyage has been a satisfactory one, I may almost say very satisfactory, and that you must have disposed of the goods to much advantage. It has been a new and somewhat extraordinary way of doing business, but I am bound to say that the result has exceeded our expectations, and we trust that you will command the *Jane* for many more voyages.'

"Not for me, says I. You can hand me over the wages due to me, and you will find the *Jane* moored in the stream just above the Tower. You will find her in order and shipshape; but never again do I set my foot on board her or on any other vessel belonging to men who have doubted my honesty.

"Nor did I. I had a pretty good name among traders, and ten days later I started for the Levant again in command of a far smarter vessel than the *Jane* had ever been."

"And we all went with you, Captain," John Wilkes said, "every man jack of us. And on her very next voyage the *Jane* was captured by the Algerines, and I reckon there are some of the poor fellows working as slaves there now; for though Blake did blow the place pretty nigh out of water a few years afterwards, it is certain that the Christian slaves handed over to him were not half those the Moors had in their hands."

"It would seem, Captain Dowsett, from your story, that you can manage very well without a supercargo?" Cyril said quietly.

"Aỳ, lad; but you see that was a ready-money business. I handed over the goods and took the cash; there was no accounts to be kept. It was all clear and above board. But it is a different thing in this ship altogether, when, instead of paying down on the nail for what they get, you have got to keep an account of everything and send in all their items jotted down in order. Why, Nellie, your tongue seems quieter than usual."

"You have not given me a chance, father. You have been talking ever since we sat down to table."

Supper was now over. The two apprentices at once retired. Cyril would have done the same, but Mistress Dowsett said,—

"Sit you still, Cyril. The Captain says that you are to be considered as one of the officers of the ship, and we shall be always glad to have you here, though of course you can always go up to your own room, or go out, when you feel inclined."

"I have to go out three times a week to work," Cyril said; "but all the other evenings I shall be glad indeed to sit here, Mistress Dowsett. You cannot tell what a pleasure it is to me to be in an English home like this."

It was not long before John Wilkes went out.

"He is off to smoke his pipe," the Captain said. "I never light mine till he goes. I can't persuade him to take his with me; he insists it would not be manners to smoke in the cabin."

"He is quite right, father," Nellie said. "It is bad enough having you smoke here. When mother's friends or mine come in they are well-nigh choked; they are not accustomed to it as we are, for a respectable London citizen does not think of taking tobacco."

"I am a London citizen, Nellie, but I don't set up any special claim to respectability. I am a sea-captain, though that rascally Greek cannon-ball and other circumstances have made a trader of me, sorely against my will; and if I could not have my pipe and my glass of grog here I would go and sit with John Wilkes in the tavern at the corner of the street, and I suppose that would not be even as respectable as smoking here."

" Nellie doesn't mean, David, that she wants you to give up smoking; only she thinks that John is quite right to go out to take his pipe. And I must say I think so too. You know that when you have sea-captains of your acquaintance here, you always send the maid off to bed and smoke in the kitchen."

"Ay, ay, my dear, I don't want to turn your room into a fo'castle. There is reason in all things. I suppose you don't smoke, Master Cyril?"

"No, Captain Dave, I have never so much as thought of such a thing. In France it is the fashion to take snuff, but the habit seemed to me a useless one, and I don't think that I should ever have taken to it."

"I wonder," Captain Dave said, after they had talked for some time, "that after living in sight of the sea for so long your thoughts never turned that way."

"I cannot say that I have never thought of it," Cyril said. "I have thought that I should greatly like to take foreign voyages, but I should not have cared to go as a ship's boy, and to live with men so ignorant that they could not even write their own names. My thoughts have turned rather to the Army; and when I get older I think of entering some foreign service, either that of Sweden or of one of the Protestant German princes. I could obtain introductions through which I might enter as a cadet, or gentleman volunteer. I have learnt German, and though I cannot speak it as I can French or English, I know enough to make my way in it."

"Can you use your sword, Cyril?" Nellie Dowsett asked.

"I have had very good teaching," Cyril replied, "and hope to be able to hold my own."

"Then you are not satisfied with this mode of life?" Mistress Dowsett said.

"I am satisfied with it, Mistress, inasmuch as I can earn

money sufficient to keep me. But rather than settle down for life as a city scrivener, I would go down to the river and ship on board the first vessel that would take me, no matter where she sailed for."

"I think you are wrong," Mistress Dowsett said gravely. "My husband tells me how clever you are at figures, and you might some day get a good post in the house of one of our great merchants."

"Maybe it would be so," Cyril said; "but such a life would ill suit me. I have truly a great desire to earn money; but it must be in some way to suit my taste."

"And why do you want to earn a great deal of money, Cyril?" Nellie laughed, while her mother shook her head disapprovingly.

"I wish to have enough to buy my father's estate back again," he said, "and though I know well enough that it is not likely I shall ever do it, I shall fight none the worse that I have such a hope in my mind."

"Bravo, lad!" Captain Dave said. "I knew not that there was an estate in the case, though I did hear that you were the son of a Royalist. It is a worthy ambition, boy, though if it is a large one 'tis scarce like that you will get enough to buy it back again."

"It is not a very large one," Cyril said. "'Tis down in Norfolk, but it was a grand old house—at least, so I have heard my father say, though I have but little remembrance of it, as I was but three years old when I left it. My father, who was Sir Aubrey Shenstone, had hoped to recover it; but he was one of the many who sold their estates for far less than their value in order to raise money in the King's service, and, as you are aware, none of those who did so have been reinstated, but only those who, having had their land taken from them by Parliament, recovered them because their owners had no title-deeds to show, save the grant of Parliament that was of no effect in the Courts. Thus the most loyal men—those who sold their estates to aid the King

—have lost all, while those that did not so dispossess themselves in his service are now replaced on their land."

"It seems very unfair," Nellie said indignantly.

"It is unfair to them, assuredly, Mistress Nellie. And yet it would be unfair to the men who bought, though often they gave but a tenth of their value, to be turned out again unless they received their money back. It is not easy to see where that money could come from, for assuredly the King's privy purse would not suffice to pay all the money, and equally certain is it that Parliament would not vote a great sum for that purpose."

"It is a hard case, lad—a hard case," Captain Dave said, as he puffed the smoke from his pipe. "Now I know how you stand, I blame you in no way that you long more for a life of adventure than to settle down as a city scrivener. I don't think even my wife, much as she thinks of the city, could say otherwise."

"It alters the case much," Mistress Dowsett said. "I did not know that Cyril was the son of a Knight, though it was easy enough to see that his manners accord not with his present position. Still there are fortunes made in the city, and no honest work is dishonouring even to a gentleman's son."

"Not at all, Mistress," Cyril said warmly. "'Tis assuredly not on that account that I would fain seek more stirring employment; but it was always my father's wish and intention that, should there be no chance of his ever regaining the estate, I should enter foreign service, and I have always looked forward to that career."

"Well, I will wager that you will do credit to it, lad," Captain Dave said. "You have proved that you are ready to turn your hand to any work that may come to you. You have shown a manly spirit, my boy, and I honour you for it; and by St. Anthony I believe that some day, unless a musket-ball or a pike-thrust brings you up with a round turn, you will live to get your own back again."

Cyril remained talking for another two hours, and then

betook himself to bed. After he had gone, Mistress Dowsett said, after a pause,—

"Do you not think, David, that, seeing that Cyril is the son of a Knight, it would be more becoming to give him the room downstairs instead of the attic where he is now lodged?"

The old sailor laughed.

"That is woman-kind all over," he said. "It was good enough for him before, and now forsooth, because the lad mentioned, and assuredly in no boasting way, that his father had been a Knight, he is to be treated differently. He would not thank you himself for making the change, dame. In the first place, it would make him uncomfortable, and he might make an excuse to leave us altogether; and in the second, you may be sure that he has been used to no better quarters than those he has got. The Royalists in France were put to sore shifts to live, and I fancy that he has fared no better since he came home. His father would never have consented to his going out to earn money by keeping the accounts of little city traders like myself had it not been that he was driven to it by want. No, no, wife; let the boy go on as he is, and make no difference in any way. I liked him before, and I like him all the better now, for putting his gentlemanship in his pocket and setting manfully to work instead of hanging on the skirts of some Royalist who has fared better than his father did. He is grateful as it is—that is easy to see —for our taking him in here. We did that partly because he proved a good worker and has taken a lot of care off my shoulders, partly because he was fatherless and alone. I would not have him think that we are ready to do more because he is a Knight's son. Let the boy be, and suffer him to steer his ship his own course. If, when the time comes, we can further his objects in any way we will do it with right good will. What do you think of him, Nellie?" he asked, changing the subject.

"He is a proper young fellow, father, and I shall be well content to go abroad escorted by him instead of having your apprentice, Robert Ashford, in attendance on me. He has not a word to say for himself, and truly I like him not in any way."

"He is not a bad apprentice, Nellie, and John Wilkes has but seldom cause to find fault with him, though I own that I have no great liking myself for him; he never seems to look one well in the face, which, I take it, is always a bad sign. I know no harm of him; but when his apprenticeship is out, which it will be in another year, I shall let him go his own way, for I should not care to have him on the premises."

"Methinks you are very unjust, David. The lad is quiet and regular in his ways; he goes twice every Sunday to the Church of St. Alphage, and always tells me the texts of the sermons."

The Captain grunted.

"Maybe so, wife; but it is easy to get hold of the text of a sermon without having heard it. I have my doubts whether he goes as regularly to St. Alphage's as he says he does. Why could he not go with us to St. Bennet's?"

"He says he likes the administrations of Mr. Catlin better, David. And, in truth, our parson is not one of the stirring kind."

"So much the better," Captain Dave said bluntly. "I like not these men that thump the pulpit and make as if they were about to jump out head foremost. However, I don't suppose there is much harm in the lad, and it may be that his failure to look one in the face is not so much his fault as that of nature, which endowed him with a villainous squint. Well, let us turn in; it is past nine o'clock, and high time to be a-bed."

Cyril seemed to himself to have entered upon a new life when he stepped across the threshold of David Dowsett's store. All his cares and anxieties had dropped from him. For the past two years he had lived the life of an automaton, starting early to his work, returning in the middle of the day to his dinner,—to which as often as not he sat down alone,—and spending his evenings in utter loneliness in the bare garret, where he was generally in bed long before his father returned. He blamed himself sometimes during the first fortnight of his stay here for the feeling of light-heartedness that at times

came over him. He had loved his father in spite of his
faults, and should, he told himself, have felt deeply depressed
at his loss; but nature was too strong for him. The pleasant
evenings with Captain Dave and his family were to him delightful; he was like a traveller who, after a cold and cheerless
journey, comes in to the warmth of a fire, and feels a glow
of comfort as the blood circulates briskly through his veins.
Sometimes, when he had no other engagements, he went out
with Nellie Dowsett, whose lively chatter was new and very
amusing to him. Sometimes they went up into Cheapside,
and into St. Paul's, but more often sallied out of the city at
Aldgate, and walked into the fields. On these occasions he
carried a stout cane that had been his father's, for Nellie tried
in vain to persuade him to gird on a sword.

"You are a gentleman, Cyril," she would argue, "and have
a right to carry one."

"I am for the present a sober citizen, Mistress Nellie, and
do not wish to assume to be of any other condition. Those
one sees with swords are either gentlemen of the Court, or
common bullies, or maybe highwaymen. After nightfall it is
different; for then many citizens carry their swords, which
indeed are necessary to protect them from the ruffians who,
in spite of the city watch, oftentimes attack quiet passers-by;
and if at any time I escort you to the house of one of your
friends, I shall be ready to take my sword with me. But in
the daytime there is no occasion for a weapon, and, moreover,
I am full young to carry one, and this stout cane would, were
it necessary, do me good service, for I learned in France the
exercise that they call the *bâton*, which differs little from our
English singlestick."

While Cyril was received almost as a member of the family
by Captain Dave and his wife, and found himself on excellent
terms with John Wilkes, he saw that he was viewed with
dislike by the two apprentices. He was scarcely surprised
at this. Before his coming, Robert Ashford had been in the
habit of escorting his young mistress when she went out, and

had no doubt liked these expeditions, as a change from the measuring out of ropes and weighing of iron in the store. Then, again, the apprentices did not join in the conversation at table unless a remark was specially addressed to them; and as Captain Dave was by no means fond of his elder apprentice, it was but seldom that he spoke to him. Robert Ashford was between eighteen and nineteen. He was no taller than Cyril, but it would have been difficult to judge his age by his face, which had a wizened look; and, as Nellie said one day, in his absence, he might pass very well for sixty.

It was easy enough for Cyril to see that Robert Ashford heartily disliked him; the covert scowls that he threw across the table at meal-time, and the way in which he turned his head and feigned to be too busy to notice him as he passed through the shop, were sufficient indications of ill-will. The younger apprentice, Tom Frost, was but a boy of fifteen; he gave Cyril the idea of being a timid lad. He did not appear to share his comrade's hostility to him, but once or twice, when Cyril came out from the office after making up the accounts of the day, he fancied that the boy glanced at him with an expression of anxiety, if not of terror.

"If it were not," Cyril said to himself, " that Tom is clearly too nervous and timid to venture upon an act of dishonesty, I should say that he had been pilfering something; but I feel sure that he would not attempt such a thing as that, though I am by no means certain that Robert Ashford, with his foxy face and cross eyes, would not steal his master's goods or any one else's did he get the chance. Unless he were caught in the act, he could do it with impunity, for everything here is carried on in such a free-and-easy fashion that any amount of goods might be carried off without their being missed."

After thinking the matter over, he said, one afternoon when his employer came in while he was occupied at the accounts,—

"I have not seen anything of a stock-book, Captain Dave. Everything else is now straight, and balanced up to to-day. Here is the book of goods sold, the book of goods

A CHANGE FOR THE BETTER.

received, and the ledger with the accounts; but there is no stock-book such as I find in almost all the other places where I work."

"What do I want with a stock-book?" Captain Dave asked.

"You cannot know how you stand without it," Cyril replied. "You know how much you have paid, and how much you have received during the year; but unless you have a stock-book you do not know whether the difference between the receipts and expenditure represents profit, for the stock may have so fallen in value during the year that you may really have made a loss while seeming to make a profit."

"How can that be?" Captain Dave asked. "I get a fair profit on every article."

"There ought to be a profit, of course," Cyril said; "but sometimes it is found not to be so. Moreover, if there is a stock-book you can tell at any time, without the trouble of opening bins and weighing metal, how much stock you have of each article you sell, and can order your goods accordingly."

"How would you do that?"

"It is very simple, Captain Dave," Cyril said. "After taking stock of the whole of the goods, I should have a ledger in which each article would have a page or more to itself, and every day I should enter from John Wilkes's sales-book a list of the goods that have gone out, each under its own heading. Thus, at any moment, if you were to ask how much chain you had got in stock I could tell you within a fathom. When did you take stock last?"

"I should say it was about fifteen months since. It was only yesterday John Wilkes was saying we had better have a thorough overhauling."

"Quite time, too, I should think, Captain Dave. I suppose you have got the account of your last stock-taking, with the date of it?"

"Oh yes, I have got that;" and the Captain unlocked his desk and took out an account-book. "It has been lying there ever since. It took a wonderful lot of trouble to do, and I had a clerk and two men in for a fortnight, for of course John and the boys were attending to their usual duties. I have often wondered since why I should have had all that trouble over a matter that has never been of the slightest use to me."

"Well, I hope you will take it again, sir; it is a trouble, no doubt, but you will find it a great advantage."

"Are you sure you think it needful, Cyril?"

"Most needful, Captain Dave. You will see the advantage of it afterwards."

"Well, if you think so, I suppose it must be done," the Captain said, with a sigh; "but it will be giving you a lot of trouble to keep this new book of yours."

"That is nothing, sir. Now that I have got all the back work up it will be a simple matter to keep the daily work straight. I shall find ample time to do it without any need of lengthening my hours."

Cyril now set to work in earnest, and telling Mrs. Dowsett he had some books that he wanted to make up in his room before going to bed, he asked her to allow him to keep his light burning.

Mrs. Dowsett consented, but shook her head and said he would assuredly injure his health if he worked by candle light.

Fortunately, John Wilkes had just opened a fresh sales-book, and Cyril told him that he wished to refer to some particulars in the back books. He first opened the ledger by inscribing under their different heads the amount of each description of goods kept in stock at the last stock-taking, and then entered under their respective heads all the sales that had been made, while on an opposite page he entered the amount purchased. It took him a month's hard work, and he finished it on the very day that the new stock-taking concluded.

CHAPTER III.

A THIEF SOMEWHERE.

TWO days after the conclusion of the stock-taking, Cyril said, after breakfast was over,—
"Would it trouble you, Captain Dave, to give me an hour up here before you go downstairs to the counting-house. I am free for two hours now, and there is a matter upon which I hould like to speak to you privately."

"Certainly, lad," the old sailor said, somewhat surprised. "We shall be quiet enough here, as soon as the table is cleared. My dame and Nellie will be helping the maid do up the cabins, and will then be sallying out marketing."

When the maid had cleared the table, Cyril went up to his room and returned with a large ledger and several smaller books.

"I have, for the last month, Captain Dave, been making up this stock-book for my own satisfaction."

"Bless me, lad, why have you taken all that trouble? This accounts, then, for your writing so long at night, for which my dame has been quarrelling with you!"

"It was interesting work," Cyril said quietly. "Now, you see, sir," he went on, opening the big ledger, "here are the separate accounts under each head. Those pages, you see, are for heavy cables for hawsers; of these, at the date of the last stock-taking, there were, according to the book you handed to me, five hundred fathoms in stock. These are the amounts you have purchased since. Now, upon the other side are all the sales of this cable entered in the sales-book. Adding them together, and deducting them from the other side, you will see there should remain in stock four hundred and fifty fathoms. According to the new stock-taking there are four hundred and thirty-eight. That is, I take it, as near as you could expect to get, for, in the measuring out of so many thousand fathoms of cable during the fifteen months between the two stock-takings, there may well have been a loss of the twelve fathoms in giving good measurement."

"That is so," Captain Dave said. "I always say to John Wilkes, 'Give good measurement, John—better a little over than a little under.' Nothing can be clearer or more satisfactory."

Cyril closed the book.

"I am sorry to say, Captain Dave, all the items are not so satisfactory, and that I greatly fear that you have been robbed to a considerable amount."

"Robbed, lad!" the Captain said, starting up from his chair. "Who should rob me? Not John Wilkes, I can be sworn! Not the two apprentices for a surety, for they never go out during the day, and John keeps a sharp look-out upon them, and the entrance to the shop is always locked and barred after work is over, so that none can enter without getting the key, which, as you know, John always brings up and hands to me as soon as he has fastened the door! You are mistaken, lad, and although I know that your intentions are good, you should be careful how you make a charge that might bring ruin to innocent men. Carelessness there may be; but robbery! No; assuredly not."

"I have not brought the charge without warrant, Captain Dave," Cyril said gravely, "and if you will bear with me for a few minutes, I think you will see that there is at least something that wants looking into."

"Well, it is only fair after the trouble you have taken, lad, that I should hear what you have to say; but it will need strong evidence indeed to make me believe that there has been foul play."

"Well, sir," Cyril said, opening the ledger again, "in the first place, I would point out that in all the heavy articles, such as could not conveniently be carried away, the tally of the stock-takers corresponds closely with the figures in this book. In best bower anchors the figures are absolutely the same, and, as you have seen, in heavy cables they closely correspond. In the large ship's compasses, the ship's boilers, and ship's galleys, the numbers tally exactly. So it is with all the heavy articles; the main blocks are correct, and all other heavy gear. This shows that John Wilkes's book is carefully kept, and it would be strange indeed if heavy goods had all been properly entered, and light ones omitted; but yet when we turn to small articles, we find that there is a great discrepancy between the figures. Here is the account, for instance, of the half-inch rope. According to my ledger, there should be eighteen hundred fathoms in stock, whereas the stock-takers found but three hundred and eighty. In two-inch rope there is a deficiency of two hundred and thirty fathoms, in one-inch rope of six hundred and twenty. These sizes, as you know, are always in requisition, and a thief would find ready purchasers for a coil of any of them. But, as might be expected, it is in copper that the deficiency is most serious. Of fourteen-inch bolts, eighty-two are short, of twelve-inch bolts a hundred and thirty, of eight-inch three hundred and nine; and so on throughout almost all the copper stores. According to your expenditure and receipt-book, Captain Dave, you have made, in the last fifteen months, twelve hundred and thirty pounds; but according to this book your stock is less in value, by two thousand and thirty-four pounds, than it should have been. You are, therefore, a poorer man than you were at the beginning of this fifteen months' trading, by eight hundred and four pounds."

Captain Dave sat down in his chair, breathing hard. He took out his handkerchief and wiped the drops of perspiration from his forehead.

"Are you sure of this, boy?" he said hoarsely. "Are you sure that you have made no mistake in your figures?"

"Quite sure," Cyril said firmly. "In all cases in which I have found deficiences I have gone through the books three times and compared the figures, and I am sure that if you put the books into the hands of any city accountant, he will bear out my figures."

For a time Captain Dave sat silent.

"Hast any idea," he said at last, " how this has come about?"

"I have none," Cyril replied. "That John Wilkes is not concerned in it I am as sure as you are; and, thinking the matter over, I see not how the apprentices could have carried off so many articles, some heavy and some bulky, when they left the shop in the evening, without John Wilkes noticing them. So sure am I, that my advice would be that you should take John Wilkes into your confidence, and tell him how matters stand. My only objection to that is that he is a hasty man, and that I fear he would not be able to keep his countenance, so that the apprentices would remark that something was wrong. I am far from saying that they have any hand in it; it would be a grievous wrong to them to have suspicions when there is no shadow of evidence against them; but at any rate, if this matter is to be stopped and the thieves detected, it is most important that they should have, if they are guilty, no suspicion that they are in any way being watched, or that these deficiencies have been discovered. If they have had a hand in the matter they most assuredly had accomplices, for such goods could not be disposed of by an apprentice to any dealer without his being sure that they must have been stolen."

"You are right there, lad—quite right. Did John Wilkes know that I had been robbed in this way he would get into a fury, and no words could restrain him from falling upon the apprentices and beating them till he got some of the truth out of them."

"They may be quite innocent," Cyril said. " It may be that the thieves have discovered some mode of entry into the store either by opening the shutters at the back, or by loosening a board, or even by delving up under the ground. It is surely easier to believe this than that the boys can have contrived to carry off so large a quantity of goods under John Wilkes's eye."

"That is so, lad. I have never liked Robert Ashford, but

God forbid that I should suspect him of such crime only because his forehead is as wrinkled as an ape's, and Providence has set his eyes crossways in his head. You cannot always judge a ship by her upper works; she may be ugly to the eye and yet have a clear run under water. Still, you can't help going by what you see. I agree with you that if we tell John Wilkes about this, those boys will know five minutes afterwards that the ship is on fire; but if we don't tell him, how are we to get to the bottom of what is going on?"

"That is a difficult question, but a few days will not make much difference, when we know that it has been going on for over a year, and may, for aught we know, have been going on much longer. The first thing, Captain Dave, is to send these books to an accountant, for him to go through them and check my figures."

"There is no need for that, lad. I know how careful you are, and you cannot have gone so far wrong as all this."

"No, sir, I am sure that there is no mistake; but, for your own sake as well as mine, it were well that you should have the signature of an accountant to the correctness of the books. If you have to lay the matter before the magistrates, they would not take my testimony as to your losses, and might even say that you were rash in acting upon the word of a boy like myself, and you might then be obliged to have the accounts made up anew, which would cost you more, and cause much delay in the process; whereas, if you put in your books and say that their correctness is vouched for by an accountant, no question would arise on it; nor would there be any delay now, for while the books are being gone into, we can be trying to get to the bottom of the matter here."

"Ay, ay, it shall be done, Master Cyril, as you say. But for the life of me I don't see how we are to get at the bottom of the ship to find out where she is leaking!"

"It seems to me that the first thing, Captain Dave, is to see to the warehouse. As we agreed that the apprentices cannot have carried out all these goods under John Wilkes's eye, and cannot have come down night after night through the house, the warehouse must have been entered from without. As I never go in there, it would be best that you should see to this matter yourself. There are the fastenings of the shutters in the first place, then the boardings all round. As for me, I will look round outside. The window of my room looks into the street, but if you will take me to one of the rooms at the back we can look at the surroundings of the yard, and may gather some idea whether the goods can have been passed over into any of the houses abutting on it, or, as is more likely, into the lane that runs up by its side."

The Captain led the way into one of the rooms at the back of the house, and opening the casement, he and Cyril leaned out. The store occupied fully half the yard, the rest being occupied by anchors, piles of iron, ballast, etc. There were two or three score of guns of various sizes piled on each other. A large store of cannon-ball was ranged in a great pyramid close by. A wall some ten feet high separated the yard from the lane Cyril had spoken of. On the left, adjoining the warehouse, was the yard of the next shop, which belonged to a wool-stapler. Behind were the backs of a number of small houses crowded in between Tower Street and Leadenhall Street.

"I suppose you do not know who lives in those houses, Captain Dave?"

"No, indeed. The land is not like the sea. Afloat, when one sees a sail, one wonders what is her nationality, and whither she is bound, and still more whether she is an honest trader or a rascally pirate; but here on land, one scarcely gives a thought as to who may dwell in the houses round."

"I will walk round presently," Cyril said, "and gather, as far as I can, who they are that live there; but, as I have said, I fancy it is over that wall and into the alley that your goods have departed. The apprentices' room is this side of the house, is it not?"

"Yes; John Wilkes sleeps in the room next to yours, and the door opposite to his is that of the lads' room."

"Do the windows of any of the rooms look into that lane?"

"No; it is a blank wall on that side."

"There is the clock striking nine," Cyril said, starting. "It is time for me to be off. Then you will take the books to-day, Captain Dave?"

"I will carry them off at once, and when I return will look narrowly into the fastenings of the two windows and door from the warehouse into the yard; and will take care to do so when the boys are engaged in the front shop."

When his work was done, Cyril went round to the houses behind the yard, and he found that they stood in a small court, with three or four trees growing in the centre, and were evidently inhabited by respectable citizens. Over the door of one was painted, "Joshua Heddings, Attorney"; next to him was Gilbert Cushing, who dealt in jewels, silks, and other precious commodities from the East; next to him was a doctor, and beyond a dealer in spices. This was enough to assure him that it was not through such houses as these that the goods had been carried.

Cyril had not been back at the mid-day meal, for his work that day lay up by Holborn Bar, where he had two customers whom he attended with but half an hour's interval between the visits, and on the days on which he went there he was accustomed to get something to eat at a tavern hard by.

Supper was an unusually quiet meal. Captain Dave now and then asked John Wilkes a question as to the business matters of the day, but evidently spoke with an effort. Nellie rattled on as usual; but the burden of keeping up the conversation lay entirely on her shoulders and those of Cyril. After the apprentices had left, and John Wilkes had started for his usual resort, the Captain lit his pipe. Nellie signed to Cyril to come and seat himself by her in the window that projected out over the street, and enabled the occupants of the seats at either side to have a view up and down it.

"What have you been doing to father, Cyril?" she asked, in low tones; "he has been quite unlike himself all day. Generally when he is out of temper he rates every one heartily, as if we were a mutinous crew, but to-day he has gone about scarcely speaking; he hasn't said a cross word to any of us, but several times when I spoke to him I got no answer, and it is easy to see that he is terribly put out about something. He was in his usual spirits at breakfast; then, you know, he was talking with you for an hour, and it does not take much guessing to see that it must have been something that passed between you that has put him out. Now what was it?"

"I don't see why you should say that, Mistress Nellie. It is true we did have a talk together, and he examined some fresh books I have been making out and said that he was mightily pleased with my work. I went away at nine o'clock, and something may have occurred to upset him between that and dinner."

"All which means that you don't mean to tell me anything about it, Master Cyril. Well, then, you may consider yourself in my black books altogether," she said petulantly.

"I am sorry that you should say so," he said. "If it were true that anything that I had said to him had ruffled him, it would be for him to tell you, and not for me."

"Methinks I have treated Robert Ashford scurvily, and I shall take him for my escort to see His Majesty attend service at St. Paul's to-morrow."

Cyril smiled.

"I think it would be fair to give him a turn, Mistress, and I am glad to see that you have such a kind thought."

Nellie rose indignantly, and taking her work sat down by the side of her mother.

"It is a fine evening," Cyril said to Captain Dave, "and I think I shall take a walk round. I shall return in an hour."

The Captain understood, by a glance Cyril gave him, that he was going out for some purpose connected with the matter they had in hand.

"Ay, ay, lad," he said. "It is not good for you to be sitting moping at home every evening. I have often wondered before that you did not take a walk on deck before you turned in. I always used to do so myself."

"I don't think there is any moping in it, Captain Dave," Cyril said, with a laugh. "If you knew how pleasant the evenings have been to me after the life I lived before, you would not say so."

Cyril's only object in going out, however, was to avoid the necessity of having to talk with Dame Dowsett and Nellie. His thoughts were running on nothing but the robbery, and he had found it very difficult to talk in his usual manner, and to answer Nellie's sprightly sallies. It was dark already. A few oil lamps gave a feeble light here and there. At present he had formed no plan whatever of detecting the thieves; he was as much puzzled as the Captain himself as to how the goods could have been removed. It would be necessary, of course, to watch the apprentices, but he did not think that anything was likely to come out of this. It was the warehouse itself that must be watched, in order to discover how the thieves made an entry. His own idea was that they got over the wall by means of a rope, and in some way managed to effect an entry into the warehouse. The apprentices could hardly aid them unless they came down through the house.

If they had managed to get a duplicate key of the door leading from the bottom of the stairs to the shop, they could, of course, unbar the windows, and pass things out—that part of the business would be easy; but he could not believe that they would venture frequently to pass down through the house. It was an old one, and the stairs creaked. He himself was a light sleeper; he had got into the way of waking at the slightest sound, from the long watches he had had for his father's return, and felt sure that he should have heard them open their door and steal along the passage past his room, however quietly they might do it. He walked up the

Exchange, then along Cheapside as far as St. Paul's, and back. Quiet as it was in Thames Street there was no lack of animation elsewhere. Apprentices were generally allowed to go out for an hour after supper, the regulation being that they returned to their homes by eight o'clock. Numbers of these were about. A good many citizens were on their way home after supping with friends. The city watch, with lanterns, patrolled the streets, and not infrequently interfered in quarrels which broke out among the apprentices. Cyril felt more solitary among the knots of laughing, noisy lads than in the quiet streets, and was glad to be home again. Captain Dave himself came down to open the door.

"I have just sent the women to bed," he said. "The two boys came in five minutes ago. I thought you would not be long."

"I did not go out for anything particular," Cyril said; "but Mistress Nellie insisted that there was something wrong with you, and that I must know what it was about, so, feeling indeed indisposed to talk, I thought it best to go out for a short time."

"Yes, yes. Women always want to know, lad. I have been long enough at sea, you may be sure, to know that when anything is wrong, it is the best thing to keep it from the passengers as long as you can."

"You took the books away this morning, Captain Dave?" Cyril asked as they sat down.

"Ay, lad, I took them to Master Skinner, who bears as good a reputation as any accountant in the city, and he promised to take them in hand without loss of time; but I have been able to do nothing here. John, or one or other of the boys, was always in the warehouse, and I have had no opportunity of examining the door and shutters closely. When the house is sound asleep we will take a lantern and go down to look at them. I have been thinking that we must let John Wilkes into this matter; it is too much to bear on my mind by myself. He is my first mate, you see, and in time of danger, the first mate, if he is worth anything, is the man the captain relies on for help."

"By all means tell him, then," Cyril said. "I can keep books, but I have no experience in matters like this, and shall be very glad to have his opinion and advice."

"There he is—half-past eight. He is as punctual as clockwork."

Cyril ran down and let John in.

"The Captain wants to speak to you," he said, "before you go up to bed."

John, after carefully bolting the door, followed him upstairs.

"I have got some bad news for you, John. There, light your pipe again, and sit down. My good dame has gone off to bed, and we have got the cabin to ourselves."

John touched an imaginary hat and obeyed orders.

"The ship has sprung a bad leak, John. This lad here has found it out, and it is well he did, for unless he had done so we should have had her foundering under our feet without so much as suspecting anything was going wrong."

The sailor took his newly-lighted pipe from between his lips and stared at the Captain in astonishment.

"Yes, it is hard to believe, mate, but, by the Lord Harry, it is as I say. There is a pirate about somewhere, and the books show that, since the stock-taking fifteen months ago, he has eased the craft of her goods to the tune of two thousand pounds and odd."

John Wilkes flung his pipe on to the table with such force that it shivered into fragments.

"Dash my timbers!" he exclaimed. "Who is the man? You only give me the orders, sir, and I am ready to range alongside and board him."

"That is what we have got to find out, John. That the goods have gone is certain, but how they can have gone beats us altogether."

"Do you mean to say, Captain, that they have stolen them out of the place under my eyes and me know nothing about it? It can't be, sir. There must be some mistake. I know naught about figures, save enough to put down the things I sell, but I don't believe as a thing has gone out of the shop unbeknown to me. That yarn won't do for me, sir," and he looked angrily at Cyril.

"It is true enough, John, for all that. The books have been balanced up. We knew what was in stock fifteen months ago, and we knew from your sale-book what has passed out of the shop, and from your entry-book what has come in. We know now what there is remaining. We find that in bulky goods, such as cables and anchors and ship's boilers and such-like, the accounts tally exactly, but in the small rope, and above all in the copper, there is a big shrinkage. I will read you the figures of some of them."

John's face grew longer and longer as he heard the totals read.

"Well, I'm jiggered!" he said, when the list was concluded. "I could have sworn that the cargo was right according to the manifest. Well, Captain, all I can say is, if that 'ere list be correct, the best thing you can do is to send me adrift as a blind fool. I have kept my tallies as correct as I could, and I thought I had marked down every package that has left the ship, and here they must have been passing out pretty nigh in cart-loads under my very eyes, and I knew nothing about it."

"I don't blame you, John, more than I blame myself. I am generally about on deck, and had no more idea that the cargo was being meddled with than you had. I have been wrong in letting matters go on so long without taking stock of them and seeing that it was all right; but I never saw the need for it. This is what comes of taking to a trade you know nothing about; we have just been like two children, thinking that it was all plain and above board, and that we had nothing to do but to sell our goods and to fill up again when the hold got empty. Well, it is of no use talking over that part of the business. What we have got to do is to find out this leak and stop it. We are pretty well agreed, Cyril and me, that the things don't go out of the shop by daylight. The question is, how do they go out at night?"

"I always lock up the hatches according to orders, Captain."

"Yes, I have no doubt you do, John; but maybe the fastenings have been tampered with. The only way in which we see it can have been managed is that some one has been in the habit of getting over the wall between the yard and the lane, and then getting into the warehouse somehow. It must have been done very often, for if the things had been taken in considerable quantities you would have noticed that the stock was short directly the next order came in. Now I propose we light these two lanterns I have got here, and that we go down and have a look round the hold."

Lighting the candles, they went downstairs. The Captain took out the key and turned the lock. It grated loudly as he did so.

"That is a noisy lock," Cyril said.

"It wants oiling," John replied. "I have been thinking of doing it for the last month, but it has always slipped out of my mind."

"At any rate," Cyril said, "it is certain that thieves could not have got into the shop this way, for the noise would have been heard all over the house."

The door between the shop and the warehouse was next unlocked. The fastenings of the shutters and doors were first examined; there was no sign of their having been tampered with. Each bolt and hasp was tried, and the screws examined. Then they went round trying every one of the stout planks that formed the side; all were firm and in good condition.

"It beats me altogether," the Captain said, when they had finished their examination. "The things cannot walk out of themselves; they have got to be carried. But how the fellows who carry them get in is more than I can say. There is nowhere else to look, is there, John?"

"Not that I can see, Captain."

They went to the door into the shop, and were about to close it, when Cyril said,—

"Some of the things that are gone are generally kept in here, Captain—the rope up to two inch, for example, and a good deal of canvas, and most of the smaller copper fittings; so that, whoever the thief is, he must have been in the habit of coming in here as well as into the warehouse."

"That is so, lad. Perhaps they entered from this side."

"Will you hold the lantern here, John," Cyril said.

The sailor held the lantern to the lock.

"There are no scratches nor signs of tools having been used here," Cyril said, examining both the lock and the door-post. Whether the thief came into the warehouse first, or not, he must have had a key."

The Captain nodded

"Thieves generally carry a lot of keys with them, Cyril; and if one does not quite fit they can file it until it does."

The shutters of the shop window and its fastenings, and those of the door, were as secure as those of the warehouse, and, completely puzzled, the party went upstairs again.

"There must be some way of getting in and out, although we can't find it," Captain Dave said. "Things can't have gone off by themselves."

"It may be, Captain," John Wilkes said, "that some of the planks may be loose."

"But we tried them all, John."

"Ay, they seem firm enough, but it may be that one of them is wedged in, and that when the wedges are taken out it could be pulled off."

"I think you would have noticed it, John. If there was anything of that sort it must be outside. However, we will take a good look round the yard to-morrow. The warehouse is strongly built, and I don't believe that any plank could be taken off and put back again, time after time, without making a noise that would be heard in the house. What do you think, Cyril?"

"I agree with you, Captain Dave. How the thieves make an entry I can't imagine, but I don't believe that it is through the wall of the warehouse. I am convinced that the robberies must have been very frequent. Had a large amount been taken at a time, John Wilkes would have been sure to notice it. Then, again, the thieves would not come so often, and each time for a comparatively small amount of booty, unless it could be managed without any serious risk or trouble. However, now that we do know that they come, we shall have, I should think, very little difficulty in finding out how it is done."

"You may warrant we will keep a sharp look-out," John Wilkes said savagely. "If the Captain will give me the use of a room at the back of the house, you may be sure I sha'n't close an eye till I have got to the bottom of the matter. I am responsible for the cargo below, and if I had kept as sharp an eye on the stores as I ought to have done, this would not have happened. Only let me catch them trying to board, and I will give them such a reception that I warrant me they will sheer off with a bullet or two in them. I have got that pair of boarding pistols, and a cutlass, hung up over my bed."

"You must not do that, John," the Captain said. "It isn't a matter of beating off the pirates by pouring a broadside into them. Maybe you might cripple them, more likely they would make off, and we want to capture them. Therefore, I say, let us watch, and find out how they do it. When we once know that, we can lay our plans for capturing them the next time they come. I will take watch and watch with you."

"Well, if it goes on long, Captain, I won't say no to that; but for to-night anyhow I will sit up alone."

"Very well, let it be so, John. But mind, whatever you see, you keep as still as a mouse. Just steal to my room in your stockinged feet directly you see anything moving. Open the door and say, 'Strange sail in sight!' and I will be over at your window in no time. And now, Cyril, you and I may as well turn in."

The night passed quietly.

"You saw nothing, I suppose, John?" the Captain said next morning, after the apprentices had gone down from breakfast.

"Not a thing, Captain."

"Now we will go and have a look in the yard. Will you come, Cyril?"

"I should like to come," Cyril replied, "but, as I have never been out there before, had you not better make some pretext for me to do so. You might say, in the hearing of the apprentices, 'We may as well take the measurements for that new shed we were talking about, and see how much boarding it will require.' Then you can call to me out from the office to come and help you to measure."

"Then you still think the apprentices are in it?" John Wilkes asked sharply.

"I don't say I think so, John. I have nothing against them. I don't believe they could come down at night without being heard; I feel sure they could not get into the shop without that stiff bolt making a noise. Still, as it is possible they may be concerned in the matter, I think that, now we have it in good train for getting to the bottom of it, it would be well to keep the matter altogether to ourselves."

"Quite right," Captain Dave said approvingly. "When you suspect treachery, don't let a soul think that you have got such a matter in your mind, until you are in a position to take the traitor by the collar and put a pistol to his ear. That idea of yours is a very good one; I will say something about the shed to John this morning, and then when you go down to the counting-house after dinner I will call to you to come out o the yard with us."

After dinner, Captain Dave went with Cyril into the counting-house.

"We had an order in this morning for a set of ship's anchors, and John and I have been in the yard looking them out; we looked over the place pretty sharply, as you may be sure, but as far as we could see the place is as solid as when it was built, fifty years ago, by my father."

The Captain went out into the store, and ten minutes afterwards re-entered the shop and shouted,—

"Come out here, Cyril, and lend a hand. We are going to take those measurements. Bring out your ink-horn, and a bit of paper to put them down as we take them."

The yard was some sixty feet long by twenty-five broad, exclusive of the space occupied by the warehouse. This, as Cyril had observed from the window above, did not extend as far as the back wall; but on walking round there with the two men, he found that the distance was greater than he had expected, and that there was a space of some twenty feet clear.

"This is where we are thinking of putting the shed," the Captain said in a loud voice.

"But I see that you have a crane and door into the loft over the warehouse there," Cyril said, looking up.

"We never use that now. When my father first began business, he used to buy up old junk and such-like stores, and store them up there, but it didn't pay for the trouble; and, besides, as you see, he wanted every foot of the yard room, and of course at that time they had to leave a space clear for the carts to come up from the gate round here, so it was given up, and the loft is empty now."

Cyril looked up at the crane. It was swung round so as to lie flat against the wooden shutters. The rope was still through the block, and passed into the loft through a hole cut at the junction of the shutters.

They now measured the space between the warehouse and the wall, the Captain repeating the figures, still in a loud voice; then they discussed the height of the walls, and after some argument between the Captain and John Wilkes agreed that this should be the same as the rest of the building. Still talking on the subject, they returned through the warehouse, Cyril on the way taking a look at the massive gate that opened into the lane. In addition to a heavy bar it had a strong hasp, fastened by a great padlock. The apprentices were busy at work coiling up some rope when they passed by.

"When we have knocked a door through the end there, John," Captain Dave said, " it will give you a deal more room, and you will be able to get rid of all these cables and heavy dunnage, and to have matters more ship-shape here."

While they had been taking the measurements, all three had carefully examined the wall of the warehouse.

" There is nothing wrong there, Cyril," his employer said, as, leaving John Wilkes in the warehouse, they went through the shop into the little office.

" Certainly nothing that I could see, Captain Dave. I did not before know the loft had any opening to the outside. Of course I have seen the ladder going up from the warehouse to that trap-door; but as it was closed I thought no more of it."

" I don't suppose any one has been up there for years, lad. What, are you thinking that some one might get in through those shutters? Why, they are twenty feet from the ground, so that you would want a long ladder, and when you got up there you would find that you could not open the shutters. I said nobody had been up there, but I did go up myself to have a look round when I first settled down here, and there is a big bar with a padlock."

Cyril thought no more about it, and after supper it was arranged that he and Captain Dave should keep watch by turns at the window of the room that had been now given to John Wilkes, and that the latter should have a night in his berth, as the Captain expressed it. John Wilkes had made some opposition, saying that he would be quite willing to take his watch.

" You will just obey orders, John," the Captain said. " You have had thirty-six hours off the reel on duty, and you have got to be at work all day to-morrow again. You shall take the middle watch to-morrow night if you like, but one can see with half an eye that you are not fit to be on the look-out to-night. I doubt if any of us could see as far as the length of the bowsprit. It is pretty nearly pitch dark; there is not a star to be seen, and it looked to me, when I turned out before supper, as if we were going to have a storm."

CHAPTER IV.

CAPTURED.

IT was settled that Cyril was to take the first watch, and that the Captain should relieve him at one o'clock. At nine, the family went to bed. A quarter of an hour later, Cyril stole noiselessly from his attic down to John Wilkes's room. The door had been left ajar, and the candle was still burning.

"I put a chair by the window," the sailor said, from his bed, "and left the light, for you might run foul of something or other in the dark, though I have left a pretty clear gangway for you."

Cyril blew out the candle, and seated himself at the window. For a time he could see nothing, and told himself that the whole contents of the warehouse might be carried off without his being any the wiser.

"I shall certainly see nothing," he said to himself; "but, at least, I may hear something."

So saying, he turned the fastening of the casement and opened it about half an inch. As his eyes became accustomed to the darkness, he was able to make out the line of the roof of the warehouse, which was some three or four feet below the level of his eyes, and some twenty feet away on his left. The time passed slowly. He kept himself awake by thinking over the old days in France, the lessons he had learnt with his friend, Harry Parton, and the teaching of the old clergyman.

He heard the bell of St. Paul's strike ten and eleven. The last stroke had scarcely ceased to vibrate when he rose to his feet suddenly. He heard, on his left, a scraping noise. A moment later it ceased, and then was renewed again. It lasted but a few seconds; then he heard an irregular, shuffling noise, that seemed to him upon the roof of the warehouse. Pressing his face to the casement, he suddenly became aware that the straight line of the ridge was broken by something moving along it, and a moment later he made out a second object, just behind the first. Moving with the greatest care, he made his way out of the room, half closed the door behind him, crossed the passage, and pushed at a door opposite.

"Captain Dave," he said, in a low voice, "get up at once, and please don't make a noise."

"Ay, ay, lad."

There was a movement from the bed, and a moment later the Captain stood beside him.

"What is it, lad?" he whispered.

"There are two figures moving along on the ridge of the roof of the warehouse. I think it is the apprentices. I heard a slight noise, as if they were letting themselves down from their window by a rope. It is just over that roof, you know."

There was a rustling sound as the Captain slipped his doublet on.

"That is so. The young scoundrels! What can they be doing on the roof?"

They went to the window behind. Just as they reached it there was a vivid flash of lightning. It sufficed to show them a figure lying at full length at the farther end of the roof; then all was dark again, and a second or two later came a sharp, crashing roar of thunder.

"We had better stand well back from the window," Cyril whispered. "Another flash might show us to any one looking this way."

"What does it mean, lad? What on earth is that boy doing there? I could not see which it was."

"I think it is Ashford," Cyril said. "The figure in front seemed the smaller of the two."

"But where on earth can Tom have got to?"

"I should fancy, sir, that Robert has lowered him so that he can get his feet on the crane and swing it outwards; then he might sit down on it and swing himself by the rope into the loft if the doors are not fastened inside. Robert, being taller, would have no difficulty in lowering himself——

There!" he broke off, as another flash of lightning lit up the sky. "He has gone, now; there is no one on the roof."

John Wilkes was by this time standing beside them, having started up at the first flash of lightning.

"Do you go up, John, into their room," the Captain said. "I think there can be no doubt that these fellows on the roof are Ashford and Frost, but it is as well to be able to swear to it."

The foreman returned in a minute or two.

"The room is empty, Captain; the window is open, and there is a rope hanging down from it. Shall I cast it adrift?"

"Certainly not, John. We do not mean to take them to-night, and they must be allowed to go back to their beds without a suspicion that they have been watched. I hope and trust that it is not so bad as it looks, and that the boys have only broken out from devilry. You know, boys will do things of that sort just because it is forbidden."

"There must be more than that," John Wilkes said. "If it had been just after they went to their rooms, it might be that they went to some tavern or other low resort, but the town is all asleep now."

They again went close to the window, pushed the casement a little more open, and stood listening there. In two or three minutes there was a very slight sound heard.

"They are unbolting the door into the yard," John Wilkes whispered. "I would give a month's pay to be behind them with a rope's end."

Half a minute later there was a sudden gleam of light below, and they could see the door open. The light disappeared again, but they heard footsteps; then they saw the light thrown on the fastening to the outer gate, and could make out that two figures below were applying a key to the padlock. This was taken off and laid down; then the heavy wooden bar was lifted, and also laid on the ground. The gate opened as if pushed from the other side. The two figures went out; the sound of a low murmur of conversation could be heard; then they returned, the gate was closed and fastened again, they entered the warehouse, the light disappeared, and the door was closed.

"That's how the things went, John."

"Ay, ay, sir," the foreman growled.

"As they were undoing the gate, the light fell on a coil of rope they had set down there, and a bag which I guess had copper of some kind in it. They have done us cleverly, the young villains! There was not noise enough to wake a cat. They must have had every bolt and hinge well oiled."

"We had better close the casement now, sir, for as they come back along the ridge they will be facing it, and if a flash of lightning came they would see that it was half open, and even if they did not catch sight of our faces they would think it suspicious that the window should be open, and it might put them on their guard."

"Yes; and we may as well turn in at once, John. Like enough when they get back they will listen for a bit at their door, so as to make sure that everything is quiet before they turn in. There is nothing more to see now. Of course they will get in as they got out. You had better turn in as you are, Cyril; they may listen at your door."

Cyril at once went up to his room, closed the door, placed a chair against it, and then lay down on his bed. He listened intently, and four or five minutes later thought that he heard a door open; but he could not be sure, for just at that moment heavy drops began to patter down upon the tiles. The noise rose louder and louder until he could scarce have heard himself speak. Then there was a bright flash and the deep rumble of the thunder mingled with the sharp rattle of the raindrops overhead. He listened for a time to the storm, and then dropped off to sleep.

Things went on as usual at breakfast the next morning. During the meal, Captain Dave gave the foreman several instructions as to the morning's work.

"I am going on board the *Royalist*," he said. "John Browning wants me to overhaul all the gear, and see what will do for another voyage or two, and what must be new. His skipper asked for new running rigging all over, but he thinks that there can't be any occasion for its all being renewed. I don't expect I shall be in till dinner-time, so any one that wants to see me must come again in the afternoon."

Ten minutes later, Cyril went out, on his way to his work. Captain Dave was standing a few doors away.

"Before I go on board the brig, lad, I am going up to the Chief Constable's to arrange about this business. I want to get four men of the watch. Of course, it may be some nights before this is tried again, so I shall have the men stowed away in the kitchen. Then we must keep watch, and as soon as we see those young villains on the roof, we will let the men out at the front door. Two will post themselves this end of the lane, and two go round into Leadenhall Street and station themselves at the other end. When the boys go out after supper we will unlock the door at the bottom of the stairs into the shop, and the door into the warehouse. Then we will steal down into the shop and listen there until we hear them open the door into the yard, and then go into the warehouse and be ready to make a rush out as soon as they get the gate open. John will have his boatswain's whistle ready, and will give the signal. That will bring the watch up, so they will be caught in a trap."

"I should think that would be a very good plan, Captain Dave, though I wish that it could have been done without Tom Frost being taken. He is a timid sort of boy, and I have no doubt that he has been entirely under the thumb of Robert."

"Well, if he has he will get off lightly," the Captain said. "Even if a boy is a timid boy, he knows what will be the consequences if he is caught robbing his master. Cowardice is no excuse for crime, lad. The boys have always been well treated, and though I daresay Ashford is the worst of the two, if the other had been honest he would not have seen him robbing me without letting me know."

For six nights' watch was kept without success. Every evening, when the family and apprentices had retired to rest, John Wilkes went quietly downstairs and admitted the four constables, letting them out in the morning before any one was astir. Mrs. Dowsett had been taken into her husband's confidence so far as to know that he had discovered he had been robbed, and was keeping a watch for the thieves. She was not told that the apprentices were concerned in the matter, for Captain Dave felt sure that, however much she might try to conceal it, Robert Ashford would perceive, by her looks that something was wrong.

Nellie was told a day or two later, for, although ignorant of her father's nightly watchings, she was conscious from his manner, and that of her mother, that something was amiss, and was so persistent in her inquiries, that the Captain consented to her mother telling her that he had a suspicion he was being robbed, and warning her that it was essential that the subject must not be in any way alluded to.

"Your father is worrying over it a good deal, Nellie, and it is better that he should not perceive that you are aware of it. Just let things go on as they were."

"Is the loss serious, mother?"

"Yes; he thinks that a good deal of money has gone. I don't think he minds that so much as the fact that, so far, he doesn't know who the people most concerned in it may be. He has some sort of suspicion in one quarter, but has no clue whatever to the men most to blame."

"Does Cyril know anything about it?" Nellie asked suddenly.

"Yes, he knows, my dear; indeed, it was owing to his cleverness that your father first came to have suspicions."

"Oh! that explains it," Nellie said. "He had been talking to father, and I asked what it was about and he would not tell me, and I have been very angry with him ever since."

"I have noticed that you have been behaving very foolishly," Mrs. Dowsett said quietly, "and that for the last week you have been taking Robert with you as an escort when you went out of an evening. I suppose you did that to annoy Cyril, but I don't think that he minded much."

"I don't think he did, mother," Nellie agreed, with a laugh which betrayed a certain amount of irritation. "I saw that he smiled, two or three evenings back, when I told Robert at supper that I wanted him to go out with me, and I was rarely angry, I can tell you."

Cyril had indeed troubled himself in no way about Nellie's coolness; but when she had so pointedly asked Robert to go with her, he had been amused at the thought of how greatly she would be mortified, when Robert was haled up to the Guildhall for robbing her father, at the thought that he had been accompanying her as an escort.

"I rather hope this will be our last watch, Captain Dave," he said, on the seventh evening.

"Why do you hope so specially to-night, lad?"

"Of course I have been hoping so every night. But I think it is likely that the men who take the goods come regularly once a week; for in that case there would be no occasion for them to meet at other times to arrange on what night they should be in the lane."

"Yes, that is like enough, Cyril; and the hour will probably be the same, too. John and I will share your watch to-night, so as to be ready to get the men off without loss of time."

Cyril had always taken the first watch, which was from half-past nine till twelve. The Captain and Wilkes had taken the other watches by turns.

As before, just as the bell finished striking eleven, the three watchers again heard through the slightly open casement the scraping noise on the left. It had been agreed that they should not move, lest the sound should be heard outside. Each grasped the stout cudgel he held in his hand, and gazed at the roof of the warehouse, which could now be plainly seen, for the moon was half full and the sky was clear. As before, the two figures went along, and this time they could clearly recognise them. They were both sitting astride of the ridge tiles, and moved themselves along by means of their hands. They waited until they saw one after the other disappear at the end of the roof, and then John Wilkes quietly stole downstairs. The four constables had been warned to be specially wakeful.

"They are at it again to-night," John said to them, as he entered. "Now, do you two who go round into Leadenhall Street start at once, but don't take your post at the end of the lane for another five or six minutes. The thieves outside may not have come up at present. As you go out, leave the door ajar; in five minutes you others should stand ready. Don't go to the corner, but wait in the doorway below until you hear the whistle. They will be only fifteen or twenty yards up the lane, and would see you if you took up your station at the corner; but the moment you hear the whistle, rush out and have at them. We shall be there before you will."

John went down with the last two men, entered the shop, and stood there waiting until he should be joined by his master. The latter and Cyril remained at the window until they saw the door of the warehouse open, and then hurried downstairs. Both were in their stockinged feet, so that their movements should be noiseless.

"Come on, John; they are in the yard," the Captain whispered; and they entered the warehouse and went noiselessly on, until they stood at the door. The process of unbarring the gate was nearly accomplished. As it swung open, John Wilkes put his whistle to his lips and blew a loud, shrill call, and the three rushed forward. There was a shout of alarm, a fierce imprecation, and three of the four figures at the gate sprang at them. Scarce a blow had been struck when the two constables ran up and joined in the fray. Two men fought stoutly, but were soon overpowered. Robert Ashford, knife in hand, had attacked John Wilkes with fury, and would have

"ROBERT ASHFORD, KNIFE IN HAND, ATTACKED JOHN WILKES WITH FURY."

stabbed him, as his attention was engaged upon one of the men outside, had not Cyril brought his cudgel down sharply on his knuckles, when, with a yell of pain, he dropped the knife and fled up the lane. He had gone but a short distance, however, when he fell into the hands of the two constables, who were running towards him. One of them promptly knocked him down with his cudgel, and then proceeded to bind his hands behind him, while the other ran on to join in the fray. It was over before he got there, and his comrades were engaged in binding the two robbers. Tom Frost had taken no part in the fight. He stood looking on, paralysed with terror, and when the two men were overpowered he fell on his knees beseeching his master to have mercy on him.

"It is too late, Tom," the Captain said. "You have been robbing me for months, and now you have been caught in the act you will have to take your share in the punishment. You are a prisoner of the constables' here, and not of mine, and even if I were willing to let you go, they would have their say in the matter. Still, if you make a clean breast of what you know about it, I will do all I can to get you off lightly; and seeing that you are but a boy, and have been, perhaps, led into this, they will not be disposed to be hard on you. Pick up that lantern and bring it here, John; let us see what plunder they were making off with."

There was no rope this time, but a bag containing some fifty pounds' weight of brass and copper fittings. One of the constables took possession of this.

"You had better come along with us to the Bridewell, Master Dowsett, to sign the charge sheet, though I don't know whether it is altogether needful, seeing that we have caught them in the act; and you will all three have to be at the Court to-morrow at ten o'clock."

"I will go with you," the Captain said; "but I will first slip in and put my shoes on; I brought them down in my hand and shall be ready in a minute. You may as well lock up this gate again, John. I will go out through the front door and join them in the lane." As he went into the house, John Wilkes closed the gate and put up the bar, then took up the lantern and said to Cyril,—

"Well, Master Cyril, this has been a good night's work, and mighty thankful I am that we have caught the pirates. It was a good day for us all when you came to the Captain, or they might have gone on robbing him till the time came that there was nothing more to rob; and I should never have held up my head again, for though the Captain would never believe that I had had a hand in bringing him to ruin, other people would not have thought so, and I might never have got a chance of proving my innocence. Now we will just go to the end of the yard and see if they did manage to get into the warehouse by means of that crane, as you thought they did."

They found that the crane had been swung out just far enough to afford a foot-hold to those lowering themselves on to it from the roof. The door of the loft stood open.

"Just as you said. You could not have been righter, not if you had seen them at it. And now I reckon we may as well lock up the place again, and turn in. The Captain has got the key of the front door, and we will leave the lantern burning at the bottom of the stairs."

Cyril got up as soon as he heard a movement in the house, and went down to the shop, which had been already opened by John Wilkes.

"It seems quiet here, without the apprentices, John. Is there any way in which I can help?"

"No, thank you, sir. We sha'n't be moving the goods about till after breakfast, and then, no doubt, the Captain will get an extra man in to help me. I reckon he will have to get a neighbour in to give an eye to the place while we are all away at the Court."

"I see there is the rope still hanging from their window," Cyril said, as he went out into the yard.

"I thought it best to leave it there," John Wilkes replied;

"and I ain't been up into the loft either. It is best to leave matters just as they were. Like enough, they will send an officer down from the Court to look at them."

When the family assembled at breakfast, Mrs. Dowsett was looking very grave. The Captain, on the other hand, was in capital spirits. Nellie, as usual, was somewhat late.

"Where is everybody?" she asked in surprise, seeing that Cyril alone was in his place with her father and mother.

"John Wilkes is downstairs, looking after the shop, and will come up and have his breakfast when we have done," her father replied.

"Are both the apprentices out, then?" she asked.

"The apprentices are in limbo," the Captain said grimly.

"In limbo, father! What does that mean?"

"It means that they are in gaol, my dear."

Nellie put down the knife and fork that she had just taken up.

"Are you joking, father?"

"Very far from it, my dear; it is no joke to any of us— certainly not to me, and not to Robert Ashford, or Tom Frost. They have been robbing me for the last year, and, for aught I know, before that. If it had not been for Master Cyril it would not have been very long before I should have had to put my shutters up."

"But how could they rob you, father?"

"By stealing my goods, and selling them, Nellie. The way they did it was to lower themselves by a rope from their window on to the roof of the warehouse, and to get down at the other end on to the crane, and then into the loft. Then they went down and took what they had a fancy to, undid the door, and went into the yard, and then handed over their booty to the fellows waiting at the gate for it. Last night we caught them at it, after having been on the watch for ten days."

"That is what I heard last night, then," she said. "I was woke by a loud whistle, and then I heard a sound of quarrelling and fighting in the lane. I thought it was some roysterers going home late. Oh, father, it is dreadful to think of! And what will they do to them?"

"It is a hanging matter," the Captain said; "it is not only theft, but mutiny. No doubt the judges will take a lenient view of Tom Frost's case, both on the ground of his youth, and because, no doubt, he was influenced by Ashford; but I would not give much for Robert's chances. No doubt it will be a blow to you, Nellie, for you seem to have taken to him mightily of late."

Nellie was about to give an emphatic contradiction, but as she remembered how pointedly she had asked for his escort during the last few days, she flushed up, and was silent.

"It is terrible to think of," she said, after a pause. "I suppose this is what you and Cyril were consulting about, father. I have to ask your pardon, Master Cyril, for my rudeness to you; but of course I did not think it was anything of consequence, or that you could not have told me if you had wished to do so."

"You need not beg my pardon, Mistress Nellie. No doubt you thought it churlish on my part to refuse to gratify your curiosity, and I am not surprised that you took offence. I knew that when you learned how important it was to keep silence over the matter, that you would acquit me of the intention of making a mystery about nothing."

"I suppose you knew, mother?" Nellie asked.

"I knew that your father believed that he was being robbed, Nellie, and that he was keeping watch for some hours every night, but I did not know that he suspected the apprentices. I am glad that we did not, for assuredly we should have found it very hard to school our faces so that they should not guess that aught was wrong."

"That was why we said nothing about it, Nellie. It has been as much as I have been able to do to sit at table, and talk in the shop as usual, with boys I knew were robbing me; and I know honest John Wilkes must have felt it still more. But till a week ago we would not believe that they had a hand in the matter. It is seven nights since Cyril caught them creeping along the roof, and called me to the window in John Wilkes's room, whence he was watching the yard, not thinking the enemy was in the house."

"And how did you come to suspect that robbery was going on, Cyril?"

"Simply because, on making up the books, I found there was a great deficiency in the stores."

"That is what he was doing when he was sitting up at night, after you were in bed, Miss Nellie," her father said. "You may thank your stars that he took a berth in this ship, for the scoundrels would have foundered her to a certainty, if he had not done so. I tell you, child, he has saved this craft from going to the bottom. I have not said much to him about it, but he knows that I don't feel it any the less."

"And who were the other men who were taken, father?"

"That I can't tell you, Nellie. I went to the Bridewell with them, and as soon as I saw them safely lodged there I came home. They will be had up before the Lord Mayor this morning, and then I daresay I shall know all about them. Now I must go and take my watch below, and let John Wilkes come off duty."

"Why, John, what is the matter?" Mrs. Dowsett said, when the foreman entered.

"Nothing worth speaking of, Mistress. I got a clip over the eye from one of the pirates we were capturing. The thing mattered nothing, one way or the other, but it might have cost me my life, because, for a moment, it pretty well dazed me. That young villain, Bob, was just coming at me with his knife, and I reckon it would have gone hard with me if Master Cyril here hadn't, just in the nick of time, brought his stick down on Robert's knuckles, and that so sharply that the fellow dropped his knife with a yell, and took to his heels, only to fall into the hands of two of the watch coming from the other end of the lane. You did me a good turn, lad, and if ever I get the chance of ranging up alongside of you in a fray, you may trust me to return it."

He held out his hand to Cyril, and gave a warm grip to the hand the latter laid in it.

"It is a rum start, Mistress," John went on, as he sat down to his meal, "that two old hands like the Captain and I were sailing on, not dreaming of hidden rocks or sand-banks, when this lad, who I used to look upon as a young cockerel who was rather above his position, should have come forward and have saved us all from shipwreck."

"It is indeed, John," his mistress said earnestly, "and I thank God indeed that He put the thought into the minds of Captain Dave and myself to ask him to take up his abode with us. It seemed to us then that we were doing a little kindness that would cost us nothing, whereas it has turned out the saving of us."

"Dear, dear!" Nellie, who had been sitting with a frown on her pretty face, said pettishly. "What a talk there will be about it all, and how Jane Greenwood and Martha Stebbings and the rest of them will laugh at me! They used to say they wondered how I could go about with such an ugly wretch behind me, and of course I spoke up for him and said that he was an honest knave and faithful; and now it turns out that he is a villain and a robber. I shall never hear the last of him."

"You will get over that, Nellie," her mother said severely. "It would be much better if, instead of thinking of such trifles, you would consider how sad a thing it is that two lads should lose their character, and perhaps their lives, simply for their greed of other people's goods. I could cry when I think of it. I know that Robert Ashford has neither father nor mother to grieve about him, for my husband's father took him out of sheer charity; but Tom's parents are living, and it will be heart-breaking indeed to them when they hear of their son's misdoings."

"I trust that Captain Dave will get him off," Cyril said.

"As he is so young he may turn King's evidence, and I feel sure that he did not go willingly into the affair. I have noticed many times that he had a frightened look, as if he had something on his mind. I believe that he acted under fear of the other."

As soon as John Wilkes had finished his breakfast he went with Captain Dave and Cyril to the Magistrates' Court at the Guildhall. Some other cases were first heard, and then the apprentices, with the two men who had been captured in the lane, were brought in and placed in the dock. The men bore marks that showed they had been engaged in a severe struggle, and that the watch had used their staves with effect. One was an elderly man with shaggy grey eyebrows; the other was a very powerfully built fellow, who seemed, from his attire, to follow the profession of a sailor. Tom Frost was sobbing bitterly. One of Robert Ashford's hands was bandaged up. As he was placed in the dock he cast furtive glances round with his shifty eyes, and as they fell upon Cyril an expression of deadly hate came over his face. The men of the watch who had captured them first gave their evidence as to finding them in the act of robbery, and testified to the desperate resistance they had offered to capture. Captain Dave then entered the witness-box, and swore first to the goods that were found on them being his property, and then related how, it having come to his knowledge that he was being robbed, he had set a watch, and had, eight days previously, seen his two apprentices getting along the roof, and how they had come out from the warehouse door, had opened the outer gate, and had handed over some goods they had brought out to persons unknown waiting to receive them.

"Why did you not stop them in their commission of the theft?" the Alderman in the Chair asked.

"Because, sir, had I done so, the men I considered to be the chief criminals, and who had doubtless tempted my apprentices to rob me, would then have made off. Therefore, I thought it better to wait until I could lay hands on them also, and so got four men of the watch to remain in the house at night."

Then he went on to relate how, after watching seven nights, he had again seen the apprentices make their way along the roof, and how they and the receivers of their booty were taken by the watch, aided by himself, his foreman, and Master Cyril Shenstone, who was dwelling in his house.

After John Wilkes had given his evidence, Cyril went into the box and related how, being engaged by Captain David Dowsett to make up his books, he found, upon stock being taken, that there was a deficiency to the amount of many hundreds of pounds in certain stores, notably such as were valuable without being bulky.

"Is anything known as to the prisoners?" the magistrate asked the officer of the city watch in charge of the case.

"Nothing is known of the two boys, your honour; but the men are well known. The elder, who gave the name of Peter Johnson, is one Joseph Marner; he keeps a marine shop close to the Tower. For a long time he has been suspected of being a receiver of stolen goods, but we have never been able to lay finger on him before. The other man has, for the last year, acted as his assistant in the shop; he answers closely to the description of a man, Ephraim Fowler, who has long been wanted. This man was a seaman in a brig trading to Yarmouth. After an altercation with the captain he stabbed him, and then slew the mate who was coming to his assistance; then with threats he compelled the other two men on board to let him take the boat. When they were off Brightlingsea he rowed away, and has not been heard of since. If you will remand them, before he comes up again I hope to find the men who were on board, and see if they identify him. We are in possession of Joseph Marner's shop, and have found large quantities of goods that we have reason to believe are the proceeds of these and other robberies."

After the prisoners had left the dock, Captain Dave went up to the officer.

"I believe," he said, "that the boy has not voluntarily taken part in these robberies, but has been led away, or perhaps obliged by threats to take part in them; he may be able to give you some assistance, for maybe these men are not the only persons to whom the stolen goods have been sold, and he may be able to put you on the track of other receivers."

"The matter is out of my hands now," the officer said, "but I will represent what you say in the proper quarter; and now you had better come round with me; you may be able to pick out some of your property. We only made a seizure of the place an hour ago. I had all the men who came in on duty this morning to take a look at the prisoners. Fortunately two or three of them recognised Marner, and you may guess we lost no time in getting a search warrant and going down to his place. It is the most important capture we have made for some time, and may lead to the discovery of other robberies that have been puzzling us for months past. There is a gang known as the Black Gang, but we have never been able to lay hands on any of their leaders, and such fellows as have been captured have refused to say a word, and have denied all knowledge of it. There have been a number of robberies of a mysterious kind, none of which have we been able to trace, and they have been put down to the same gang. The Chief Constable is waiting for me there, and we shall make a thorough search of the premises, and it is like enough we shall come across some clue of importance. At any rate, if we can find some of the articles stolen in the robberies I am speaking of, it will be a strong proof that Marner is one of the chiefs of the gang, and that may lead to further discoveries."

"You had better come with us, John," Captain Dave said. "You know our goods better than I do myself. Will you come, Cyril?"

"I should be of no use in identifying the goods, sir, and I am due in half an hour at one of my shops."

The search was an exhaustive one. There was no appearance of an underground cellar, but on some of the boards of the shop being taken up, it was found that there was a large one extending over the whole house. This contained an immense variety of goods. In one corner was a pile of copper bolts that Captain Dave and John were able to claim at once, as they bore the brand of the maker from whom they obtained their stock. There were boxes of copper and brass ship and house fittings, and a very large quantity of rope, principally of the sizes in which the stock had been found deficient; but to these Captain Dave was unable to swear. In addition to these articles the cellar contained a number of chests, all of which were found to be filled with miscellaneous articles of wearing apparel—rolls of silk, velvet, cloth, and other materials—curtains, watches, clocks, ornaments of all kinds, and a considerable amount of plate. As among these were many articles which answered to the descriptions given of goods that had been stolen from country houses, the whole were impounded by the Chief Constable, and carried away in carts. The upper part of the house was carefully searched, the walls tapped, wainscotting pulled down, and the floors carefully examined. Several hiding-places were found, but nothing of any importance discovered in them.

"I should advise you," the Chief Constable said to Captain Dave, "to put in a claim for every article corresponding with those you have lost. Of course, if any one else comes forward and also puts in a claim, the matter will have to be gone into, and if neither of you can absolutely swear to the things, I suppose you will have to settle it somehow between you. If no one else claims them, you will get them all without question, for you can swear that, to the best of your knowledge and belief, they are yours, and bring samples of your own goods to show that they exactly correspond with them. I have no doubt that a good deal of the readily saleable stuff, such as ropes, brass sheaves for blocks, and things of that sort, will have been sold, but as it is clear that there is a good deal of your stuff in the stock found below, I hope your loss will not be very great. There is no doubt it has been a splendid find for us. It is likely enough that we shall discover among those boxes goods that have been obtained from a score of robberies in London, and likely enough in the country. We have arrested three men we found in the place, and two women, and may get from some of them information that will enable us to lay hands on some of the others concerned in these robberies."

CHAPTER V.

KIDNAPPED.

THAT afternoon Captain Dave went down to the Bridewell, and had an interview with Tom Frost, in the presence of the Master of the prison.

"Well, Tom, I never expected to have to come to see you in a place like this."

"I am glad I am here, master," the boy said earnestly, with tears in his eyes. "I don't mind if they hang me; I would rather anything than go on as I have been doing. I knew it must come, and whenever I heard any one walk into the shop I made sure it was a constable. I am ready to tell everything, master; I know I deserve whatever I shall get, but that won't hurt me half as much as it has done, having to go on living in the house with you, and knowing I was helping to rob you all along."

"Anything that you say must be taken down," the officer said; "and I can't promise that it will make any difference in your sentence."

"I do not care anything about that; I am going to tell the truth."

"Very well, then, I will take down anything you say. But wait a minute."

He went to the door of the room and called.

"Is the Chief Constable in?" he asked a man who came up. "If he is, ask him to step here."

A minute later the Chief Constable came in.

"This prisoner wishes to make a confession, Master Holmes. I thought it best that you should be here. You can hear what he says then, and it may help you in your inquiry. Besides, you may think of questions on points he may not mention; he understands that he is speaking entirely of his own free will, and that I have given him no promise whatever that his so doing will alter his sentence, although no doubt it will be taken into consideration."

"Quite so," the constable said. "This is not a case where one prisoner would be ordinarily permitted to turn King's evidence against the others, because, as they were caught in the act, no such evidence is necessary. We know all about how the thing was done, and who did it."

"I want to tell how I first came to rob my master," the boy said. "I never thought of robbing him. When I came up to London, my father said to me, 'Whatever you do, Tom, be honest. They say there are rogues up in London; don't you have anything to do with them.' One evening, about a year ago I went out with Robert, and we went to a shop near the wall at Aldgate. I had never been there before, but Robert knew the master, who was the old man that was taken in the lane. Robert said the man was a relation of his father's, and had been kind to him. We sat down and talked for a time, and then Robert, who was sitting close to me, moved for something, and put his hand against my pocket.

"'Hullo!' he said; 'what have you got there?'

"'Nothing,' I said.

"'Oh, haven't you?' and he put his hand in my pocket, and brought out ten guineas. 'Hullo!' he said; 'where did you get these? You told me yesterday you had not got a groat. Why, you young villain, you must have been robbing the till!'

"I was so frightened that I could not say anything, except that I did not know how they came there, and I could swear that I had not touched the till. I was too frightened to think then, but I have since thought that the guineas were never in my pocket at all, but were in Robert's hand.

"'That won't do, boy,' the man said. 'It is clear that you are a thief. I saw Robert take them from your pocket, and, as an honest man, it is my duty to take you to your master and tell him what sort of an apprentice he has. You are young, and you will get off with a whipping at the pillory, and that will teach you that honesty is the best policy.'

"So he got his hat and put it on, and took me by the collar as if to haul me out into the street. I went down on my knees to beg for mercy, and at last he said that he would keep the matter quiet if I would swear to do everything that Robert told me; and I was so frightened that I swore to do so.

"For a bit there wasn't any stealing, but Robert used to take me out over the roof, and we used to go out together and go to places where there were two or three men, and they gave us wine. Then Robert proposed that we should have a look through the warehouse. I did not know what he meant, but as we went through he filled his pockets with things and told me to take some too. I said I would not. Then he threatened to raise the alarm, and said that when Captain Dave came down he should say he heard me get up to come down by the rope on to the warehouse, and that he had followed me to see what I was doing, and had found me in the act of taking goods, and that, as he had before caught me with money stolen from the till, as a friend of his could testify, he felt that it was his duty to summon you at once. I know I ought to have refused, and to have let him call you down, but I was too frightened. At last I agreed to do what he told me, and ever since then we have been robbing you."

"What have you done with the money you got for the things?" the constable asked.

"I had a groat sometimes," the boy said, "but that is all. Robert said first that I should have a share, but I said I would have nothing to do with it. I did as he ordered me because I could not help it. Though I have taken a groat or two sometimes, that is all I have had."

"Do you know anything about how much Robert had?"

"No, sir; I never saw him paid any money. I supposed that he had some because he has said sometimes he should set up a shop for himself, down at some seaport town, when he was out of his apprenticeship; but I have never seen him with any money beyond a little silver. I don't know what he used to do when we had given the things to the men that met us in the lane. I used always to come straight back to bed, but generally he went out with them. I used to fasten the gate after him, and he got back over the wall by a rope. Most times he didn't come in till a little before daybreak."

"Were they always the same men that met you in the lane?"

"No, sir. The master of the shop was very seldom there. The big man has come for the last three or four months, and there were two other men. They used to be waiting for us together until the big man came, but since then one or other of them came with him, except when the master of the shop was there himself."

"Describe them to me?"

The boy described them as well as he could.

"Could you swear to them if you saw them?"

"I think so. Of course, sometimes it was moonlight, and I could see their faces well; and besides, the light of the lantern often fell upon their faces."

The constable nodded.

"The descriptions answer exactly," he said to Captain Dave, "to the two men we found in the shop. The place was evidently the headquarters of a gang of thieves."

"Please, sir," the boy said, "would you have me shut up in another place? I am afraid of being with the others. They have sworn they will kill me if I say a word, and when I get back they will ask me who I have seen and what I have said."

Captain Dave took the other two men aside.

"Could you not let the boy come home with me?" he said. "I believe his story is a true one. He has been terrified into helping that rascal, Robert Ashford. Of course he himself was of no good to them, but they were obliged to force him into it, as otherwise he would have found out Robert's absences and might have reported them to me. I will give what bail you like, and will undertake to produce him whenever he is required."

"I could not do that myself," the constable said, "but I will go round to the Court now with the boy's confession, and I have no doubt the Alderman will let him go. But let me give you a word of advice: don't let him stir out of the house after dark. We have no doubt that there is a big gang concerned in this robbery, and the others of which we found the booty at the receiver's. They would not know how much this boy could tell about them, but if he went back to you they would guess that he had peached. If he went out after dark, the chances would be against his ever coming back again. No, now I think of it, I am sure you had better let him stay where he is. The Master will put him apart from the others, and make him comfortable. You see, at present we have no clue as to the men concerned in the robberies. You may be sure that they are watching every move on our part, and if they knew that this boy was out, they might take the alarm and make off."

"Well, if you think so, I will leave him here."

"I am sure that it would be the best plan."

"You will make him comfortable, Master Holroyd?"

"Yes; you need not worry about him, Captain Dowsett."

They then turned to the boy.

"You will be moved away from the others, Tom," Captain Dave said, "and Mr. Holroyd has promised to make you comfortable."

"Oh, Captain Dave," the boy burst out, "will you forgive me? I don't mind being punished, but if you knew how awfully miserable I have been all this time, knowing that I was robbing you while you were so kind to me, I think you would forgive me."

"I forgive you, Tom," Captain Dave said, putting his hand on the boy's shoulder. "I hope that this will be a lesson to you, all your life. You see all this has come upon you because you were a coward. If you had been a brave lad you would have said, 'Take me to my master.' You might have been sure that I would have heard your story as well as theirs, and I don't think I should have decided against you under the circumstances. It was only your word against Robert's; and his taking you to this man's, and finding the money in your pocket in so unlikely a way, would certainly have caused me to have suspicions. There is nothing so bad as cowardice; it is the father of all faults. A coward is certain to be a liar, for he will not hesitate to tell any falsehood to shelter him from the consequences of a fault. In your case, you see, cowardice has made you a thief; and in some cases it might drive a man to commit a murder. However, lad, I forgive you freely. You have been weak, and your weakness has made you a criminal; but it has been against your own will. When all this is over, I will see what can be done for you. You may live to be an honest man and a good citizen yet."

Two days later Cyril was returning home late in the evening after being engaged longer than usual in making up a number of accounts for one of his customers. He had come through Leadenhall Street, and had entered the lane where the capture of the thieves had been made, when he heard a footstep behind him. He turned half round to see who was following him, when he received a tremendous blow on the head which struck him senseless to the ground.

After a time he was dimly conscious that he was being carried along. He was unable to move; there was something in his mouth that prevented him from calling out, and his head was muffled in a cloak. He felt too weak and confused to struggle. A minute later he heard a voice, that sounded below him, say,—

"Have you got him?"

"I have got him all right," was the answer of the man who was carrying him.

Then he felt that he was being carried down some stairs. Some one took him, and he was thrown roughly down; then there was a slight rattling noise, followed by a regular sound. He wondered vaguely what it was, but as his senses came back it flashed upon him; it was the sound of oars; he was in a boat. It was some time before he could think why he should be in a boat. He had doubtless been carried off by some of the friends of the prisoners', partly, perhaps, to prevent his giving evidence against them, partly from revenge for the part he had played in the discovery of the crime.

In a few minutes the sound of oars ceased, and there was a bump as the boat struck against something hard. Then he was lifted up, and some one took hold of him from above. He was carried a few steps and roughly thrust in somewhere. There was a sound of something heavy being thrown down above him, and then for a long time he knew nothing more.

When he became conscious again, he was able, as he lay there, to come to a distinct conclusion as to where he was. He had been kidnapped, carried off, taken out in a boat to some craft anchored in the river, and was now in the hold. He felt almost suffocated. The wrap round his head prevented his breathing freely, the gag in his mouth pressed on his tongue, and gave him severe pain, while his head ached acutely from the effects of the blow.

The first thing to do was, if possible, to free his hands, so as to relieve himself from the gag and muffling. An effort or two soon showed him that he was but loosely bound. Doubtless the man who had attacked him had not wasted much time in securing his arms, believing that the blow would be sufficient to keep him quiet until he was safe on board ship. It was, therefore, without much difficulty that he managed to free one of his hands, and it was then an easy task to get rid of the rope altogether. The cloak was pulled from his face, and, feeling for his knife, he cut the lashings of the gag and removed it from his mouth. He lay quiet for a few minutes, panting from his exhaustion. Putting up his hand he felt a beam about a foot above his body. He was, then, in a hold already stored with cargo. The next thing was to shift his position among the barrels and bales upon which he was lying, until he found a comparatively level spot. He was in too great pain to think of sleep; his head throbbed fiercely, and he suffered from intense thirst.

From time to time heavy footsteps passed overhead. Presently he heard a sudden rattling of blocks, and the flapping of a sail. Then he noticed that there was a slight change in the level of his position, and knew that the craft was under way on her voyage down the river.

It seemed an immense time to him before he saw a faint gleam of light, and edging himself along, found himself again under the hatchway, through a crack in which the light was shining. It was some hours before the hatch was lifted off, and he saw two men looking down.

"Water!" he said. "I am dying of thirst."

"Bring a pannikin of water," one of the men said, "but first give us a hand, and we will have him on deck."

Stooping down, they took Cyril by the shoulders and hoisted him out.

"He is a decent-looking young chap," the speaker went on. "I would have seen to him before, if I had known him to be so bad. Those fellows didn't tell us they had hurt him. Here is the water, young fellow. Can you sit up to drink it?"

Cyril sat up and drank off the contents of the pannikin.

"Why, the back of your head is all covered with blood!" the man who had before spoken said. "You must have had an ugly knock?"

"I don't care so much for that," Cyril replied. "It's the gag that hurt me. My tongue is so much swollen I can hardly speak."

"CYRIL SAT UP AND DRANK OFF THE CONTENTS OF THE PANNIKIN."

"Well, you can stay here on deck if you will give me your promise not to hail any craft we may pass. If you won't do that I must put you down under hatches again."

"I will promise that willingly," Cyril said; "the more so that I can scarce speak above a whisper."

"Mind, if you as much as wave a hand, or do anything to bring an eye on us, down you go into the hold again, and when you come up next time it will be to go overboard. Now just put your head over the rail, and I will pour a few buckets of water over it. I agreed to get you out of the way, but I have got no grudge against you, and don't want to do you harm."

Getting a bucket with a rope tied to the handle, he dipped it into the river, and poured half-a-dozen pailfuls over Cyril's head. The lad felt greatly refreshed, and, sitting down on the deck, was able to look round. The craft was a coaster of about twenty tons burden. There were three men on deck besides the man who had spoken to him, and who was evidently the skipper. Besides these a boy occasionally put up his head from a hatchway forward. There was a pile of barrels and empty baskets amidship, and the men presently began to wash down the decks and to tidy up the ropes and gear lying about. The shore on both sides was flat, and Cyril was surprised at the width of the river. Behind them was a small town, standing on higher ground.

"What place is that?" he asked a sailor who passed near him.

"That is Gravesend."

A few minutes afterwards the boy again put his head out of the hatchway and shouted,—

"Breakfast!"

"Can you eat anything, youngster?" the skipper asked Cyril.

"No, thank you, my head aches too much; and my mouth is so sore I am sure I could not get anything down."

"Well, you had best lie down, then, with your head on

that coil of rope; I allow you did not sleep much last night."

In a few minutes Cyril was sound asleep, and when he awoke the sun was setting.

"You have had a good bout of it, lad," the skipper said, as he raised himself on his elbow and looked round. "How are you feeling now?"

"A great deal better," Cyril said, as he rose to his feet.

"Supper will be ready in a few minutes, and if you can manage to get a bit down it will do you good."

"I will try, anyhow," Cyril said. "I think that I feel hungry."

The land was now but a faint line on either hand. A gentle breeze was blowing from the south-west, and the craft was running along over the smooth water at the rate of three or four miles an hour. Cyril wondered where he was being taken to, and what was going to be done with him, but determined to ask no questions. The skipper was evidently a kind-hearted man, although he might be engaged in lawless business, but it was as well to wait until he chose to open the subject.

As soon as the boy hailed, the captain led the way to the hatchway. They descended a short ladder into the fo'castle, which was low, but roomy. Supper consisted of boiled skate—a fish Cyril had never tasted before—oaten bread, and beer. His mouth was still sore, but he managed to make a hearty meal of fish, though he could not manage the hard bread. One of the men was engaged at the helm, but the other two shared the meal, all being seated on lockers that ran round the cabin. The fish were placed on an earthenware dish, each man cutting off slices with his jack-knife, and using his bread as a platter. Little was said while the meal went on; but when they went on deck again, the skipper, having put another man at the tiller, while the man released went forward to get his supper, said,—

"Well, I think you are in luck, lad."

Cyril opened his eyes in surprise.

"You don't think so?" the man went on. "I don't mean that you are in luck in being knocked about and carried off, but that you are not floating down the river at present instead of walking the deck here. I can only suppose that they thought your body might be picked up, and that it would go all the harder with the prisoners, if it were proved that you had been put out of the way. You don't look like an informer either!"

"I am not an informer," Cyril said indignantly. "I found that my employer was being robbed, and I aided him to catch the thieves. I don't call that informing. That is when a man betrays others engaged in the same work as himself."

"Well, well, it makes no difference to me," the skipper said. "I was engaged by a man, with whom I do business sometimes, to take a fellow who had been troublesome out of the way, and to see that he did not come back again for some time. I bargained that there was to be no foul play; I don't hold with things of that sort. As to carrying down a bale of goods sometimes, or taking a few kegs of spirits from a French lugger, I see no harm in it; but when it comes to cutting throats, I wash my hands of it. I am sorry now I brought you off, though maybe if I had refused they would have put a knife into you, and chucked you into the river. However, now that I have got you I must go through with it. I ain't a man to go back from my word, and what I says I always sticks to. Still, I am sorry I had anything to do with the business. You look to me a decent young gentleman, though your looks and your clothes have not been improved by what you have gone through. Well, at any rate, I promise you that no harm shall come to you as long as you are in my hands."

"And how long is that likely to be, captain?"

"Ah! that is more than I can tell you. I don't want to do you harm, lad, and more than that, I will prevent other people from doing you harm as long as you are on board this craft. But more than that I can't say. It is likely enough I shall have trouble in keeping that promise, and I can't go a step farther. There is many a man who would have chucked you overboard, and so have got rid of the trouble altogether, and of the risk of its being afterwards proved that he had a hand in getting you out of the way."

"I feel that, captain," Cyril said, "and I thank you heartily for your kind treatment of me. I promise you that if at any time I am set ashore and find my way back to London, I will say no word which can get you into trouble."

"There is Tom coming upon deck. You had better turn in. You have had a good sleep, but I have no doubt you can do with some more, and a night's rest will set you up. You take the left-hand locker. The boy sleeps on the right hand, and we have bunks overhead."

Cyril was soon soundly asleep, and did not wake when the others turned in. He was alone in the cabin when he opened his eyes, but the sun was shining brightly through the open hatchway. He sprang up and went on deck. The craft was at anchor. No land could be seen to the south, but to the north a low shore stretched away three or four miles distant. There was scarcely a breath of wind.

"Well, you have had a good sleep, lad," the captain said. "You had best dip that bucket overboard and have a wash; you will feel better after it. Now, boy, slip down and get your fire going; we shall be ready for breakfast as soon as it is ready for us."

Cyril soused his head with the cold water, and felt, as the captain had said, all the better for it, for the air in the little cabin was close and stuffy, and he had felt hot and feverish before his wash.

"The wind died out, you see," the captain said, "and we had to anchor when tide turned at two o'clock. There is a dark line behind us, and as soon as the wind reaches us, we will up anchor. The force of the tide is spent."

The wind, however, continued very light, and the vessel did little more than drift with the tide, and when it turned at two o'clock they had to drop anchor again close under some high land, on the top of which stood a lofty tower.

"That is a land-mark," the captain said. "There are some bad sands outside us, and that stands as a mark for vessels coming through."

Cyril had enjoyed the quiet passage much. The wound at the back of his head still smarted, and he had felt disinclined for any exertion. More than once, in spite of the good allowance of sleep he had had, he dosed off as he sat on the deck with his back against the bulwark, watching the shore as they drifted slowly past it, and wondering vaguely how it would all end. They had been anchored but half an hour when the captain ordered the men to the windlass.

"There is a breeze coming, lads," he said; "and even if it only lasts for an hour, it will take us round the head and far enough into the bay to get into the tide running up the rivers."

The breeze, however, when it came, held steadily, and in two hours they were off Harwich; but on coming opposite the town they turned off up the Orwell, and anchored, after dark, at a small village some six miles up the river.

"If you will give me your word, lad, that you will not try to escape, and will not communicate with any one who may come off from the shore, I will continue to treat you as a passenger; but if not, I must fasten you up in the cabin, and keep a watch over you."

"I will promise, captain. I should not know where to go if I landed. I heard you say, 'There is Harwich steeple,' when we first came in sight of it, but where that is I have no idea, nor how far we are from London. As I have not a penny in my pocket, I should find it well-nigh impossible to make my way to town, which may, for aught I know, be a hundred miles away; for, in truth, I know but little of the geography of England, having been brought up in France, and not having been out of sight of London since I came over."

Just as he was speaking, the splash of an oar was heard close by.

"Up, men," the captain said in a low tone to those in the fo'castle. "Bring up the cutlasses. Who is that?" he called, hailing the boat.

"Merry men all," was the reply.

"All right. Come alongside. You saw our signal, then?"

"Ay, ay, we saw it; but there is an officer with a boat-load of sailors ashore from the King's ship at Harwich. He is spending the evening with the revenue captain here, and we had to wait until the two men left in charge of the boat went up to join their comrades at the tavern. What have you got for us?"

"Six boxes and a lot of dunnage, such as cables, chains, and some small anchors."

"Well, you had better wait for an hour before you take the hatches off. You will hear the gig with the sailors row past soon. The tide has begun to run down strong, and I expect the officer won't be long before he moves. As soon as he has gone we will come out again. We shall take the goods up half a mile farther. The revenue man on that beat has been paid to keep his eyes shut, and we shall get them all stored in a hut, a mile away in the woods, before daybreak. You know the landing-place; there will be water enough for us to row in there for another two hours."

The boat rowed away to the shore, which was not more than a hundred yards distant. A little later they heard a stir on the strand, then came the sound of oars, and two minutes later a boat shot past close to them, and then, bearing away, rowed down the river.

"Now, lads," the captain said, "get the hatches off. The wind is coming more off shore, which is all the better for us, but do not make more noise than you can help."

The hatches were taken off, and the men proceeded to get up a number of barrels and bales, some sail-cloth being thrown on the deck to deaden the sound. Lanterns, passed down into the hold, gave them light for their operations.

"This is the lot," one of the sailors said presently.

Six large boxes were then passed up and put apart from the others. Then followed eight or ten coils of rope, a quantity of chain, some kedge anchors, a number of blocks, five rolls of canvas, and some heavy bags that, by the sound they made when they were laid down, Cyril judged to contain metal articles of some sort. Then the other goods were lowered into the hold and the hatches replaced. The work had scarcely concluded when the boat again came alongside, this time with four men on board. Scarcely a word was spoken as the goods were transferred to the boat.

"You will be going to-morrow?" one of the men in the boat asked.

"Yes, I shall get up to Ipswich on the top of the tide—that is, if I don't stick fast in this crooked channel. My cargo is all either for Ipswich or Aldborough. Now let us turn in," as the boatmen made their way up the river. "We must be under way before daylight, or else we shall not save the tide down to-morrow evening. I am glad we have got that lot safely off. I always feel uncomfortable until we get rid of that part of the cargo. If it wasn't that it paid better than all the rest together I would not have anything to do with it."

Cyril was very glad to lie down on the locker, while the men turned into their berths overhead. He had not yet fully recovered from the effects of the blow he had received, but in spite of the aching of his head he was soon sound asleep. It seemed to him that he had scarcely closed his eyes when he was roused by the captain's voice,—

"Tumble up, lads. The light is beginning to show."

Ten minutes later they were under way. The breeze had almost died out, and after sailing for some two miles in nearly a straight course, the boat was thrown over, two men got into it, and, fastening a rope to the ketch's bow, proceeded to tow her along, the captain taking the helm.

To Cyril's surprise, they turned off almost at right angles to the course they had before been following, and made straight for the opposite shore. They approached it so closely that Cyril expected that in another moment the craft would take ground, when, at a shout from the captain, the men in the boat started off parallel with the shore, taking the craft's head round. For the next three-quarters of an hour they pursued a serpentine course, the boy standing in the chains and heaving the lead continually. At last the captain shouted,—" You can come on board now, lads. We are in the straight channel at last." Twenty minutes later they again dropped their anchor opposite a town of considerable size.

"That is Ipswich, lad," the captain said. "It is as nasty a place to get into as there is in England, unless you have got the wind due aft."

The work of unloading began at once, and was carried on until after dark.

"That is the last of them," the captain said, to Cyril's satisfaction. "We can be off now when the tide turns, and if we hadn't got clear to-night we might have lost hours, for there is no getting these people on shore to understand that the loss of a tide means the loss of a day, and that it is no harder to get up and do your work at one hour than it is at another. I shall have a clean up, now, and go ashore. I have got your promise, lad, that you won't try to escape?"

Cyril assented. Standing on the deck there, with the river bank but twenty yards away, it seemed hard that he should not be able to escape. But, as he told himself, he would not have been standing there if it had not been for that promise, but would have been lying, tightly bound, down in the hold.

Cyril and the men were asleep when the captain came aboard, the boy alone remaining up to fetch him off in the boat when he hailed.

"There is no wind, captain," Cyril said, as the anchor was got up.

"No, lad, I am glad there is not. We can drop down with the tide and the boat towing us, but if there was a head wind we might have to stop here till it either dropped or shifted. I have been here three weeks at a spell. I got some news ashore," he went on, as he took his place at the helm, while the three men rowed the boat ahead. "A man I sometimes bring things to told me that he heard there had been an attempt to rescue the men concerned in that robbery. I heard, before I left London, it was likely that it would be attempted. There were a lot of people concerned in that affair, one way and another, and I knew they would move heaven and earth to get them out, for if any of them peached there would be such a haul as the constables never made in the city before. Word was passed to the prisoners to be ready, and as they were being taken from the Guildhall to Newgate there was a sudden rush made. The constables were not caught napping, and there was a tough fight, till the citizens ran out of their shops and took part with them, and the men, who were sailors, watermen, 'longshore-men, and rascals of all sorts, bolted.

"But two of the prisoners were missing. One was, I heard, an apprentice who was mixed up in the affair, and no one saw him go. They say he must have stooped down and wriggled away into the crowd. The other was a man they called Black Dick; he struck down two constables, broke through the crowd, and got clean away. There is a great hue and cry, but so far nothing has been heard of them. They will be kept in hiding somewhere till there is a chance of getting them through the gates or on board a craft lying in the river. Our men made a mess of it, or they would have got them all off. I hear that they are all in a fine taking that Marner is safely lodged in Newgate with the others taken in his house; he knows so much that if he chose to peach he could hang a score of men. Black Dick could tell a good deal, but he wasn't in all the secrets, and they say Marner is really the head of the band and had a finger in pretty nigh every robbery through the country. All those taken in his place are also in Newgate, and they say the constables are searching the city like ferrets in a rabbit-warren, and that several other arrests have been made."

"I am not sorry the apprentice got away," Cyril said. "He

is a bad fellow, there is no doubt, and, by the look he gave me, he would do me harm if he got a chance, but I suppose that is only natural. As to the other man, he looked to me to be a desperate villain, and he also gave me so evil a look that, though he was in the dock with a constable on either side of him, I felt horribly uncomfortable, especially when I heard what sort of man he was."

"What did they say of him?"

"They said they believed he was a man named Ephraim Fowler, who had murdered the skipper and mate of a coaster and then went off in the boat."

"Is that the man? Then truly do I regret that he has escaped. I knew both John Moore, the master, and George Monson, the mate, and many a flagon of beer we have emptied together. If I had known the fellow's whereabouts, I would have put the constables on his track. I am heartily sorry now, boy, that I had a hand in carrying you off, though maybe it is best for you that it has been so. If I hadn't taken you some one else would, and more than likely you would not have fared so well as you have done, for some of them would have saved themselves all further trouble and risk, by chucking you overboard as soon as they were well out of the Pool."

"Can't you put me ashore now, captain?"

"No, boy; I have given my word and taken my money, and I am not one to fail to carry out a bargain because I find that I have made a bad one. They have trusted me with thousands of pounds' worth of goods, and I have no reason to complain of their pay, and am not going to turn my back on them now they have got into trouble; besides, though I would trust you not to round upon me, I would not trust them. If you were to turn up in London they would know that I had sold them, and Marner would soon hear of it. There is a way of getting messages to a man even in prison. Then you may be sure that, if he said nothing else, he would take good care to let out that I was the man who used to carry their booty away, sometimes to quiet places on the coast, and sometimes across to Holland, and the first time I dropped anchor in the Pool I should find myself seized and thrown into limbo. No, lad; I must carry out my agreement—which is that I am not to land you in England, but that I am to take you across to Holland or elsewhere—the elsewhere meaning that if you fall overboard by the way there will be no complaints as to the breach of the agreement. That is, in fact, what they really meant, though they did not actually put it into words. They said, 'We have a boy who is an informer, and has been the means of Marner being seized and his place broken up, and there is no saying that a score of us may not get a rope round our necks. In consequence, we want him carried away. What you do with him is nothing to us so long as he don't set foot in England again.' 'Will Holland suit you? I am going across there,' I said, ' after touching at Ipswich and Aldborough.' ' It would be much safer for you and every one else if it happen that he falls over before he gets there. However, we will call it Holland.'"

" Then if I were to fall overboard," Cyril said, with a smile, " you would not be breaking your agreement, captain? I might fall overboard to-night, you know."

" I would not advise it, lad. You had much better stay where you are. I don't say I mightn't anchor off Harwich, and that if you fell overboard you couldn't manage to swim ashore, but I tell you I would not give twopence for your life when you got back to London. It is to the interest of a score of men to keep Marner's mouth shut. They have shown their willingness to help him as far as they could, by getting you out of the way, and if you got back they would have your life the first time you ventured out of doors after dark; they would be afraid Marner would suppose they had sold him if you were to turn up at his trial, and as like as not he would round on the whole lot. Besides, I don't think it would be over safe for me the first time I showed myself in London afterwards, for, though I never said that I would do it, I have no doubt they reckoned that I should chuck you overboard, and if you were to make your appearance in London they would certainly put it down that I had sold them. You keep yourself quiet, and I will land you in Holland, but not as they would expect, without a penny or a friend; I will put you into good hands, and arrange that you shall be sent back again as soon as the trial is over."

"Thank you very much, captain. I have no relations in London, and no friends, except my employer, Captain David Dowsett, and by this time he will have made up his mind that I am dead, and it won't make much difference whether I return in four or five days or as many weeks."

CHAPTER VI.

A NARROW ESCAPE.

THE *Eliza*, for this Cyril, after leaving Ipswich, learnt was her name, unloaded the rest of her cargo at Aldborough, and then sailed across to Rotterdam. The skipper fulfilled his promise by taking Cyril to the house of one of the men with whom he did business, and arranging with him to board the boy until word came that he could safely return to England. The man was a diamond-cutter, and to him packets of jewellery and gems that could not be disposed of in England had often been brought over by the captain. The latter had nothing to do with the pecuniary arrangements, which were made direct by Marner, and he had only to hand over the packets and take back sums of money to England.

"You understand," the captain said to Cyril, " that I have not said a word touching the matter for which you are here. I have only told him that it had been thought it was as well you should be out of England for a time. Of course, he understood that you were wanted for an affair in which you had taken part; but it matters not what he thinks. I have paid him for a month's board for you, and here are three pounds, which will be enough to pay for your passage back if I myself should not return. If you do not hear from me, or see the *Eliza*, within four weeks, there is no reason why you should not take passage back. The trial will be over by that time, and as the members of the gang have done their part in preventing you from appearing, I see not why they should have further grudge against you."

"I cannot thank you too much for your kindness, captain. I trust that when I get back you will call at Captain Dowsett's store in Tower Street, so that I may see you and again thank you; I know that the Captain himself will welcome you heartily when I tell him how kindly you have treated me. He will be almost as glad as I shall myself to see you. I suppose you could not take him a message or letter from me now?"

"I think not, lad. It would never do for him to be able to say at the trial that he had learnt you had been kidnapped. They might write over here to the Dutch authorities about you. There is one thing further. From what I heard when I landed yesterday, it seems that there is likely to be war between Holland and England."

"I heard a talk of it in London," Cyril said, "but I do not rightly understand the cause, nor did I inquire much about the matter."

"It is something about the colonies, and our taxing their goods, but I don't rightly understand the quarrel, except that the Dutch think, now that Blake is gone and our ships for the most part laid up, they may be able to take their revenge for the lickings we have given them. Should there be war, as you say you speak French as well as English, I should think you had best make your way to Dunkirk as a young Frenchman, and from there you would find no difficulty in crossing to England."

"I know Dunkirk well, captain, having indeed lived there all my life. I should have no difficulty in travelling through Holland as a French boy."

"If there is a war," the captain said, "I shall, of course, come here no more; but it may be that you will see me at Dunkirk. French brandy sells as well as Dutch Schiedam, and if I cannot get the one I may perhaps get the other; and there is less danger in coming to Dunkirk and making across to Harwich than there is in landing from Calais or Nantes on the south coast, where the revenue men are much more on the alert than they are at Harwich."

"Are you not afraid of getting your boat captured? You said it was your own."

"Not much, lad. I bring over a regular cargo, and the kegs are stowed away under the floor of the cabin, and I run them at Pin-mill—that is the place we anchored the night before we got to Ipswich. I have been overhauled a good many times, but the cargo always looks right, and after searching it for a bit, they conclude it is all regular. You see, I don't bring over a great quantity—fifteen or twenty kegs is as much as I can stow away—and it is a long way safer being content with a small profit than trying to make a big one."

Cyril parted with regret from the captain, whose departure had been hastened by a report that war might be declared at any moment, in which case the *Eliza* might have been detained for a considerable time. He had, therefore, been working almost night and day to get in his cargo, and Cyril had remained on board until the last moment. He had seen the diamond dealer but once, and hoped that he should not meet him often, for he felt certain that awkward questions would be asked him. This man was in the habit of having dealings with Marner, and had doubtless understood from the captain that he was in some way connected with his gang; and were he to find out the truth he would view him with the reverse of a friendly eye. He had told him that he was to take his meals with his clerk, and Cyril hoped, therefore, that he should seldom see him.

He wandered about the wharf until it became dark. Then he went in and took supper with the clerk. As the latter spoke Dutch only, there was no possibility of conversation. Cyril was thinking of going up to his bed when there was a ring at the bell. The clerk went to answer it, leaving the door open as he went out, and Cyril heard a voice ask, in English, if Herr Schweindorf was in. The clerk said something in Dutch.

"The fool does not understand English, Robert," the man said.

"Tell him," he said, in a louder voice, to the clerk, "that two persons from England—England, you understand—who have only just arrived, want to see him on particular business. There, don't be blocking up the door; just go and tell your master what I told you."

He pushed his way into the passage, and the clerk, seeing that there was nothing else to do, went upstairs.

A minute later he came down again, and made a sign for them to follow him. As they went up Cyril stole out and looked after them. The fact that they had come from England, and that one of them was named Robert, and that they had business with this man, who was in connection with Marner, had excited his suspicions, but he felt a shiver of fear run through him as he recognised the figures of Robert Ashford and the man who was called Black Dick. He remembered the expression of hatred with which they had regarded him in the Court, and felt that his danger would be great indeed did they hear that he was in Rotterdam. A moment's thought convinced him that they would almost certainly learn this at once from his host. The latter would naturally mention that the captain had left a lad in his charge who was, as he believed, connected with them. They would denounce him as an enemy instead of a friend. The diamond merchant would expel him from his house, terrified at the thought that he possessed information as to his dealings with this band in England; and once beyond the door he would, in this strange town, be at the mercy of his enemies. Cyril's first impulse was to run back into the room, seize his cap, and fly. He waited, however, until the clerk came down again; then he put his cap carelessly on his head.

"I am going for a walk," he said, waving his hand vaguely.

The man nodded, went with him to the door, and Cyril heard him put up the bar after he had gone out. He walked quietly away, for there was no fear of immediate pursuit. Black Dick had probably brought over some more jewels to dispose of, and that business would be transacted, before there would be any talk of other matters. It might be a quarter of an hour before they heard that he was an inmate of the house; then, when they went downstairs with the dealer, they would hear that he had gone out for a walk and would await his return, so that he had two or three hours at least before there would be any search.

It was early yet. Some of the boats might be discharging by torchlight. At any rate, he might hear of a ship starting in the morning. He went down to the wharf. There was plenty of bustle here; boats were landing fish, and larger craft were discharging or taking in cargo; but his inability to speak Dutch prevented his asking questions. He crossed to the other side of the road. The houses here were principally stores or drinking taverns. In the window of one was stuck up, "English and French Spoken Here." He went inside, walked up to the bar, and called for a glass of beer in English.

"You speak English, landlord?" he asked, as the mug was placed before him.

The latter nodded.

"I want to take passage either to England or to France," he said. "I came out here but a few days ago, and I hear that there is going to be trouble between the two countries. It will therefore be of no use my going on to Amsterdam. I wish to get back again, for I am told that if I delay I may be too late. I cannot speak Dutch, and therefore cannot inquire if any boat will be sailing in the morning for England or Dunkirk. I have acquaintances in Dunkirk, and speak

French, so it makes no difference to me whether I go there or to England."

"My boy speaks French," the landlord said, "and if you like he can go along the port with you. Of course, you will give him something for his trouble?"

"Willingly," Cyril said, "and be much obliged to you into the bargain."

The landlord left the bar and returned in a minute with a boy twelve years old.

"He does not speak French very well," he said, "but I daresay it will be enough for your purpose. I have told him that you want to take ship to England, or that, if you cannot find one, to Dunkirk. If that will not do, Ostend might suit you. They speak French there, and there are boats always going between there and England."

"That would do; though I should prefer the other."

"There would be no difficulty at any other time in getting a boat for England, but I don't know whether you will do so now. They have been clearing off for some days, and I doubt if you will find an English ship in port now, though of course there may be those who have been delayed for their cargo."

Cyril went out with the boy, and after making many inquiries learnt that there was but one English vessel still in port. However, Cyril told his guide that he would prefer one for Dunkirk if they could find one, for if war were declared before the boat sailed, she might be detained. After some search they found a coasting scow that would sail in the morning.

"They will touch at two or three places," the boy said to Cyril, after a talk with the captain; "but if you are not in a hurry, he will take you and land you at Dunkirk for a pound —that is, if he finds food; if you find food he will take you for eight shillings. He will start at daybreak."

"Tell him that I agree to his price. I don't want the trouble of getting food. As he will be going so early, I will come on board at once. I will get my bundle, and will be back in half an hour."

He went with the boy to one of the sailors' shops near, bought a rough coat and a thick blanket, had them wrapped up into a parcel, and then, after paying the boy, went on board.

As he expected, he found there were no beds or accommodation for passengers, so he stretched himself on a locker in the cabin, covered himself with his blanket, and put the coat under his head for a pillow. His real reason for choosing this craft in preference to the English ship was that he thought it probable that, when he did not return to the house, it would at once be suspected that he had recognised the visitors, and was not going to return at all. In that case, they might suspect that he would try to take passage to England, and would, the first thing in the morning, make a search for him on board any English vessels that might be in the port.

It would be easy then for them to get him ashore, for the diamond merchant might accuse him of theft, and so get him handed over to him. Rather than run that risk, he would have started on foot had he not been able to find a native craft sailing early in the morning. Failing Dunkirk and Ostend, he would have taken a passage to any other Dutch port, and run his chance of getting a ship from there. The great point was to get away from Rotterdam.

The four men forming the crew of the scow returned late, and by their loud talk Cyril, who kept his eyes closed, judged that they were in liquor. In a short time they climbed up into their berths, and all was quiet. At daybreak they were called up by the captain. Cyril lay quiet until, by the rippling of the water against the side, he knew that the craft was under way. He waited a few minutes, and then went up on deck. The scow, clumsy as she looked, was running along fast before a brisk wind, and in an hour Rotterdam lay far behind them.

A NARROW ESCAPE.

The voyage was a pleasant one. They touched at Dordrecht, at Steenbergen on the mainland, and Flushing, staying a few hours in each place to take in or discharge cargo. After this, they made out from the Islands, and ran along the coast, putting into Ostend and Nieuport, and, four days after starting, entered the port of Dunkirk.

Cyril did not go ashore at any of the places at which they stopped. It was possible that war might have been declared with England, and as it might be noticed that he was a foreigner he would in that case be questioned and arrested. As soon, therefore, as they neared a quay, he went down to the cabin and slept until they got under way again. The food was rough, but wholesome; it consisted entirely of fish and black bread; but the sea air gave him a good appetite, and he was in high spirits at the thought that he had escaped from danger and was on his way back again. At Dunkirk he was under the French flag, and half an hour after landing had engaged a passage to London on a brig that was to sail on the following day. The voyage was a stormy one, and he rejoiced in the possession of his great-coat, which he had only bought in order that he might have a packet to bring on board the scow, and so avoid exciting any suspicion or question as to his being entirely unprovded with luggage.

It was three days before the brig dropped anchor in the Pool. As soon as she did so, Cyril hailed a waterman, and spent almost his last remaining coin in being taken to shore. He was glad that it was late in the afternoon and so dark that his attire would not be noticed. His clothes had suffered considerably from his capture and confinement on board the *Eliza*, and his great-coat was of a rough appearance that was very much out of character in the streets of London. He had, however, but a short distance to traverse before he reached the door of the house. He rang at the bell, and the door was opened by John Wilkes.

"What is it?" the latter asked. "The shop is shut for the night, and I ain't going to open for any one. At half-past seven in the morning you can get what you want, but not before."

"Don't you know me, John?" Cyril laughed.

The old sailor stepped back as if struck with a blow.

"Eh, what?" he exclaimed. "Is it you, Cyril? Why, we had all thought you dead! I did not know you in this dim light and in that big coat you have got on. Come upstairs, master. Captain Dave and the ladies will be glad indeed to see you. They have been mourning for you sadly, I can tell you."

Cyril took off his wrap and hung it on a peg, and then followed John upstairs.

"There, Captain Dave," the sailor said, as he opened the door of the sitting-room. "There is a sight for sore eyes!—a sight you never thought you would look on again."

For a moment Captain Dave, his wife, and daughter stared at Cyril as if scarce believing their eyes. Then the Captain sprang to his feet.

"It's the lad, sure enough. Why, Cyril," he went on, seizing him by the hand, and shaking it violently, "we had never thought to see you alive again; we made sure that those pirates had knocked you on the head, and that you were food for fishes by this time. There has been no comforting my good wife; and as to Nellie, if it had been a brother she had lost, she could not have taken it more hardly."

"They did knock me on the head, and very hard too, Captain Dave. If my skull hadn't been quite so thick, I should, as you say, have been food for fishes before now, for that is what they meant me for, and there is no thanks to them that I am here at present. I am sorry that you have all been made so uncomfortable about me."

"We should have been an ungrateful lot indeed if we had not, considering that in the first place you saved us from being ruined by those pirates, and that it was, as we thought, owing to the services you had done us that you had come to your end."

"But where have you been, Master Cyril?" Nellie broke in. "What has happened to you? We have been picturing all sorts of horrors, mother and I. That evil had befallen you we were sure, for we knew that you would not go away of a sudden, in this fashion, without so much as saying good-bye. We feared all the more when, two days afterwards, the wretches were so bold as to attack the constables, and to rescue Robert Ashford and another from their hands. Men who would do this in broad daylight would surely hesitate at nothing."

"Let him eat his supper without asking further questions, Nellie," her father said. "It is ill asking one with victuals before him to begin a tale that may, for aught I know, last an hour. Let him have his food, lass, and then I will light my pipe, and John Wilkes shall light his here instead of going out for it, and we will have the yarn in peace and comfort. It spoils a good story to hurry it through. Cyril is here, alive and well; let that content you for a few minutes."

"If I must, I must," Nellie said, with a little pout. "But you should remember, father, that, while you have been all your life having adventures of some sort, this is the very first that I have had; for though Cyril is the one to whom it befell, it is all a parcel with the robbery of the house and the capture of the thieves."

"When does the trial come off, Captain Dave?"

"It came off yesterday. Marner is to be hung at the end of the week. He declared that he was but in the lane by accident when two lads opened the gate. He and the man with him, seeing that they were laden with goods, would have seized them, when they themselves were attacked and beaten down. But this ingenuity did not save him. Tom Frost had been admitted as King's evidence, and testified that Marner had been several times at the gate with the fellow that escaped, to receive the stolen goods. Moreover, there were many articles among those found at his place that I was able to swear to, besides the proceeds of over a score of burglaries. The two men taken in his house will have fifteen years in gaol. The women got off scot-free; there was no proof that they had taken part in the robberies, though there is little doubt they knew all about them."

"But how did they prove the men were concerned?"

"They got all the people whose property had been found there, and four of these, on seeing the men in the yard at Newgate, were able to swear to them as having been among those who came into their rooms and frightened them well-nigh to death. It was just a question whether they should be hung or not, and there was some wonder that the Judge let them escape the gallows."

"And what has become of Tom?"

"They kept Tom in the prison till last night. I saw him yesterday, and I am sure the boy is mighty sorry for having been concerned in the matter, being, as I truly believe, terrified into it. I had written down to an old friend of mine who has set up in the same way as myself at Plymouth. Of course I told him all the circumstances, but assured him, that according to my belief, the boy was not so much to blame, and that I was sure the lesson he had had, would last him for life; so I asked him to give Tom another chance, and if he did so, to keep the knowledge of this affair from every one. I got his answer yesterday morning, telling me to send him down to him; he would give him a fair trial, and if he wasn't altogether satisfied with him, would then get him a berth as ship's boy. So, last night after dark, he was taken down by John Wilkes, and put on board a coaster bound for Plymouth. I would have taken him back here, but after your disappearance I feared that his life would not be safe; for although they had plenty of other cases they could have proved against Marner, Tom's evidence brought this business home to him."

Captain Dave would not allow Cyril to begin his story until the table had been cleared and he and John Wilkes had lighted their pipes. Then Cyril told his adventure, the earlier part of which elicited many exclamations of pity from Dame Dowsett and Mistress Nellie, and some angry ejaculations from the Captain when he heard that Black Dick and Robert Ashford had got safely off to Holland.

"By St. Anthony, lad," he broke out, when the story was finished, "you had a narrow escape from those villains at Rotterdam. Had it chanced that you were out at the time they came, I would not have given a groat for your life. By all accounts, that fellow Black Dick is a desperate villain. They say that they had got hold of evidence enough against him to hang a dozen men, and it seems that there is little doubt that he was concerned in several cases, where, not content with robbing, the villain had murdered the inmates of lonely houses round London. He had good cause for hating you. It was through you that he had been captured, and had lost his share in all that plunder at Marner's. Well, I trust the villain will never venture to show his face in London again; but there is never any saying. I should like to meet that captain who behaved so well to you, and I will meet him too, and shake him by the hand and tell him that any gear he may want for that ketch of his, he is free to come in here to help himself. There is another thing to be thought of. I must go round in the morning to the Guildhall and notify the authorities that you have come back. There has been a great hue and cry for you. They have searched the thieves' dens of London from attic to cellar; there have been boats out looking for your body; and on the day after you were missing they overhauled all the ships in the port. Of course the search has died out now, but I must go and tell them, and you will have to give them the story of the affair."

"I sha'n't say a word that will give them a clue that will help them to lay hands on the captain. He saved my life, and no one could have been kinder than he was. I would rather go away for a time altogether, for I don't see how I am to tell the story without injuring him."

"No; it is awkward, lad. I see that, even if you would not give them the name of the craft, they might find out what vessels went into Ipswich on that morning, and also the names of those that sailed from Rotterdam on the day she left."

"It seems to me, Captain, that the only way will be for me to say the exact truth, namely, that I gave my word to the captain that I would say naught of the matter. I could tell how I was struck down, and how I did not recover consciousness until I found myself in a boat, and was lifted on board a vessel and put down into the hold, and was there kept until morning. I could say that when I was let out I found we were far down the river, that the captain expressed great regret when he found that I had been hurt so badly, that he did everything in his power for me, and that after I had been some days on board the ship he offered to land me in Holland, and to give me money to pay my fare back here if I would give him my word of honour not to divulge his name or the name of the ship, or that of the port at which he landed me. Of course, they can imprison me for a time if I refuse to tell, but I would rather stay in gaol for a year than say aught that might set them upon the track of Captain Madden. It was not until the day he left me in Holland that I knew his name, for of course the men always called him captain, and so did I."

"That is the only way I can see out of it, lad. I don't think they will imprison you after the service you have done in enabling them to break up this gang, bring the head of it to justice, and recover a large amount of property."

So indeed, on their going to the Guildhall next morning, it turned out. The sitting Alderman threatened Cyril with committal to prison unless he gave a full account of all that had happened to him, but Captain Dowsett spoke up for him, and said boldly that instead of punishment he deserved honour for the great service he had done to justice, and that, moreover, if he were punished for refusing to keep the promise of secrecy he had made, there was little chance in the future of desperate men sparing the lives of those who fell into their hands. They would assuredly murder them in self-defence if they knew that the law would force them to break any promise of silence they might have made. The Magistrate, after a consultation with the Chief Constable, finally came round to this view, and permitted Cyril to leave the Court, after praising him warmly for the vigilance he had shown in the protection of his employer's interests. He regretted that he had not been able to furnish them with the name of a man who had certainly been, to some extent, an accomplice of those who had assaulted him, but this was not, however, so much to be regretted, since the man had done all in his power to atone for his actions.

"There is no further information you can give us, Master Cyril?"

"Only this, your worship: that on the day before I left Holland, I caught sight of the two persons who had escaped from the constables. They had just landed."

"I am sorry to hear it," the Alderman said. "I had hoped that they were still in hiding somewhere in the City, and that the constables might yet be able to lay hands on them. However, I expect they will be back again ere long. Your ill-doer is sure to return here sooner or later, either with the hope of further gain, or because he cannot keep away from his old haunts and companions. If they fall into the hands of the City constables, I will warrant they won't escape again."

He nodded to Cyril, who understood that his business was over and left the Court with Captain Dave.

"I am not so anxious as the Alderman seemed to be that Black Dick and Robert Ashford should return to London, Captain Dave."

"No; I can understand that, Cyril. And even now that you know they are abroad, it would be well to take every precaution, for the others whose business has been sorely interrupted by the capture of that villain Marner may again try to do you harm. No doubt other receivers will fill his place in time, but the loss of a ready market must incommode them much. Plate they can melt down themselves, and I reckon they would have but little difficulty in finding knaves ready to purchase the products of the melting-pot; but it is only a man with premises specially prepared for it who will buy goods of all kinds, however bulky, without asking questions about them."

Cyril was now in high favour with Mistress Nellie, and whenever he was not engaged when she went out he was invited to escort her.

One day he went with her to hear a famous preacher hold forth at St. Paul's. Only a portion of the cathedral was used for religious services; the rest was utilised as a sort of public promenade, and here people of all classes met—gallants of the Court, citizens, their wives and daughters, idlers and loungers, thieves and mendicants.

As Nellie walked forward to join the throng gathered near the pulpit, Cyril noticed a young man in a Court suit, standing among a group who were talking and laughing much louder than was seemly, take off his plumed hat, and make a deep bow, to which she replied by a slight inclination of the head, and passed on with somewhat heightened colour.

Cyril waited until the service was over, when, as he left the cathedral with her, he asked,—

"Who was that ruffler in gay clothes, who bowed so deeply to you, Mistress Nellie?—that is, if there is no indiscretion in my asking."

"I met him in a throng while you were away," she said, with an attempt at carelessness which he at once detected. "There was a great press, and I well-nigh fainted, but he very courteously came to my assistance, and brought me safely out of the crowd."

"And doubtless you have seen him since, Mistress?"

Nellie tossed her head.

"I don't see what right you have to question me, Master Cyril?"

"No right at all," Cyril replied good-temperedly, "save that I am an inmate of your father's house, and have received great kindness from him, and I doubt if he would be pleased if he knew that you bowed to a person unknown to him and unknown, I presume, to yourself, save that he has rendered you a passing service."

"He is a gentleman of the Court, I would have you know," she said angrily.

"I do not know that that is any great recommendation if the tales one hears about the Court are true," Cyril replied calmly. "I cannot say I admire either his companions or his manners, and if he is a gentleman he should know that if he wishes to speak to an honest citizen's daughter it were only right that he should first address himself to her father."

"Heigh ho!" Nellie exclaimed, with her face flushed with indignation. "Who made you my censor, I should like to know? I will thank you to attend to your own affairs, and to leave mine alone."

"The affairs of Captain Dave's daughter are mine so long as I am abroad with her," Cyril said firmly. "I am sorry to displease you, but I am only doing what I feel to be my duty. Methinks that, were John Wilkes here in charge of you, he would say the same, only probably he would express his opinion as to yonder gallant more strongly than I do;" he nodded in the direction of the man, who had followed them out of the cathedral, and was now walking on the other side of the street, and evidently trying to attract Nellie's attention.

Nellie bit her lips. She was about to answer him passionately, but restrained herself with a great effort.

"You are mistaken in the gentleman, Cyril," she said, after a pause; "he is of a good family, and heir to a fine estate."

"Oh, he has told you as much as that, has he? Well, Mistress Nellie, it may be as he says, but surely it is for your father to inquire into that, when the gentleman comes forward in due course and presents himself as a suitor. Fine feathers do not always make fine birds, and a man may ruffle it at King Charles's Court without ten guineas to shake in his purse."

At this moment the young man crossed the street, and, bowing deeply to Nellie, was about to address her when Cyril said gravely,—

"Sir, I am not acquainted with your name, nor do I know more about you save that you are a stranger to this lady's family. That being so, and as she is at present under my escort, I must ask you to abstain from addressing her."

"You insolent young varlet!" the man said furiously. "Had I a cane instead of a sword I would chastise you for your insolence."

"That is as it may be," Cyril said quietly. "That sort of thing may do down at Whitehall, but if you attempt to make trouble here in Cheapside you will very speedily find yourself in the hands of the watch."

"For Heaven's sake, sir," Nellie said anxiously, as several passers-by paused to see what was the matter, "do not cause trouble. For my sake, if not for your own, pray leave me."

"I obey you, Mistress," the man said again, lifting his hat and bowing deeply. "I regret that the officiousness of this blundering varlet should have mistaken my intentions, which were but to salute you courteously."

So saying, he replaced his hat, and, with a threatening scowl at Cyril, pushed his way roughly through those standing round, and walked rapidly away.

Nellie was very pale, and trembled from head to foot.

"Take me home, Cyril," she murmured.

He offered her his arm, and he made his way along the street, while his face flushed with anger at some jeering remarks he heard from one or two of those who looked on at the scene. It was not long before Nellie's anger gained the upper hand of her fears.

"A pretty position you have placed me in, with your interference!"

"You mean, I suppose, Mistress Nellie, a pretty position that man placed you in, by his insolence. What would

"FOR HEAVEN'S SAKE, SIR, DO NOT CAUSE TROUBLE."

Captain Dave say if he heard that his daughter had been accosted by a Court gallant in the streets?"

"Are you going to tell him?" she asked, removing her hand sharply from his arm.

"I have no doubt I ought to do so, and if you will take my advice you will tell him yourself as soon as you reach home, for it may be that among those standing round was some one who is acquainted with both you and your father; and you know as well as I do what Captain Dave would say if it came to his ears in such fashion."

Nellie walked for some time in silence. Her anger rose still higher against Cyril at the position in which his interference had placed her, but she could not help seeing that his advice was sound. She had indeed met this man several times, and had listened without chiding to his protestations of admiration and love. Nellie was ambitious. She had been allowed to have her own way by her mother, whose sole companion she had been during her father's absence at sea. She knew that she was remarkably pretty, and saw no reason why she, like many another citizen's daughter, should not make a good match. She had readily given the man her promise to say nothing at home until he gave her leave to do so, and she had been weak enough to take all that he said for gospel. Now she felt that, at any rate, she must smooth matters over and put it so that as few questions as possible should be asked. After a long pause, then, she said,—

"Perhaps you are right, Cyril. I will myself tell my father and mother. I can assure you that I had no idea I should meet him to-day."

This Cyril could readily believe, for certainly she would not have asked him to accompany her if she had known. However, he only replied gravely,—

"I am glad to hear that you will tell them, Mistress Nellie, and trust that you will take them entirely into your confidence."

This Nellie had no idea of doing; but she said no further word until they reached home.

CHAPTER VII.

SAVED FROM A VILLAIN.

"I FIND that I have to give you thanks for yet another service, Cyril," Captain Dave said heartily, when they met the next morning. "Nellie tells me a young Court gallant had the insolence to try to address her yesterday in Cheapside, on her way back from St. Paul's, that you prevented his doing so, and that there was quite a scene in the street. If I knew who he was I would break his sconce for him, were he Rochester himself. A pretty pass things have come to, when a citizen's daughter cannot walk home from St. Paul's without one of these impudent vagabonds of the Court venturing to address her! Know you who he was?"

"No; I have never seen the fellow before, Captain Dave. I do know many of the courtiers by sight, having, when we first came over, often gone down to Whitehall with my father when he was seeking to obtain an audience with the King; but this man's face is altogether strange to me."

"Well, well! I will take care that Nellie shall not go abroad again except under her mother's escort or mine. I know, Cyril, that she would be as safe under your charge as in ours, but it is better that she should have the presence of an older person. It is not that I doubt your courage or your address, lad, but a ruffling gallant of this sort would know naught of you, save that you are young, and besides, did you interfere, there might be a scene that would do serious harm to Nellie's reputation."

"I agree with you thoroughly, Captain Dave," Cyril said warmly. "It will be far better that you or Mrs. Dowsett should be by her side as long as there is any fear of further annoyance from this fellow. I should ask nothing better than to try a bout with him myself, for I have been right well taught how to use my sword; but, as you say, a brawl in the street is of all things to be avoided."

Three or four weeks passed quietly. Nellie seldom went abroad; when she did so her mother always accompanied her if it were in the daytime, and her father whenever she went to the house of any friend after dusk.

Cyril one day caught sight of the gallant in Tower Street, and although he was on his way to one of his customers, he at once determined to break his appointment and to find out who the fellow was. The man sauntered about looking into the shops for full half an hour, but it was apparent to Cyril that he paid little attention to their contents, and was really waiting for some one. When the clock struck three he started, stamped his foot angrily on the ground, and, walking away rapidly to the stairs of London Bridge, took a seat in a boat, and was rowed up the river.

Cyril waited until he had gone a short distance, and then hailed a wherry rowing two oars.

"You see that boat over there?" he said. "I don't wish to overtake it at present. Keep a hundred yards or so behind it, but row inshore so that it shall not seem that you are following them."

The men obeyed his instructions until they had passed the Temple; then, as the other boat still kept in the middle of the stream, Cyril had no doubt that it would continue its course to Westminster.

"Now stretch to your oars," he said to the watermen. "I want to get to Westminster before the other boat, and to be well away from the stairs before it comes up."

The rest of the journey was performed at much greater speed, and Cyril alighted at Westminster while the other boat was some three or four hundred yards behind. Paying the watermen, he went up the stairs, walked away fifty or sixty yards, and waited until he saw the man he was following appear. The latter walked quietly up towards Whitehall and entered a tavern frequented by young bloods of the Court.

Cyril pressed his hat down over his eyes. His dress was not the same as that in which he had escorted Nellie to the Cathedral, and he had but small fear of being recognised.

When he entered he sat down at a vacant table, and, having ordered a stoup of wine, looked round. The man had joined a knot of young fellows like himself, seated at a table. They were dissipated-looking blades, and were talking loudly and boisterously.

"Well, Harvey, how goes it? Is the lovely maiden we saw when we were with you at St. Paul's ready to drop into your arms?"

"Things are going on all right," Harvey said, with an air of consciousness; "but she is watched by two griffins, her father and mother. 'Tis fortunate they do not know me by sight, and I have thus chances of slipping a note in her hand when I pass her. I think it will not be long before you will have to congratulate me."

"She is an heiress and only daughter, is she not, honest John?" another asked.

"She is an only child, and her father bears the reputation of doing a good business; but as to what I shall finally do, I shall not yet determine. As to that, I shall be guided by circumstances."

"Of course, of course," the one who had first spoken said.

Cyril had gained the information he required. The man's name was John Harvey, and Nellie was keeping up a clandestine correspondence with him. Cyril felt that were he to listen longer he could not restrain his indignation, and, without touching the wine he had paid for, he hastily left the tavern.

As he walked towards the city, he was unable to decide what he had better do. Were he to inform Captain Dave of what he had heard there would be a terrible scene, and there was no saying what might happen. Still, Nellie must be saved from falling into the hands of this fellow, and if he abstained from telling her father he must himself take steps to prevent the possibility of such a thing taking place. The more he thought of it the more he felt of the heavy responsibility it would be. Anxious as he was to save Nellie from the anger of her father, it was of far greater consequence to save her from the consequences of her own folly. At last he resolved to take John Wilkes into his counsels. John was devoted to his master, and even if his advice were not of much value, his aid in keeping watch would be of immense service. Accordingly, that evening, when John went out for his usual pipe after supper, Cyril, who had to go to a trader in Holborn, followed him out quickly and overtook him a few yards from the door.

"I want to have a talk with you, John."

"Ay, ay, sir. Where shall it be? Nothing wrong, I hope? That new apprentice looks to me an honest sort of chap, and the man we have got in the yard now is an old mate of mine. He was a ship's boy on board the *Dolphin* twenty-five years back, and he sailed under the Captain till he left the sea. I would trust that chap just as I would myself."

"It is nothing of that sort, John. It is another sort of business altogether, and yet it is quite as serious as the last. I have got half an hour before I have to start to do those books at Master Hopkins'. Where can we have a talk in a quiet place where there is no chance of our being overheard?"

"There is a little room behind the bar at the place I go to, and I have no doubt the landlord will let us have it, seeing as I am a regular customer."

"At any rate we can see, John. It is too cold for walking about talking here; and, besides, I think one can look at a matter in all lights much better sitting down than one can walking about."

"That is according to what you are accustomed to," John said, shaking his head. "It seems to me that I can look further into the innards of a question when I am walking up and down the deck on night watch with just enough wind aloft to take her along cheerful, and not too much of it, than I can at any other time; but then, you see, that is just what one is accustomed to. This is the place."

He entered a quiet tavern, and, nodding to five or six weather-beaten-looking men, who were sitting smoking long pipes, each with a glass of grog before him, went up to the landlord, who formed one of the party. He had been formerly the master of a trader, and had come into the possession of the tavern by marriage with its mistress, who was still the acting head of the establishment.

"We have got a piece of business we want to overhaul, Peter. I suppose we can have that cabin in yonder for a bit?"

"Ay, ay. There is a good fire burning. You will find pipes on the table. You will want a couple of glasses of grog, of course?"

John nodded, and then led the way into the little snuggery at the end of the room. It had a glass door, so that, if desired, a view could be obtained of the general room, but there was a curtain to draw across this. There was a large oak settle on either side of the fire, and there was a table, with pipes and a jar of tobacco standing between them.

"This is a tidy little crib," John said, as he seated himself and began to fill a pipe. "There is no fear of being disturbed here. There has been many a voyage talked over and arranged in this 'ere room. They say that Blake himself, when the Fleet was in the river, would drop in here sometimes, with one of his captains, for a quiet talk."

A minute later a boy entered and placed two steaming glasses of grog on the table. The door closed after him, and John said,—

"Now you can get under way, Master Cyril. You have got a fair course now, and nothing to bring you up."

"It is a serious matter, John. And before I begin, I must tell you that I rely on your keeping absolute silence as to what I am going tell you."

"That in course," John said, as he lifted his glass to his lips. "You showed yourself a first-rate pilot in that last job, and I am content to sail under you this time without asking any questions as to the ship's course, and to steer according to orders."

Cyril told the story, interrupted frequently by angry ejaculations on the part of the old bo'swain.

"Dash my wig!" he exclaimed, when Cyril came to an end. "But this is a bad business altogether, Master Cyril. One can engage a pirate and beat him off if the crew is staunch, but when there is treason on board ship, it makes it an awkward job for those in command."

"The question is this, John: ought we to tell the Captain, or shall we try to take the affair into our own hands, and so to manage it that he shall never know anything about it?"

The sailor was silent for a minute or two, puffing his pipe meditatively.

"I see it is an awkward business to decide," he said. "On one side, it would pretty nigh kill Captain Dave to know that Mistress Nellie has been steering wild and has got out of hand. She is just the apple of his eye. Then, on the other hand, if we undertook the job without telling him, and one fine morning we was to find out she was gone, we should be in a mighty bad fix, for the Captain would turn round and say, 'Why didn't you tell me? If you had done so, I would have locked her up under hatches, and there she would be, safe now.'"

"That is just what I see, and it is for that reason I come to you. I could not be always on the watch, but I think that you and I together would keep so sharp a look-out that we might feel pretty sure that she could not get away without our knowledge."

"We could watch sharply enough at night, Master Cyril. There would be no fear of her getting away then without our knowing it. But how would it be during the day? There am I in the shop or store from seven in the morning until we lock up before supper-time. You are out most of your time, and when you are not away, you are in the office at the books, and she is free to go in and out of the front door without either of us being any the wiser."

"I don't think he would venture to carry her off by daylight," Cyril said. "She never goes out alone now, and could scarcely steal away unnoticed. Besides, she would know that she would be missed directly, and a hue and cry set up. I should think she would certainly choose the evening, when we are all supposed to be in bed. He would have a chair waiting somewhere near; and there are so often chairs going about late, after city entertainments, that they would get off unnoticed. I should say the most dangerous time is between nine o'clock and midnight. She generally goes off to bed at nine or soon after, and she might very well put on her hood and cloak and steal downstairs at once, knowing that she would not be missed till morning. Another dangerous time would be when she goes out to a neighbour's. The Captain always takes her, and goes to fetch her at nine o'clock, but she might make some excuse to leave quite early, and go off in that way."

"That would be awkward, Mr. Cyril, for neither you nor I could be away at supper-time without questions being asked. It seems to me that I had better take Matthew into the secret. As he don't live in the house he could very well watch wherever she is, till I slip round after supper to relieve him, and he could watch outside here in the evening till either you or I could steal downstairs and take his place. You can count on him keeping his mouth shut just as you can on me. The only thing is, how is he to stop her if he finds her coming out from a neighbour's before the Captain has come for her?"

"If he saw her coming straight home he could follow her to the door without being noticed, John, but if he found her going some other way he must follow her till he sees some one speak to her, and must then go straight up and say, 'Mistress Dowsett, I am ready to escort you home.' If she orders him off, or the man she meets threatens him, as is like enough, he must say, 'Unless you come I shall shout for aid, and call upon passers-by to assist me'; and, rather than risk the exposure, she would most likely return with him. Of course, he would carry with him a good heavy cudgel, and choose a thoroughfare where there are people about to speak to her, and not an unfrequented passage, for you may be sure the fellow would have no hesitation in running him through if he could do so without being observed."

"Matthew is a stout fellow," John Wilkes said, "and was as smart a sailor as any on board till he had his foot smashed by being jammed by a spare spar that got adrift in a gale, so that the doctors had to cut off the leg under the knee, and leave him to stump about on a timber toe for the rest of his life. I tell you what, Master Cyril: we might make the thing safer still if I spin the Captain a yarn as how Matthew has strained his back and ain't fit to work for a bit; then I can take on another hand to work in the yard, and we can put him on watch all day. He might come on duty at nine o'clock in the morning, and stop until I relieve him as soon as supper is over. Of course, he would not keep opposite the house, but might post himself a bit up or down the street, so that he could manage to keep an eye on the door."

"That would be excellent," Cyril said. "Of course, at the supper-hour he could go off duty, as she could not possibly leave the house between that time and nine o'clock. You always come in about that hour, and I hear you go up to bed. When you get there, you should at once take off your boots, slip downstairs again with them, and go quietly out. I often sit talking with Captain Dave till half-past nine or ten, but directly I can get away I will come down and join you. I think in that way we need feel no uneasiness as to harm coming from our not telling Captain Dave, for it would be impossible for her to get off unnoticed. Now that is all arranged I must be going, for I shall be late at my appointment unless I hurry."

"Shall I go round and begin my watch at once, Master Cyril?"

"No, there is no occasion for that. We know that he missed her to-day, and therefore can have made no appointment; and I am convinced by what he said to the fellows he met, that matters are not settled yet. However, we will begin to-morrow.

You can take an opportunity during the day to tell Matthew about it, and he can pretend to strain his back in the afternoon, and you can send him away. He can come round again next morning early, and when the Captain comes down you can tell him that you find that Matthew will not be able to work for the present, and ask him to let you take another man on until he can come back again."

Cyril watched Nellie closely at meal-times and in the evening for the next few days. He thought that he should be certain to detect some slight change in her manner, however well she might play her part, directly she decided on going off with this man. She would not dream that she was suspected in any way, and would therefore be the less cautious. Matthew kept watch during the day, and followed if she went out with her father to a neighbour's, remaining on guard outside the house until John Wilkes relieved him as soon as he had finished his supper. If she remained at home in the evening John went out silently, after his return at his usual hour, and was joined by Cyril as soon as Captain Dave said good-night and went into his bedroom. At midnight they re-entered the house and stole up to their rooms, leaving their doors open and listening attentively for another hour before they tried to get to sleep.

On the sixth morning Cyril noticed that Nellie was silent and abstracted at breakfast-time. She went out marketing with her mother afterwards, and at dinner her mood had changed. She talked and laughed more than usual. There was a flush of excitement on her cheeks, and he drew the conclusion that in the morning she had not come to an absolute decision, but had probably given an answer to the man during the time she was out with her mother, and that she felt the die was now cast.

"Pass the word to Matthew to keep an extra sharp watch this afternoon and to-morrow, John. I think the time is close at hand," he said, as they went downstairs together after dinner.

"Do you think so? Well, the sooner the better. It is trying work, this here spying, and I don't care how soon it is over. I only hope it will end by our running down this pirate and engaging him."

"I hope so too, John. I feel it very hard to be sitting at table with her and Captain Dave and her mother, and to know that she is deceiving them."

"I can't say a word for her," the old sailor said, shaking his head. "She has as good parents as a girl could want to have. They would give their lives for her, either of them, cheerful, and there she is thinking of running away from them with a scamp she knows nothing of and has probably never spoken with for an hour. I knew her head was a bit turned with young fellows dangling after her, and by being noticed by some of the Court gallants at the last City ball, and by being made the toast by many a young fellow in City taverns—'Pretty Mistress Nellie Dowsett'; but I did not think her head was so turned that she would act as she is doing. Well, well, we must hope that this will be a lesson, Master Cyril, that she will remember all her life."

"I hope so, John, and I trust that we shall be able to manage it all so that the matter will never come to her parents' ears."

"I hope so, and I don't see why it should. The fellow may bluster, but he will say nothing about it because he would get into trouble for trying to carry off a citizen's daughter."

"And besides that, John,—which would be quite as serious in the eyes of a fellow of this sort,—he would have the laugh against him among all his companions for having been outwitted in the City. So I think when he finds the game is up he will be glad enough to make off without causing trouble."

"Don't you think we might give him a sound thrashing? It would do him a world of good."

"I don't think it would do a man of that sort much good, John, and he would be sure to shout, and then there would be trouble, and the watch might come up, and we should all get hauled off together. In the morning the whole story would be known, and Mistress Nellie's name in the mouth of every apprentice in the City. No, no; if he is disposed to go off quietly, by all means let him go."

"I have no doubt that you are right, Master Cyril, but it goes mightily against the grain to think that a fellow like that is to get off with a whole skin. However, if one should fall foul of him some other time, one might take it out of him."

Captain Dave found Cyril but a bad listener to his stories that evening, and, soon after nine, said he should turn in.

"I don't know what ails you to-night, Cyril," he said. "Your wits are wool-gathering, somewhere. I don't believe that you heard half that last story I was telling you."

"I heard it all, sir; but I do feel a little out of sorts this evening."

"You do too much writing, lad. My head would be like to go to pieces if I were to sit half the hours that you do at a desk."

When Captain Dave went into his room, Cyril walked upstairs and closed his bedroom door with a bang, himself remaining outside. Then he took off his boots, and, holding them in his hand, went noiselessly downstairs to the front door. The lock had been carefully oiled, and, after putting on his boots again, he went out.

"You are right, Master Cyril, sure enough," John Wilkes said when he joined him, fifty yards away from the house. "It is to-night she is going to try to make off. I thought I had best keep Matthew at hand, so I bid him stop till I came out, then sent him round to have a pint of ale at the tavern, and when he came back told him he had best cruise about, and look for signs of pirates. He came back ten minutes ago, and told me that a sedan chair had just been brought to the other end of the lane. It was set down some thirty yards from Fenchurch Street. There were the two chairmen and three fellows wrapped up in cloaks."

"That certainly looks like action, John. Well, I should say that Matthew had better take up his station at the other end of the lane, there to remain quiet until he hears an uproar at the chair; then he can run up to our help if we need it. We will post ourselves near the door. No doubt Harvey, and perhaps one of his friends, will come and wait for her. We can't interfere with them here, but must follow and come up with her just before they reach the chair. The further they are away from the house the better. Then if there is any trouble Captain Dave will not hear anything of it.".

"That will be a good plan of operations," John agreed. "Matthew is just round the next corner. I will send him to Fenchurch Street at once."

He went away, and rejoined Cyril in two or three minutes. They then went along towards the house, and took post in a doorway on the other side of the street, some thirty yards from the shop. They had scarcely done so, when they heard footsteps, and presently saw two men come along in the middle of the street. They stopped and looked round.

"There is not a soul stirring," one said. "We can give the signal."

So saying, he sang a bar or two of a song popular at the time, and they then drew back from the road into a doorway and waited.

Five minutes later, Cyril and his fellow-watcher heard a very slight sound, and a figure stepped out from Captain Dowsett's door. The two men crossed at once and joined her. A few low words were spoken, and they moved away together, and turned up the lane.

As soon as they disappeared from sight, Cyril and John Wilkes issued out. The latter had produced some long strips of cloth, which he wound round both their boots, so as, he said, to muffle the oars. Their steps, therefore, as they followed, were almost noiseless. Walking fast, they came up to the three persons ahead of them just as they reached the sedan chair. The two chairmen were standing at the poles, and a third man was holding the door open with his hat in his hand.

"Avast heaving, mates!" John Wilkes said. "It seems to me as you are running this cargo without proper permits."

Nellie gave a slight scream on hearing the voice, while the man beside her stepped forward, exclaiming furiously:

"S'death, sir! who are you, and what are you interfering about?"

"I am an honest man I hope, master. My name is John Wilkes, and, as that young lady will tell you, I am in the employ of her father."

"Then I tell you, John Wilkes, or John the Devil, or whatever your name may be, that if you don't at once take yourself off, I will let daylight into you," and he drew his sword, as did his two companions.

John gave a whistle, and the wooden-legged man was heard hurrying up from Fenchurch Street.

"Cut the scoundrel down, Penrose," Harvey exclaimed, "while I put the lady into the chair."

The man addressed sprang at Wilkes, but in a moment his Court sword was shivered by a blow from the latter's cudgel, which a moment later fell again on his head, sending him reeling back several paces.

"Stay, sir, or I will run you through," Cyril said, pricking Harvey sharply in the arm as he was urging Nellie to enter the chair.

"Oh, it's you, is it?" the other exclaimed, in a tone of fury. "My boy of Cheapside! Well, I can spare a moment to punish you."

"Oh, do not fight with him, my lord!" Nellie exclaimed.

"My lord!" Cyril laughed. "So he has become a lord, eh?"

Then he changed his tone.

"Mistress Nellie, you have been deceived. This fellow is no lord. He is a hanger-on of the Court, one John Harvey, a disreputable blackguard whom I heard boasting to his boon-companions of his conquest. I implore you to return home as quietly as you went. None will know of this."

He broke off suddenly, for, with an oath, Harvey rushed at him. Their swords clashed, there was a quick thrust and parry, and then Harvey staggered back with a sword-wound through the shoulder, dropping his sword to the ground.

"Your game is up, John Harvey," Cyril said. "Did you have your deserts I would pass my sword through your body. Now call your fellows off, or it will be worse for them."

"Oh, it is not true? Surely it cannot be true?" Nellie cried, addressing Harvey. "You cannot have deceived me?"

The fellow, smarting with pain, and seeing that the game was up, replied with a savage curse.

"You may think yourself lucky that you are only disabled, you villain!" Cyril said, taking a step towards him with his sword menacingly raised. "Begone, sir, before my patience is exhausted, or, by heaven! it will be your dead body that the chairmen will have to carry away."

"Disabled or not," John Wilkes exclaimed, "I will have a say in the matter;" and, with a blow with his cudgel, he stretched Harvey on the ground, and belaboured him furiously until Cyril dragged him away by force. Harvey rose slowly to his feet.

"Take yourself off, sir," Cyril said. "One of your brave companions has long ago bolted; the other is disarmed, and has his head broken. You may thank your stars that you have escaped with nothing worse than a sword-thrust through your shoulder, and a sound drubbing. Hanging would be a fit punishment for knaves like you. I warn you, if you ever address or in any way molest this lady again, you won't get off so easily."

Then he turned and offered his arm to Nellie, who was leaning against the wall in a half-fainting state. Not a word was spoken until they emerged from the lane.

"No one knows of this but ourselves, Mistress Nellie, and you will never hear of it from us. Glad indeed I am that I have saved you from the misery and ruin that must have resulted from your listening to that plausible scoundrel. Go quietly upstairs. We will wait here till we are sure that you have gone safely into your room; then we will follow. I doubt not that you are angry with me now, but in time you will feel that you have been saved from a great danger."

The door was not locked. He lifted the latch silently, and held the door open for her to pass in. Then he closed it again, and turned to the two men who followed them.

"This has been a good night's work, John."

"That has it. I don't think that young spark will be coming after City maidens again. Well, it has been a narrow escape for her. It would have broken the Captain's heart if she had gone in that way. What strange things women are! I have always thought Mistress Nellie as sensible a girl as one would want to see. Given a little over-much, perhaps, to thinking of the fashion of her dress, but that was natural enough, seeing how pretty she is and how much she is made of; and yet she is led, by a few soft speeches from a man she knows nothing of, to run away from home, and leave father, and mother, and all. Well, Matthew, lad, we sha'n't want any more watching. You have done a big service to the master, though he will never know it. I know I can trust you to keep a stopper on your jaws. Don't you let a soul know of this—not even your wife."

"You trust me, mate," the man replied. "My wife is a good soul, but her tongue runs nineteen to the dozen, and you might as well shout a thing out at Paul's Cross as drop it into her ear. I think my back will be well enough for me to come to work again to-morrow," he added, with a laugh.

"All right, mate. I shall be glad to have you again, for the chap who has been in your place is a landsman, and he don't know a marling-spike from an anchor. Good-night, mate."

"Well, Master Cyril," he went on, as the sailor walked away, "I don't think there ever was such a good wind as that which blew you here. First of all you saved Captain Dave's fortune, and now you save his daughter. I look on Captain Dave as being pretty nigh the same as myself, seeing as I have been with him man and boy for over thirty years, and I feel what you have done for him just as if you had done it for me. I am only a rough sailor-man, and I don't know how to put it in words, but I feel just full up with a cargo of thankfulness."

"That is all right," Cyril said, holding out his hand, which John Wilkes shook with a heartiness that was almost painful. "Captain Dave offered me a home when I was alone without a friend in London, and I am glad indeed that I have been able to render him service in return. I myself have done little enough, though I do not say that the consequences have not been important. It has been just taking a little trouble and keeping a few watches—a thing not worth talking about one way or the other. I hope this will do Mistress Nellie good. She is a nice girl, but too fond of admiration, and inclined to think that she is meant for higher things than to marry a London citizen. I think to-night's work will cure her of that. This fellow evidently made himself out to her to be a nobleman of the Court. Now she sees that he is neither a nobleman nor a gentleman, but a ruffian who took advantage of her vanity and inexperience, and that she would have done better to have jumped down the well in the yard than to have put herself in his power. Now we can go up to bed. There is no more probability of our waking the Captain than there has been on other nights; but mind, if we should do so, you stick to the story we agreed on, that you thought there was some one by the gate in the lane again, and so called me to go down with you to investigate, not thinking it worth while to rouse up the Captain on what might be a false alarm."

Everything remained perfectly quiet as they made their way upstairs to their rooms as silently as possible.

"Where is Nellie?" Captain Dave asked, when they assembled at breakfast.

"She is not well," his wife replied. "I went to her room just now and found that she was still a-bed. She said that she had a bad headache, and I fear that she is going to have a fever, for her face is pale and her eyes red and swollen, just as if she had been well-nigh crying them out of her head; her hands are hot and her pulse fast. Directly I have had breakfast I shall make her some camomile tea, and if that does not do her good I shall send for the doctor."

"Do so, wife, without delay. Why, the girl has never ailed a day for years! What can have come to her?"

"She says it is only a bad headache—that all she wants is to be left alone."

"Yes, yes; that is all very well, but if she does not get better soon she must be seen to. They say that there were several cases last week of that plague that has been doing so much harm in foreign parts, and if that is so it behoves us to be very careful, and see that any illness is attended to without delay."

"I don't think that there is any cause for alarm," his wife said quietly. "The child has got a headache and is a little feverish, but there is no occasion whatever for thinking that it is anything more. There is nothing unusual in a girl having a headache, but Nellie has had such good health that if she had a prick in the finger you would think it was serious."

"By the way, John," Captain Dave said suddenly, "did you hear any noise in the lane last night? Your room is at the back of the house, and you were more likely to have heard it than I was. I have just seen one of the watch, and he tells me that there was a fray there last night, for there is a patch of blood and marks of a scuffle. It was up at the other end. There is some mystery about it, he thinks, for he says that one of his mates last night saw a sedan chair escorted by three men turn into the lane from Fenchurch Street just before ten o'clock, and one of the neighbours says that just after that hour he heard a disturbance and a clashing of swords there. On looking out, he saw something dark that might have been a chair standing there, and several men engaged in a scuffle. It seemed soon over, and directly afterwards three people came down the lane this way. Then he fancied that some one got into the chair, which was afterwards carried out into Fenchurch Street."

"I did hear something that sounded like a quarrel or a fray," John Wilkes said, "but there is nothing unusual about that. As everything was soon quiet again, I gave no further thought to it."

"Well, it seems a curious affair, John. However, it is the business of the City watch and not mine, so we need not bother ourselves about it. I am glad to see you have got Matthew at work again this morning. He tells me that he thinks he has fairly got over that sprain in his back."

CHAPTER VIII.

THE CAPTAIN'S YARN.

MINDFUL of the fact that this affair had added a new enemy to those he had acquired by the break-up of the Black Gang, Cyril thought it as well to go round and give notice to the two traders whose books he attended to in the evening, that unless they could arrange for him to do them in the daytime he must give up the work altogether. Both preferred the former alternative, for they recognised the advantage they had derived from his work, and that at a rate of pay for which they could not have obtained the services of any scrivener in the City.

It was three or four days before Nellie Dowsett made her appearance at the general table.

"I can't make out what ails the girl," her mother said, on the previous evening. "The fever speedily left her, as I told you, but she is weak and languid, and seems indisposed to talk."

"She will soon get over that, my dear," Captain Dave said.

"Girls are not like men. I have seen them on board ship. One day they are laughing and fidgeting about like wild things, the next day they are poor, woebegone creatures. If she gets no better in a few days, I will see when my old friend, Jim Carroll, is starting in his brig for Yarmouth, and will run down with her myself—and of course with you, wife, if you will go—and stay there a few days while he is unloading and filling up again. The sea-air will set her up again, I warrant."

"Not at this time of year," Dame Dowsett said firmly. "With these bitter winds it is no time for a lass to go a-sailing; and they say that Yarmouth is a great deal colder than we are here, being exposed to the east winds."

"Well, well, Dame, then we will content ourselves with a run in the hoy down to Margate. If we choose well the wind and tide we can start from here in the morning and maybe reach there late in the evening, or, if not, the next morning to breakfast. Or if you think that too far we will stop at Sheerness, where we can get in two tides easily enough if the wind be fair."

"That would be better, David; but it were best to see how she goes on. It may be, as you say, that she will shortly gain her strength and spirits again."

It was evident, when Nellie entered the room at breakfast-time the next morning, that her mother's reports had not been exaggerated. She looked, indeed, as if recovering from a severe illness, and when she said good-morning to her father her voice trembled and her eyes filled with tears.

"Tut, tut, lass! This will never do. I shall soon hardly own you for my Nellie. We shall have to feed you up on capons and wine, child, or send you down to one of the baths for a course of strengthening waters."

She smiled faintly, and then turning, gave her hand to Cyril. As she did so, a slight flush of colour came into her cheeks.

"I am heartily glad to see you down again, Mistress Nellie," he said, "and wish you a fair and speedy recovery."

"I shall be better presently," she replied, with an effort. "Good-morning, John."

"Good-morning, Mistress Nellie. Right glad are we to see you down again, for it makes but a dull table without your merry laugh to give an edge to our appetites."

She sat down now, and the others, seeing that it was best to let her alone for a while, chatted gaily together.

"There is no talk in the City but of the war, Cyril," the Captain said presently. "They say that the Dutch make sure of eating us up, but they won't find it as easy a job as they fancy. The Duke of York is to command the Fleet. They say that Prince Rupert will be second. To my mind they ought to have entrusted the whole matter to him. He proved himself as brave a captain at sea as he was on land, and I will warrant he would lead his ships into action as gallantly as he rode at the head of his Cavaliers on many a stricken field. The ships are fitting out in all haste, and they are gathering men at every sea-port. I should say they will have no lack of hands, for there are many ships laid up, that at other times trade with Holland, and Dantzic, and Dunkirk, and many a bold young sailor who will be glad to try whether he can fight as stoutly against the Dutch under York and Rupert as his father did under Blake."

"For my part," Cyril said, "I cannot understand it; for it seems to me that the English and Dutch have been fighting for the last year. I have been too busy to read the Journal, and have not been in the way of hearing the talk of the coffee-houses and taverns; but, beyond that it is some dispute about the colonies, I know little of the matter."

"I am not greatly versed in it myself, lad. Nellie here reads the Journal, and goes abroad more than any of us, and should be able to tell us something about it. Now, girl, can't you do something to set us right in this matter, for I like not to be behind my neighbours, though I am such a stay-at-home, having, as I thank the Lord, much happiness here, and no occasion to go out to seek it."

"There was much discourse about it, father, the evening I went to Dame King's. There were several gentlemen there who had trade with the East, and one of them held shares in the English Company trading thither. After supper was over, they discoursed more fully on the matter than was altogether pleasing to some of us, who would much rather that, as we had hoped, we might have dancing or singing. I could see that Dame King herself was somewhat put out that her husband should have, without her knowing of his intention, brought in these gentlemen. Still, the matter of their conversation was new to us, and we became at last so mightily interested in it that we listened to the discourse without bemoaning ourselves that we had lost the amusement we looked for. I know I wished at the time that you had been there. I say not that I can repeat all that I heard, but as I had before read some of the matters spoken of in the Journal, I could follow what the gentlemen said more closely. Soon after the coming of the King to the throne the friendship between us and the Spaniards, that had been weakened during the mastership of Cromwell, was renewed, and they gave our ships many advantages at their ports, while, on the other hand, they took away the privileges the Dutch had enjoyed there, and thus our commerce with Spain increased, while that of the Dutch diminished."

"That is certainly true, Nellie," her father said. "We have three ships sailing through the Mediterranean now to one that sailed there ten years ago, and doubtless the Dutch must have suffered by the increase in our trade."

"Then he said that, as we had obtained the Island of Bombay in the East Indies and the City of Tangier in Africa as the dowry of the Queen, and had received the Island of Poleron for our East India Company by the treaty with Holland, our commerce everywhere increased, and raised their jealousy higher and higher. There was nothing in this of which complaint could be made by the Dutch Government, but nevertheless they gave encouragement to their East and

West India Companies to raise trouble. Their East India Company refused to hand over the Island, and laid great limitations as to the places at which our merchants might trade in India. The other Company acted in the same manner, and lawlessly took possession of Cape Coast Castle, belonging to our English Company.

"The Duke of York, who was patron and governor of our African Company, sent Sir Robert Holmes with four frigates to Guinea to make reprisals. He captured a place from the Dutch and named it James's Fort, and then, proceeding to the River Gambia, he turned out the Dutch traders there and built a fort. A year ago, as the Dutch still held Cape Coast Castle, Sir Robert was sent out again with orders to take it by force, and on the way he overhauled a Dutch ship and found she carried a letter of secret instructions from the Dutch Government to the West India Company to take the English Fort at Cormantin. Seeing that the Hollanders, although professing friendship, were thus treacherously inclined, he judged himself justified in exceeding the commission he had received, and on his way south he touched at Cape Verde. There he first captured two Dutch ships and then attacked their forts on the Island of Gorse and captured them, together with a ship lying under their guns.

"In the fort he found a great quantity of goods ready to be shipped. He loaded his own vessels, and those that he had captured, with the merchandise, and carried it to Sierra Leone. Then he attacked the Dutch fort of St. George del Mena, the strongest on the coast, but failed there; but he soon afterwards captured Cape Coast Castle, though, as the gentlemen said, a mightily strong place. Then he sailed across to America, and, as you know, captured the Dutch Settlements of New Netherlands, and changed the name into that of New York. He did this not so much out of reprisal for the misconduct of the Dutch in Africa, but because the land was ours by right, having been discovered by the Cabots and taken possession of in the name of King, Henry VII., and our title always maintained until the Dutch seized it thirty years ago.

"Then the Dutch sent orders to De Ruyter, who commanded the fleet which was in the Mediterranean, to sail away privately and to make reprisals on the Coast of Guinea and elsewhere. He first captured several of our trading forts, among them that of Cormantin, taking great quantities of goods belonging to our Company; he then sailed to Barbadoes, where he was beaten off by the forts. Then he captured twenty of our ships off Newfoundland, and so returned to Holland, altogether doing damage, as the House of Commons told His Majesty, to the extent of eight hundred thousand pounds. All this time the Dutch had been secretly preparing for war, which they declared in January, which has forced us to do the same, although we delayed a month in hopes that some accommodation might be arrived at. I think, father, that is all that he told us, though there were many details that I do not remember."

"And very well told, lass, truly. I wonder that your giddy head should have taken in so much matter. Of course, now you tell them over, I have heard these things before—the wrong that the Dutch did our Company by seizing their post at Cape Coast, and the reprisals that Sir Robert Holmes took upon them with our Company's ships—but they made no great mark on my memory, for I was just taking over my father's work when the first expedition took place. At any rate, none can say that we have gone into this war unjustly, seeing that the Dutch began it, altogether without cause, by first attacking our trading posts."

"It seems to me, Captain Dave," John Wilkes said, "that it has been mighty like the war that our English buccaneers waged against the Spaniards in the West Indies, while the two nations were at peace at home."

"It is curious," Cyril said, "that the trouble begun in Africa should have shifted to the other side of the Atlantic."

"Ay, lad; just as that first trouble was at last fought out

in the English Channel, off the coast of France, so this is likely to be decided in well-nigh the same waters."

"The gentlemen, the other night, were all of opinion," Nellie said, "that the matter would never have come to such a head had it not been that De Witt, who is now the chief man in Holland, belongs to the French party there, and has been urged on by King Louis, for his own interest, to make war with us."

"That may well be, Nellie. In all our English wars France has ever had a part either openly or by intrigues. France never seems to be content with attending to her own business, but is ever meddling with her neighbours', and, if not fighting herself, trying to set them by the ears against each other. If I were a bit younger, and had not lost my left flipper, I would myself volunteer for the service. As for Master Cyril here, I know he is burning to lay aside the pen and take to the sword."

"That is so, Captain Dave. As you know, I only took up the pen to keep me until I was old enough to use a sword. I have been two years at it now, and I suppose it will be as much longer before I can think of entering the service of one of the Protestant princes; but as soon as I am fit to do so, I shall get an introduction and be off; but I would tenfold rather fight for my own country, and would gladly sail in the Fleet, though I went but as a ship's boy."

"That is the right spirit, Master Cyril," John Wilkes exclaimed. "I would go myself if the Captain could spare me and they would take such a battered old hulk."

"I couldn't spare you, John," Captain Dave said. "I have been mighty near making a mess of it, even with you as chief mate, and I might as well shut up shop altogether if you were to leave me. I should miss you, too, Cyril," he went on, stretching his arm across the table to shake hands with the lad. "You have proved a real friend and a true; but were there a chance of your going as an officer, I would not balk you, even if I could do so. It is but natural that a lad of spirit should speak and think as you do; besides, the war may not last for long, and when you come back, and the ships are paid off, you would soon wipe off the arrears of work, and get the books into ship-shape order. But, work or no work, that room of yours will always stand ready for you while I live, and there will always be a plate for you on this table."

"Thank you, Captain Dave. You always overrate my services, and forget that they are but the consequence of the kindness that you have shown to me. But I have no intention of going. It was but a passing thought. I have but one friend who could procure me a berth as a volunteer, and as it is to him I must look for an introduction to some foreign prince, I would not go to him twice for a favour, especially as I have no sort of claim on his kindness. To go as a cabin boy would be to go with men under my own condition, and although I do not shirk hard work and rough usage, I should not care for them in such fashion. Moreover, I am doing work which, even without your hospitality, would suffice to keep me comfortably, and if I went away, though but for a month, I might find that those for whom I work had engaged other assistance. Spending naught, I am laying by money for the time when I shall have to travel at my own expense and to provide myself necessaries, and, maybe, to keep myself for a while until I can procure employment. I have the prospect that, by the end of another two years, I shall have gathered a sufficient store for all my needs, and I should be wrong to throw myself out of employment merely to embark on an adventure, and so to make a break, perhaps a long one, in my plans."

"Don't you worry yourself on that score," Captain Dave said warmly, and then checked himself. "It will be time to talk about that when the time comes. But you are right, lad. I like a man who steadfastly holds on the way he has chosen, and will not turn to the right or left. There is not much that a man cannot achieve if he keeps his aim steadily in view. Why, Cyril, if you said you had made up your mind to be Lord Mayor of London, I would wager that you would some day be elected."

Cyril laughed.

"I shall never set my eyes in that direction, nor do I think the thing I have set myself to do will ever be in my power—that is, to buy back my father's estate; but so long as I live I shall keep that in view."

"More unlikely things have happened, lad. You have got first to rise to be a General; then, what with your pay and your share in the sack of a city or two, and in other ways, you may come home with a purse full enough even for that. But it is time for us to be going down below. Matthew will think that we have forgotten him altogether."

Another fortnight passed. Nellie had, to a considerable extent, recovered from the shock that she had suffered, but her manner was still quiet and subdued, her sallies were less lively, and her father noticed, with some surprise, that she no longer took any great interest in the gossip he retailed of the gay doings of the Court.

"I can't think what has come over the girl," he said to his wife. "She seems well in health again, but she is changed a good deal, somehow. She is gentler and softer. I think she is all the better for it, but I miss her merry laugh and her way of ordering things about, as if her pleasure only were to be consulted."

"I think she is very much improved," Mrs. Dowsett said decidedly; "though I can no more account for it than you can. She never used to have any care about the household, and now she assists me in my work, and is in all respects dutiful and obedient, and is not for ever bent upon gadding about as she was before. I only hope it will continue so, for, in truth, I have often sighed over the thought that she would make but a poor wife for an honest citizen."

"Tut, tut, wife. It has never been as bad as that. Girls will be girls, and if they are a little vain of their good looks, that will soften down in time, when they get to have the charge of a household. You yourself, dame, were not so staid when I first wooed you, as you are now; and I think you had your own little share of vanity, as was natural enough in the prettiest girl in Plymouth."

When Nellie was in the room Cyril did his best to save her from being obliged to take part in the conversation, by inducing Captain Dave to tell him stories of some of his adventures at sea.

"You were saying, Captain Dave, that you had had several engagements with the Tunis Rovers," he said one evening. "Were they ever near taking you?"

"They did take me once, lad, and that without an engagement; but, fortunately, I was not very long a prisoner. It was not a pleasant time though, John, was it?"

"It was not, Captain Dave. I have been in sore danger of wreck several times, and in three big sea-fights; but never did I feel so out of heart as when I was lying, bound hand and foot, on the ballast in the hold of that corsair. No true sailor is afraid of being killed; but the thought that one might be all one's life a slave among the cruel heathen was enough to take the stiffness out of any man's courage."

"But how was it that you were taken without an engagement, Captain Dave? And how did you make your escape?"

"Well, lad, it was the carelessness of my first mate that did it; but as he paid for his fault with his life let us say naught against him. He was a handsome, merry young fellow, and had shipped as second mate, but my first had died of fever in the Levant, and of course he got the step, though all too young for the responsibility. We had met with some bad weather when south of Malta, and had had a heavy gale for three days, during which time we lost our main topmast, and badly strained the mizzen. The weather abated when we were off Pantellaria, which is a bare rock rising like a mountain peak out of the sea, and with only one place where a landing can be safely effected. As the gale had blown itself out, and it was likely we should have a spell of settled weather, I decided to anchor close in to the Island, and to repair damages.

"We were hard at work for two days. All hands had had a stiff time of it, and the second night, having fairly repaired damages, I thought to give the crew a bit of a rest, and, not dreaming of danger, ordered that half each watch might remain below. John Wilkes was acting as my second mate. Pettigrew took the first watch; John had the middle watch; and then the other came up again. I turned out once or twice, but everything was quiet—we had not seen a sail all day. There was a light breeze blowing, but no chance of its increasing, and as we were well sheltered in the only spot where the anchorage was good, I own that I did not impress upon Pettigrew the necessity for any particular vigilance. Anyhow, just as morning was breaking I was woke by a shout. I ran out on deck, but as I did so there was a rush of dark figures, and I was knocked down and bound before I knew what had happened. As soon as I could think it over, it was clear enough. The Moor had been coming into the anchorage, and, catching sight of us in the early light, had run alongside and boarded us.

"The watch, of course, must have been asleep. There was not a shot fired nor a drop of blood shed, for those on deck had been seized and bound before they could spring to their feet, and the crew had all been caught in their bunks. It was bitter enough. There was the vessel gone, and the cargo, and with them my savings of twenty years' hard work, and the prospect of slavery for life. The men were all brought aft and laid down side by side. Young Pettigrew was laid next to me.

"'I wish to heaven, captain,' he said, 'you had got a pistol and your hand free, and would blow out my brains for me. It is all my fault, and hanging at the yard-arm is what I deserve. I never thought there was the slightest risk—not a shadow of it—and feeling a bit dozy, sat down for five minutes' caulk. Seeing that, no doubt the men thought they might do the same; and this is what has come of it. I must have slept half an hour at least, for there was no sail in sight when I went off, and this Moor must have come round the point and made us out after that.'

"The corsair was lying alongside of us, her shrouds lashed to ours. There was a long jabbering among the Moors when they had taken off our hatches and seen that we were pretty well full up with cargo; then, after a bit, we were kicked, and they made signs for us to get on our feet and to cross over into their ship. The crew were sent down into the forward hold, and some men went down with them to tie them up securely. John Wilkes, Pettigrew, and myself were shoved down into a bit of a place below the stern cabin. Our legs were tied, as well as our arms. The trap was shut, and there we were in the dark. Of course I told Pettigrew that, though he had failed in his duty, and it had turned out badly, he wasn't to be blamed as if he had gone to sleep in sight of an enemy.

"'I had never given the Moors a thought myself,' I said, ' and it was not to be expected that you would. But no sailor, still less an officer, ought to sleep on his watch, even if his ship is anchored in a friendly harbour, and you are to blame that you gave way to drowsiness. Still, even if you hadn't, it might have come to the same thing in the long run, for the corsair is a large one, and might have taken us even if you had made her out as she rounded the point.'

"But, in spite of all I could say to cheer him, he took it to heart badly, and was groaning and muttering to himself when they left us in the dark, so I said to him,—

"'Look here, lad, the best way to retrieve the fault you have committed is to try and get us out of the scrape. Set your brains to work, and let us talk over what had best be done. There is no time to be lost, for with a fair wind they can run from here to Tunis in four-and-twenty hours, and once there one may give up all hope. There are all our crew on board this ship. The Moor carried twice as many men as we do, but we may reckon they will have put more than half of them on board our barque; they don't understand her sails as well as they do their own, and will therefore want a strong prize crew on board.'

"'I am ready to do anything, captain,' the young fellow said firmly. 'If you were to give me the word, I would get into their magazine if I could, and blow the ship into the air.'

"'Well, I don't know that I will give you that order Pettigrew. To be a heathen's slave is bad, but, at any rate, I would rather try that life for a bit than strike my colours at once. Now let us think it over. In the first place we have to get rid of these ropes; then we have to work our way forward to the crew; and then to get on deck and fight for it. It is a stiff job, look at it which way one will, but at any rate it will be better to be doing something—even if we find at last that we can't get out of this dog-kennel—than to lie here doing nothing.'

"After some talk, we agreed that it was not likely the Moors would come down to us for a long time, for they might reckon that we could hold on without food or water easy enough until they got to Tunis; having agreed as to that point, we set to work to get our ropes loose. Wriggling wouldn't do it, though we tried until the cords cut into our flesh.

" At last Pettigrew said,—

"'What a fool I am! I have got my knife hanging from a lanyard round my neck. It is under my blouse, so they did not notice it when they turned my pockets out.'

"It was a long job to get at that knife. At last I found the string behind his neck, and, getting hold of it with my teeth, pulled till the knife came up to his throat. Then John got it in his teeth, and the first part of the job was done. The next was easy enough. John held the handle of the knife in his teeth and Pettigrew got hold of the blade in his, and between them they made a shift to open it; then, after a good deal of trouble, Pettigrew shifted himself till he managed to get the knife in his hands. I lay across him and worked myself backwards and forwards till the blade cut through the rope at my wrist; then, in two more minutes, we were free. Then we felt about, and found that the boarding between us and the main hold was old and shaky, and, with the aid of the knife and of our three shoulders, we made a shift at last to wrench one of the boards from its place.

"Pettigrew, who was slightest, crawled through, and we soon got another plank down. The hold was half full of cargo, which, no doubt, they had taken out of some ship or other. We made our way forward till we got to the bulkhead, which, like the one we had got through, was but a makeshift sort of affair, with room to put your fingers between the planks. So we hailed the men and told them how we had got free, and that if they didn't want to work all their lives as slaves they had best do the same. They were ready enough, you may be sure, and, finding a passage between the planks wider in one place than the rest, we passed the knife through to them, and told them how to set about cutting the rope. They were a deal quicker over it than we had been, for in our place there had been no height where we could stand upright, but they were able to do so. Two men, standing back to back and one holding the knife, made quick work of cutting the rope.

"We had plenty of strength now, and were not long in getting down a couple of planks. The first thing was to make a regular overhaul of the cargo—as well as we could do it, without shifting things and making a noise—to look for weapons or for anything that would come in handy for the fight. Not a thing could we find, but we came upon a lot of kegs that we knew, by their feel, were powder. If there had been arms and we could have got up, we should have done it at once, trusting to seize the ship before the other could come up to her help. But without arms it would be madness to try in broad daylight, and we agreed to wait till night, and to lie down again where we were before, putting the ropes round our legs again and our hands behind our backs, so that, if they did look in, everything should seem secure.

"'We shall have plenty of time,' one of the sailors said, 'for they have coiled a big hawser down on the hatch.'

"When we got back to our lazaret, we tried the hatch by which we had been shoved down, but the three of us couldn't move it any more than if it had been solid stone. We had a goodish talk over it, and it was clear that the hatchway of the main hold was our only chance of getting out; and we might find that a tough job.

"'If we can't do it in any other way,' Pettigrew said, 'I should say we had best bring enough bales and things to fill this place up to within a foot of the top; then on that we might put a keg of powder, bore a hole in it, and make a slow match that would blow the cabin overhead into splinters, while the bales underneath it would prevent the force of the explosion blowing her bottom out.'

"We agreed that, if the worst came to the worst, we would try this, and having settled that, went back to have a look at the main hatch. Feeling about round it, we found the points of the staple on which the hatchway bar worked above; they were not fastened with nuts as they would have been with us, but were simply turned over and clinched. We had no means of straightening them out, but we could cut through the woodwork round them. Setting to work at that, we took it by turns till we could see the light through the wood; then we left it to finish after dark. All this time we knew we were under sail by the rippling of the water along the sides. The men on board were evidently in high delight at their easy capture, and kicked up so much noise that there was no fear of their hearing any slight stir we made below.

"Very carefully we brought packages and bales under the hatchway, till we built up a sort of platform about four feet below it. We reckoned that, standing as thick as we could there, and all lifting together, we could make sure of hoisting the hatchway up, and could then spring out in a moment.

Pettigrew still stuck to his plan, and talked us into carrying it out, both under the fore and aft hatches, pointing out that the two explosions would scare the crew out of their wits, that some would be killed, and many jump overboard in their fright. We came to see that the scheme was really a good one, so set all the crew to carry out the business, and they, working with stockinged feet, built up a platform under their hatch, as well as in our den aft. Then we made holes in two of the kegs of powder, and, shaking a little out, damped it, and rubbed it into two strips of cotton. Putting an end of a slow match into each of the holes, we laid the kegs in their places and waited.

"We made two other fuses, so that a man could go forward, and another aft, to fire them both together. Two of the men were told off for this job, and the rest of us gathered under the main hatch, for we had settled now that if we heard them making any move to open the hatches we would fire the powder at once, whatever hour it was. In order to be ready, we cut deeper into the woodwork round the staple till there was but the thickness of a card remaining, and we could tell by this how light it was above.

"It don't take long to tell you, but all this had taken us a good many hours; and so baked were we by the heat down below, and parched by thirst, that it was as much as I could do to persuade the men to wait until nightfall. At last we saw the light in the cut fade and darken. Again the men wanted to be at work, but I pointed out that if we waited till the crew had laid down on the deck, we might carry it through without losing a life, but if they were all awake, some of them would be sure to come at us with their weapons, and, unarmed as we were, might do us much harm. Still, though I succeeded in keeping the men quiet, I felt it was hard work to put a stopper on my own impatience.

"At last even John here spoke up for action.

"'I expect those who mean to sleep are off by this time,' he said. 'As to reckoning upon them all going off, there ain't no hope of it; they will sit and jabber all night. They have made a good haul, and have taken a stout ship with a full hold, and five-and-twenty stout slaves, and that without losing a man. There won't be any sleep for most of them. I reckon it is two bells now. I do think, Captain, we might as well begin, for human nature can't stand this heat and thirst much longer.'

"'All right, John,' I said, 'Now, lads, remember that when the first explosion comes—for we can't reckon on the two slow matches burning just the same time—we all heave together till we find the hatch lifts; then, when the second comes, we chuck it over and leap out. If you see a weapon, catch it up, but don't waste time looking about, but go at them with your fists. They will be scared pretty well out of their senses, and you will not be long before you all get hold of weapons of some sort. Now, Pettigrew, shove your blade up through the wood and cut round the staple. Now, Jack Brown, get out that tinder-box you said you had about you, and get a spark going.'

"Three or four clicks were heard as the sailor struck his flint against the steel lid of the tinder-box.

"'All right, yer honour,' he said, 'I have got the spark.'

"Then the two hands we had given the slow matches to, lit them at the tinder-box, and went fore and aft, while as many of the rest of us as could crowded under the hatch.

"'Are you ready, fore and aft?' I asked.

"The two men hailed in reply.

"'Light the matches, then, and come here.'

"I suppose it was not above a minute, but it seemed ten before there was a tremendous explosion aft. The ship shook from stem to stern. There was a moment's silence, and then came yells and screams mixed with the sound of timbers and wreckage falling on the deck.

"'Now lift,' I said. 'But not too high. That is enough—she is free. Wait for the other.'

"There was a rush of feet overhead as the Moors ran forward. Then came the other explosion.

"'Off with her, lads!' I shouted, and in a moment we flung the hatch off and leapt out with a cheer. There was no fighting to speak of. The officers had been killed by the first explosion under their cabin, and many of the men had either been blown overboard or lay crushed under the timber and wreckage.

"The second explosion had been even more destructive, for it happened just as the crew, in their terror, had rushed forward. Many of those unhurt had sprung overboard at once, and as we rushed up most of the others did the same. There was no difficulty about arms, for the deck was strewn with weapons. Few of us, however, stopped to pick one up, but, half mad with rage and thirst, rushed forward at the Moors. That finished them; and before we got to them the last had sprung overboard. There was a rush on the part of the men to the scuttle butt.

"'Take one drink, lads,' I shouted, 'and then to the buckets.'

"It took us a quarter of an hour's hard work to put out the flames, and it was lucky the powder had blown so much of the decks up that we were enabled to get at the fire without difficulty, and so extinguish it before it got any great hold.

"As soon as we had got it out I called a muster. There was only one missing;—it was Pettigrew, he being the first to leap out and rush aft. There had been but one shot fired by the Moors. One fellow, as he leapt on to the rail, drew his pistol from his belt and fired before he sprang overboard. In the excitement and confusion no one had noticed whether the shot took effect, for two or three men had stumbled and fallen over fragments of timber or bodies as we rushed aft. But now we searched, and soon came on the poor young fellow. The ball had struck him fair on the forehead, and he had fallen dead without a word or a cry.

"There was, however, no time to grieve. We had got to re-capture the barque, which had been but a cable's length away when we rushed on deck; while we had been fighting the fire she had sailed on, regardless of the shrieks and shouts of the wretches who had sprung overboard from us. But she was still near us; both vessels had been running before the wind, for I had sent John Wilkes to the tiller the moment that we got possession of the corsair, and the barque was but about a quarter of a mile ahead.

"The wind was light, and we were running along at four knots an hour. The Moors on board the *Kate* had, luckily, been too scared by the explosion to think of getting one of the guns aft and peppering us while we were engaged in putting out the fire; and indeed, they could not have done us much harm if they had, for the high fo'castle hid us from their view.

"As soon as we had found Pettigrew's body and laid it on the hatch we had thrown off, I went aft to John.

"'Are we gaining on her, John?'

"'No; she has drawn away a little. But this craft is not doing her best. I expect they wanted to keep close to the barque, and so kept her sheets in. If you square the sails, captain, we shall soon be upon her.'

"That was quickly done, and then the first thing was to see that the men were all armed. We could have got a gun forward, but I did not want to damage the *Kate*, and we could soon see that we were closing on her. We shoved a bag of musket-balls into each cannon, so as to sweep her decks as we came alongside, for we knew that her crew was a good deal stronger than we were. Still, no one had any doubt as to the result, and it was soon evident that the Moors had got such a scare from the fate of their comrades that they had no stomach for fighting.

"'They are lowering the boats,' John shouted.

"'All the better,' I said. 'They would fight like rats caught in a trap if we came up to them, and though we are men enough to capture her, we might lose half our number.'

"As soon as the boats reached the water they were all pulled up to the starboard side, and then the helm was put down, and the barque came round till she was broadside on to us.

"'Down with your helm, John Wilkes!' I shouted. 'Hard down, man!'

"John hesitated, for he had thought that I should have gone round to the other side of her and so have caught all the boats; but, in truth, I was so pleased at the thought of getting the craft back again that I was willing to let the poor villains go, since they were of a mind to do so without giving us trouble. We had punished them enough, and the shrieks and cries of those left behind to drown were ringing in my ears then. So we brought the corsair up quietly by the side of the *Kate*, lashed her there, and then, with a shout of triumph, sprang on board the old barky.

"Not a Moor was left on board. The boats were four or five hundred yards away, rowing at the top of their speed. The men would have run to the guns, but I shouted,—

"'Let them go, lads. We have punished them heavily enough; we have taken their ship, and sent half of them to Eternity. Let them take the tale back to Tunis how a British merchantman re-captured their ship. Now set to work to get some of the sail off both craft, and then, when we have got things snug, we will splice the main brace and have a meal.'

"There is no more to tell. We carried the rover into Gibraltar and sold her and her cargo there. It brought in a good round sum, and, except for the death of Pettigrew, we had no cause to regret the corsair having taken us by surprise that night off Pantellaria."

"That was an exciting business, indeed, Captain Dave," Cyril said, when the Captain brought his story to a conclusion. "If it had not been for your good fortune in finding those kegs of powder, and Pettigrew's idea of using them as he did, you and John might now, if you had been alive, have been working as slaves among the Moors."

"Yes, lad. And not the least lucky thing was that Pettigrew's knife and Jack Brown's tinder-box had escaped the notice of the Moors. Jack had it in an inside pocket sewn into his shirt so as to keep it dry. It was a lesson to me, and for the rest of the time I was at sea I always carried a knife, with a lanyard round my neck, and stowed away in an inside pocket of my shirt, together with a tinder-box. They are two as useful things as a sailor can have about him, for, if cast upon a desert shore after a wreck, a man with a knife and tinder-box may make shift to live, when, without them, he and his comrades might freeze to death."

CHAPTER IX.

THE FIRE IN THE SAVOY.

THE next evening John Wilkes returned after an absence of but half an hour.

"Why, John, you can but have smoked a single pipe! Did you not find your cronies there?"

"I hurried back, Captain, because a man from one of the ships in the Pool landed and said there was a great light in the sky, and that it seemed to him it was either a big fire in the Temple, or in one of the mansions beyond the walls; so methought I would come in and ask Cyril if he would like to go with me to see what was happening."

"I should like it much, John. I saw a great fire in Holborn just after I came over from France, and a brave sight it was, though very terrible; and I would willingly see one again."

He took his hat and cloak and was about to be off, when Captain Dave called after him,—

"Buckle on your sword, lad, and leave your purse behind you. A fire ever attracts thieves and cut-throats, who flock round in hopes of stealing something in the confusion. Besides, as I have told you before, you should never go out after dark without your sword, even were it but to cross the road."

Cyril ran upstairs to his room, buckled on his weapon, and ran down again.

"The Captain is right," John Wilkes said, as he joined him at the door. "After your two adventures, it would be folly for you to go out unarmed."

"Oh, I expect they have forgotten about me long ago," Cyril laughed lightly.

"I don't know," John Wilkes said seriously. "As to Marner's gang, I think that there is not much fear from them, unless that young rascal Robert and the scoundrel who was with him have returned from Holland; and that they are not likely to do for some time to come. But it would not be in human nature if the man you call John Harvey should take his defeat without trying to pay you back for that wound you gave him, for getting Mistress Nellie out of his hands, and for making him the laughing-stock of his comrades. I tell you that there is scarce an evening that I have gone out but some fellow passes me before I have gone twenty yards, and, as he brushes my sleeve, turns his head to look at me. But yesternight I said to one who so behaved, 'Look here, mate, this is not the first time you have run against me. I warn you that if it happens again I will crack your head with my cudgel.' The fellow went off, muttering and grumbling, but 1 have no doubt that he and the others, for it certainly was not always the same man, were watching for you. To-night there was no one about, or, if there was, he did not come near me, and it may be that, finding you never leave the house after nightfall, they have decided to give it up for the present. But I thought I heard a footfall lower down the street, just as we came out of the house, and it is like enough that we are followed now."

"At any rate, they would scarce attack two of us, John, and I should not mind if they did. It is a stab in the back that I am afraid of more than an open quarrel."

"You may have a better swordsman to deal with next time. The fellow himself would scarcely care to cross swords with you again, but he would have no difficulty in getting half-a-dozen cut-throats from the purlieus of the Temple or Westminster, professional bullies, who are ready to sell their swords to those who care to purchase them, and who would cut a throat for a few crowns, without caring a jot whose throat it was. Some of these fellows are disbanded soldiers. Some are men who were ruined in the wars. Some are tavern bullies—broken men, reckless and quarrelsome gamblers so long as they have a shilling in their pockets, but equally ready to take to the road or to rob a house when their pockets are empty."

By this time they had passed the Exchange into Cheapside. Many people were hurrying in the same direction and wondering where the fire was. Presently one of the Fire Companies, with buckets, ladders, and axes, passed them at a run. Even in Cheapside the glow in the sky ahead could be plainly seen, but it was not until they passed St. Paul's and stood at the top of Ludgate Hill that the flames, shooting up high in the air, were visible. They were almost straight ahead.

"It must be at the other end of Fleet Street," Cyril said, as they broke into a run.

"Farther than that, lad. It must be one of the mansions along the Strand. A fire always looks closer than it is. I have seen a ship in flames that looked scarce a mile away, and yet, sailing with a brisk wind, it took us over an hour to come up to it."

The crowd became thicker as they approached Temple Bar. The upper windows of the houses were all open, and women were leaning out looking at the sight. From every lane and alley men poured into the street and swelled the hurrying current. They passed through the Bar, expecting to find that the fire was close at hand. They had, however, some distance farther to go, for the fire was at a mansion in the Savoy. Another Fire Company came along when they were within a hundred yards of the spot.

"Join in with them," Cyril said; and he and John Wilkes managed to push their way into the ranks, joining in the shout, "Way there, way! Make room for the buckets!"

Aided by some of the City watch the Company made its

way through the crowd, and hurried down the hill from the Strand into the Savoy. A party of the King's Guard, who had just marched up, kept back the crowd, and, when once in the open space, Cyril and his companion stepped out from the ranks and joined a group of people who had arrived before the constables and soldiers had come up.

The mansion from which the fire had originated was in flames from top to bottom. The roof had fallen in. Volumes of flame and sparks shot high into the air, threatening the safety of several other houses standing near. The Fire Companies were working their hand-pumps, throwing water on to the doors and woodwork of these houses. Long lines of men were extended down to the edge of the river and passed the buckets backwards and forwards. City officials, gentlemen of the Court, and officers of the troops, moved to and fro shouting directions and superintending the work. From many of the houses the inhabitants were bringing out their furniture and goods, aided by the constables and spectators.

"It is a grand sight," Cyril said, as, with his companion, he took his place in a quiet corner where a projecting portico threw a deep shadow.

"It will soon be grander still. The wind is taking the sparks and flames westwards, and nothing can save that house over there. Do you see the little jets of flame already bursting through the roof?"

"The house seems empty. There is not a window open."

"It looks so, Cyril, but there may be people asleep at the back. Let us work round and have a look from behind."

They turned down an alley, and in a minute or two came out behind the house. There was a garden and some high trees, but it was surrounded by a wall, and they could not see the windows.

"Here, Cyril, I will give you a hoist up. If you stand on my shoulders, you can reach to the top of the wall and pull yourself up. Come along here to where that branch projects over. That's it. Now drop your cloak, and jump on to my back. That is right. Now get on to my shoulders."

Cyril managed to get up.

"I can just touch the top, but I can't get my fingers on to it."

"Put your foot on my head. I will warrant it is strong enough to bear your weight."

Cyril did as he was told, grasped the top of the wall, and, after a sharp struggle, seated himself astride on it. Just as he did so, a window in a wing projecting into the garden was thrown open, and a female voice uttered a loud scream for help. There was light enough for Cyril to see that the lower windows were all barred. He shouted back,—

"Can't you get down the staircase?"

"No; the house is full of smoke. There are some children here. Help! Help!" and the voice rose in a loud scream again.

Cyril dropped down into the roadway by the side of John Wilkes.

"There are some women and children in there, John. They can't get out. We must go round to the other side and get some axes and break down the door."

Snatching up his cloak, he ran at full speed to his former position, followed by Wilkes. The roof of the house was now in flames. Many of the shutters and window-frames had also caught fire, from the heat. He ran up to two gentlemen who seemed to be directing the operations.

"There are some women and children in a room at the back of that house," he said. "I have just been round there to see. They are in the second storey, and are crying for help."

"I fear the ladders are too short."

"I can tie two or three of them together," Wilkes said. "I am an old sailor and can answer for the knots."

The firemen were already dashing water on the lower windows of the front of the house. A party with axes were cutting at the door, but this was so massive and solid that it resisted their efforts. One of the gentlemen went down to them. At his orders eight or ten men seized ladders. Cyril snatched some ropes from a heap that had been thrown down by the firemen, and the party, with one of the gentlemen, ran round to the back of the house. Two ladders were placed against the wall. John Wilkes, running up one of them, hauled several of the others up, and lowered them into the garden.

The flames were now issuing from some of the upper windows. Cyril dropped from the wall into the garden, and, running close up to the house, shouted to three or four women, who were screaming loudly, and hanging so far out that he thought they would fall, that help was at hand, and that they would be speedily rescued. John Wilkes rapidly tied three of the short ladders together. These were speedily raised, but it was found that they just reached the window. One of the firemen ran up, while John set to work to prepare another long ladder. As there was no sign of life at any other window he laid it down on the grass when finished.

"If you will put it up at the next window," Cyril said, "I will mount it. The woman said there were children in the house, and possibly I may find them. Those women are so frightened that they don't know what they are doing."

One woman had already been got on to the other ladder, but instead of coming down, she held on tightly, screaming at the top of her voice, until the fireman with great difficulty got up by her side, wrenched her hands from their hold, threw her across his shoulder, and carried her down.

The room was full of smoke as Cyril leapt into it, but he found that it was not, as he had supposed, the one in which the women at the next window were standing. Near the window, however, an elderly woman was lying on the floor insensible, and three girls of from eight to fourteen lay across her. Cyril thrust his head out of the window.

"Come up, John," he shouted. "I want help."

He lifted the youngest of the girls, and as he got her out of the window, John's head appeared above the sill.

"Take her down quick, John," he said, as he handed the

"TAKE HER DOWN QUICK, JOHN, THERE ARE THREE OTHERS."

child to him. "There are three others. They are all insensible from the smoke."

Filling his lungs with fresh air, he turned into the blinding smoke again, and speedily reappeared at the window with another of the girls. John was not yet at the bottom; he placed her with her head outside the window, and was back with the eldest girl by the time Wilkes was up again. He handed her to him, and then, taking the other, stepped out on to the ladder and followed Wilkes down.

"Brave lad!" the gentleman said, patting him on the shoulder. "Are there any more of them?"

"One more—a woman, sir. Do you go up, John. I will follow, for I doubt whether I can lift her by myself."

He followed Wilkes closely up the ladder. There was a red glow now in the smoke. Flames were bursting through the door. John was waiting at the window.

"Which way, lad? There is no seeing one's hand in the smoke."

"Just in front, John, not six feet away. Hold your breath."

They dashed forward together, seized the woman between them, and, dragging her to the window, placed her head and shoulders on the sill.

"You go first, John. She is too heavy for me," Cyril gasped.

John stumbled out, half suffocated, while Cyril thrust his head as far as he could outside the window.

"That is it, John; you take hold of her shoulder, and I will help you get her on to your back."

Between them they pushed her nearly out, and then, with Cyril's assistance, John got her across his shoulders. She was a heavy woman, and the old sailor had great difficulty in carrying her down. Cyril hung far out of the window till he saw him put his foot on the ground; then he seized a rung of the ladder, swung himself out on to it, and was soon down.

For a time he felt confused and bewildered, and was conscious that if he let go the ladder he should fall. He heard a voice say, "Bring one of those buckets of water," and directly afterwards, "Here, lad, put your head into this," and a handful of water was dashed into his face. It revived him, and, turning round, he plunged his head into a bucket that a man held up for him. Then he took a long breath or two, pressed the water from his hair, and felt himself again. The women at the other window had by this time been brought down. A door in the garden wall had been broken down with axes, and the women and girls were taken away to a neighbouring house.

"There is nothing more to do here," the gentleman said. "Now, men, you are to enter the houses round about. Wherever a door is fastened, break it in. Go out on to the roofs with buckets, put out the sparks as fast as they fall. I will send some more men to help you at once." He then put his hand on Cyril's shoulder, and walked back with him to the open space.

"We have saved them all," he said to the other gentleman who had now come up, "but it has been a close touch, and it was only by the gallantry of this young gentleman and another with him that the lives of three girls and a woman were rescued. I think all the men that can be spared had better go round to the houses in that direction. You see, the wind is setting that way, and the only hope of stopping the progress of the fire is to get plenty of men with buckets out on the roofs and at all the upper windows."

The other gentleman gave the necessary orders to an officer.

"Now, young sir, may I ask your name?" the other said to Cyril.

"Cyril Shenstone, sir," he replied respectfully; for he saw that the two men before him were persons of rank.

"Shenstone? I know the name well. Are you any relation of Sir Aubrey Shenstone?"

"He was my father, sir."

"A brave soldier, and a hearty companion," the other said warmly. "He rode behind me scores of times into the thick of the fight. I am Prince Rupert, lad."

Cyril doffed his hat in deep respect. His father had always

spoken of the Prince in terms of boundless admiration, and had over and over again lamented that he had not been able to join the Prince in his exploits at sea.

"What has become of my old friend?" the Prince asked.

"He died six months ago, Prince."

"I am sorry to hear it. I did hear that, while I was away, he had been suing at Court. I asked for him, but could get no tidings of his whereabouts. But we cannot speak here. Ask for me to-morrow at Whitehall. Do you know this gentleman?"

"No, sir, I have not the honour."

"This is the Duke of Albemarle, my former enemy, but now my good friend. You will like the lad no worse, my Lord, because his father more than once rode with me into the heart of your ranks."

"Certainly not," the Duke said. "It is clear that the son will be as gallant a gentleman as his father was before him, and, thank God! it is not against Englishmen that he will draw his sword. You may count me as your friend, sir, henceforth."

Cyril bowed deeply and retired, while Prince Rupert and the Duke hurried away again to see that the operations they had directed were properly carried out.

CHAPTER X.

HOW JOHN WILKES FOUGHT THE DUTCH.

AFTER leaving Prince Rupert, Cyril returned to John Wilkes, who was standing a short distance away.

"John! John!" he said eagerly, as he joined him. "Who do you think those gentlemen are?"

"I don't know, lad. It is easy to see that they are men of importance by the way they order every one about."

"The one who went with us to the garden is Prince Rupert; the other is the Duke of Albemarle. And the Prince has told me to call upon him to-morrow at Whitehall."

"That is a stroke of luck, indeed, lad, and right glad am I that I took it into my head to fetch you out to see the fire. But more than that, you have to thank yourself, for, indeed, you behaved right gallantly. You nearly had the Prince for your helper, for just before I went up the ladder the last time he stepped forward and said to me, 'You must be well-nigh spent, man. I will go up this time.' However, I said that I would finish the work, and so, without more ado, I shook off the hand he had placed on my arm, and ran up after you. Well, it is a stroke of good fortune to you, lad, that you should have shown your courage under his eye—no one is more able to appreciate a gallant action. This may help you a long way towards bringing about the aim you were talking about the other night, and I may live to see you Sir Cyril Shenstone yet."

"You can see me that now," Cyril said, laughing. "My father was a baronet, and therefore at his death I came into the title, though I am not silly enough to go about the City as Sir Cyril Shenstone when I am but a poor clerk. It will be time enough to call myself 'Sir' when I see some chance of buying back our estate, though, indeed, I have thought of taking the title again when I embark on foreign service, as it may help me somewhat in obtaining promotion. But do not say anything about it at home. I am Cyril Shenstone, and have been fortunate enough to win the friendship of Captain Dave, and I should not be so comfortable were there any change made in my position in the family. A title is an empty thing, John, unless there are means to support it, and plain Cyril Shenstone suits my position far better than a title without a guinea in my purse. Indeed, till you spoke just now, I had well-nigh forgotten that I have the right to call myself 'Sir.'"

They waited for two hours longer. At the end of that time

four mansions had been burnt to the ground, but the further progress of the flames had been effectually stayed. The crowd had already begun to scatter, and as they walked eastward the streets were full of people making their way homeward. The bell of St. Paul's was striking midnight as they entered. The Captain and his family had long since gone off to bed.

"This reminds one of that last business," John whispered, as they went quietly upstairs.

"It does, John. But it has been a pleasanter evening in every way than those fruitless watches we kept in the street below."

The next morning the story of the fire was told, and excited great interest.

"Who were the girls you saved, Cyril?" Nellie asked.

"I don't know. I did not think of asking to whom the house belonged, nor, indeed, was there any one to ask. Most of the people were too busy to talk to, and the rest were spectators who had, like ourselves, managed to make their way in through the lines of the soldiers and watch."

"Were they ladies?"

"I really don't know," Cyril laughed. "The smoke was too thick to see anything about them, and I should not know them if I met them to-day; and, besides, when you only see a young person in her nightdress, it is hard to form any opinion as to her rank."

Nellie joined in the laugh.

"I suppose not, Cyril. It might make a difference to you, though. Those houses in the Savoy are almost all the property of noblemen, and you might have gained another powerful friend if they had been the daughters of one."

"I should not think they were so," Cyril said. "There seemed to be no one else in the house but three maid servants and the woman who was in the room with them. I should say the family were all away and the house left in charge of servants. The woman may have been a housekeeper, and the girls her children; besides, even had it been otherwise, it was merely by chance that I helped them out. It was John who tied the ladders together and who carried the girls down, one by one. If I had been alone I should only have had time to save the youngest, for I am not accustomed to running up and down ladders, as he is, and by the time I had got her down it would have been too late to have saved the others. Indeed, I am not sure that we did save them; they were all insensible, and, for aught I know, may not have recovered from the effects of the smoke. My eyes are smarting even now."

"And so you are to see Prince Rupert to-day, Cyril?" Captain Dave said. "I am afraid we shall be losing you, for he will, I should say, assuredly appoint you to one of his ships if you ask him."

"That would be good fortune indeed," Cyril said. "I cannot but think myself that he may do so, though it would be almost too good to be true. Certainly he spoke very warmly, and, although he may not himself have the appointment of his officers, a word from him at the Admiralty would, no doubt, be sufficient. At any rate, it is a great thing indeed to have so powerful a friend at Court. It may be that, at the end of another two years, we may be at war with some other foreign power, and that I may be able to enter our own army instead of seeking service abroad. If not, much as I should like to go to sea to fight against the Dutch, service in this Fleet would be of no real advantage to me, for the war may last but for a short time, and as soon as it is over the ships will be laid up again and the crews disbanded."

"Ay, but if you find the life of a sailor to your liking, Cyril, you might do worse than go into the merchant service. I could help you there, and you might soon get the command of a trader. And, let me tell you, it is a deal better to walk the decks as captain than it is to be serving on shore with twenty masters over you; and there is money to be made, too. A captain is always allowed to take in a certain amount of cargo on his own account; that was the way I scraped together money enough to buy my own ship at last, and to be master as well as owner, and there is no reason why you should not do the same."

"Thank you, Captain Dave. I will think it over when I find out whether I like a sea life, but at present it seems to me that my inclinations turn rather towards the plan that my father recommended, and that, for the last two years, I have always had before me. You said, the other day, you had fought the Dutch, John?"

"Ay, ay, Master Cyril; but, in truth, it was from no wish or desire on my part that I did so. I had come ashore from Captain Dave's ship here in the Pool, and had been with some of my messmates who had friends in Wapping and had got three days' leave ashore, as the cargo we expected had not come on board the ship. We had kept it up a bit, and it was latish when I was making my way down to the stairs. I expect that I was more intent on making a straight course down the street than in looking about for pirates, when suddenly I found myself among a lot of men. One of them seized me by the arm.

"'Hands off, mate!' says I, and I lifted my fist to let fly at him, when I got a knock at the back of the head. The next thing I knew was, I was lying in the hold of a ship, and, as I made out presently, with a score of others, some of whom were groaning, and some cursing.

"'Hullo, mates!' says I. 'What port is this we are brought up in?'

"'We are on board the *Tartar*,' one said.

"I knew what that meant, for the *Tartar* was the receiving hulk where they took the pressed men.

"The next morning, without question asked, we were brought up on deck, tumbled into a small sloop, and taken down to Gravesend, and there put, in batches of four or five, into the ships of war lying there. It chanced that I was put on board Monk's flagship the *Resolution*. And that is how it was I came to fight the Dutch."

"What year was that in, John?"

"'53—in May it was. Van Tromp, at that time, with ninety-eight ships of war, and six fire-ships, was in the Downs, and felt so much Master of the Sea that he sailed in and battered Dover Castle."

"Then you were in the fight of the 2nd of June?"

"Ay; and in that of the 31st of July, which was harder still."

"Tell me all about it, John."

"Lor' bless you, sir, there is nothing to tell as far as I was concerned. I was at one of the guns on the upper deck, but I might as well have been down below for anything I saw of it. It was just load and fire, load and fire. Sometimes, through the clouds of smoke, one caught a sight of the Dutchman one was firing at; more often one didn't. There was no time for looking about, I can tell you, and if there had been time there was nothing to see. It was like being in a big thunderstorm, with thunderbolts falling all round you, and a smashing and a grinding and a ripping that would have made your hair stand on end if you had only had time to think of it. But we hadn't time. It was 'Now then, my hearties, blaze away! Keep it up, lads! The Dutchmen have pretty near had enough of it!' And then, at last, 'They are running, lads. Run in your guns, and tend the sails.' And then a cheer as loud as we could give—which wasn't much, I can tell you, for we were spent with labour, and half choked with powder, and our tongues parched up with thirst."

"How many ships had you?"

"We had ninety-five war-ships, and five fire-ships, so the game was an equal one. They had Tromp and De Ruyter to command them, and we had Monk and Deane. Both Admirals were on board our ship, and in the very first broadside the Dutch fired a chain-shot, and pretty well cut Admiral Deane in two. I was close to him at the time. Monk, who was standing by his side, undid his own cloak in a moment, threw it over his comrade, and held up his hand to the few of us that had seen what had happened, to take no notice of it.

"It was a good thing that Deane and Monk were on board the same ship. If it had not been so, Deane's flag would have been hauled down and all the Fleet would have known of his death, which, at the commencement of the fight, would have greatly discouraged the men.

"They told me, though I know naught about it, that Rear-Admiral Lawson charged with the Blue Squadron right through the Dutch line, and so threw them into confusion. However, about three o'clock, the fight having begun at eleven, Van Tromp began to draw off, and we got more sail on the *Resolution* and followed them for some hours, they making a sort of running fight of it, till one of their big ships blew up, about nine in the evening, when they laid in for shore. Blake came up in the night with eighteen ships. The Dutch tried to draw off, but at eight o'clock we came up to them, and, after fighting for four hours, they hauled off and ran, in great confusion, for the flats, where we could not follow them, and so they escaped to Zeeland. We heard that they had six of their best ships sunk, two blown up and eleven taken, but whether it was so or not I knew not, for, in truth, I saw nothing whatever of the matter.

"We sailed to the Texel, and there blocked in De Ruyter's squadron of twenty-five large ships, and we thought that there would be no more fighting, for the Dutch had sent to England to ask for terms of peace. However, we were wrong, and, to give the Dutchmen their due, they showed resolution greater than we gave them credit for, for we were astonished indeed to hear, towards the end of July, that Van Tromp had sailed out again with upwards of ninety ships.

"On the 29th they came in view, and we sailed out to engage them, but they would not come to close quarters, and it was seven at night before the *Resolution*, with some thirty other ships, came up to them and charged through their line. By the time we had done that it was quite dark, and we missed them altogether and sailed south, thinking Van Tromp had gone that way; but, instead, he had sailed north, and in the morning we found he had picked up De Ruyter's fleet, and was ready to fight. But we had other things to think of besides fighting that day, for the wind blew so hard that it was as much as we could do to keep off the shore, and if the gale had continued a good part of the ships would have left their bones there. However, by nightfall the gale abated somewhat, and by the next morning the sea had gone down sufficient for the main deck ports to be opened. So the Dutch, having the weather gauge, sailed down to engage us.

"I thought it rough work in the fight two months before, but it was as nothing to this. To begin with, the Dutch fireships came down before the wind, and it was as much as we could do to avoid them. They did, indeed, set the *Triumph* on fire, and most of the crew jumped overboard; but those that remained managed to put out the flames.

"Lawson, with the Blue Squadron, began the fighting, and that so briskly, that De Ruyter's flagship was completely disabled and towed out of the fight. However, after I had seen that, our turn began, and I had no more time to look about. I only know that ship after ship came up to engage us, seeming bent upon lowering Monk's flag. Three Dutch Admirals, Tromp, Evertson, and De Ruyter, as I heard afterwards, came up in turn. We did not know who they were, but we knew they were Admirals by their flags, and pounded them with all our hearts; and so good was our aim that I myself saw two of the Admirals' flags brought down, and they say that all three of them were lowered. But you may guess the pounding was not all on our side, and we suffered very heavily.

"Four men were hurt at the gun I worked, and nigh half the crew were killed or wounded. Two of our masts were shot away, many of our guns disabled, and towards the end of the fight, we were towed out of the line. How the day would have gone if Van Tromp had continued in command of the

Dutch, I cannot say, but about noon he was shot through the body by a musket-ball, and this misfortune greatly discouraged the Dutchmen, who fight well as long as things seem to be going their way, but lose heart very easily when they think the matter is going against them.

"By about two o'clock the officers shouted to us that the Dutch were beginning to draw off, and it was not long before they began to fly, each for himself, and in no sort of order. Some of our light frigates, that had suffered less than the line-of-battle ships, followed them until the one Dutch Admiral whose flag was left flying, turned and fought them till two or three of our heavier ships came up and he was sunk.

"We could see but little of the chase, having plenty of work, for, had a gale come on, our ship, and a good many others would assuredly have been driven ashore, in the plight we were in. Anyhow, at night their ships got into the Texel, and our vessels, which had been following them, anchored five or six leagues out, being afraid of the sands. Altogether we had burnt or sunk twenty-six of their ships of war, while we lost only two frigates, both of which were burnt by their fire-ships.

"As it was certain that they would not come out for some time again, and many of our ships being unfit for further contention until repaired, we returned to England, and I got my discharge and joined Captain Dave again a fortnight later, when his ship came up the river.

"Monk is a good fighter, Master Cyril, and should have the command of the Fleet instead of, as they say, the Duke of York. Although he is called General, and not Admiral, he is as good a sea-dog as any of them, and he can think as well as fight.

"Among our ships that day were several merchantmen that had been taken up for the service at the last moment and had guns slapped on board, with gunners to work them. Some of them had still their cargoes in the hold, and Monk, thinking that it was likely the captains would think more of saving their ships and goods than of fighting the Dutch, changed the captains all round, so that no man commanded his own vessel. And the consequence was that, as all admitted, the merchantmen were as willing to fight as any, and bore themselves right stoutly.

"Don't you think, Master Cyril, if you go with the Fleet, that you are going to see much of what goes on. It will be worse for you than it was for me, for there was I, labouring and toiling like a dumb beast, with my mind intent upon working the gun, and paying no heed to the roar and confusion around, scarce even noticing when one beside me was struck down. You will be up on the poop, having naught to do but to stand with your hand on your sword-hilt, and waiting to board an enemy or to drive back one who tries to board you. You will find that you will be well-nigh dazed and stupid with the din and uproar."

"It does not sound a very pleasant outlook, John," Cyril laughed. "However, if I ever do get into an engagement, I will think of what you have said, and will try and prevent myself from getting either dazed or stupid; though, in truth, I can well imagine that it is enough to shake any one's nerves to stand inactive in so terrible a scene."

"You will have to take great care of yourself, Cyril," Nellie said gravely.

Captain Dave and John Wilkes both burst into a laugh.

"How is he to take care of himself, Nellie?" her father said. "Do you suppose that a man on deck would be any the safer were he to stoop down with his head below the rail, or to screw himself up on the leeward side of a mast? No, no, lass; each man has to take his share of danger, and the most cowardly runs just as great a risk as the man who fearlessly exposes himself."

CHAPTER XI.

PRINCE RUPERT.

THE next day Cyril went down to breakfast in what he had often called, laughingly, his Court suit. This suit he had had made for him a short time before his father's death, to replace the one he had when he came over, that being altogether outgrown. He had done so to please Sir Aubrey, who had repeatedly expressed his anxiety that Cyril should always be prepared to take advantage of any good fortune that might befall him. This was the first time he had put it on.

"Well, truly you look a pretty fellow, Cyril," the Captain said, as he entered. "Don't you think so, Nellie?"

The girl nodded.

"I don't know that I like him better than in his black suit, father. But he looks very well."

"Hullo, lass! This is a change of opinion, truly! For myself I care not one jot for the fashion of a man's clothes, but I had thought that you always inclined to gay attire, and Cyril now would seem rather to belong to the Court than to the City."

"If it had been any other morning, father, I might have thought more of Cyril's appearance; but what you were telling us but now of the continuance of the Plague is so sad, that mourning, rather than Court attire, would seem to be the proper wear."

"Is the Plague spreading fast, then, Captain Dave?"

"No; but it is not decreasing, as we had hoped it would do. From the beginning of December the deaths rose steadily until the end of January. While our usual death-rate is under three hundred it went to four hundred and seventy-four. Then the weather setting in very severe checked it till the end of February, and we all hoped that the danger was over, and that we should be rid of the distemper before the warm weather set in; but for the last fortnight there has been a rise rather than a fall—not a large one, but sufficient to cause great alarm that it will continue until warm weather sets in, and may then grow into terrible proportions. So far, there has been no case in the City, and it is only in the West that it has any hold, the deaths being altogether in the parishes of St. Giles's, St. Andrew's, St. Bride's, and St. James's, Clerkenwell. Of course, there have been cases now and then for many years past, and nine years ago it spread to a greater extent than now, and were we at the beginning of winter instead of nearing summer there would be no occasion to think much of the matter; but, with the hot weather approaching, and the tales we hear of the badness of the Plague in foreign parts one cannot but feel anxious."

"And they say, too, that there have been prophecies of grievous evils in London," Nellie put in.

"We need not trouble about that," her father replied. "The Anabaptists prophesied all sorts of evils in Elizabeth's time, but naught came of it. There are always men and women with disordered minds, who think that they are prophets, and have power to see further into the future than other people, but no one minds them or thinks aught of their wild words save at a time like the present, when there is a danger of war or pestilence. You remember Bill Vokes, John?"

"I mind him, yer honour. A poor, half-crazed fellow he was, and yet a good seaman, who would do his duty blow high or blow low. He sailed six voyages with us, Captain."

"And never one of them without telling the crew that the ship would never return to port. He had had dreams about it, and the black cat had mewed when he left home, and he saw the three magpies in a tree hard by when he stepped from the door, and many other portents of that kind. The first time he well-nigh scared some of the crew, but after the first voyage—from which we came back safely, of course—they did but laugh at him; and as in all other respects he was a good sailor, and a willing fellow, I did not like to discharge him, for, once the men found out that his prophecies came to naught, they did no harm, and, indeed, they afforded them much amusement. Just as it is on board a ship, so it is elsewhere. If our vessel had gone down that first voyage, any man who escaped drowning would have said that Bill Vokes had not been without reason in his warnings, and that it was nothing less than flying in the face of Providence, to put to sea when the loss of the ship had been so surely foretold. So, on shore, the fools or madmen who have dreams and visions are not heeded when times are good, and men's senses sound, whereas, in troubled times, men take their ravings to heart. If all the scatterbrains had a good whipping at the pillory it would be well, both for them and for the silly people who pay attention to their ravings."

A few minutes later, Cyril took a boat to the Whitehall steps, and after some delay was shown up to Prince Rupert's room.

"None the worse for your exertions yester-even, young gentleman, I hope?" the Prince said, shaking hands with him warmly.

"None, sir. The exertion was not great, and it was but the inconvenience of the smoke that troubled me in any way."

"Have you been to inquire after the young ladies who owe their lives to you?"

"No, sir; I know neither their names nor their condition, nor, had I wished it, could I have made inquiries, for I know not whither they were taken."

"I sent round early this morning," the Prince said, "and heard that they were as well as might be expected after the adventure they went through. And now tell me about yourself, and what you have been doing. 'Tis one of the saddest things to me, since I returned to England, that so many good men who fought by my side have been made beggars in the King's service, and that I could do naught for them. 'Tis a grievous business, and yet I see not how it is to be mended.

The hardest thing is, that those who did most for the King's service are those who have suffered most deeply. None of those who were driven to sell their estates at a fraction of their value, in order to raise money for the King's treasury or to put men into the field, have received any redress. It would need a vast sum to buy back all their lands, and Parliament would not vote money for that purpose; nor would it be fair to turn men out of the estates that they bought and paid for. Do you not think so?" he asked suddenly, seeing, by the lad's face, that he was not in agreement with him.

"No, sir; it does not seem to me that it would be unfair. These men bought the lands for, as you say, but a fraction of their value; they did so in the belief that Parliament would triumph, and their purchase was but a speculation grounded on that belief. They have had the enjoyment of the estates for years, and have drawn from them an income which has, by this time, brought them in a sum much exceeding that which they have adventured, and it does not seem to me that there would be any hardship whatever were they now called upon to restore them to their owners. 'Tis as when a man risks his money in a venture at sea. If all goes as he hopes he will make a great profit on his money. If the ship is cast away or taken by pirates, it is unfortunate, but he has no reason to curse his ill-luck if the ship had already made several voyages which have more than recouped the money he ventured."

"Well and stoutly argued!" the Prince said approvingly. "But you must remember, young sir, that the King, on his return, was by no means strongly seated on the throne. There was the Army most evilly affected towards him; there were the Puritans, who lamented the upset of the work they or their fathers had done. All those men who had purchased the estates of the Royalists had families and friends, and, had these estates been restored to their rightful owners, there might have been an outbreak that would have shaken the throne again. Many would have refused to give up possession, save to force; and where was the force to come from? Even had the King had troops willing to carry out such a measure, they might have been met by force, and had blood once been shed, none can say how the trouble might have spread, or what might have been the end of it. And now, lad, come to your own fortunes."

Cyril briefly related the story of his life since his return to London, stating his father's plan that he should some day take foreign service.

"You have shown that you have a stout heart, young sir, as well as a brave one, and have done well, indeed, in turning your mind to earn your living by such talents as you have, rather than in wasting your time in vain hopes and in ceaseless importunities for justice. It may be that you have acted wisely in thinking of taking service on the Continent, seeing that we have no Army; and when the time comes, I will further your wishes to the utmost of my power. But in the meantime there is opportunity for service at home, and I will gladly appoint you as a Volunteer in my own ship. There are many gentlemen going with me in that capacity, and it would be of advantage to you, if, when I write to some foreign prince on your behalf, I can say that you have fought under my eye."

"Thank you greatly, Prince. I have been wishing, above all things, that I could join the Fleet, and it would be, indeed, an honour to begin my career under the Prince of whom I heard so often from my father."

Prince Rupert looked at his watch.

"The King will be in the Mall now," he said. "I will take you across and present you to him. It is useful to have the *entrée* at Court, though perhaps the less you avail yourself of it the better."

So saying, he rose, put on his hat, and, throwing his cloak over his shoulder, went across to the Mall, asking questions of Cyril as he went, and extracting from him a sketch of the adventure of his being kidnapped and taken to Holland.

Presently they arrived at the spot where the King, with

three or four nobles and gentlemen, had been playing. Charles was in a good humour, for he had just won a match with the Earl of Rochester.

"Well, my grave cousin," he said merrily, "what brings you out of your office so early? No fresh demands for money, I hope?"

"Not at present. And indeed, it is not to you that I should come on such a quest, but to the Duke of York."

"And he would come to me," said the King; "so it is the same thing."

"I have come across to present to your Majesty a very gallant young gentleman, who yesterday evening, at the risk of his life, saved the three daughters of the Earl of Wisbech from being burned at the fire in the Savoy, where his Lordship's mansion was among those that were destroyed. I beg to present to your Majesty Sir Cyril Shenstone, the son of the late Sir Aubrey Shenstone, a most gallant gentleman, who rode under my banner in many a stern fight in the service of your royal father."

"I knew him well," the King said graciously, "but had not heard of his death. I am glad to hear that his son inherits his bravery. I have often regretted deeply that it was out of my power to requite, in any way, the services Sir Aubrey rendered, and the sacrifices he made for our House."

His brow clouded a little, and he looked appealingly at Prince Rupert.

"Sir Cyril Shenstone has no more intention of asking for favours than I have, Charles," the latter said. "He is going to accompany me as a Volunteer against the Dutch, and if the war lasts I shall ask for a better appointment for him."

"That he shall have," the King said warmly. "None have a better claim to commissions in the Navy and Army than sons of gentlemen who fought and suffered in the cause of our royal father. My Lords," he said to the little group of gentlemen, who had been standing a few paces away while this conversation had been going on, "I would have you know

"CYRIL RAISED THE KING'S HAND TO HIS LIPS."

Sir Cyril Shenstone, the son of a faithful adherent of my father, and who, yesterday evening, saved the lives of the three daughters of My Lord of Wisbech in the fire at the Savoy. He is going as a Volunteer with my cousin Rupert when he sails against the Dutch."

The gentlemen all returned Cyril's salute courteously.

"He will be fortunate in beginning his career under the eyes of so brave a Prince," the Earl of Rochester said, bowing to Prince Rupert.

"It would be well if you all," the latter replied bluntly, "were to ship in the Fleet for a few months instead of wasting your time in empty pleasures."

The Earl smiled. Prince Rupert's extreme disapproval of the life at Court was well known.

"We cannot all be Bayards, Prince, and most of us would, methinks, be too sick at sea to be of much assistance, were we to go. But if the Dutchmen come here, which is not likely—for I doubt not, Prince, that you will soon send them flying back to their own ports—we shall all be glad to do our best to meet them when they land."

The Prince made no reply, but, turning to the King, said,—

"We will not detain you longer from your game, Cousin Charles. I have plenty to do, with all the complaints as to the state of the ships, and the lack of stores and necessaries."

"Remember, I shall be glad to see you at my *leveés*, Sir Cyril," the King said, holding out his hand. "Do not wait for the Prince to bring you, for if you do you will wait long."

Cyril doffed his hat, raised the King's hand to his lips, then, with a deep bow and an expression of thanks, followed Prince Rupert, who was already striding away.

"You might have been better introduced," the Prince said when he overtook him. "Still it is better to be badly introduced than to have no introduction at all. I am too old for the flippancies of the Court. You had better show yourself there sometimes; you will make friends that may be useful. By the way, I have not your address, and it may be a fortnight or more before the *Henrietta* is ready to take her crew on board." He took out his tablet and wrote down the address. "Come and see me if there is anything you want to ask me. Do not let the clerks keep you out with the pretence that I am busy, but send up your name to me, and tell them that I have ordered it shall be taken up, however I may be engaged."

Having no occasion for haste, Cyril walked back to the City after leaving Prince Rupert. A great change had taken place in his fortunes in the last twenty-four hours. Then he had no prospects save continuing his work in the City for another two years, and even after that time he foresaw grave difficulties in the way of his obtaining a commission in a foreign army; for Sir John Parton, even if ready to carry out the promise he had formerly made him, might not have sufficient influence to do so. Now he was to embark in Prince Rupert's own ship. He would be the companion of many other gentlemen going out as Volunteers, and, at a bound, spring from the position of a writer in the City to that occupied by his father before he became involved in the trouble between King and Parliament. He was already admitted to Court, and Prince Rupert himself had promised to push his fortunes abroad.

And yet he felt less elated than he would have expected from his sudden change. The question of money was the cloud that dulled the brightness of his prospects. As a Volunteer he would receive no pay, and yet he must make a fair show among the young noblemen and gentlemen who would be his companions. Doubtless they would be victualled on board, but he would have to dress well and probably pay a share in the expenses that would be incurred for wine and other things on board. Had it not been for the future he would have been inclined to regret that he had not refused the tempting offer; but the advantages to be gained by Prince Rupert's patronage were so large that he felt no sacrifice would be too great to that end—even that of accepting the assistance that Captain Dave had more than once hinted he should give him. It was just the dinner-hour when he arrived home.

"Well, Cyril, I see by your face that the Prince has said nothing in the direction of your wishes," Captain Dave said, as he entered.

"Then my face is a false witness, Captain Dave, for Prince Rupert has appointed me a Volunteer on board his own ship."

"I am glad, indeed, lad, heartily glad, though your going will be a heavy loss to us all. But why were you looking so grave over it?"

"I have been wondering whether I have acted wisely in accepting it," Cyril said. "I am very happy here, I am earning my living, I have no cares of any sort, and I feel that it is a very serious matter to make a change. The Prince has a number of noblemen and gentlemen going with him as Volunteers, and I feel that I shall be out of my element in such company. At the same time I have every reason to be thankful, for Prince Rupert has promised that he will, after the war is over, give me introductions which will procure me a commission abroad."

"Well, then, it seems to me that things could not look better," Captain Dave said heartily. "When do you go on board?"

"The Prince says it may be another fortnight; so that I shall have time to make my preparations, and warn the citizens I work for, that I am going to leave them."

"I should say the sooner the better, lad. You will have to get your outfit and other matters seen to. Moreover, now that you have been taken under Prince Rupert's protection, and have become, as it were, an officer on his ship—for gentlemen Volunteers, although they have no duties in regard to working the ship, are yet officers—it is hardly seemly that you should be making up the accounts of bakers and butchers, ironmongers, and ship's storekeepers."

"The work is honest, and I am in no way ashamed of it," Cyril said; "but as I have many things to see about, I suppose I had better give them notice at once. Prince Rupert presented me to the King to-day, and His Majesty requested me to attend at Court, which I should be loath to do, were it not that the Prince urged upon me that it was of advantage that I should make myself known."

"One would think, Master Cyril, that this honour which has suddenly befallen you is regarded by you as a misfortune," Mrs. Dowsett said, laughing. "Most youths would be overjoyed at such a change in their fortune."

"It would be all very pleasant," Cyril said, "had I the income of my father's estate at my back; but I feel that I shall be in a false position, thus thrusting myself among men who have more guineas in their pockets than I have pennies. However, it seems that the matter has been taken out of my own hands, and that, as things have turned out, so I must travel. Who would have thought, when John Wilkes fetched me out last night to go to the fire, it would make an alteration in my whole life, and that such a little thing as climbing up a ladder and helping to get three girls out of a room full of smoke—and John Wilkes did the most difficult part of the work—was to change all my prospects?"

"There was a Providence in it, Cyril," Mrs. Dowsett said gently. "Why, else, should you have gone up that ladder, when, to all seeming, there was no one there. The maids were so frightened, John says, that they would never have said a word about there being any one in that room, and the girls would have perished had you not gone up. Now as, owing to that, everything has turned out according to your wishes, it would be a sin not to take advantage of it, for you may be sure that, as the way has thus been suddenly opened to you, so will all other things follow in due course."

"Thank you, madam," Cyril said simply. "I had not thought of it in that light, but assuredly you are right, and I will not suffer myself to be daunted by the difficulties there may be in my way."

John Wilkes now came in and sat down to the meal. He

was vastly pleased when he heard of the good fortune that had befallen Cyril.

"It seems to me," Cyril said, "that I am but an impostor, and that at least some share in the good luck ought to have fallen to you, John, seeing that you carried them all down the ladder."

"I have carried heavier bales, many a time, much longer distances than that—though I do not say that the woman was not a tidy weight, for, indeed, she was; but I would have carried down ten of them for the honour I had in being shaken by the hand by Prince Rupert, as gallant a sailor as ever sailed a ship. No, no; what I did was all in a day's work, and no more than lifting anchors and chains about in the storehouse. As for honours, I want none of them. I am moored in a snug port here, and would not leave Captain Dave if they would make a Duke of me."

Nellie had said no word of congratulation to Cyril, but as they rose from dinner, she said, in low tones,—

"You know I am pleased, and hope that you will have all the good fortune you deserve."

Cyril set out at once to make a round of the shops where he worked. The announcement that he must at once terminate his connection with them, as he was going on board the Fleet, was everywhere received with great regret.

"I would gladly pay double," one said, "rather than that you should go, for, indeed, it has taken a heavy load off my shoulders, and I know not how I shall get on in the future."

"I should think there would be no difficulty in getting some other young clerk to do the work," Cyril said.

"Not so easy," the man replied. "I had tried one or two before, and found they were more trouble than they were worth. There are not many who write as neatly as you do, and you do as much in an hour as some would take a day over. However, I wish you good luck, and if you should come back, and take up the work again, or start as a scrivener in the City, I can promise you that you shall have my books again, and that among my friends I can find you as much work as you can get through."

Something similar was said to him at each of the houses where he called, and he felt much gratified at finding that his work had given such satisfaction.

When he came in to supper, Cyril was conscious that something had occurred of an unusual nature. Nellie's eyes were swollen with crying; Mrs. Dowsett had also evidently been in tears; while Captain Dave was walking up and down the room restlessly.

The servant was placing the things upon the table, and, just as they were about to take their seats, the bell of the front door rang loudly.

"See who it is, John," Captain Dave said. "Whoever it is seems to be in a mighty hurry."

In a minute or two John returned, followed by a gentleman. The latter paused at the door, and then said, bowing courteously, as he advanced, to Mrs. Dowsett,—

"I must ask pardon for intruding on your meal, madam, but my business is urgent. I am the Earl of Wisbech, and I have called to see Sir Cyril Shenstone, to offer him my heartfelt thanks for the service he has rendered me by saving the lives of my daughters."

All had risen to their feet as he entered, and there was a slight exclamation of surprise from the Captain, his wife, and daughter, as the Earl said "Sir Cyril Shenstone."

Cyril stepped forward.

"I am Cyril Shenstone, my Lord," he said, "and had the good fortune to be able, with the assistance of my friend here, John Wilkes, to rescue your daughters, though, at the time, indeed, I was altogether ignorant of their rank. It was a fortunate occurrence, but I must disclaim any merit in the action, for it was by mere accident that, mounting to the window by a ladder, I saw them lying insensible on the ground."

"Your modesty does you credit, sir," the Earl said, shaking

him warmly by the hand. "But such is not the opinion of Prince Rupert, who described it to me as a very gallant action; and, moreover, he said that it was you who first brought him the news that there were females in the house, which he and others had supposed to be empty, and that it was solely owing to you that the ladders were taken round."

"Will you allow me, my Lord, to introduce to you Captain Dowsett, his wife, and daughter, who have been to me the kindest of friends?"

"A kindness, my Lord," Captain Dave said earnestly, "that has been repaid a thousandfold by this good youth, of whose rank we were indeed ignorant until you named it. May I ask you to honour us by joining in our meal?"

"That will I right gladly, sir," the Earl said, "for, in truth, I have scarce broke my fast to-day. I was down at my place in Kent when I was awoke this morning by one of my grooms, who had ridden down with the news that my mansion in the Savoy had been burned, and that my daughters had had a most narrow escape of their lives. Of course, I mounted at once and rode to town, where I was happy in finding that they had well-nigh recovered from the effects of their fright and the smoke. Neither they nor the nurse who was with them could give me any account of what had happened, save that they had, as they supposed, become insensible from the smoke. When they recovered, they found themselves in the Earl of Surrey's house, to which it seems they had been carried. After inquiry, I learned that the Duke of Albemarle and Prince Rupert had both been on the scene directing operations. I went to the latter, with whom I have the honour of being well acquainted, and he told me the whole story, saying that had it not been for Sir Cyril Shenstone, my daughters would certainly have perished. He gave credit, too, to Sir Cyril's companion, who, he said, carried them down the ladder, and himself entered the burning room the last time, to aid in bringing out the nurse, who was too heavy for the rescuer of my daughters to lift. Save a cup of wine and a piece of bread, that I took on my first arrival, I have not broken my fast to-day."

Then he seated himself on a chair that Cyril had placed for him between Mrs. Dowsett and Nellie.

Captain Dave whispered to John Wilkes, who went out, and returned in two or three minutes with three or four flasks of rare Spanish wine which the Captain had brought back on his last voyage, and kept for drinking on special occasions. The Dame always kept an excellent table, and although she made many apologies to the Earl, he assured her that none were needed, for that he could have supped no better in his own house.

"I hear," he said presently to Cyril, "that you are going out as a Volunteer in Prince Rupert's ship. My son is also going with him, and I hope, in a day or two, to introduce him to you. He is at present at Cambridge, but, having set his mind on sailing with the Prince, I have been fain to allow him to give up his studies. I heard from Prince Rupert that you had recently been kidnapped and taken to Holland. He gave me no particulars, nor did I ask them, being desirous of hurrying off at once to express my gratitude to you. How was it that such an adventure befell you—for it would hardly seem likely that you could have provoked the enmity of persons capable of such an outrage?"

"It was the result of his services to me, my Lord," Captain Dave said. "Having been a sea-captain, I am but a poor hand at accounts; but, having fallen into this business at the death of my father, it seemed simple enough for me to get on without much book-learning. I made but a bad shape at it; and when Master Shenstone, as he then called himself, offered to keep my books for me, it seemed to me an excellent mode of saving myself worry and trouble. However, when he set himself to making up the accounts of my stock, he found that I was nigh eight hundred pounds short; and, setting himself to watch, discovered that my apprentices were in alliance with a band of thieves, and were nightly robbing me. We caught them and two of the thieves in the act. One of the latter was the receiver, and on his premises the proceeds of a great number of robberies were found, and there was no doubt that he was the chief of a notorious gang, called the 'Black Gang,' which had for a long time infested the City and the surrounding country. It was to prevent Sir Cyril from giving evidence at the trial that he was kidnapped and sent away. He was placed in the house of a diamond merchant, to whom the thieves were in the habit of consigning jewels; and this might well have turned out fatal to him, for to the same house came my elder apprentice and one of the men captured with him— a notorious ruffian—who had been rescued from the constables by a gang of their fellows, in open daylight, in the City. These, doubtless, would have compassed his death had he not happily seen them enter the house, and made his escape, taking passage in a coaster bound for Dunkirk, from which place he took another ship to England. Thus you see, my Lord, that I am indebted to him for saving me from a further loss that might well have ruined me."

He paused, and glanced at Nellie, who rose at once, saying to the Earl,—

"I trust that your Lordship will excuse my mother and myself. My father has more to tell you; at least, I should wish him to do so."

Then, taking her mother's hand, she curtsied deeply, and they left the room together.

"Such, my Lord, as I have told you, is the service, so far as I knew till this afternoon, Sir Cyril Shenstone has rendered me. That was no small thing, but it is very little to what I know now that I am indebted to him. After he went out I was speaking with my wife on money matters, desiring much to be of assistance to him in the matter of the expedition on which he is going. Suddenly my daughter burst into tears and left the room. I naturally bade my wife follow her and learn what ailed her. Then, with many sobs and tears, she told her mother that we little knew how much we were indebted to him. She said she had been a wicked girl, having permitted herself to be accosted several times by a well-dressed gallant, who told her that he was the Earl of Harwich, who had professed great love for her, and urged her to marry him privately.

"He was about to speak to her one day when she was out under Master Cyril's escort. The latter interfered, and there was well-nigh a *fracas* between them. Being afraid that some of the lookers-on might know her, and bring the matter to our ears, she mentioned so much to us, and, in consequence, we did not allow her to go out afterwards, save in the company of her mother. Nevertheless, the man continued to meet her, and, as he was unknown to her mother, passed notes into her hand. To these she similarly replied, and at last consented to fly with him. She did so at night, and was about to enter a sedan chair in the lane near this house when they were interrupted by the arrival of Master Shenstone and my friend John Wilkes. The former, it seems, had his suspicions, and setting himself to watch, had discovered that she was corresponding with this man—whom he had found was not the personage he pretended to be, but a disreputable hanger-on of the Court, one John Harvey—and had then kept up an incessant watch, with the aid of John Wilkes, outside the house at night, until he saw her come out and join the fellow with two associates, when he followed her to the chair they had in readiness for her.

"There was, she says, a terrible scene. Swords were drawn. John Wilkes knocked down one of the men, and Master Shenstone ran John Harvey through the shoulder. Appalled now at seeing how she had been deceived, and how narrowly she had escaped destruction, she returned with her rescuers to the house, and no word was ever said on the subject until she spoke this afternoon. We had noticed that a great change had come over her, and that she seemed to have lost all her tastes for shows and finery, but little did we dream of the cause. She said that she could not have kept the secret much longer in any case, being utterly miserable at the thought of how she had degraded herself and deceived us.

"It was a sad story to have to hear, my Lord, but we have fully forgiven her, having, indeed, cause to thank God both for her preservation and for the good that this seems to have wrought in her. She had been a spoilt child, and, being well-favoured, her head had been turned by flattery, and she indulged in all sorts of foolish dreams. Now she is truly penitent for her folly. Had you not arrived, my Lord, I should, when we had finished our supper, have told Master Shenstone that I knew of this vast service he has rendered us—a service to which the other was as nothing. That touched my pocket only; this my only child's happiness. I have told you the story, my Lord, by her consent, in order that you might know what sort of a young fellow this gentleman who has rescued your daughter is. John, I thank you for your share in this matter," and, with tears in his eyes, he held out his hand to his faithful companion.

"I thank you deeply, Captain Dowsett, for having told me this story," the Earl said gravely. "It was a painful one to tell, and I feel sure that the circumstance will, as you say, be of lasting benefit to your daughter. It shows that her heart is a true and loyal one, or she would not have had so painful a story told to a stranger, simply that the true character of her preserver should be known. I need not say that it has had the effect she desired of raising Sir Cyril Shenstone highly in my esteem. Prince Rupert spoke of him very highly and told me how he had been honourably supporting himself and his father, until the death of the latter. Now I see that he possesses unusual discretion and acuteness, as well as bravery. Now I will take my leave, thanking you for the good entertainment that you have given me. I am staying at the house of the Earl of Surrey, Sir Cyril, and I hope that you will call to-morrow morning, in order that my daughters may thank you in person."

Captain Dave and Cyril escorted the Earl to the door and then returned to the chamber above.

CHAPTER XII.

NEW FRIENDS.

ON arriving at the room upstairs, Captain Dave placed his hand on Cyril's shoulder and said:

"How can I thank you, lad, for what you have done for us?"

"By saying nothing further about it, Captain Dave. I had hoped that the matter would never have come to your ears, and yet I rejoice, for her own sake, that Mistress Nellie has told you all. I thought that she would do so some day, for I, too, have seen how much she has been changed since then, and though it becomes me not to speak of one older than myself, I think that the experience has been for her good, and, above all, I am rejoiced to find that you have fully forgiven her, for indeed I am sure that she has been grievously punished."

"Well, well, lad, it shall be as you say, for indeed I am but a poor hand at talking, but believe me that I feel as grateful as if I could express myself rightly, and that the Earl of Wisbech cannot feel one wit more thankful to you for having saved the lives of his three children than I do for your having saved my Nellie from the consequences of her own folly. There is one thing that you must let me do—it is but a small thing, but at present I have no other way of showing what I feel: you must let me take upon myself, as if you had been my son, the expenses of this outfit of yours. I was talking of the matter, as you may have guessed by what I said to the Earl, when Nellie burst into tears; and if I contemplated this when I knew only you had saved me from ruin, how much more do I feel it now that you have done this greater thing? I trust that you will not refuse me and my wife this small opportunity of showing our gratitude. What say you, John Wilkes?"

"I say, Captain Dave, that it is well spoken, and I am sure Master Cyril will not refuse your offer."

"I will not, Captain Dave, providing that you let it be as a loan that I may perhaps some day be enabled to repay you. I feel that it would be churlish to refuse so kind an offer, and it will relieve me of the one difficulty that troubled me when the prospects in all other respects seemed so fair."

"That is right, lad, and you have taken a load off my mind. You have not acted quite fairly by us in one respect, Master Cyril!"

"How is that?" Cyril asked in surprise.

"In not telling us that you were Sir Cyril Shenstone, and in letting us put you up in an attic, and letting you go about as Nellie's escort, as if you had been but an apprentice."

Cyril laughed.

"I said that my father was Sir Aubrey Shenstone, though I own that I did not say so until I had been here some time; but the fact that he was a Baronet and not a Knight made little difference. It was a friendless lad whom you took in and gave shelter to, Captain Dave, and it mattered not whether he was plain Cyril or Sir Cyril. I had certainly no thought of taking my title again until I entered a foreign army, and indeed it would have been a disservice to me here in London. I should have cut but a poor figure asking for work and calling myself Sir Cyril Shenstone. I should have had to enter into all sorts of explanations before anyone would have believed me, and I don't think that, even with you, I should have been so comfortable as I have been."

"Well, at any rate, no harm has been done," Captain Dave said; "but I think you might have told me."

"If I had, Captain Dave, you would assuredly have told your wife and Mistress Nellie; and it was much more pleasant for me that things should be as they were."

"Well, perhaps you were right, lad. And I own that I might not have let you work at my books, and worry over that robbery, had I known that you were of a station above me."

"That you could never have known," Cyril said warmly. "We have been poor ever since I can remember. I owed my education to the kindness of friends of my mother, and in no way has my station been equal to that of a London trader like yourself. As to the title, it was but a matter of birth, and went but ill with an empty purse and a shabby doublet. In the future it may be useful, but until now, it has been naught, and indeed worse than naught, to me."

The next morning when Cyril went into the parlour he found that Nellie was busy assisting the maid to lay the table. When the latter had left the room, the girl went up to Cyril and took his hand.

"I have never thanked you yet," she said. "I could not bring myself to speak of it, but now that I have told them I can do so. Ever since that dreadful night I have prayed for you, morning and evening, and thanked God for sending you to my rescue. What a wicked girl you must have thought me—and with reason! But you could not think of me worse than I thought of myself. Now that my father and mother have forgiven me I shall be different altogether. I had before made up my mind to tell them. Still, it did not seem to me that I should ever be happy again. But now that I have had the courage to speak out, and they have been so good to me, a great weight is lifted off my mind, and I mean to learn to be a good housewife like my mother, and to try to be worthy, some day, of an honest man's love."

"I am sure you will be," Cyril said warmly. "And so, Mistress Nellie, it has all turned out for the best, though it did not seem so at one time."

At this moment Captain Dave came in.

"I am glad to see you two talking together as of old," he said. "We had thought that there must be some quarrel between you, for you had given up rating him, Nellie. Give her a kiss, Cyril; she is a good lass, though she has been a foolish one. Nay, Nellie, do not offer him your cheek—it is the fashion to do that to every idle acquaintance. Kiss him heartily, as if you loved him. That is right, lass. Now let us to breakfast. Where is your mother? She is late."

"I told her that I would see after the breakfast in future, father, and I have begun this morning—partly because it is my duty to take the work off her hands, and partly because I wanted a private talk with Sir Cyril."

"I won't be called Sir Cyril under this roof," the lad said, laughing. "And I warn you that if any one calls me so I will not answer. I have always been Cyril with you all, and I intend to remain so to the end, and you must remember that it is but a few months that I have had the right to the title, and was never addressed by it until by Prince Rupert. I was for the moment well nigh as much surprised as you were last night."

An hour later Cyril again donned his best suit, and started to pay his visit to the Earl. Had he not seen him over-night, he would have felt very uncomfortable at the thought of the visit; but he had found him so pleasant and friendly, and so entirely free from any air of pride or condescension, that it seemed as if he were going to meet a friend. He was particularly struck with the manner in which he had placed Captain Dave and his family at their ease, and got them to talk as freely and naturally with him as if he had been an acquaintance of long standing. It seemed strange to him to give his name as Sir Cyril Shenstone to the lackeys at the door, and he almost expected to see an expression of amusement on their faces. They had, however, evidently received instructions respecting him, for he was without question at once ushered into the room in which the Earl of Wisbech and his daughters were sitting.

The Earl shook him warmly by the hand, and then, turning to his daughters, said,—

"This is the gentleman to whom you owe your lives, girls. Sir Cyril, these are my daughters—Lady Dorothy, Lady Bertha, and Lady Beatrice. It seems somewhat strange to have to introduce you, who have saved their lives, to them; but you have the advantage of them, for you have seen them before, but they have not until now seen your face."

Each of the girls as she was named made a deep curtsey, and then presented her cheek to be kissed, as was the custom of the times.

"They are somewhat tongue-tied," the Earl said, smiling, as the eldest of the three cast an appealing glance to him, "and have begged me to thank you in their names, which I do with all my heart, and beg you to believe that their gratitude is none the less deep because they have no words to express it. They generally have plenty to say, I can assure you, and will find their tongues when you are a little better acquainted."

"I am most happy to have been of service to you, ladies," Cyril said, bowing deeply to them. "I can hardly say that I have the advantage your father speaks of, for in truth the smoke was so thick, and my eyes smarted so with it, that I could scarce see your faces."

"Their attire, too, in no way helped you," the Earl said, with a laugh, "for, as I hear, their costume was of the slightest. I believe that Dorothy's chief concern is that she did not have time to attire herself in a more becoming toilette before the smoke overpowered her."

"Now, father," the girl protested, with a pretty colour in her cheeks, "you know I have never said anything of the sort, though I did say that I wished I had thrown a cloak round me. It is not pleasant, whatever you may think, to know that one was handed down a ladder in one's nightdress."

"I don't care about that a bit," Beatrice said; "but you did not say, father, that it was a young gentleman, no older than Sydney, who found us and carried us out. I had expected to see a great big man."

"I don't think I said anything about his age, Beatrice, but simply told you that I had found out that it was Sir Cyril Shenstone that had saved you."

"Is the nurse recovering, my Lord?"

"She is still in bed, and the doctor says she will be some time before she quite recovers from the fright and shock. They were all sleeping in the storey above. It was Dorothy who first woke, and, after waking her sisters, ran into the nurse's room, which was next door, and roused her. The silly woman was so frightened that she could do nothing but stand at the window and scream until the girls almost dragged her away, and forced her to come downstairs. The smoke, however, was so thick that they could get no farther than the next floor; then, guided by the screams of the other servants, they opened a door and ran in, but, as you know, it was not the room into which the women had gone. The nurse fell down in a faint as soon as she got in. The girls, as it seems, dragged her as far as they could towards the window, but she was too heavy for them; and as they had not shut the door, the smoke poured in and overpowered them, and they fell beside her. The rest you know. She is a silly woman, and she has quite lost my confidence by her folly and cowardice, but she has been a good servant, and the girls, all of whom she nursed, were fond of her. Still, it is evident that she is not to be trusted in an emergency, and it was only because the girls' governess is away on a visit to her mother that she happened to be left in charge of them. Now, young ladies, you can leave us, as I have other matters to talk over with Sir Cyril."

The three girls curtsied deeply, first to their father, and then to Cyril, who held the door for them to pass out.

"Now, Sir Cyril," the Earl said, as the door closed behind them, "we must have a talk together. You may well believe that, after what has happened, I look upon you almost as part of my family, and that I consider you have given me the right to look after your welfare as if you were a near relation of my own; and glad I am to have learned yesterday evening that you are, in all respects, one whom I might be proud indeed to call a kinsman. Had you been a cousin of mine, with parents but indifferently off in worldly goods, it would have been my duty, of course, to push you forward and to aid you in every way to make a proper figure on this expedition. I think that, after what has happened, I have equally the right to do so, and what would have been my duty, had you been a relation, is no less a duty, and will certainly be a great gratification to me to do now. You understand me, do you not? I wish to take upon myself all the charges connected with your outfit, and to make you an allowance, similar to that which I shall give to my son, for your expenses on board ship. All this is of course but a slight thing, but, believe me, that when the expedition is over it will be my pleasure to help you forward to advancement in any course which you may choose."

"I thank you most heartily, my Lord," Cyril said, "and would not hesitate to accept your help in the present matter, did I need it. However, I have saved some little money during the past two years, and Captain Dowsett has most generously offered me any sum I may require for my expenses, and has consented to allow me to take it as a loan to be repaid at some future time, should it be in my power to do so. Your offer, however, to aid me in my career afterwards, I most thankfully accept. My idea has always been to take service under some foreign prince, and Prince Rupert has most kindly promised to aid me in that respect; but after serving for a time at sea I shall be better enabled to judge than at present as to whether that course is indeed the best, and I shall be most thankful for your council in this and all other matters, and feel myself fortunate indeed to have obtained your good will and patronage."

"Well, if it must be so, it must," the Earl said. "Your friend Captain Dowsett seems to me a very worthy man. You have placed him under an obligation as heavy as my own, and he has the first claim to do you service. In this matter, then, I must be content to stand aside, but on your return from sea it will be my turn, and I shall be hurt and grieved indeed if you do not allow me an opportunity of proving my gratitude to you. As to the career you speak of, it is a precarious one. There are indeed many English and Scotch officers who have risen to high rank and honour in foreign service; but to every one that so succeeds, how many fall unnoticed, and lie in unmarked graves, in well nigh every country in Europe? Were you like so many of your age, bent merely on adventure and pleasure, the case would be different, but it is evident that you have a clear head for business, that you are steady and persevering, and such being the case, there are many offices under the Crown in which you might distinguish yourself and do far better than the vast majority of those who sell their swords to foreign princes, and become mere soldiers of fortune, fighting for a cause in which they have no interest, and risking their lives in quarrels that are neither their own nor their country's.

"However, all this we can talk over when you come back after having, as I hope, aided in destroying the Dutch Fleet. I expect my son up to-morrow, and trust that you will accompany him to the King's *levée* next Monday. Prince Rupert tells me that he has already presented you to the King, and that you were well received by him, as indeed you had a right to be, as the son of a gentleman who had suffered and sacrificed much in the Royal cause. But I will take the opportunity of introducing you to several other gentlemen who will sail with you. On the following day I shall be going down into Kent, and shall remain there until it is time for Sydney to embark. If you can get your preparations finished by that time, I trust that you will give us the pleasure of your company, and will stay with me until you embark with Sydney. In this way you will come to know us better, and to feel, as I wish you to feel, as one of the family."

Cyril gratefully accepted the invitation, and then took his leave.

Captain Dave was delighted when he heard the issue of his visit to the Earl.

"I should never have forgiven you, lad, if you had accepted the Earl's offer to help you in the matter of this expedition. It is no great thing, and comes well within my compass, and I should have been sorely hurt had you let him come between us; but in the future I can do little, and he much. I have spoken to several friends who are better acquainted with public affairs than I am, and they all speak highly of him. He holds, for the most part, aloof from Court, which is to his credit seeing how matters go on there; but he is spoken of as a very worthy gentleman and one of merit, who might take a prominent part in affairs were he so minded. He has broad estates in Kent and Norfolk, and spends the greater part of his life at one or other of his country seats. Doubtless, he will be able to assist you greatly in the future."

"I did not like to refuse his offer to go down with him to Kent," Cyril said, "though I would far rather have remained here with you until we sail."

"You did perfectly right, lad. It will cut short your stay here but a week, and it would be madness to refuse the opportunity of getting to know him and his family better. The Countess died three years ago, I hear, and he has shown no disposition to take another wife, as he might well do, seeing he is but a year or two past forty, and has as pleasant a face and manner as I have ever seen. He is not the sort of man to promise what he will not perform, Cyril, and more than ever do I think that it was a fortunate thing for you that John Wilkes fetched you to that fire in the Savoy. And now, lad, you have no time to lose. You must come with me at once to Master Woods, the tailor, in Eastcheap, who makes clothes not only for the citizens but for many of the nobles and gallants of the Court. In the first place, you will need a fitting dress for the King's *levée*; then you will need at least one more suit similar to that you now wear, and three for on board ship and for ordinary occasions, made of stout cloth, but in the fashion; then you must have helmet, and breast- and back-pieces for the fighting, and for these we will go to Master Lawrence, the armourer, in Cheapside. All these we will order to-day in my name, and put them down in your account to me. As to arms, you have your sword, and there is but a brace of pistols to be bought. You will want a few things such as thick cloaks for sea service; for though I suppose that Volunteers do not keep their watch, you may meet with rains and heavy weather, and you will need something to keep you dry."

They sallied out at once. So the clothes were ordered, and the Court suit, with the best of the others promised by the end of the week; the armour was fitted on and bought, and a stock of fine shirts with ruffles, hose, and shoes, was also purchased. The next day Sidney Oliphant, the Earl's son, called upon Cyril. He was a frank, pleasant young fellow, about a year older than Cyril. He was very fond of his sisters, and expressed in lively terms his gratitude for their rescue.

"This expedition has happened in the nick of time for me," he said, when, in accordance with his invitation, Cyril and he embarked in the Earl's boat in which he had been rowed to the City, "for I was in bad odour with the authorities, and was like, ere long, to have been sent home far less pleasantly; and although the Earl, my father, is very indulgent, he would have been terribly angry with me had it been so. To tell you the truth, at the University we are divided into two sets—those who read and those who don't—and on joining I found myself very soon among the latter. I don't think it was quite my fault, for I naturally fell in with companions whom I had known before, and it chanced that some of these were among the wildest spirits in the University.

"Of course I had my horses, and, being fond of riding, I was more often in the saddle than in my seat in the college schools. Then there were constant complaints against us for sitting up late and disturbing the college with our melodies, and altogether we stood in bad odour with the Dons; and when they punished us we took our revenge by playing them pranks, until lately it became almost open war, and would certainly have ended before long in a score or more of us being sent down. I should not have minded that myself, but it would have grieved the Earl, and I am not one of the new-fashioned ones who care naught for what their fathers may say. He has been praising you up to the skies this morning, I can tell you—

I don't mean only as to the fire but about other things—and says he hopes we shall be great friends, and I am sure I hope so too, and think so. He had been telling me about your finding out about their robbing that good old sea-captain you live with, and how you were kidnapped afterwards, and sent to Holland; and how, in another adventure, although he did not tell me how that came about, you pricked a ruffling gallant through the shoulder; so that you have had a larger share of adventure, by a great deal, than I have. I had expected to see you a rather solemn personage, for the Earl told me you had more sense in your little finger than I had in my whole body, which was not complimentary to me, though I daresay it is true."

"Now, as a rule, they say that sensible people are very disagreeable; but I hope I shall not be disagreeable," Cyril laughed, "and I am certainly not aware that I am particularly sensible."

"No, I am sure you won't be disagreeable, but I should have been quite nervous about coming to see you if it had not been for the girls. Little Beatrice told me she thought you were a prince in disguise, and had evidently a private idea that the good fairies had sent you to her rescue. Bertha said that you were a very proper young gentleman, and that she was sure you were nice. Dorothy didn't say much, but she evidently approved of the younger girls' sentiments, so I felt that you must be all right, for the girls are generally pretty severe critics, and very few of my friends stand at all high in their good graces. What amusement are you most fond of?"

"I am afraid I have had very little time for amusements," Cyril said. "I was very fond of fencing when I was in France, but have had no opportunity of practising since I came to England. I went to a bull-bait once, but thought it a cruel sport."

"I suppose you go to a play-house sometimes?"

"No; I have never been inside one. A good deal of my work has been done in the evening, and I don't know that the thought ever occurred to me to go. I know nothing of your English sports, and neither ride nor shoot, except with a pistol, with which I used to be a good shot when I was in France."

They rowed down as low as Greenwich, then, as the tide turned, made their way back; and by the time Cyril alighted from the boat at London Bridge stairs the two young fellows had become quite intimate with each other.

Nellie looked with great approval at Cyril as he came downstairs in a full Court dress. Since the avowal she had made of her fault she had recovered much of her brightness. She bustled about the house, intent upon the duties she had newly taken up, to the gratification of Mrs. Dowsett, who protested that her occupation was gone.

"Not at all, mother. It is only that you are now captain of the ship, and have got to give your orders instead of carrying them out yourself. Father did not pull up the ropes or go aloft to furl the sails, while I have no doubt he had plenty to do in seeing that his orders were carried out. You will be worse off than he was, for he had John Wilkes, and others, who knew their duty, while I have got almost everything to learn."

Although her cheerfulness had returned, and she could again be heard singing snatches of song about the house, her voice and manner were gentler and softer, and Captain Dave said to Cyril,—

"It has all turned out for the best, lad. The ship was very near wrecked, but the lesson has been a useful one, and there is no fear of her being lost from want of care or good seamanship in future. I feel, too, that I have been largely to blame in the matter. I spoilt her as a child, and I spoilt her all along. Her mother would have kept a firmer hand upon the helm if I had not always spoken up for the lass, and said, 'Let her have her head; don't check the sheets in too tautly.' I see I was wrong now. Why, lad, what a blessing it is to us all that it happened when it did! for if that fire had been but a month earlier, you would probably have gone away with the Earl, and we should have known nothing of Nellie's peril until we found that she was gone."

"Sir Cyril—no, I really cannot call you Cyril now," Nellie said, curtseying almost to the ground after taking a survey of the lad, "your costume becomes you rarely; and I am filled with wonder at the thought of my own stupidity in not seeing all along that you were a prince in disguise. It is like the fairy tales my old nurse used to tell me of the king's son who went out to look for a beautiful wife, and who worked as a scullion in the king's palace without any one suspecting his rank. I think fortune has been very hard upon me, in that I was born five years too soon. Had I been but fourteen instead of nineteen, your Royal Highness might have cast favourable eyes upon me."

"But then, Mistress Nellie," Cyril said, laughing, "you would be filled with grief now at the thought that I am going away to the wars."

The girl's face changed. She dropped her saucy manner and said earnestly,—

"I am grieved Cyril; and if it would do any good I would sit down and have a hearty cry. The Dutchmen are brave fighters, and their fleet will be stronger than ours; and there will be many who sail away to sea who will never come back again. I have never had a brother; but it seems to me that if I had had one who was wise, and thoughtful, and brave, I should have loved him as I love you. I think the princess must always have felt somehow that the scullion was not what he seemed; and though I have always laughed at you and scolded you, I have known all along that you were not really a clerk. I don't know that I thought you were a prince; but I somehow felt a little afraid of you. You never said that you thought me vain and giddy, but I knew you did think so, and I used to feel a little malice against you; and yet, somehow, I respected and liked you all the more, and now it seems to me that you are still in disguise, and that, though you seem to be but a boy, you are really a man to whom some good fairy has given a boy's face. Methinks no boy could be as thoughtful and considerate, and as kind as you are."

"You are exaggerating altogether," Cyril said; "and yet, in what you say about my age, I think you are partly right. I have lived most of my life alone; I have had much care always on my shoulders, and grave responsibility; thus it is that I am older in many ways than I should be at my years. I would it were not so. I have not had any boyhood, as other boys have, and I think it has been a great misfortune for me."

"It has not been a misfortune for us, Cyril; it has been a blessing indeed to us all that you have not been quite like other boys, and I think that all your life it will be a satisfaction for you to know that you have saved one house from ruin, one woman from misery and disgrace. Now it is time for you to be going; but although you are leaving us to-morrow, Cyril, I hope that you are not going quite out of our lives."

"That you may be sure I am not, Nellie. If you have reason to be grateful to me, truly I have much reason to be grateful to your father. I have never been so happy as since I have been in this house, and I shall always return to it as to a home where I am sure of a welcome—as the place to which I chiefly owe any good fortune that may ever befall me."

The *levée* was a brilliant one, and was attended, in addition to the usual throng of courtiers, by most of the officers and gentlemen who were going with the Fleet. Cyril was glad indeed that he was with the Earl of Wisbech and his son, for he would have felt lonely and out of place in the brilliant throng, in which Prince Rupert's face would have been the only one with which he was familar. The Earl introduced him to several of the gentlemen who would be his shipmates, and by all he was cordially received when the Earl named him as the gentleman who had rescued his daughters from death.

At times, when the Earl was chatting with his friends

Cyril moved about through the rooms with Sydney, who knew by appearance a great number of those present, and was able to point out all the distinguished persons of the Court to him.

"There is the Prince," he said, "talking with the Earl of Rochester. What a grave face he has now! It is difficult to believe that he is the Rupert of the wars, and the headstrong prince whose very bravery helped to lose well nigh as many battles as he won. We may be sure that he will take us into the very thick of the fight, Cyril. Even now his wrist is as firm, and, I doubt not, his arm as strong as when he led the Cavaliers. I have seen him in the tennis-court; there is not one at the Court, though many are well nigh young enough to be his sons, who is his match at tennis. There is the Duke of York. They say he is a Catholic, but I own that makes no difference to me. He is fond of the sea, and is never so happy as when he is on board ship, though you would hardly think it by his grave face. The King is fond of it, too. He has a pleasure vessel that is called a yacht, and so has the Duke of York, and they have races one against the other; but the King generally wins. He is making it a fashionable pastime. Some day I will have one myself—that is, if I find I like the sea; for it must be pleasant to sail about in your own vessel, and to go wheresoever one may fancy without asking leave from any man."

When it came to his turn Cyril passed before the King with the Earl and his son. The Earl presented Sydney, who had not before been at Court, to the King, mentioning that he was going out as a Volunteer in Prince Rupert's vessel.

"That is as it should be, my Lord," the King said. "England need never fear so long as her nobles and gentlemen are ready themselves to go out to fight her battles, and to set an example to the seamen. You need not present this young gentleman to me; my cousin Rupert has already done so, and told me of the service he has rendered to your daughters. He, too, sails with the Prince, and after what happened there can be no doubt that he can stand fire well. I would that this tiresome dignity did not prevent my being of the party. I would gladly, for once, lay my kingship down and go out as one of the company to help give the Dutchmen a lesson that will teach them that, even if caught unexpectedly, the sea-dogs of England can well hold their own, though they have no longer a Blake to command them."

"I wonder that the King ventures to use Blake's name," Sydney whispered, as they moved away, "considering the indignities that he allowed the judges to inflict on the body of the grand old sailor."

"It was scandalous!" Cyril said warmly; "and I burned with indignation when I heard of it in France. They may call him a traitor because he sided with the Parliament, but even Royalists should never have forgotten what great deeds he did for England. However, though they might have dishonoured his body, they could not touch his fame, and his name will be known and honoured as long as England is a nation and when the names of the men who condemned him have been long forgotten."

After leaving the *leveé*, Cyril went back to the City, and the next morning started on horseback, with the Earl and his son, to the latter's seat, near Sevenoaks, the ladies having gone down in the Earl's coach on the previous day. Wholly unaccustomed as Cyril was to riding, he was so stiff that he had difficulty in dismounting when they rode up to the mansion. The Earl had provided a quiet and well-trained horse for his use, and he had therefore found no difficulty in retaining his seat.

"You must ride every day while you are down here," the Earl said, "and by the end of the week you will begin to be fairly at home in the saddle. A good seat is one of the prime necessities of a gentleman's education, and if it should be that you ever carry out your idea of taking service abroad it will be essential for you, because, in most cases, the officers are mounted. You can hardly expect ever to become a brilliant rider. For that it is necessary to begin young; but if you can keep your seat under all circumstances, and be able to use your sword on horseback, as well as on foot, it will be all that is needful."

The week passed very pleasantly. Cyril rode and fenced daily with Sydney, who was surprised to find that he was fully his match with the sword. He walked in the gardens with the girls, who had now quite recovered from the effects of the fire. Bertha and Beatrice, being still children, chatted with him as freely and familiarly as they did with Sydney. Of Lady Dorothy he saw less, as she was in charge of her *governante*, who always walked beside her, and was occupied in training her into the habits of preciseness and decorum in vogue at the time.

"I do believe, Dorothy," Sydney said, one day, "that you are forgetting how to laugh. You walk like a machine, and seem afraid to move your hands or your feet except according to rule. I like you very much better as you were a year ago, when you did not think yourself too fine for a romp, and could laugh when you were pleased. That dragon of yours is spoiling you altogether."

"That is a matter of opinion, Sydney," Dorothy said, with a deep curtsey. "When you first began to fence, I have no doubt you were stiff and awkward, and I am sure if you had always had some one by your side, saying, 'Keep your head up!' 'Don't poke your chin forward!' 'Pray do not swing your arms!' and that sort of thing, you would be just as awkward as I feel. I am sure I would rather run about with the others; the process of being turned into a young lady is not a pleasant one. But perhaps some day, when you see the finished article, you will be pleased to give your Lordship's august approval," and she ended with a merry laugh that would have shocked her *governante* if she had heard it.

CHAPTER XIII.

THE BATTLE OF LOWESTOFT.

THE Earl returned with his son and Cyril to town, and the latter spent the night in the City.

"I do not know, Cyril," Captain Dave said, as they talked over his departure, "that you run much greater risk in going than do we in staying here. The Plague makes progress, and although it has not invaded the City, we can hardly hope that it will be long before it appears here. There are many evil prophesies abroad, and it is the general opinion that a great misfortune hangs over us, and they say that many have prepared to leave London. I have talked the matter over with my wife. We have not as yet thought of going, but should the Plague come heavily, it may be that we shall for a time go away. There will be no business to be done, for vessels will not come up the Thames and risk infection, nor, indeed, would they be admitted into ports, either in England or abroad, after coming from an infected place. Therefore I could leave without any loss in the way of trade. It will, of course, depend upon the heaviness of the malady, but if it becomes widespread we shall perhaps go for a visit to my wife's cousin, who lives near Gloucester, and who has many times written to us urging us to go down with Nellie for a visit to her. Hitherto, business has prevented my going, but if all trade ceases, it would be a good occasion for us, and such as may never occur again. Still, I earnestly desire that it may not arise, for it cannot do so without sore trouble and pain alighting on the City. Did the Earl tell you, Cyril, what he has done with regard to John?"

"No; he did not speak to me on the subject."

"His steward came here three days since with a gold watch and chain, as a gift from the Earl. The watch has an inscription on the case, saying that it is presented to John Wilkes from the Earl of Wisbech, as a memorial of his gratitude for the great services rendered to his daughters. Moreover, he brought a letter from the Earl saying that if John should at any time leave my service, owing to my death or retirement from business, or from John himself wishing, either from age or other reason, to leave me, he would place at his service a cottage and garden on his estate, and a pension of twenty pounds a year, to enable him to live in comfort for the remainder of his days. John is, as you may suppose, mightily pleased, for though I would assuredly never part with him as long as I live, and have by my will made provision that will keep him from want in case I die before him, it was mighty pleasant to receive so handsome a letter and offer of service from the Earl. Nellie wrote for him a letter in which he thanked the Earl for the kindness of his offer, for which, although he hoped he should never be forced to benefit from it, he was none the less obliged and grateful, seeing that he had done nothing that any other bystander would not have done, to deserve it."

Early the next morning Sydney Oliphant rode up to the door, followed by two grooms, one of whom had a led horse, and the other a sumpter-mule, which was partly laden. Captain Dave went down with Cyril to the door.

"I pray you to enter, my Lord," he said. "My wife will not be happy unless you take a cup of posset before you start. Moreover, she and my daughter desire much to see you, as you are going to sail with Sir Cyril, whom we regard as a member of our family."

"I will come up right willingly," the young noble said, leaping lightly from his horse. "If your good dame's posset is as good as the wine the Earl, my father, tells me you gave him, it must be good indeed; for he told me he believed he had none in his cellar equal to it."

He remained for a few minutes upstairs, chatting gaily, vowing that the posset was the best he had ever drank, and declaring to Nellie that he regarded as a favourable omen for his expedition that he should have seen so fair a face the last thing before starting. He shook hands with John Wilkes heartily when he came up to say that Cyril's valises were all securely packed on the horses, and then went off, promising to send Captain Dave a runnet of the finest schiedam from the Dutch Admiral's ship.

"Truly, I am thankful you came up," Cyril said, as they mounted and rode off. "Before you came we were all dull, and the Dame and Mistress Nellie somewhat tearful. Now we have gone off amidst smiles, which is vastly more pleasant."

Crossing London Bridge, they rode through Southwark, and then out into the open country. Each had a light valise strapped behind the saddle, and the servants had saddle-bags containing the smaller articles of luggage, while the sumpter-mule carried two trunks with their clothes and sea necessaries. It was late in the evening when they arrived at Chatham. Here they put up at an hotel which was crowded with officers of the Fleet, and with Volunteers like themselves.

"I should grumble at these quarters, Cyril," Sydney said, as the landlord, with many apologies, showed them into a tiny attic, which was the only place he had unoccupied, "were it not that we are going to sea to-morrow, and I suppose that our quarters will be even rougher there. However, we may have elbow-room for a time, for most of the Volunteers will not join, I hear, until the last thing before the Fleet sails, and it may be a fortnight yet before all the ships are collected. I begged my father to let me do the same, but he goes back again to-day to Sevenoaks, and he liked not the idea of my staying in town, seeing that the Plague is spreading so rapidly. I would even have stayed in the country had he let me, but he was of opinion that I was best on board—in the first place, because I may not get news down there in time to join the Fleet before it sails, and in the second, that I might come to get over this sickness of the sea, and so be fit and able to do my part when we meet the Dutch. This was so reasonable that I could urge nothing against it; for, in truth, it would be a horrible business if I were lying like a sick dog, unable to lift my head, while our men were fighting the Dutch. I have never been to sea, and know not how I shall bear it. Are you a good sailor?"

"Yes; I used to go out very often in a fishing-boat at Dunkirk, and never was ill from the first. Many people are not ill at all, and it will certainly be of an advantage to you to be on board for a short time in quiet waters before setting out for sea."

On going downstairs, Lord Oliphant found several young men of his acquaintance among those staying in the house. He introduced Cyril to them. But the room was crowded and noisy; many of those present had drunk more than was good for them, and it was not long before Cyril told his friend that he should go up to bed.

"I am not accustomed to noisy parties, Sydney, and feel quite confused with all this talk."

"You will soon get accustomed to it, Cyril. Still, do as you like. I daresay I shall not be very long before I follow you."

The next morning after breakfast they went down to the quay, and took a boat to the ship, which was lying abreast of the dockyard. The captain, on their giving their names, consulted the list.

"That is right, gentlemen, though indeed I know not why you should have come down until we are ready to sail, which may not be for a week or more, though we shall go out from here to-morrow and join those lying in the Hope; for indeed you can be of no use while we are fitting, and would but do damage to your clothes and be in the way of the sailors. It is but little accommodation you will find on board here, though we will do the best we can for you."

"We do not come about accommodation, captain," Lord Oliphant laughed, "and we have brought down gear with us that will not soil, or rather, that cannot be the worse for soiling. There are three or four others at the inn where we stopped last night who are coming on board, but I hear that the rest of the Volunteers will probably join when the fleet assembles in Yarmouth roads"

"Then they must be fonder of journeying on horseback than I am," the captain said. "While we are in the Hope, where, indeed, for aught I know, we may tarry but a day or two, they could come down by boat conveniently without trouble, whereas to Yarmouth it is a very long ride, with the risk of losing their purses to the gentlemen of the road. Moreover, though the orders are at present that the Fleet gather at Yarmouth, and many are already there, 'tis like that it may be changed in a day for Harwich or the Downs. I pray you get your meals at your inn to-day, for we are, as you see, full of work taking on board stores. If it please you to stay and watch what is doing here you are heartily welcome, but please tell the others that they had best not come off until late in the evening, by which time I will do what I can to have a place ready for them to sleep. We shall sail at the turn of the tide, which will be at three o'clock in the morning."

Oliphant wrote a few lines to the gentlemen on shore, telling them that the captain desired that none should come on board until the evening, and having sent it off by their boatmen, telling them to return in time to take them back to dinner, he and Cyril mounted to the poop and surveyed the scene round them. The ship was surrounded with lighters and boats from the dockyards, and from these casks and barrels, boxes and cases, were being swung on board by blocks from the yards, or rolled in at the port-holes. A large number of men were engaged at the work, and as fast as the stores came on board they were seized by the sailors and carried down into the hold, the provisions piled in tiers of barrels, the powder-kegs packed in the magazine.

" 'Tis like an ant-hill," Cyril said. " 'Tis just as I have seen when a nest has been disturbed. Every ant seizes a white egg as big as itself, and rushes off with it to the passage below."

"They work bravely," his companion said. "Every man seems to know that it is important that the ship should be filled up by to-night. See! the other four vessels lying above us are all alike at work, and may, perhaps, start with us in the morning. The other ships are busy, too, but not as we are. I suppose they will take them in hand when they have got rid of us."

"I am not surprised that the captain does not want idlers here, for, except ourselves, every man seems to have his appointed work."

"I feel half inclined to take off my doublet and to go and help to roll those big casks up the planks."

"I fancy, Sydney, we should be much more in the way there than here. There is certainly no lack of men, and your strength and mine together would not equal that of one of those strong fellows; besides, we are learning something here. It is good to see how orderly the work is being carried on, for, in spite of the number employed, there is no confusion. You see there are three barges on each side; the upper tiers of barrels and bales are being got on board through the port-holes, while the lower ones are fished up from the bottom by the ropes from the yards and swung into the waist, and so passed below; and as fast as one barge is unloaded another drops alongside to take its place."

They returned to the inn to dinner, after which they paid a visit to the victualling yard and dockyard, where work was everywhere going on. After supper they, with the other gentlemen for Prince Rupert's ship, took boat and went off together. They had learned that, while they would be victualled on board, they must take with them wine and other matters they required over and above the ship's fare. They had had a consultation with the other gentlemen after dinner, and concluded that it would be best to take but a small quantity of things, as they knew not how they would be able to stow them away, and would have opportunities of getting, at Gravesend or at Yarmouth, further stores, when they saw what things were required. They therefore took only a cheese, some butter, and a case of wine. As soon as they got on board they were taken below. They found that a curtain of sail-cloth had been hung across the main deck, and hammocks slung between the guns. Three or four lanterns were hung along the middle.

"This is all we can do for you, gentlemen," the officer who conducted them down said. "Had we been going on a pleasure trip we could have knocked up separate cabins, but as we must have room to work the guns, this cannot be done. In the morning the sailors will take down these hammocks, and will erect a table along the middle, where you will take your meals. At present, as you see, we have only slung hammocks for you, but when you all come on board there will be twenty. We have, so far, only a list of sixteen, but as the Prince said that two or three more might come at the last moment we have railed off space enough for ten hammocks on each side. We will get the place cleaned for you to-morrow, but the last barge was emptied but a few minutes since, and we could do naught but just sweep the deck down. To-morrow everything shall be scrubbed and put in order."

"It will do excellently well," one of the gentlemen said. "We have not come on board ship to get luxuries, and had we to sleep on the bare boards you would hear no grumbling."

"Now, gentlemen, as I have shown you your quarters, will you come up with me to the captain's cabin? He has bade me say that he will be glad if you will spend an hour with him there before you retire to rest."

On their entering, the captain shook hands with Lord Oliphant and Cyril.

"I must apologise, gentlemen, for being short with you when you came on board this morning; but my hands were full, and I had no time to be polite. They say you can never get a civil answer from a housewife on her washing-day, and it is the same thing with an officer on board a ship when she is taking in her stores. However, that business is over, and now I am glad to see you all, and will do my best to make you as comfortable as I can, which indeed will not be much; for as we shall, I hope, be going into action in the course of another ten days, the decks must all be kept clear, and as we have the Prince on board, we have less cabin room than we should have were we not an admiral's flagship."

Wine was placed on the table, and they had a pleasant chat. They learnt that the Fleet was now ready for sea.

"Four ships will sail with ours to-morrow," the captain said, "and the other five will be off the next morning. They have all their munitions on board, and will take in the rest of their provisions to-morrow. The Dutch had thought to take us by surprise, but from what we hear they are not so forward as we, for things have been pushed on with great zeal at all our ports, the war being generally popular with the nation, and especially with the merchants, whose commerce has been greatly injured by the pretensions and violence of the Dutch. The Portsmouth ships, and those from Plymouth, are already on their way round to the mouth of the Thames, and in a week we may be at sea. I only hope the Dutch will not be long before they come out to fight us. However, we are likely to pick up a great many prizes, and, next to fighting, you know, sailors like prize-money."

After an hour's talk the five gentlemen went below to their hammocks, and then to bed, with much laughter at the difficulty they had in mounting into their swinging cots.

It was scarce daylight when they were aroused by a great stir on board the ship, and, hastily putting on their clothes, went on deck. Already a crowd of men were aloft loosening the sails. Others had taken their places in boats in readiness to tow the ship, for the wind was, as yet, so light that it was like she would scarce have steerage way, and there were many sharp angles in the course down the river to be rounded, and shallows to be avoided. A few minutes later the moorings were cast off, the sails sheeted home, and the crew gave a great cheer, which was answered from the dockyard, and from boats alongside, full of the relations and friends of the sailors, who stood up and waved their hats and shouted good-bye.

The sails still hung idly, but the tide swept the ship along, and the men in the boats ahead simply lay on their oars until the time should come to pull her head round in one direction or another. They had not long to wait, for, as they reached the sharp corner at the end of the reach, orders were shouted, the men bent to their oars, and the vessel was taken round the curve until her head pointed east. Scarcely had they got under way when they heard the cheer from the ship astern of them, and by the time they had reached the next curve, off the village of Gillingham, the other four ships had rounded the point behind them, and were following at a distance of about a hundred yards apart. Soon afterwards the wind sprang up and the sails bellied out, and the men in the boats had to row briskly to keep ahead of the ship. The breeze continued until they passed Sheerness, and presently they dropped anchor inside the Nore sands. There they remained until the tide turned, and then sailed up the Thames to the Hope, where some forty men-of-war were already at anchor.

The next morning some barges arrived from Tilbury, laden with soldiers, of whom a hundred and fifty came on board, their quarters being on the main deck on the other side of the canvas division. A cutter also brought down a number of impressed men, twenty of whom were put on board the *Henrietta* to complete her crew. Cyril was standing on the poop watching them come on board, when he started as his eye fell on two of their number. One was Robert Ashford; the other was Black Dick. They had doubtless returned from Holland when war was declared. Robert Ashford had assumed the dress of a sailor the better to disguise himself, and the two had been carried off together from some haunt of sailors at Wapping. He pointed them out to his friend Sydney.

"So those are the two scamps? The big one looks a truculent ruffian. Well, they can do you no harm here, Cyril. I should let them stay and do their share of the fighting, and then, when the voyage is over, if they have not met with a better death than they deserve at the hands of the Dutch, you can, if you like, denounce them, and have them handed over to the City authorities."

"That I will do, as far as the big ruffian they call Black Dick is concerned. He is a desperate villain, and for aught I know may have committed many a murder, and if allowed to go free might commit many more. Besides, I shall never feel quite safe as long as he is at large. As to Robert Ashford, he is a knave, but I know no worse of him, and will therefore let him go his way."

In the evening the other ships from Chatham came up, and the captain told them later that the Earl of Sandwich, who was in command, would weigh anchor in the morning, as the contingent from London, Chatham, and Sheerness, was now complete. Cyril thought that he had never seen a prettier sight, as the Fleet, consisting of fifty men-of-war, of various sizes, and eight merchant vessels that had been bought and converted into fire-ships, got under weigh and sailed down the river. That night they anchored off Felixstowe, and the next day proceeded, with a favourable wind, to Yarmouth, where already a great number of ships were at anchor. So far the five Volunteers had taken their meals with the captain, but as the others would be coming on board, they were now to mess below, getting fresh meat and vegetables from the shore as they required them. As to other stores, they resolved to do nothing till the whole party arrived.

They had not long to wait, for, on the third day after their arrival, the Duke of York and Prince Rupert, with a great train of gentlemen, arrived in the town, and early the next morning embarked on board their respective ships. A council was held by the Volunteers in their quarters, three of their number were chosen as caterers, and, a contribution of three pounds a head being agreed upon, these went ashore in one of the ship's boats, and returned presently with a barrel or two of good biscuits, the carcasses of five sheep, two or three score of ducks and chicken, and several casks of wine, together with a large quantity of vegetables. The following morning the signal was hoisted on the mast-head of the *Royal Charles*, the Duke of York's flagship, for the Fleet to prepare to weigh anchor, and they presently got under way in three squadrons, the red under the special orders of the Duke, the white under Prince Rupert, and the blue under the Earl of Sandwich.

The Fleet consisted of one hundred and nine men-of-war and frigates, and twenty-eight fire-ships and ketches, manned by 21,006 seamen and soldiers. They sailed across to the coast of Holland, and cruised, for a few days, off Texel, capturing ten or twelve merchant vessels that tried to run in. So far, the weather had been very fine, but there were now signs of a change of weather. The sky became overcast, the wind rose rapidly, and the signal was made for the Fleet to scatter, so that each vessel should have more sea-room, and the chance of collision be avoided. By nightfall the wind had increased to the force of a gale, and the vessels were soon labouring heavily. Cyril and two or three of his comrades who, like himself, did not suffer from sickness, remained on deck; the rest were prostrate below.

For forty-eight hours the gale continued, and when it abated and the ships gradually closed up round the three admirals' flags, it was found that many had suffered sorely in the gale. Some had lost their upper spars, others had had their sails blown away, some their bulwarks smashed in, and two or three had lost their bowsprits. There was a consultation between the admirals and the principal captains, and it was agreed that it was best to sail back to England for repairs, as many of the ships were unfitted to take their place in line of battle, and as the Dutch Fleet was known to be fully equal to their own in strength, it would have been hazardous to risk an engagement. So the ketches and some of the light frigates were at once sent off to find the ships that had not yet joined, and give them orders to make for Yarmouth, Lowestoft, or Harwich. All vessels uninjured were to gather off Lowestoft, while the others were to make for the other ports, repair their damages as speedily as possible, and then rejoin at Lowestoft.

No sooner did the Dutch know that the English Fleet had sailed away than they put their fleet to sea. It consisted of one hundred and twelve men-of-war, and thirty fire-ships, and small craft manned by 22,365 soldiers and sailors. It was commanded by Admiral Obdam, having under him Tromp, Evertson, and other Dutch admirals. On their nearing England they fell in with nine ships from Hamburg, with rich cargoes, and a convoy of a thirty-four gun frigate. These they captured, to the great loss of the merchants of London.

The *Henrietta* had suffered but little in the storm, and speedily repaired her damages without going into port. With so much haste and energy did the crews of the injured ships set to work at refitting them, that in four days after the main body had anchored off Lowestoft, they were rejoined by all the ships that had made for Harwich and Yarmouth.

At midnight on June 2nd, a fast-sailing fishing-boat brought in the news that the Dutch Fleet were but a few miles away, sailing in that direction, having apparently learnt the position of the English from some ship or fishing-boat they had captured.

The trumpets on the admiral's ship at once sounded, and Prince Rupert and the Earl of Sandwich immediately rowed to her. They remained but a few minutes, and on their return to their respective vessels made the signals for their captains to come on board. The order, at such an hour, was sufficient to notify all that news must have been received of the whereabouts of the Dutch Fleet, and by the time the captains returned to their ships the crews were all up and ready to execute any order. At two o'clock day had begun to break, and soon from the mastheads of several of the vessels the lookout shouted that they could perceive the Dutch Fleet but four miles away. A mighty cheer rose throughout the Fleet, and

THE BATTLE OF LOWESTOFT. 225

as it subsided a gun from the *Royal Charles* gave the order to weigh anchor, and a few minutes later the three squadrons, in excellent order, sailed out to meet the enemy.

They did not, however, advance directly towards them, but bore up closely into the wind until they had gained the weather gauge of the enemy. Having obtained this advantage, the Duke flew the signal to engage. The Volunteers were all in their places on the poop, being posted near the rail forward, that they might be able either to run down the ladder to the waist and aid to repel boarders, or to spring on to a Dutch ship should one come alongside, and also that the after part of the poop, where Prince Rupert and the captain had taken their places near the wheel, should be free. The Prince himself had requested them so to station themselves.

"At other times, gentlemen, you are my good friends and comrades," he said, "but, from the moment that the first gun fires, you are soldiers under my orders; and I pray you take your station and remain there until I call upon you for action, for my whole attention must be given to the manœuvring of the ship, and any movement or talking near me might distract my thoughts. I shall strive to lay her alongside of the biggest Dutchman I can pick out, and as soon as the grapnels are thrown, and their sides grind together, you will have the post of honour, and will lead the soldiers aboard her. Once among the Dutchmen, you will know what to do without my telling you."

" 'Tis a grand sight, truly, Cyril," Sydney said, in a low tone, as the great fleets met each other.

"A grand sight, truly, Sydney, but a terrible one. I do not think I shall mind when I am once at it, but at present I feel that, despite my efforts, I am in a tremor, and that my knees shake as I never felt them before."

"I am glad you feel like that, Cyril, for I feel much like it myself, and began to be afraid that I had, without knowing it, been born a coward. There goes the first gun."

As he spoke, a puff of white smoke spouted out from the

bows of one of the Dutch ships, and a moment later the whole of their leading vessels opened fire. There was a rushing sound overhead, and a ball passed through the main topsail of the *Henrietta*. No reply was made by the English ships until they passed in between the Dutchmen; then the *Henrietta* poured her broadsides into the enemy on either side of her, receiving theirs in return. There was a rending of wood, and a quiver through the ship. One of the upper-deck guns was knocked off its carriage, crushing two of the men working it as it fell. Several others were hurt with splinters, and the sails pierced with holes. Again and again as she passed, did the *Henrietta* exchange broadsides with the Dutch vessels, until—the two fleets having passed through each other—she bore up, and prepared to repeat the manœuvre.

"I feel all right now," Cyril said, "but I do wish I had something to do instead of standing here useless. I quite envy the men there, stripped to the waist, working the guns. There is that fellow Black Dick, by the gun forward; he is a scoundrel, no doubt, but what strength and power he has! I saw him put his shoulder under that gun just now, and slew it across by sheer strength, so as to bear upon the stern of the Dutchman. I noticed him and Robert looking up at me just before the first gun was fired, and speaking together. I have no doubt he would gladly have pointed the gun at me instead of at the enemy, for he knows that, if I denounce him, he will get the due reward of his crimes."

As soon as the ships were headed round they passed through the Dutch as before, and this manœuvre was several times repeated. Up to one o'clock in the day no great advantage had been gained on either side. Spars had been carried away; there were yawning gaps in the bulwarks; portholes had been knocked into one, guns dismounted, and many killed; but as yet no vessel on either side had been damaged to an extent that obliged her to strike her flag, or to fall out of the fighting line. There had been a pause after each encounter, in which both fleets had occupied themselves in repairing damages, as far as possible, reeving fresh ropes in place of those that had been shot away, clearing the wreckage of fallen spars and yards, and carrying the wounded below. Four of the Volunteers had been struck down—two of them mortally wounded, but after the first passage through the enemy's fleet, Prince Rupert had ordered them to arm themselves with muskets from the racks, and to keep up a fire at the Dutch ships as they passed, aiming specially at the man at the wheel. The order had been a very welcome one, for, like Cyril, they had all felt inactivity in such a scene to be a sore trial. They were now ranged along on both sides of the poop.

At one o'clock Lord Sandwich signalled to the Blue Squadron to close up together as they advanced, as before, against the enemy's line. His position at the time was in the centre, and his squadron, sailing close together, burst into the Dutch line before their ships could make any similar disposition. Having thus broken it in sunder, instead of passing through it, the squadron separated, and the ships, turning to port and starboard, each engaged an enemy. The other two squadrons similarly ranged up among the Dutch, and the battle now became furious all along the line. Fire-ships played an important part in the battles of the time, and the thoughts of the captain of a ship were not confined to struggles with a foe of equal size, but were still more engrossed by the need for avoiding any fire-ship that might direct its course towards him.

Cyril had now no time to give a thought as to what was passing elsewhere. The *Henrietta* had ranged up alongside a Dutch vessel of equal size, and was exchanging broadsides with her. All round were vessels engaged in an equally furious encounter. The roar of the guns and the shouts of the seamen on both sides were deafening. One moment the vessel reeled from the recoil of her own guns, the next she quivered as the balls of the enemy crashed through her sides.

Suddenly, above the din, Cyril heard the voice of Prince Rupert sound like a trumpet.

"Hatchets and pikes on the starboard quarter! Draw in the guns and keep off this fire-ship."

Laying their muskets against the bulwarks, he and Sydney sprang to the mizzen-mast, and each seized a hatchet from those ranged against it. They then rushed to the starboard side, just as a small ship came out through the cloud of smoke that hung thickly around them.

There was a shock as she struck the *Henrietta*, and then, as she glided alongside, a dozen grapnels were thrown by men on her yards. The instant they had done so, the men disappeared, sliding down the ropes and running aft to their boat. Before the last leaped in he stooped. A flash of fire ran along the deck, there was a series of sharp explosions, and then a bright flame sprang up from the hatchways, ran up the shrouds and ropes, that had been soaked with oil and tar, and in a moment the sails were on fire. In spite of the flames, a score of men sprang on to the rigging of the *Henrietta* and cut the ropes of the grapnels, which, as yet—so quickly had the explosion followed their throwing—had scarce begun to check the way the fire-ship had on her as she came up.

Cyril, having cast over a grapnel that had fallen on the poop, looked down on the fire-ship as she drifted along. The deck, which, like everything else, had been smeared with tar, was in a blaze, but the combustible had not been carried as far as the helm, where doubtless the captain had stood to direct her course. A sudden thought struck him. He ran along the poop until opposite the stern of the fire-ship, climbed over the bulwark and leapt down on to the deck, some fifteen feet below him. Then he seized the helm and jammed it hard down. The fire-ship had still steerage way on her, and he saw her head at once begin to turn away from the *Henrietta*; the movement was aided by the latter's crew, who, with poles and oars, pushed her off.

The heat was terrific, but Cyril's helmet and breast-piece

sheltered him somewhat; yet though he shielded his face with his arm, he felt that it would speedily become unbearable. His eye fell upon a coil of rope at his feet. Snatching it up, he fastened it to the tiller and then round a belaying-pin in the bulwark, caught up a bucket with a rope attached, threw it over the side and soused its contents over the tiller-rope, then, unbuckling the straps of his breast- and back-pieces, he threw them off, cast his helmet on the deck, blistering his hands as he did so, and leapt overboard. It was with a delicious sense of coolness that he rose to the surface and looked round. Hitherto he had been so scorched by the flame and smothered by the smoke that it was with difficulty he had kept his attention upon what he was doing, and would doubtless, in another minute, have fallen senseless. The plunge into the sea seemed to restore his faculties, and as he came up he looked eagerly to see how far success had attended his efforts.

He saw with delight that the bow of the fire-ship was thirty or forty feet distant from the side of the *Henrietta* and her stern half that distance. Two or three of the sails of the man-of-war had caught fire, but a crowd of seamen were beating the flames out of two of them while another, upon which the fire had got a better hold, was being cut away from its yard. As he turned to swim to the side of the *Henrietta*, three or four ropes fell close to him. He twisted one of these round his body, and, a minute later, was hauled up into the waist. He was saluted with a tremendous cheer, and was caught up by three or four strong fellows, who, in spite of his remonstrances, carried him up on to the poop. Prince Rupert was standing on the top of the ladder.

"Nobly done, Sir Cyril!" he exclaimed. "You have assuredly saved the *Henrietta* and all our lives. A minute later, and we should have been on fire beyond remedy. But I will speak more to you when we have finished with the Dutchman on the other side."

CHAPTER XIV.

HONOURABLE SCARS.

DURING the time that the greater part of the crew of the *Henrietta* had been occupied with the fire-ship, the enemy had redoubled their efforts, and as the sailors returned to their guns, the mizzen-mast fell with a crash. A minute later, a Dutch man-of-war ran alongside, fired a broadside, and grappled. Then her crew, springing over the bulwarks, poured on to the deck of the *Henrietta*. They were met boldly by the soldiers, who had hitherto borne no part in the fight, and who, enraged at the loss they had been compelled to suffer, fell upon the enemy with fury. For a moment, however, the weight of numbers of the Dutchmen bore them back, but the sailors, who had at first been taken by surprise, snatched up their boarding pikes and axes.

Prince Rupert, with the other officers and Volunteers, dashed into the thick of the fray, and, step by step, the Dutchmen were driven back, until they suddenly gave way and rushed back to their own ship. The English would have followed them, but the Dutch who remained on board their ship, seeing that the fight was going against their friends, cut the ropes of the grapnels, and the ships drifted apart, some of the last to leave the deck of the *Henrietta* being forced to jump into the sea. The cannonade was at once renewed on both sides, but the Dutch had had enough of it—having lost very heavily in men—and drew off from the action.

Cyril had joined in the fray. He had risen to his feet and drawn his sword, but he found himself strangely weak. His hands were blistered and swollen, his face was already so puffed that he could scarce see out of his eyes; still, he had staggered down the steps to the waist, and, recovering his strength from the excitement, threw himself into the fray.

Scarce had he done so, when a sailor next to him fell heavily

"A DUTCH MAN-OF-WAR RAN ALONGSIDE AND FIRED A BROADSIDE.

against him, shot through the head by one of the Dutch soldiers. Cyril staggered, and before he could recover himself, a Dutch sailor struck at his head. He threw up his sword to guard the blow, but the guard was beaten down as if it had been a reed. It sufficed, however, slightly to turn the blow, which fell first on the side of the head, and then, glancing down, inflicted a terrible wound on the shoulder.

He fell at once, unconscious, and, when he recovered his senses, found himself laid out on the poop, where Sydney, assisted by two of the other gentlemen, had carried him. His head and shoulder had already been bandaged, the Prince having sent for his doctor to come up from below to attend upon him.

The battle was raging with undiminished fury all round, but, for the moment, the *Henrietta* was not engaged, and her crew were occupied in cutting away the wreckage of the mizzen-mast, and trying to repair the more important of the damages that she had suffered. Carpenters were lowered over the side, and were nailing pieces of wood over the shot-holes near the water-line. Men swarmed aloft knotting and splicing ropes and fishing damaged spars.

Sydney, who was standing a short distance away, at once came up to him.

"How are you, Cyril?"

"My head sings, and my shoulder aches, but I shall do well enough. Please get me lifted up on to that seat by the bulwark, so that I can look over and see what is going on."

"I don't think you are strong enough to sit up, Cyril."

"Oh yes I am; besides, I can lean against the bulwark."

Cyril was placed in the position he wanted, and, leaning his arm on the bulwark and resting his head on it, was able to see what was passing.

Suddenly a tremendous explosion was heard a quarter of a mile away.

"The Dutch admiral's ship has blown up," one of the men aloft shouted, and a loud cheer broke from the crew.

It was true. The Duke of York in the *Royal Charles*, of eighty guns, and the *Eendracht*, of eighty-four, the flagship of Admiral Obdam, had met and engaged each other fiercely. For a time the Dutchmen had the best of it. A single shot killed the Earl of Falmouth, Lord Muskerry, and Mr. Boyle, three gentlemen Volunteers, who at the moment were standing close to the Duke, and the *Royal Charles* suffered heavily until a shot from one of her guns struck the Dutchman's magazine, and the *Eendracht* blew up, only five men being rescued out of the five hundred that were on board of her.

This accident in no small degree decided the issue of the engagement, for the Dutch at once fell into confusion. Four of their ships, a few hundred yards from the *Henrietta*, fell foul of each other, and while the crews were engaged in trying to separate them an English fire-ship sailed boldly up and laid herself alongside. A moment later the flames shot up high, and the boat with the crew of the fire-ship rowed to the *Henrietta*. The flames instantly spread to the Dutch men-of-war, and the sailors were seen jumping over in great numbers. Prince Rupert ordered the boats to be lowered, but only one was found to be uninjured. This was manned and pushed off at once, and, with others from British vessels near, rescued a good many of the Dutch sailors.

Still the fight was raging all round; but a short time afterwards three other of the finest ships in the Dutch fleet ran into each other. Another of the English fire-ships hovering near observed the opportunity, and was laid alongside, with the same success as her consort, the three men-of-war being all destroyed.

This took place at some distance from the *Henrietta*, but the English vessels near them succeeded in saving, in their boats, a portion of the crews. The Dutch ship *Orange*, of seventy-five guns, was disabled after a sharp fight with the *Mary*, and was likewise burnt. Two Dutch vice-admirals were killed, and a panic spread through the Dutch fleet. About eight o'clock in the evening between thirty and forty of their ships made off in a body, and the rest speedily followed. During the fight and the chase eighteen Dutch ships were taken, though some of these afterwards escaped, as the vessels to which they had struck joined the rest in the chase. Fourteen were sunk, besides those burnt and blown up. Only one English ship, the *Charity*, had struck, having, at the beginning of the fight been attacked by three Dutch vessels, and lost the greater part of her men, and was then compelled to surrender to a Dutch vessel of considerably greater strength that came up and joined the others. The English loss was, considering the duration of the fight, extremely small, amounting to but 250 killed, and 340 wounded. Among the killed were the Earl of Marlborough, the Earl of Portland, who was present as a Volunteer, Rear-Admiral Sampson, and Vice-Admiral Lawson, the latter of whom died after the fight, from his wounds.

The pursuit of the Dutch was continued for some hours, and then terminated abruptly, owing to a Member of Parliament named Brounker, who was in the suite of the Duke of York, giving the captain of the *Royal Charles* orders, which he falsely stated emanated from the Duke, for the pursuit to be abandoned. For this he was afterwards expelled the House of Commons, and was ordered to be impeached, but after a time the matter was suffered to drop.

As soon as the battle was over Cyril was taken down to a hammock below. He was just dosing off to sleep when Sydney came to him.

"I am sorry to disturb you, Cyril, but an officer tells me that a man who is mortally wounded wishes to speak to you; and from his description I think it is the fellow you call Black Dick. I thought it right to tell you, but I don't think you are fit to go to see him."

"I will go," Cyril said, "if you will lend me your arm. I should like to hear what the poor wretch has to say."

"He lies just below; the hatchway is but a few yards distant."

There had been no attempt to remove Cyril's clothes, and, by the aid of Lord Oliphant and of a sailor he called to his aid, he made his way below, and was led through the line of wounded, until a doctor, turning round, said,—

"This is the man who wishes to see you, Sir Cyril."

Although a line of lanterns hung from the beams, so nearly blind was he that Cyril could scarce distinguish the man's features.

"I have sent for you," the latter said faintly, "to tell you that if it hadn't been for your jumping down on to that fireship you would not have lived through this day's fight. I saw that you recognised me, and knew that, as soon as we went back, you would hand us over to the constables. So I made up my mind that I would run you through in the *mêlée* if we got hand to hand with the Dutchmen, or would put a musket-ball into you while the firing was going on. But when I saw you standing there with the flames round you, giving your life, as it seemed, to save the ship, I felt that, even if I must be hung for it, I could not bring myself to hurt so brave a lad; so there is an end of that business. Robert Ashford was killed by a gun that was knocked from its carriage, so you have got rid of us both. I thought I should like to tell you before I went that the brave action you did saved your life, and that, bad as I am, I had yet heart enough to feel that I would rather take hanging than kill you."

The last words had been spoken in a scarcely audible whisper. The man closed his eyes; and the doctor, laying his hand on Cyril's arm, said,—

"You had better go back to your hammock now, Sir Cyril. He will never speak again. In a few minutes the end will come."

Cyril spent a restless night. The wind was blowing strongly from the north, and the crews had hard work to keep the vessels off the shore. His wounds did not pain him much, but his hands, arms, face, and legs, smarted intolerably, for his clothes had been almost burnt off him, and, refreshing as the sea-bath had been at the moment, it now added to the smarting of the wounds.

In the morning Prince Rupert came down to see him.

"It was madness of you to have joined in that *mêlée*, lad, in the state in which you were. I take the blame on myself in not ordering you to remain behind; but when the Dutchmen poured on board I had no thought of aught but driving them back again. It would have marred our pleasure in the victory we have won had you fallen, for to you we all owe our lives and the safety of the ship. No braver deed was performed yesterday than yours. I fear it will be some time before you are able to fight by my side again; but, at least, you have done your share, and more, were the war to last a lifetime."

Cyril was in less pain now, for the doctor had poured oil over his burns, and had wrapped up his hands in soft bandages.

"It was the thought of a moment, Prince," he said. "I saw the fire-ship had steerage way on her, and if the helm were put down she would drive away from our side, so without stopping to think about it one way or the other, I ran along to the stern, and jumped down to her tiller."

"Yes, lad, it was but a moment's thought, no doubt, but it is one thing to think, and another to execute, and none but the bravest would have ventured that leap on to the fire-ship. By to-morrow morning we shall be anchored in the river. Would you like to be placed in the hospital at Sheerness, or to be taken up to London?"

"I would rather go to London, if I may," Cyril said. "I know that I shall be well nursed at Captain Dave's, and hope, ere long, to be able to rejoin."

"Not for some time, lad—not for some time. Your burns will doubtless heal apace, but the wound in your shoulder is serious. The doctor says that the Dutchman's sword has cleft right through your shoulder-bone. 'Tis well that it is your left, for it may be that you will never have its full use again. You are not afraid of the Plague, are you? for on the day we left town there was a rumour that it had at last entered the City."

"I am not afraid of it," Cyril said; "and if it should come to Captain Dowsett's house, I would rather be there, that I may do what I can to help those who were so kind to me."

"Just as you like, lad. Do not hurry to rejoin. It is not likely there will be any fighting for some time, for it will be long before the Dutch are ready to take the sea again after the hammering we have given them, and all there will be to do will be to blockade their coast and to pick up their ships from foreign ports as prizes."

The next morning Cyril was placed on board a little yacht, called the *Fan Fan*, belonging to the Prince, and sailed up the river, the ship's company mustering at the side and giving him a hearty cheer. The wind was favourable, and they arrived that afternoon in town. According to the Prince's instructions, the sailors at once placed Cyril on a litter that had been brought for the purpose, and carried him up to Captain Dowsett's.

The City was in a state of agitation. The news of the victory had arrived but a few hours before, and the church bells were all ringing, flags were flying, the shops closed, and the people in the streets. John Wilkes came down in answer to the summons of the bell.

"Hullo!" he said; "whom have we here?"

"Don't you know me, John?" Cyril said.

John gave a start of astonishment.

"By St. Anthony, it is Master Cyril! At least, it is his voice, though it is little I can see of him, and what I see in no way resembles him."

"It is Sir Cyril Shenstone," the captain of the *Fan Fan*, who had come with the party, said sternly, feeling ruffled at the familiarity with which this rough-looking servitor of a City trader spoke of the gentleman in his charge. "It is Sir Cyril Shenstone, as brave a gentleman as ever drew sword, and who, as I hear, saved Prince Rupert's ship from being burnt by the Dutchmen."

"He knows me," John Wilkes said bluntly, "and he knows no offence is meant. The Captain and his dame, and Mistress Nellie are all out, Sir Cyril, but I will look after you till they return. Bring him up, lads. I am an old sailor myself, and fought the Dutch under Blake and Monk more than once."

He led the way upstairs into the best of the spare rooms. Here Cyril was laid on a bed. He thanked the sailors heartily for the care they had taken of him, and the captain handed a letter to John, saying,—

"The young Lord Oliphant asked me to give this to Captain Dowsett, but as he is not at home I pray you to give it him when he returns."

As soon as they had gone, John returned to the bed.

"This is terrible, Master Cyril. What have they been doing to you? I can see but little of your face for those bandages, but your eyes look mere slits, your flesh is all red and swollen, your eyebrows have gone, your arms and legs are all swathed up in bandages—— Have you been blown up with gunpowder?—for surely no wound could have so disfigured you."

"I have not been blown up John, but I was burnt by the flames of a Dutch fire-ship that came alongside. It is a matter that a fortnight will set right, though I doubt not that I am an unpleasant-looking object at present, and it will be some time before my hair grows again."

"And you are not hurt otherwise, Master?" John asked anxiously.

"Yes; I am hurt gravely enough, though not so as to imperil my life. I have a wound on the side of my head, and the same blow, as the doctor says, cleft through my shoulder-bone."

"I had best go and get a surgeon at once," John said; "though it will be no easy matter, for all the world is agog in the streets."

"Leave it for the present, John. There is no need whatever

for haste. In that trunk of mine is a bottle of oils for the burns, though most of the sore places are already beginning to heal over, and the doctor said that I need not apply it any more, unless I found that they smarted too much for bearing. As for the other wounds, they are strapped up and bandaged, and he said that unless they inflamed badly, they would be best let alone for a time. So sit down quietly, and let me hear the news."

"The news is bad enough, though the Plague has not yet entered the City."

"The Prince told me that there was a report, before he came on board at Lowestoft, that it had done so."

"No, it is not yet come; but people are as frightened as if it was raging here. For the last fortnight they have been leaving in crowds from the West End, and many of the citizens are also beginning to move. They frighten themselves like a parcel of children. The comet seemed to many a sign of great disaster."

Cyril laughed.

"If it could be seen only in London there might be something in it, but as it can be seen all over Europe, it is hard to say why it should augur evil to London especially. It was shining in the sky three nights ago when we were chasing the Dutch, and they had quite as good reason for thinking it was a sign of misfortune to them as have the Londoners."

"That is true enough," John Wilkes agreed; "though, in truth, I like not to see the thing in the sky myself. Then people have troubled their heads greatly because, in Master Lilly's Almanack, and other books of prediction, a great pestilence is foretold."

"It needed no great wisdom for that," Cyril said, "seeing that the Plague has been for some time busy in foreign parts, and that it was here, though not so very bad, in the winter, when these books would have been written."

"Then," John Wilkes went on, "there is a man going

through the streets, night and day. He speaks to no one, but cries out continually, 'Oh! the great and dreadful God!' This troubles many men's hearts greatly."

"It is a pity, John, that the poor fellow is not taken and shut up in some place where madmen are kept. Doubtless, it is some poor coward whose brain has been turned by fright. People who are frightened by such a thing as that must be poor-witted creatures indeed."

"That may be, Master Cyril, but methinks it is as they say, one fool makes many. People get together and bemoan themselves till their hearts fail them altogether. And yet, methinks they are not altogether without reason, for if the pestilence is so heavy without the walls, where the streets are wider and the people less crowded than here, it may well be that we shall have a terrible time of it in the City when it once passes the walls."

"That may well be, John, but cowardly fear will not make things any better. We knew, when we sailed out against the Dutch the other day, that very many would not see the setting sun, yet I believe there was not one man throughout the Fleet who behaved like a coward."

"No doubt, Master Cyril; but there is a difference. One can fight against men, but one cannot fight against the pestilence, and I do not believe that if the citizens knew that a great Dutch army was marching on London, and that they would have to withstand a dreadful siege, they would be moved with fear as they are now."

"That may be so," Cyril agreed. "Now, John, I think that I could sleep for a bit."

"Do so, Master, and I will go into the kitchen and see what I can do to make you a basin of broth when you awake; for the girl has gone out too. She wanted to see what was going on in the streets; and as I had sooner stay quietly at home I offered to take her place, as the shop was shut and I had nothing to do. Maybe by the time you wake again Captain Dave and the others will be back from their cruise."

It was dark when Cyril woke at the sound of the bell. He heard voices and movements without, and then the door was quietly opened.

"I am awake," he said. "You see, I have taken you at your word, and come back to be patched up."

"You are heartily welcome," Mrs. Dowsett said. "Nellie, bring the light. Cyril is awake. We were sorry indeed when John told us that you had come in our absence. It was but a cold welcome for you to find that we were all out."

"There was nothing I needed, madam. Had there been, John would have done it for me."

Nellie now appeared at the door with the light, and gave an exclamation of horror as she approached the bedside.

"It is not so bad as it looks, Nellie," Cyril said. "Not that I know how it looks, for I have not seen myself in a glass since I left here; but I can guess that I am an unpleasant object to look at."

Mrs. Dowsett made a sign to Nellie to be silent.

"John told us that you were badly burned and were all wrapped up in bandages, but we did not expect to find you so changed. However, that will soon pass off, I hope."

"I expect I shall be all right in another week, save for this wound in my shoulder. As for that on my head, it is but of slight consequence. My skull was thick enough to save my brain."

"Well, Master Cyril," Captain Dave said heartily, as he entered the room with a basin of broth in his hand, and then stopped abruptly.

"Well, Captain Dave, here I am, battered out of all shape, you see, but not seriously damaged in my timbers. There, you see, though I have only been a fortnight at sea, I am getting quite nautical."

"That is right, lad—that is right," Captain Dave said, a little unsteadily. "My dame and Nellie will soon put you into ship-shape trim again. So you got burnt, I hear, by one of those rascally Dutch fire-ships? and John tells me that the captain of the sailors who carried you here said that you had gained mighty credit for yourself."

"I did my best, as every one did, Captain Dave. There was not a man on board the Fleet who did not do his duty, or we should never have beaten the Dutchmen so soundly."

"You had better not talk any more," Mrs. Dowsett said. "You are in my charge now, and my first order is that you must keep very quiet, or else you will be having fever come on. You had best take a little of this broth now. Nellie will sit with you while I go out to prepare you a cooling drink."

"I will take a few spoonfuls of the soup since John has taken the trouble to prepare it for me," Cyril said; "though, indeed, my lips are so parched and swollen that the cooling drink will be much more to my taste."

"I think it were best first, dame," the Captain said, "that John and I should get him comfortably into bed, instead of lying there wrapped up in the blanket in which they brought him ashore. The broth will be none the worse for cooling a bit."

"That will be best," his wife agreed. "I will fetch some more pillows, so that we can prop him up. He can swallow more comfortably so, and will sleep all the better when he lies down again."

As soon as Cyril was comfortably settled John Wilkes was sent to call in a doctor, who, after examining him, said that the burns were doing well, and that he would send in some cooling lotion to be applied to them frequently. As to the wounds, he said they had been so skilfully bandaged that it were best to leave them alone, unless great pain set in.

Another four days, and Cyril's face had so far recovered its usual condition that the swelling was almost abated, and the bandages could be removed. The peak of the helmet had sheltered it a good deal, and it had suffered less than his hands and arms. Captain Dave and John had sat up with him by turns at night, while the Dame and her daughter had taken care of him during the day. He had slept a great deal and had not been allowed to talk at all. This prohibition was now removed, as the doctor said that the burns were now all healing fast, and that he no longer had any fear of fever setting in.

"By the way, Captain," John Wilkes said, that day, at dinner, "I have just bethought me of this letter, that was given me by the sailor who brought Cyril here. It is for you, from young Lord Oliphant. It has clean gone out of my mind till now. I put it in the pocket of my doublet, and have forgotten it ever since."

"No harm can have come of the delay, John," Captain Dave said. "It was thoughtful of the lad. He must have been sure that Cyril would not be in a condition to tell us aught of the battle, and he may have sent us some details of it, for the Gazette tells us little enough, beyond the ships taken and the names of gentlemen and officers killed. Here, Nellie, do you read it. It seems a long epistle, and my eyes are not as good as they were."

Nellie took the letter and read aloud:—

"'DEAR AND WORTHY SIR,—I did not think when I was so pleasantly entertained at your house that it would befall me to become your correspondent, but so it has happened, for, Sir Cyril being sorely hurt, and in no state to tell you how the matter befell him—if indeed his modesty would allow him, which I greatly doubt—it is right that you should know how the business came about, and what great credit Sir Cyril has gained for himself. In the heat of the fight, when we were briskly engaged in exchanging broadsides with a Dutchman of our own size, one of their fire-ships, coming unnoticed through the smoke, slipped alongside of us, and, the flames breaking out, would speedily have destroyed us, as indeed they went near doing. The grapnels were briskly thrown over, but she had already touched our sides, and the flames were blowing across us when Sir Cyril, perceiving that she had still some way on her, sprang down on to her deck and put over the helm. She was then a pillar of flame, and the decks, which were plentifully besmeared with pitch, were all in a blaze, save just round the tiller where her captain had stood to steer her. It was verily a furnace, and it seemed impossible that one could stand there for only half a minute and live. Every one on board was filled with astonishment, and the Prince called out loudly that he had never seen a braver deed. As the fire-ship drew away from us, we saw Sir Cyril fasten the helm down with a rope, and then, lowering a bucket over, throw water on to it; then he threw off his helmet and armour—his clothes being, by this time, all in a flame—and sprang into the sea, the fire-ship being now well nigh her own length from us. She had sheered off none too soon, for some of our sails were on fire, and it was with great difficulty that we succeeded in cutting them from the yards and so saving the ship.

"'All, from the Prince down, say that no finer action was ever performed, and acknowledge that we all owe our lives, and His Majesty owes his ship, to it. Then, soon after we had hauled Sir Cyril on board, the Dutchmen boarded us, and there was a stiff fight, all hands doing their best to beat them back, in which we succeeded.

"'Sir Cyril, though scarce able to stand, joined in the fray, unnoticed by us all, who in the confusion had not thought of him, and being, indeed, scarce able to hold his sword, received a heavy wound, of which, however, the doctor has all hopes that he will make a good recovery.

"'It would have done you good to hear how the whole crew cheered Sir Cyril as we dragged him on board. The Prince is mightily taken with him, and is sending him to London in his own yacht, where I feel sure that your good dame and fair daughter will do all that they can to restore him to health. As soon as I get leave—though I do not know when that will be, for we cannot say as yet how matters will turn out, or what ships will keep the sea—I shall do myself the honour of waiting upon you. I pray you give my respectful compliments to Mrs. Dowsett and Mistress Nellie, who are, I hope, enjoying good health.

"'Your servant to command,
"'SYDNEY OLIPHANT.'"

The tears were standing in Nellie's eyes, and her voice trembled as she read. When she finished she burst out crying.

"There!" John Wilkes exclaimed, bringing his fist down upon the table. "I knew, by what that skipper said, the lad had been doing something quite out of the way, but when I spoke to him about it before you came in he only said that he had tried his best to do his duty, just as every other man in the Fleet had done. Who would have thought, Captain Dave, that that quiet young chap, who used to sit down below making out your accounts, was going to turn out a hero?"

"Who, indeed?" the Captain said, wiping his eyes with the back of his hands. "Why, he wasn't more than fifteen then, and, as you say, such a quiet fellow. He used to sit there and write, and never speak unless I spoke to him. 'Tis scarce two years ago, and look what he has done! Who would have thought it? I can't finish my breakfast," he went on, getting up from his seat, "till I have gone in and shaken him by the hand."

"You had better not, David," Mrs. Dowsett said gently. "We had best say but little to him about it now. We can let him know we have heard how he came by his burns from Lord Oliphant, but do not let us make much of it. Had he wished it he would have told us himself."

Captain Dave sat down again.

"Perhaps you are right, my dear. At any rate, till he is getting strong we will not tell him what we think of him. Anyhow, it can't do any harm to tell him we know it, and may do him good, for it is clear he does not like telling it himself, and may be dreading our questioning about the affair."

Mrs. Dowsett and Nellie went into Cyril's room as soon as they had finished breakfast. Captain Dave followed them a few minutes later.

"We have been hearing how you got burnt," he began. "Your friend, Lord Oliphant, sent a letter about it by the skipper of his yacht. That stupid fellow, John, has been carrying it about ever since, and only remembered it just now, when we were at breakfast. It was a plucky thing to do, lad."

"It turned out a very lucky one," Cyril said hastily, "for it was the means of saving my life."

"Saving your life, lad! What do you mean?"

Cyril then told how Robert Ashford and Black Dick had been brought on board as impressed men, how the former had been killed, and the confession that Black Dick had made to him before dying.

"He said he had made up his mind to kill me during the fight, but that, after I had risked my life to save the *Henrietta*, he was ashamed to kill me, and that, rather than do so, he had resolved to take his chance of my denouncing him when he returned to land."

"There was some good in the knave, then," Captain Dave said. "Yes, it was a fortunate as well as a brave action, as it turned out."

"Fortunate in one respect, but not in another," Cyril put in, anxious to prevent the conversation reverting to the question of his bravery. "I put down this wound in my shoulder to it, for if I had been myself I don't think I should have got hurt. I guarded the blow, but I was so shaky that he broke my guard down as if I had been a child, though I think that it did turn the blow a little, and saved it from falling fair on my skull. Besides, I should have had my helmet and armour on if it had not been for my having to take a swim. So, you see, Captain Dave, things were pretty equally balanced, and there is no occasion to say anything more about them."

"We have one piece of bad news to tell you, Cyril," Mrs. Dowsett remarked, in order to give the conversation the turn which she saw he wished for. "We heard this morning that the Plague has come at last into the City. Dr. Burnet was attacked yesterday."

"That is bad news indeed, Dame, though it was not to be expected that it would spare the City. If you will take my advice, you will go away at once, before matters get worse, for if the Plague gets a hold here the country people will have nothing to do with Londoners, fearing that they will bring the infection among them."

"We shall not go until you are fit to go with us, Cyril," Nellie said indignantly.

"Then you will worry me into a fever," Cyril replied. "I am getting on well now, and as you said, when you were talking of it before, you should leave John in charge of the house and shop, he will be able to do everything that is necessary for me. If you stay here, and the Plague increases, I shall keep on worrying myself at the thought that you are risking your lives needlessly for me, and if it should come into the house, and any of you die, I shall charge myself all my life with having been the cause of your death. I pray you, for my sake as well as your own, to lose no time in going to the sister Captain Dave spoke of, down near Gloucester."

"Do not agitate yourself," Mrs. Dowsett said gently, pressing him quietly back on to the pillows from which he had risen in his excitement. "We will talk it over, and see what is for the best. It is but a solitary case yet, and may spread no further. In a few days we shall see how matters go. Things have not come to a bad pass yet."

Cyril, however, was not to be consoled. Hitherto he had given comparatively small thought to the Plague, but now that it was in the City, and he felt that his presence alone prevented the family from leaving, he worried incessantly over it.

"Your patient is not so well," the doctor said to Mrs. Dowsett, next morning. "Yesterday he was quite free from fever—his hands were cool; now they are dry and hard. If this goes on, I fear that we shall have great trouble."

"He is worrying himself because we do not go out of town.

We had, indeed, made up our minds to do so, but we could not leave him here."

"Your nursing would be valuable certainly, but if he goes on as he is he will soon be in a high fever; his wounds will grow angry and fester. While yesterday he seemed in a fair way to recovery, I should be sorry to give any favourable opinion as to what may happen if this goes on. Is there no one who could take care of him if you went?"

"John Wilkes will remain behind, and could certainly be trusted to do everything that you directed; but that is not like women, doctor."

"No, I am well aware of that; but if things go on well he will really not need nursing, while, if fever sets in badly, the best nursing may not save him. Moreover, wounds and all other ailments of this sort do badly at present; the Plague in the air seems to affect all other maladies. If you will take my advice, Dame, you will carry out your intention, and leave at once. I hear there are several new cases of the Plague to-day in the City, and those who can go should lose no time in doing so; but, even if not for your own sakes, I should say go for that of your patient."

"Will you speak to my husband, doctor? I am ready to do whatever is best for your patient, whom we love dearly, and regard almost as a son."

"If he were a son I should give the same advice. Yes, I will see Captain Dowsett."

Half an hour later, Cyril was told what the doctor's advice had been, and, seeing that he was bent on it, and that if they stayed they would do him more harm than good, they resolved to start the next day for Gloucestershire.

CHAPTER XV.

THE PLAGUE.

RELUCTANT as they were to leave Cyril, Mrs. Dowsett and her daughter speedily saw that the doctor's advice was good. Cyril did not say much, but an expression of restful satisfaction came over his face, and it was not long before he fell into a quiet sleep that contrasted strongly with the restless and fretful state in which he had passed the night.

"You see I was right, madam," the doctor said that evening. "The fever has not quite left him, but he is a different man to what he was this morning; another quiet night's rest, and he will regain the ground he has lost. I think you can go in perfect comfort so far as he is concerned. Another week and he will be up, if nothing occurs to throw him back again; but of course it will be weeks before he can use his arm."

John Wilkes had been sent off as soon as it was settled that they would go, and had bought, at Epping, a waggon and a pair of strong horses. It had a tilt, and the ladies were to sleep in it on the journey, as it was certain that, until they were far away from London, they would be unable to obtain lodgings. A man was engaged to drive them down, and a sail and two or three poles were packed in the waggon to make a tent for him and Captain Dowsett. A store of provisions was cooked, and a cask of beer, another of water, and a case of wine, were also placed in. Mattresses were laid down for the ladies to sit on during the day and to sleep on at night; so they would be practically independent during the journey. Early next morning they started.

"It seems heartless to leave you, Cyril," Nellie said, as they came in to say good-bye.

"Not heartless at all," Cyril replied. "I know that you are going because I wish it."

"It is more than wishing, you tiresome boy. We are going

because you have made up your mind that you will be ill if we don't. You are too weak to quarrel with now, but when we meet again, tremble, for I warn you I shall scold you terribly then."

"You shall scold me as much as you please, Nellie; I shall take it all quite patiently."

Nellie and her mother went away in tears, and Captain Dave himself was a good deal upset. They had thought the going away from home on such a long journey would be a great trial, but this was now quite lost sight of in their regret at what they considered deserting Cyril, and many were the injunctions that were given to John Wilkes before the waggon drove off. They were somewhat consoled by seeing that Cyril was undoubtedly better and brighter. He had slept all night without waking, his hands were cool, and the flush had entirely left his cheek.

"If they were starting on a voyage to the Indies they could not be in a greater taking," John Wilkes said, on returning to Cyril's bedside. "Why, I have seen the Captain go off on a six months' voyage and less said about it."

"I am heartily glad they are gone, John. If the Plague grows there will be a terrible time here. Is the shop shut?"

"Ay; the man went away two days ago, and we sent off the two 'prentices yesterday. There is naught doing. Yesterday half the vessels in the Pool cleared out on the news of the Plague having got into the City, and I reckon that, before long, there won't be a ship in the port. We shall have a quiet time of it, you and I; we shall be like men in charge of an old hulk."

Another week, and Cyril was up. All his bandages, except those on the shoulder and head, had been thrown aside, and the doctor said that, ere long, the former would be dispensed with. John had wanted to sit up with him, but as Cyril would not hear of this he had moved his bed into the same room, so that he could be up in a moment if anything was wanted. He went out every day to bring in the news.

"There is little enough to tell, Master Cyril," he said one day. "So far, the Plague grows but slowly in the City, though, indeed, it is no fault of the people that it does not spread rapidly. Most of them seem scared out of their wits; they gather together and talk, with white faces, and one man tells of a dream that his wife has had, and another of a voice that he says he has heard; and some have seen ghosts. Yesterday I came upon a woman with a crowd round her; she was staring up at a white cloud, and swore that she could plainly see an angel with a white sword, and some of the others cried that they saw it too. I should like to have been a gunner's mate with a stout rattan, and to have laid it over their shoulders, to give them something else to think about for a few hours. It is downright pitiful to see such cowards. At the corner of one street there was a quack, vending pills and perfumes that he warranted to keep away the Plague, and the people ran up and bought his nostrums by the score; I hear there are a dozen such in the City, making a fortune out of the people's fears. I went into the tavern I always use, and had a glass of Hollands and a talk with the landlord. He says that he does as good a trade as ever, though in a different way. There are no sailors there now, but neighbours come in and drink down a glass of strong waters, which many think is the best thing against the Plague, and then hurry off again. I saw the Gazette there, and it was half full of advertisements of people who said they were doctors from foreign parts, and all well accustomed to cure the Plague. They say the magistrates are going to issue notices about shutting up houses, as they do at St. Giles's, and to have watchmen at the doors to see none come in or go out, and that they are going to appoint examiners in every parish to go from house to house to search for infected persons."

"I suppose these are proper steps to take," Cyril said, "but it will be a difficult thing to keep people shut up in houses where one is infected. No doubt it would be a good thing at the commencement of the illness, but when it has once spread itself, and the very air become infected, it seems to me that it will do but little good, while it will assuredly cause great distress and trouble. I long to be able to get up myself, and to see about things."

"The streets have quite an empty aspect, so many have gone away; and what with that, and most of the shops being closed, and the dismal aspect of the people, there is little pleasure in being out, Master Cyril."

"I daresay, John. Still, it will be a change, and, as soon as I am strong enough, I shall sally out with you."

Another fortnight, and Cyril was able to do so. The Plague had still spread, but so slowly that people began to hope that the City would be spared any great calamity, for they were well on in July, and in another six weeks the heat of summer would be passed. Some of those who had gone into the country returned, more shops had been opened, and the panic had somewhat subsided.

"What do you mean to do, Master Cyril?" John Wilkes asked that evening. "Of course you cannot join the Fleet again, for it will be, as the doctor says, another two months before your shoulder-bone will have knit strongly enough for you to use your arm, and at sea it is a matter of more consequence than on land for a man to have the use of both arms. The ship may give a sudden lurch, and one may have to make a clutch at whatever is nearest to prevent one from rolling into the lee scuppers; and such a wrench as that would take from a weak arm all the good a three months' nursing had done it, and might spoil the job of getting the bone to grow straight again altogether. I don't say you are fit to travel yet, but you should be able before long to start on a journey, and might travel down into Gloucestershire, where, be sure, you will be gladly welcomed by the Captain, his dame, and Mistress Nellie. Or, should you not care for that, you might go aboard a ship. There are hundreds of them lying idle in the river, and many families have taken up their homes there, so as to be free from all risks of meeting infected persons in the streets."

"I think I shall stay here, John, and keep you company. If the Plague dies away, well and good. If it gets bad, we can shut ourselves up. You say that the Captain has laid in a great store of provisions, so that you could live without laying out a penny for a year, and it is as sure as anything can be, that when the cold weather comes on it will die out. Besides, John, neither you nor I are afraid of the Plague, and it is certain that it is fear that makes most people take it. If it becomes bad, there will be terrible need for help, and maybe we shall be able to do some good. If we are not afraid of facing death in battle, why should we fear it by the Plague. It is as noble a death to die helping one's fellow-countrymen in their sore distress as in fighting for one's country."

"That is true enough, Master Cyril, if folks did but see it so. I do not see what we could do, but if there be aught, you can depend on me. I was in a ship in the Levant when we had a fever, which, it seems to me, was akin to this Plague, though not like it in all its symptoms. Half the crew died, and, as you say, I verily believe that it was partly from the lowness of spirits into which they fell from fear. I used to help nurse the sick, and throw overboard the dead, and it never touched me. I don't say that I was braver than others, but it seemed to me as it was just as easy to take things comfortable as it was to fret over them."

Towards the end of the month the Plague spread rapidly, and all work ceased in the parishes most affected. But, just as it had raged for weeks in the Western parishes outside the City, so it seemed restricted by certain invisible lines, after it had made its entry within the walls, and while it raged in some parts others were entirely unaffected, and here shops were open, and the streets still retained something of their usual appearance. There had been great want among the poorer classes, owing to the cessation of work, especially along the riverside. The Lord Mayor, some of the Aldermen, and most other rich citizens, had hastened to leave the City.

While many of the clergy were deserting their flocks, and many doctors their patients, others remained firmly at their posts, and worked incessantly, and did all that was possible in order to check the spread of the Plague and to relieve the distress of the poor.

Numbers of the women were engaged as nurses. Examiners were appointed in each parish, and these, with their assistants, paid house-to-house visitations, in order to discover any who were infected; and as soon as the case was discovered the house was closed, and none suffered to go in or out, a watchman being placed before the door day and night. Two men therefore were needed to each infected house, and this afforded employment for numbers of poor. Others were engaged in digging graves, or in going round at night, with carts, collecting the dead.

So great was the dread of the people at the thought of being shut up in their houses, without communication with the world, that every means was used for concealing the fact that one of the inmates was smitten down. This was the more easy because the early stages of the disease were without pain, and people were generally ignorant that they had been attacked until within a few hours, and sometimes within a few minutes, of their death; consequently, when the Plague had once spread, all the precautions taken to prevent its increase were useless, while they caused great misery and suffering, and doubtless very much greater loss of life. For, owing to so many being shut up in the houses with those affected, and there being no escape from the infection, whole families, with the servants and apprentices, sickened and died together.

Cyril frequently went up to view the infected districts. He was not moved by curiosity, but by a desire to see if there were no way of being of use. There was not a street but many of the houses were marked with the red cross. In front of these the watchmen sat on stools or chairs lent by the inmates, or borrowed from some house whence the inhabitants had all fled. The air rang with pitiful cries.

Sometimes women, distraught with terror or grief, screamed wildly through open windows. Sometimes people talked from the upper stories to their neighbours on either hand, or opposite, prisoners like themselves, each telling their lamentable tale of misery, of how many had died and how many remained.

It was by no means uncommon to see on the pavement men and women who, in the excess of despair or pain, had thrown themselves headlong down. While such sounds and sights filled Cyril with horror, they aroused still more his feelings of pity and desire to be of some use. Very frequently he went on errands for people who called down from above to him. Money was lowered in a tin dish, or other vessel, in which it lay covered with vinegar as a disinfectant. Taking it out, he would go and buy the required articles, generally food or medicine, and, returning, place them in a basket that was again lowered.

The watchmen mostly executed these commissions, but many of them were surly fellows, and, as they were often abused and cursed by those whom they held prisoners, would do but little for them. They had, moreover, an excuse for refusing to leave the door, because, as often happened, it might be opened in their absence and the inmates escape. It was true that the watchmen had the keys, but the screws were often drawn from the locks inside; and so frequently was this done that at last chains with padlocks were fastened to all the doors as soon as the watch was set over them. But even this did not avail. Many of the houses had communications at the backs into other streets, and so eluded the vigilance of the watch; while, in other cases, communications were broken through the walls into other houses, empty either by desertion or death, and the escape could thus be made under the very eye of the watchman.

Very frequently Cyril went into a church when he saw the door open. Here very small congregations would be gathered, for there was a fear on the part of all of meeting with strangers, for these might, unknown to themselves, be already stricken with the pest, and all public meetings of any kind were, for this reason, strictly forbidden. One day, he was passing a church that had hitherto been always closed, its incumbent being one of those who had fled at the outbreak of the Plague. Upon entering he saw a larger congregation than usual, some twenty or thirty people being present.

The minister had just mounted the pulpit, and was beginning his address as Cyril entered. The latter was struck with his appearance. He was a man of some thirty years of age, with a strangely earnest face. His voice was deep, but soft and flexible, and in the stillness of the almost empty church its lowest tones seemed to come with impressive power, and Cyril thought that he had never heard such preaching before. The very text seemed strange at such a time: "*Rejoice ye, for the kingdom of heaven is at hand.*" From most of the discourses he had heard Cyril had gone out depressed rather than inspirited. They had been pitched in one tone. The terrible scourge that raged round them was held up as a punishment sent by the wrath of God upon a sinful people, and the congregation were warned to prepare themselves for the fate, that might at any moment be theirs, by repentance and humiliation. The preacher to whom Cyril was now listening spoke in an altogether different strain.

"You are all soldiers of Christ," he said, "and now is an opportunity given to you to show that you are worthy soldiers. When the troops of a worldly monarch go in to battle they do so with head erect, with proud and resolute bearing, with flashing eye, and with high courage, determined to bear aloft his banner and to crown it with victory, even though it cost them their lives. Such is the mien that soldiers of Christ should bear in the mortal strife now raging round us. Let them show the same fearlessness of death, the same high courage, the same unlimited confidence in their Leader. What matter if they die in His service? He has told them what their work should be. He has bidden them visit the sick and comfort the sorrowing. What if there be danger in the work?

Did He shrink from the Cross which was to end His work of love, and is it for His followers to do so? 'Though you go down into the pit,' He has said, 'I am there also'; and with His companionship one must be craven indeed to tremble. This is a noble opportunity for holding high the banner of Christ. There is work to be done for all, and as the work is done, men should see by the calm courage, the cheerfulness, and the patience of those that do it, that they know that they are doing His work, and that they are content to leave the issue, whatever it be, in His hands."

Such was the tone in which, for half an hour, he spoke. When he had finished he offered up a prayer, gave the blessing, and then came down from the pulpit and spoke to several of the congregation. He was evidently personally known to most of them. One by one, after a few words, they left the church. Cyril remained to the last.

"I am willing to work, sir," he said, as the preacher came up, " but, so far, no work has come in my way."

" Have you father or mother, or any dependent on you?"

" No one, sir."

"Then come along with me; I lodge close by. I have eaten nothing to-day, and must keep up my strength, and I have a long round of calls to make."

"This is the first time I have seen the church open," Cyril said, as they went out.

" It is not my church, sir, nor do I belong to the Church of England; I am an Independent. But as many of the pastors have fled and left their sheep untended, so have we—for there are others besides myself who have done so—taken possession of their empty pulpits, none gainsaying us, and are doing what good we can. You have been in the war, I see," he went on, glancing at Cyril's arm, which was carried in a sling.

"Yes; I was at the battle of Lowestoft, and having been wounded there, came to London to stay in a friend's house till I was cured. He and his family have left, but I am living with a trusty foreman who is in charge of the house. I have a great desire to be useful. I myself have little fear of the plague."

"That is the best of all preservatives from its ravages, although not a sure one; for many doctors who have laboured fearlessly have yet died. Have you thought of any way of being useful?"

"No, sir; that is what is troubling me. As you see, I have but the use of one arm, and I have not got back my full strength by a long way."

"Every one can be useful if he chooses," the minister said. "There is need everywhere among this stricken, frightened, helpless people, of men of calm courage and cool heads. Nine out of ten are so scared out of their senses, when once the Plague enters the houses, as to be well nigh useless, and yet the law hinders those who would help if they could. I am compelled to labour, not among those who are sick, but among those who are well. When one enters a house with the red cross on the door, he may leave it no more until he is either borne out to the dead-cart, or the Plague has wholly disappeared within it, and a month has elapsed. The sole exception are the doctors; they are no more exempt from spreading the infection than other men, but as they must do their work so far as they can they have free passage; and yet, so few is their number and so heavy already their losses, that not one in a hundred of those that are smitten can have their aid. Here is one coming now, one of the best—Dr. Hodges. If you are indeed willing so to risk your life, I will speak to him. But I know not your name?"

"My name is Cyril Shenstone."

The clergyman looked at him suddenly, and would have spoken, but the doctor was now close to them.

"Ah! Mr. Wallace," he said, "I am glad to see you, and to know that, so far, you have not taken the disease, although constantly going into the worst neighbourhoods."

"Like yourself, Dr. Hodges, I have no fear of it."

"I do not say I have no fear," the doctor replied. "I do my

duty so far as I can, but I do not doubt that, sooner or later, I shall catch the malady, as many of us have done already. I take such precautions as I can, but the distemper seems to baffle all precautions. My only grief is that our skill avails so little. So far we have found nothing that seems to be of any real use. Perhaps if we could attack it in the earlier stages we might be more successful. The strange nature of the disease, and the way in which it does its work well-nigh to the end, before the patient is himself aware of it, puts it out of our power to combat it. In many cases I am not sent for until the patient is at the point of death, and by the time I reach his door I am met with the news that he is dead. But I must be going."

"One moment, Dr. Hodges. This young gentleman has been expressing to me his desire to be of use. I know nothing of him save that he was one of my congregation this morning, but, as he fears not the Plague, and is moved by a desire to help his fellows in distress, I take it that he is a good youth. He was wounded in the battle of Lowestoft, and, being as ready to encounter the Plague as he was the Dutch, would now fight in the cause of humanity. Would you take him as an assistant? I doubt if he knows anything of medicine, but I think he is one that would see your orders carried out. He has no relations or friends, and therefore considers himself free to venture his life."

The doctor looked earnestly at Cyril and then raised his hat.

"Young sir," he said, "since you are willing so to venture your life, I will gladly accept your help. There are few enough clear heads in this city, God knows. As for the nurses, they are Jezebels. They have the choice of starving or nursing, and they nurse; but they neglect their patients, they rob them, and there is little doubt that in many cases they murder them, so that at the end of their first nursing they may have enough money to live on without going to another house. But I am pressed for time. Here is my card. Call on me this evening at six, and we will talk further on the matter."

Shaking hands with the minister he hurried away.

"Come as far as my lodgings," Mr. Wallace said to Cyril, "and stay with me while I eat my meal. 'Tis a diversion to one's mind to turn for a moment from the one topic that all men are speaking of.

"Your name is Shenstone. I come from Norfolk. There was a family of that name formerly had estates near my native place. One Sir Aubrey Shenstone was at its head—a brave gentleman. I well remember seeing him when I was a boy, but he took the side of the King against the Parliament, and, as we heard, passed over with Charles to France when his cause was lost. I have not heard of him since."

"Sir Aubrey was my father," Cyril said quietly; "he died a year ago. I am his only son."

"And therefore Sir Cyril," the minister said, "though you did not so name yourself."

"It was needless," Cyril said. "I have no estates to support my title, and though it is true that, when at sea with Prince Rupert, I was called Sir Cyril, it was because the Prince had known my father, and knew that I, at his death, inherited the title, though I inherited nothing else."

They now reached the door of Mr. Wallace's lodging, and went up to his room on the first floor.

"Neglect no precaution," the minister said. "No one should throw away his life. I myself, although not a smoker, nor accustomed to take snuff, use it now, and would, as the doctors advise, chew a piece of tobacco, but 'tis too nasty, and when I tried it, I was so ill that I thought even the risk of the Plague preferable. But I carry camphor in my pockets, and when I return from preaching among people of whom some may well have the infection, I bathe my face and hands with vinegar, and, pouring some on to a hot iron, fill the room with its vapour. My life is useful, I hope, and I would fain keep it, as long as it is the Lord's will, to work in His service. As a rule, I take wine and bread before I go out in the morning, though to-day I was pressed for time, and neglected it. I should advise you always to do so. I am convinced that a full man has less chance of catching the infection than a fasting one, and that it is the weakness many men suffer from their fears, and from their loss of appetite from grief, that causes them to take it so easily. When the fever was so bad in St. Giles's, I heard that in many instances, where whole families were carried away, the nurses shut up with them were untouched with the infection, and I believe that this was because they had become hardened to the work, and ate and drank heartily, and troubled not themselves at all at the grief of those around them. They say that many of these harpies have grown wealthy, loading themselves with everything valuable they could lay hands on in the houses of those they attended."

After the meal, in which he insisted upon Cyril joining him, was concluded, Mr. Wallace uttered a short prayer that Cyril might safely pass through the work he had undertaken.

"I trust," he said, "that you will come here frequently? I generally have a few friends here of an evening. We try to be cheerful, and to strengthen each other, and I am sure we all have comfort at these meetings."

"Thank you, I will come sometimes, sir; but as a rule I must return home, for my friend, John Wilkes, would sorely miss my company, and is so good and faithful a fellow that I would not seem to desert him on any account."

"Do as you think right, lad, but remember there will always be a welcome for you here when you choose to come."

John Wilkes was dismayed when he heard of Cyril's intention.

"Well, Master Cyril," he said, after smoking his pipe in silence for some time, "it is not for me to hinder you in what you have made up your mind to do. I don't say that if I wasn't on duty here that I mightn't go and do what I could for these poor creatures. But I don't know. It is one thing to face a deadly fever like this Plague if it comes on board your own ship, for there is no getting out of it; and as you have got to face it, why, says I, do it as a man; but as for going out of your way to put yourself in the middle of it, that is going a bit beyond me."

"Well, John, you didn't think it foolish when I went as a Volunteer to fight the Dutch. It was just the same thing, you know."

"I suppose it was," John said reluctantly, after a pause. "But then, you see, you were fighting for your country."

"Well, but in the present case I shall be fighting for my countrymen and countrywomen, John. It is awful to think of the misery that people are suffering, and it seems to me that, having nothing else to do here, it is specially my duty to put my hand to the work of helping as far as I can. The risk may, at present, be greater than it would be if I stayed at home, but if the Plague spreads—and it looks as if all the City would presently be affected—all will have to run the risk of contagion. There are thousands of women now who voluntarily enter the houses as nurses for a small rate of pay. Even robbers, they say, will enter and ransack the houses of the dead in search of plunder. It will be a shame indeed then if one should shrink from doing so when possibly one might do good."

"I will say nothing more against it, Master Cyril. Still, I do not see exactly what you are going to do; with one arm you could scarce hold down a raving man."

"I am not going to be a nurse, certainly, John," Cyril said, with a laugh. "I expect that the doctor wants certain cases watched. Either he may doubt the nurses, or he may want to see how some particular drug works. Nothing, so far, seems of use, but that may be partly because the doctors are all so busy that they cannot watch the patients and see, from hour to hour, how medicines act."

"When I was in the Levant, and the pest was bad there," John Wilkes said, "I heard that the Turks, when seized with the distemper, sometimes wrapped themselves up in a great number of clothes, so that they sweated heavily, and that this seemed, in some cases, to draw off the fever, and so the patient recovered."

"That seems a sensible sort of treatment, John, and worth trying with this Plague."

On calling on Dr. Hodges that afternoon, Cyril found that he had rightly guessed the nature of the work that the doctor wished him to perform.

"I can never rely upon the nurses," he said. "I give instructions with medicines, but in most cases I am sure that the instructions are never carried out. The relations and friends are too frightened to think or act calmly, too full of grief for the sick, and anxiety for those who have not yet taken the illness, to watch the changes in the patient. As to the nurses, they are often drunk the whole time they are in the house. Sometimes they fear to go near the sick man or woman; sometimes, undoubtedly, they hasten death. In most cases it matters little, for we are generally called in too late to be of any service. The poor people view us almost as enemies; they hide their malady from us in every way. Half our time, too, is wasted uselessly, for many are there who frighten themselves into the belief that they are ill, and send for us in all haste. So far, we feel that we are working altogether in the dark; none of us can see that any sort of drug avails even in the slightest degree when the malady has once got a hold. One in twenty cases may live, but why we know not. Still the fact that some do live shows that the illness is not necessarily mortal, and that, could the right remedy be found, we might yet overcome it. The first thing, however, is to try to prevent its spread. Here we have ten or more people shut up in a house with one sick person. It is a terrible necessity, for it is a sentence of death to many, if not to all. We give the nurses instructions to fumigate the room by evaporating vinegar upon hot irons, by burning spices and drugs, by sprinkling perfumes. So far, I cannot see that these measures have been of any service, but I cannot say how thoroughly they have been carried out, and I sorely need an assistant to see that the system is fairly tried. It is not necessary that he should be a doctor, but he must have influence and power over those in the house. He must be calm and firm, and he must be regarded by the people as a doctor. If you will undertake this, you must put on a wig, for you know that that is looked upon as a necessary part of a doctor's outfit by people in general. I shall introduce you as my assistant, and say that you are to be obeyed as implicitly as if I myself were present. There is another reason why you must pass as a doctor, for you would otherwise be a prisoner and unable to pass in and out. You had best wear a black suit. I will lend you one of my canes and a snuff-box, and should advise you to take snuff, even if it is not your habit, for I believe that it is good against infection, and one of the experiments I wish to try is as to what its result may be if burnt freely in the house. Are you ready to undertake this work?"

"Quite ready, sir."

"Then come round here at eight in the morning. I shall have heard by that hour from the examiners of this parish of any fresh case they have found. They begin their rounds at five o'clock."

The next day Cyril presented himself at the doctor's, dressed in black, with white ruffles to his shirt, and a flowing wig he had purchased the night before.

"Here are the cane and snuff-box," Dr. Hodges said. "Now you will pass muster very well as my assistant. Let us be off at once, for I have a long list of cases."

Cyril remained outside while Doctor Hodges went into three or four houses. Presently he came down to the door, and said to him,—

"This is a case where things are favourable for a first trial. It is a boy who is taken ill, and the parents, though in deep grief, seem to have some sense left."

He turned to the watchman, who had already been placed at the door. The man, who evidently knew him, had saluted respectfully when he entered the house.

"This gentleman is my assistant," he said, "and you will allow him to pass in and out just as you would myself. He is going to take this case entirely in hand, and you will regard him as being in charge here."

He then re-entered the house with Cyril, and led him to the room where the parents of the boy, and two elder sisters, were assembled.

"This is my assistant," he said, "and he has consented to take entire charge of the case, though I myself shall look in and consult with him every morning. In the first place, your son must be taken to the top storey of the house. You say that you are ready to nurse him yourselves, and do not wish that a paid nurse should be had in. I commend your determination, for the nurses are, for the most part, worse than useless, and carry the infection all over the house. But only one of you must go into the room, and whoever goes in must stay there. It is madness for all to be going in and out and exposing themselves to the infection when no good can be done. When this is the case, one or other is sure to take the malady, and then it spreads to all. Which of you will undertake the duty?"

All four at once offered themselves, and there was an earnest contest between them for the dangerous post. Dr. Hodges listened for a minute or two, and then decided upon the elder of the two sisters—a quiet, resolute-looking girl with a healthy face.

"This young lady shall be nurse," he said. "I feel that I can have confidence in her. She looks healthy and strong, and would, methinks, best resist the malady, should she take it. I am leaving my assistant here for a time to see to the fumigation of the house. You will please see that his orders are carried out in every respect. I have every hope that if this is done the Plague will not spread further; but much must depend upon yourselves. Do not give way to grief, but encourage each other, and go about with calm minds. I see," he said, pointing to a Bible on the table, "that you know where to go for comfort and strength. The first thing is to carry the boy up to the room that we chose for him."

"I will do that," the father said.

"He had better be left in the blankets in which he is lying. Cover him completely over with them, for, above all, it is necessary that you should not inhale his breath. You had better take the head and your daughter the feet. But first see that the room upstairs is prepared."

In a few minutes the lad was transferred to the upper room, the doctor warning the others not to enter that from which he had been carried until it had been fumigated and sprinkled with vinegar.

"Now," he said to the girl who was to remain with the patient, "keep the window wide open; as there is no fireplace, keep a brazier of charcoal burning near the window. Keep the door shut, and open it only when you have need for something. Give him a portion of this medicine every half hour. Do not lean over him—remember that his breath is a fatal poison. Put a pinch of these powdered spices into the fire every few minutes. Pour this perfume over your handkerchief, and put it over your mouth and nose whenever you approach the bed. He is in a stupor now, poor lad, and I fear that his chance of recovery is very slight; but you must remember that your own life is of value to your parents, and that it behoves you to do all in your power to preserve it, and that if you take the contagion it may spread through the house. We shall hang a sheet, soaked in vinegar, outside the door."

"We could not have a better case for a trial," he said, as he went downstairs and joined Cyril, whom he had bidden wait below. "The people are all calm and sensible, and if we succeed not here, there is small chance of our succeeding elsewhere."

The doctor then gave detailed orders as to fumigating the house, and left. Cyril saw at once that a brazier of charcoal was lighted and carried upstairs, and he called to the girl to come out and fetch it in. As soon as she had done so the sheet was hung over the door. Then he took another brazier, placed it in the room from which the boy had been carried, laid several lumps of sulphur upon it, and then left the room. All the doors of the other rooms were then thrown open, and a quantity of tobacco, spices, and herbs, were burnt on a red-hot iron at the foot of the stairs, until the house was filled with a dense smoke. Half an hour later all the windows were opened.

CHAPTER XVI.

FATHER AND SON.

THE process of fumigation had well nigh suffocated the wife and daughter of the trader, but, as soon as the smoke cleared away, Cyril set them all to work to carry up articles of furniture to another bedroom on the top floor.

"When your daughter is released from nursing, madam," he said, "she must at once come into this room, and remain there secluded for a few days. Therefore, it will be well to make it as comfortable as possible for her. Her food must be taken up and put outside the door, so that she can take it in there without any of you going near her."

The occupation was a useful one, as it distracted the thoughts of those engaged in it from the sick room.

Cyril did not enter there. He had told the girl to call him should there be any necessity, but said,—

"Do not call me unless absolutely needful, if, for instance, he becomes violent, in which case we must fasten the sheets across him so as to restrain him. But it is of no use your remaining shut up there if I go in and out of the room to carry the infection to the others."

"You have hurt your arm, doctor?" the mother said, when

the arrangements were all made, and they had returned to the room below.

"Yes," he said; "I met with an accident, and must, for a short time, keep my arm in a sling."

"You look young, sir, to be running these fearful perils."

"I am young," Cyril said, "and have not yet completed all my studies; but Dr. Hodges judged that I was sufficiently advanced to be able to be of service to him, not so much in prescribing as by seeing that his orders were carried out."

Every half hour he went upstairs, and inquired, through the door, as to the state of the boy.

Late in the afternoon he heard the girl crying bitterly within. He knocked, and she cried out,—

"He is dead, sir; he has just expired."

"Then you must think of yourself and the others," he said. "The small packet I placed on the chair contains sulphur. Close the window, then place the packet on the fire, and leave the room at once and go into the next room, which is all ready for you. There, I pray you, undress, and sponge yourself with vinegar, then make your clothes into a bundle and put them outside the door. There will be a bowl of hot broth in readiness for you there; drink that, and then go to bed at once, and keep the blankets over you and try to sleep."

He went part of the way downstairs, and, in a minute or two, heard a door open and shut, then another door shut. Knowing that the order had been carried out, he went downstairs.

"Madam," he said, "God has taken your boy. The doctor had but little hope for him. For the sake of yourself and those around you, I pray you all to bear up against the sorrow."

The mother burst into tears, and, leaving her with her husband and daughter, Cyril went into the kitchen, where the maid and an apprentice were sitting with pale faces, and bade the servant at once warm up the broth, that had already been prepared. As soon as it was ready, he carried a basin upstairs. The bundle of clothes had already been placed outside the girl's room. He took this down and put it on the kitchen fire.

"Now," he said, "take four basins up to the parlour, and do you and the boy each make a hearty meal. I think there is little fear of the Plague spreading, and your best chance of avoiding it is by keeping up your spirits and not fretting about it."

As soon as the broth had been taken into the parlour, he went in and persuaded them to eat and to take a glass of wine with it, while he himself sat down with them.

"You are all weak," he said, "for, doubtless, you have eaten nothing to-day, and you need strength as well as courage. I trust that your daughter will presently go off into a sound sleep. The last thing before you go to bed, take up with you a basin of good posset with a glass of wine in it; knock gently at her door; if she is awake, tell her to come out and take it in as soon as you have gone, but if she does not reply, do not rouse her. I can be of no further use to-night, but will return in the morning, when I hope to find all is well."

The father accompanied him to the door.

"You will of course bring the poor boy down to-night. It were best that you made some excuse to sleep in another room. Let your daughter sleep with her mother. When you go in to fetch him, be careful that you do not enter at once, for the fumes of the sulphur will scarcely have abated. As you go in, place a wet handkerchief to your mouth, and make to the window and throw it open, closing the door behind you. Sit at the window till the air is tolerable, then wrap the blankets round him and carry him downstairs when you hear the bell. After he has gone tell the servant to have a brazier lighted, and to keep up the kitchen fire. As soon as he is gone, burn on the brazier at the foot of the stairs, tobacco and spices, as we did before; then take off your clothes and burn them on the kitchen fire, and then go up to bed. You can leave the doors and windows of the rooms that are not in use open, so that the smoke may escape."

"God bless you, sir!" the man said. "You have been a comfort indeed to us, and I have good hopes that the Plague will spread no further among us."

Cyril went first to the doctor's, and reported what had taken place.

"I will go round in the morning and see how they are," he concluded, "and bring you round word before you start on your rounds."

"You have done very well indeed," the doctor said. "If people everywhere would be as calm, and obey orders as well as those you have been with, I should have good hopes that we might check the spread of the Plague; but you will find that they are quite the exception."

This, indeed, proved to be the case. In many instances, the people were so distracted with grief and fear that they ran about the house like mad persons, crying and screaming, running in and out of the sick chamber, or sitting there crying helplessly, and refusing to leave the body until it was carried out to the dead-cart. But with such cases Cyril had nothing to do, as the doctor would only send him to the houses where he saw that his instructions would be carried out.

To his great satisfaction, Cyril found that the precautions taken in the first case proved successful. Regularly, every morning, he inquired at the door, and received the answer, "All are well."

In August the Plague greatly increased in violence, the deaths rising to ten thousand a week. A dull despair had now seized the population. It seemed that all were to be swept away. Many went out of their minds. The quacks no longer drove a flourishing trade in their pretended nostrums; these were now utterly discredited, for nothing seemed of the slightest avail. Some went to the opposite extreme, and affected to defy fate. The taverns were filled again, and boisterous shouts and songs seemed to mock the dismal cries from the houses with the red cross on the door. Robberies were rife. Regardless of the danger of the pest, robbers broke into the houses where all the inmates had perished by the Plague, and rifled them of their valuables. The nurses plundered the dying. All natural affection seemed at an end. Those stricken were often deserted by all their relatives, and left alone to perish.

Bands of reckless young fellows went through the streets singing, and, dressing up in masks, performed the dance of death. The dead were too many to be carried away in carts at night to the great pits prepared for them, but the dismal tones of the bell, and the cries of "Bring out your dead!" sounded in the streets all day. It was no longer possible to watch the whole of the infected houses. Sometimes Plague-stricken men would escape from their beds and run through the streets until they dropped dead. One such man, in the height of his delirium, sprang into the river, and, after swimming about for some time, returned to the shore, marvellously cured of his malady by the shock.

Cyril went occasionally in the evening to the lodgings of Mr. Wallace. At first he met several people gathered there, but the number became fewer every time he went. He had told the minister that he thought that it would be better for him to stay away, exposed as he was to infection, but Mr. Wallace would take no excuses on this score.

"We are all in the hands of God," he said. "The streets are full of infected people, and I myself frequently go to pray with my friends in the earliest stages of the malady. There is no longer any use in precautions. We can but all go on doing our duty until we are called away, and even among the few who gather here of an evening there may be one or more who are already smitten, though unconscious yet that their summons has come."

Among others Cyril was introduced to a Mr. and Mrs. Harvey, who were, the minister told him, from the country, but were staying in town on account of a painful family business.

"I have tried to persuade them to return home and to stay there until the Plague ceases, but they conceive it their duty to remain. They are, like myself, Independents, and are not easily to be turned from a resolution they have taken."

Cyril could easily understand that Mr. Harvey was exactly what he, from the description he had heard of them, had pictured to himself that a Roundhead soldier would be. He had a stern face, eyes deeply sunk in his head, high cheekbones, a firm mouth, and a square jaw. He wore his hair cut close. His figure was bony, and he must, as a young man, have been very powerful. He spoke in a slow, deliberate way, that struck Cyril as being the result of long effort, for a certain restless action of the fingers and the quick movement of the eye, told of a naturally impulsive and fiery disposition. He constantly used scriptural texts in the course of his speech. His wife was gentle and quiet, but it was evident that there was a very strong sympathy between them, and Cyril found, after meeting them once or twice, that he liked them far better than he thought he should do on their first introduction. This was, no doubt, partly due to the fact that Mr. Harvey frequently entered into conversation with him, and appeared to interest himself in him. He was, too, a type that was altogether new to the lad. From his father, and his father's companions, he had heard nothing good of the Puritans, but the evident earnestness of this man's nature was, to some extent, in accordance with his own disposition, and he felt that, widely as he might differ from him on all points of politics, he could not but respect him. The evenings were pleasant. As if by common consent, the conversation never turned on the Plague, but they talked of other passing events, of the trials of their friends, and of the laws that were being put in force against Noncomformists.

"What think you of these persecutions, young sir?" Mr. Harvey abruptly asked Cyril, one evening, breaking off in the midst of a general conversation.

Cyril was a little confused at the unexpected question.

"I think all persecutions for conscience' sake are wrong," he said, after a moment's pause, "and generally recoil upon the persecutors. Spain lost Holland owing to her persecution of the people. France lost great numbers of her best citizens by her laws against the Protestants. I agree with you thoroughly, that the persecution of the Nonconformists at present is a grievous error, and a cruel injustice; but, at the same time, if you will excuse my saying so, it is the natural consequence of the persecution by the Nonconformists, when they were in power, of the ministers of the Church of England. My tutor in France was an English clergyman, who had been driven from his living, like thousands of other ministers, because he would not give up his opinions. Therefore, you see, I very early was imbued with a hatred of persecution in any form. I trust that I have not spoken too boldly; but you asked for my opinion, and I was forced to give it."

"At any rate, young sir, you have spoken manfully, and I like you none the worse for it. Nor can I altogether gainsay your words. But you must remember that we had before been oppressed, and that we have been engaged in a desperate struggle for liberty of conscience."

"Which, having won for ourselves, we proceeded to deny to others," Mr. Wallace said, with a smile. "Cyril has us fairly, Mr. Harvey. We are reaping what our fathers sowed. They thought that the power they had gained was to be theirs to hold always, and they used it tyrannously, being thereby false to all their principles. It is ever the persecuted, when he attains power, who becomes the persecutor, and, hard as is the pressure of the laws now, we should never forget that we have, in our time, been persecutors, and that in defiance of the rights of conscience we had fought to achieve. Man's nature is, I fear, unchangeable. The slave longs, above all things, for freedom, but when he rises successfully against his master he, in turn, becomes a tyrant, and not infrequently a cruel and bloodthirsty one. Still, we must hope. It may be in the good days that are to come, we may reach a point when each will be free to worship in his own fashion, without any fear or hindrance, recognising the fact that each has a right to follow his own path to Heaven, without its being a subject of offence to those who walk in other ways."

One or two of the other visitors were on the point of speaking, when Mr. Wallace put a stop to further argument by fetching a Bible from his closet, and preparing for the short service of prayer with which the evening always closed.

One evening, Mr. Harvey and his wife were absent from the usual gathering.

"I feel anxious about them," Mr. Wallace said; "they have never, since they arrived in town, missed coming here at seven o'clock. The bells are usually striking the hour as they come. I fear that one or other of them may have been seized by the Plague."

"With your permission, sir, I will run round and see," Cyril said. "I know their lodging, for I have accompanied them to the door several times. It is but five minutes' walk from here. If one or other is ill I will run round to Dr. Hodges, and I am sure, at my request, he will go round at once to see them."

Cyril walked fast towards the lodging occupied by the Harveys. It was at the house of a mercer, but he and his family had, three weeks before, gone away, having gladly permitted his lodgers to remain, as their presence acted as a guard to the house. They had brought up an old servant with them, and were therefore able to dispense with other attendants. Cyril hurried along, trying, as usual, to pay as little heed as he could to the doleful cries that arose from many of the houses. Although it was still broad daylight there was scarce a soul in the streets, and those he met were, like himself, walking fast, keeping as far as possible from any one they met, so as to avoid contact.

As he neared the house he heard a woman scream. A moment later a casement was thrown open, and Mrs. Harvey's head appeared. She gave another piercing cry for help, and was then suddenly dragged back, and the casement was violently closed. Cyril had so frequently heard similar cries that he would have paid no attention to it had it come from a stranger, but he felt that Mrs. Harvey was not one to give way to wild despair, even had her husband been suddenly attacked with the Plague. Her sudden disappearance, and the closing of the casement, too, were unaccountable, unless, indeed, her husband were in a state of violent delirium. He ran to the door and flung himself against it.

"Help me to force it down," he cried, to a man who was passing.

"You are mad," the man replied. "Do you not see that they have got the Plague? You may hear hundreds of such cries every day."

Cyril drew his sword, which he always carried when he went out of an evening—for, owing to the deaths among the City watch, deeds of lawlessness and violence were constantly perpetrated—and struck, with all his strength, with the hilt upon the fastening of the casement next the door. Several of the small panes of glass fell in, and the whole window shook. Again and again he struck upon the same spot, when the fastening gave way, and the window flew open. He sprang in at once, ran through the shop into the passage, and then upstairs. The door was open, and he nearly fell over the body of a man. As he ran into the room he heard the words,—

"For the last time: Will you sign the deed? You think I will not do this, but I am desperate."

As the words left his mouth, Cyril sprang forward between the man and Mr. Harvey, who was standing with his arms folded, looking steadfastly at his opponent, who was menacing him with a drawn sword. The man, with a terrible oath, turned to defend himself, repeating the oath when he saw who was his assailant.

"I let you off last time lightly, you scoundrel!" Cyril exclaimed. "This time it is your life or mine."

The man made a furious lunge at him. Cyril parried it, and would at the next moment have run him through had not

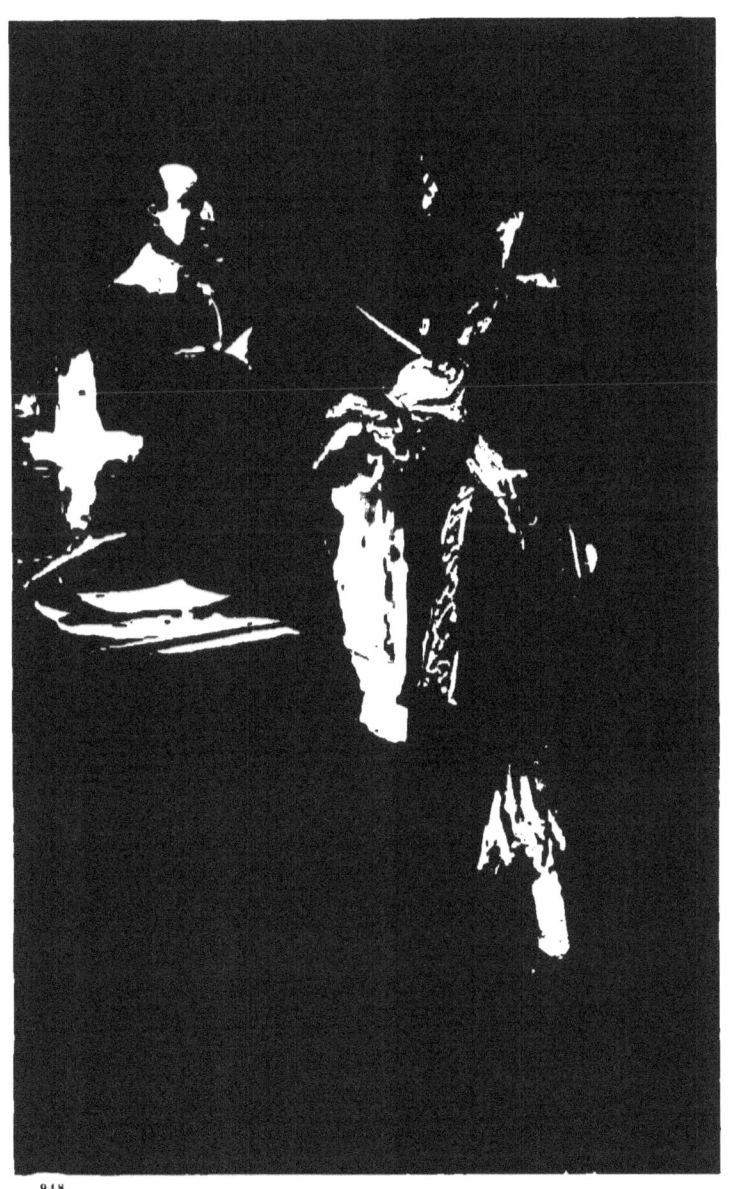

"FOR THE LAST TIME: WILL YOU SIGN THE DEED?"

Mr. Harvey suddenly thrown himself between them, hurling Cyril's antagonist to the ground.

"Put up your sword," he said to Cyril. "This man is my son; scoundrel and villain, yet still my son, even though he has raised his hand against me. Leave him to God."

Cyril had stepped a pace back in his surprise. At first he thought that Mr. Harvey's trouble had turned his brain; then it flashed across him that this ruffian's name was indeed John Harvey. The man was about to rise from the floor when Cyril again sprang forward.

"Drop that sword," he exclaimed, "or I will run you through. Now, sir," he said to Mr. Harvey, "will you draw out that pistol, whose butt projects from his pocket, or your son may do one of us mischief yet?"

That such had been the man's intention was evident from the glance of baffled rage he threw at Cyril.

"Now, sir, go," his father said sternly. "Remember that, henceforth, you are no son of mine. Did I do my duty I should hand you over to the watch—not for your threats to me, but for the sword-thrust you have given to Joseph Edmonds, who has many times carried you on his shoulder when a child. You may compass my death, but be assured that not one farthing will you gain thereby. 'Vengeance is mine, saith the Lord.' I leave it to Him to pay it. Now go."

John Harvey rose to his feet, and walked to the door. Then he turned and shook his fist at Cyril.

"Curse you!" he said. "I will be even with you yet."

Cyril now had time to look round. His eye fell upon the figure of Mrs. Harvey, who had fallen insensible. He made a step towards her, but her husband said, "She has but fainted. This is more pressing," and he turned to the old servant. Cyril aided him in lifting the old man up and laying him on the couch.

"He breathes," said he.

"He is wounded to death," Mr. Harvey said sadly; "and my son hath done it."

Cyril opened the servant's coat.

"Here is the wound, high up on the left side. It may not touch a vital part. It bleeds freely, and I have heard that that is a good sign."

"It is so," Mr. Harvey said excitedly. "Perhaps he may yet recover. I would give all that I am worth that it might be so, and that, bad as he may be, the sin of this murder should not rest on my son's soul."

"I will run for the doctor, sir, but before I go let me help you to lift your wife. She will doubtless come round shortly, and will aid you to stanch the wound till the doctor comes."

Mrs. Harvey was indeed already showing signs of returning animation. She was placed on a couch, and water sprinkled on her face. As soon as he saw her eyes open Cyril caught up his hat and ran to Dr. Hodges. The doctor had just finished his supper, and was on the point of going out again to see some of his patients. On hearing from Cyril that a servant of some friends of his had been wounded by a robber, he put some lint and bandages in his pocket, and started with him.

"These robberies are becoming more and more frequent," he said; "and so bold and reckless are the criminals that they seem to care not a jot whether they add murder to their other crimes. Where do you say the wound is?"

Cyril pointed below his own shoulder.

"It is just about there, doctor."

"Then it may be above the upper edge of the lung. If so, we may save the man. Half an inch higher or lower will make all the difference between life and death. As you say that it was bleeding freely, it is probable that the sword has missed the lung, for had it pierced it, the bleeding would have been chiefly internal, and the hope of saving him would have been slight indeed."

When they reached the house Cyril found that Mrs. Harvey had quite recovered. They had cut open the man's clothes and her husband was pressing a handkerchief, closely folded, upon the wound.

"It is serious, but, I think, not vital," Dr. Hodges said, after examining it. "I feel sure that the sword has missed the lung."

After cutting off the rest of the man's upper garments, he poured, from a phial he had brought with him, a few drops of a powerful styptic into the wound, placed a thick pad of lint over it, and bandaged it securely. Then, giving directions that a small quantity of spirits and water should be given to the patient from time to time, and, above all things, that he should be kept perfectly quiet, he hurried away.

"Is there anything more I can do, sir?" Cyril asked Mr. Harvey.

"Nothing more. You will understand, sir, what our feelings are, and that our hearts are too full of grief and emotion for us to speak. We shall watch together to-night, and lay our case before the Lord."

"Then I will come early in the morning and see if there is aught I can do, sir. I am going back now to Mr. Wallace, who was uneasy at your absence. I suppose you would wish me to say only that I found that there was a robber in the place who, having wounded your servant, was on the point of attacking you when I entered, and that he fled almost immediately."

"That will do. Say to him that for to-night we shall be busy nursing, and that my wife is greatly shaken; therefore I would not that he should come round, but I pray him to call here in the morning."

"I will do so, sir."

Cyril went downstairs, closed the shutters of the window into which he had broken, and put up the bars, and then went out at the door, taking special pains to close it firmly behind him.

He was glad to be out of the house. He had seen many sad scenes during the last few weeks, but it seemed to him that this was the saddest of all. Better, a thousand times, to see a son stricken by the Plague than this. He walked slowly back to the minister's. He met Mr. Wallace at the door of his house.

"I was coming round," the latter said. "Of course one or other of them are stricken?"

"No, sir; it was another cause that prevented their coming. Just as I reached the house I heard a scream, and Mrs. Harvey appeared at the casement calling for help. I forced open a window and ran up. I found that a robber had entered the house. He had seriously wounded the old servant, and was on the point of attacking Mr. Harvey when I entered. Taken by surprise, the man fled almost immediately. Mrs. Harvey had fainted. At first, we thought the servant was killed, but, finding that he lived, I ran off and fetched Dr. Hodges, who has dressed the wound, and thinks that the man has a good chance of recovery. As Mrs. Harvey had now come round, and was capable of assisting her husband, they did not accept my offer to stay and do anything I could. I said I was coming to you, and Mr. Harvey asked me to say that, although they were too much shaken to see you this evening, they should be glad if you would go round to them the first thing in the morning."

"Then the robber got away unharmed?" Mr. Wallace asked.

"He was unharmed, sir. I would rather that you did not question me on the subject. Mr. Harvey will doubtless enter fully into the matter with you in the morning. We did not exchange many words, for he was greatly disturbed in spirit at the wounding of his old servant, and the scene he had gone through; and, seeing that he and his wife would rather be alone with their patient, I left almost directly after Dr. Hodges went away. However, I may say that I believe that there are private matters in the affair, which he will probably himself communicate to you."

"Then I will ask no more questions, Cyril. I am well content to know that it is not as I feared, and that the Plague has not attacked them."

"I said that I would call round in the morning, sir; but I have been thinking of it as I came along, and consider that, as you will be there, it is as well that I should not do so. I will come round here at ten o'clock, and should you not have returned, will wait until you do. I do not know that I can be of any use whatever, and do not wish to intrude there. Will you kindly say this to them, but add that should they really wish me to go, I will of course do so?"

Mr. Wallace looked a little puzzled.

"I will do as you ask me, but it seems to me that they will naturally wish to see you, seeing that, had it not been for your arrival, they might have been robbed and perhaps murdered."

"You will understand better when you have seen Mr. Harvey, sir. Now I will be making for home; it is about my usual hour, and John Wilkes will be beginning to wonder and worry about me."

To John, Cyril told the same story as to Mr. Wallace.

"But how was it that you let the villain escape, Master Cyril? Why did you not run him through the body?"

"I had other things to think of, John. There was Mrs. Harvey lying insensible, and the servant desperately wounded, and I thought more of these than of the robber, and was glad enough, when he ran out, to be able to turn my attention to them."

"Ay, ay, that was natural enough, lad; but 'tis a pity the villain got off scot-free. Truly it is not safe for two old people to be in an empty house by themselves in these times, specially as, maybe, the houses on either side are also untenanted, and robbers can get into them and make their way along the roof, and so enter any house they like by the windows there. It was a mercy you chanced to come along. Men are so accustomed now to hear screams and calls for aid, that none trouble themselves as to such sounds. And you still feel quite well?"

"Never better, John, except for occasional twitches in my shoulder."

"It does not knit so fast as it should do," John said. "In

the first place, you are always on the move; then no one can go about into infected houses without his spirits being disturbed, and of all things a calm and easy disposition is essential for the proper healing of wounds. Lastly, it is certain that when there is poison in the air wounds do not heal so quickly as at other times."

"It is going on well enough, John; indeed, I could not desire it to do better. As soon as it is fairly healed I ought to join Prince Rupert again; but in truth I do not wish to go, for I would fain see this terrible Plague come to an end before I leave; for never since the days of the Black Death, hundreds of years ago, was there so strange and terrible a malady in this country."

Mr. Wallace had returned to his house when Cyril called the next morning.

"Thinking over what you said last night, Cyril, I arrived at a pretty correct conclusion as to what had happened, though I thought not that it could be as bad as it was. I knew the object with which Mr. Harvey and his wife had come up to London, at a time when most men were fleeing from it. Their son has, ever since he came up three years ago, been a source of grievous trouble to them, as he was, indeed, for a long time previously. Some natures seem naturally to turn to evil, and this boy's was one of them. It may be that the life at home was too rigid and severe, and that he revolted against it. Certain it is that he took to evil courses and consorted with bad companions. Severity was unavailing. He would break out of the house at night and be away for days. He was drunken and dissolute.

"At last, just after a considerable sum of money had come into the house from the tenants' rents, he stole it, and went up to London. His name was not mentioned at home, though his father learnt from correspondents here that he had become a hanger-on of the Court, where, his father being a man of condition, he found friends without difficulty. He was a gambler and a brawler, and bore a bad reputation even among the riffraff of the Court. His father learnt that he had disappeared from sight at the time the Court went to Oxford early in June, and his correspondent found that he was reported to have joined a band a abandoned ruffians, whose least crimes were those of robbery.

"When the Plague spread rapidly, Mr. Harvey and his wife determined to come up to London, to make one more effort to draw him from his evil courses. The only thing that they have been able to learn for certain was, that he was one of the performers in that wicked mockery the dance of death, but their efforts to trace him have otherwise failed.

" They had intended, if they had found him, and he would have made promises of amendment, to have given him money that would have enabled him to go over to America and begin a new life there, promising him a regular allowance to maintain him in comfort. As they have many friends over there, some of whom went abroad to settle before the Civil War broke out here, they would be able to have news how he was going on; and if they found he was living a decent life, and truly repented his past course, they would in five years have had him back again, and reinstated him as their heir.

" I knew their intentions in the matter, and have done my best to gain them news of him. I did not believe in the reformation of one who had shown himself to be of such evil spirit; but God is all-powerful, and might have led him out from the slough into which he had fallen.

"Yesterday evening, half an hour before you went there, his father and mother were astonished at his suddenly entering. He saluted them at first with ironical politeness, and said that having heard from one from the same part of the country that he had seen them in London, he had had the streets thereabouts watched, and having found where they lodged, had come to pay his respects.

" There was a reckless bravado in his manner that alarmed his mother, and it was not long before the purpose of his visit came out. He demanded that his father should at once sign a deed which he had brought drawn out in readiness, assigning to him at once half his property.

"'You have,' he said, 'far more than you can require. Living as you do, you must save three-quarters of your income, and it would be at once an act of charity, and save you the trouble of dealing with money that is of no use to you.'

"His father indignantly refused to take any such step, and then told him the plans he had himself formed for him. At this he laughed scoffingly.

"'You have the choice,' he said, 'of giving me half, or of my taking everything.' And then he swore with terrible oaths that unless his father signed the paper, that day should be his last. 'You are in my power,' he said, 'and I am desperate. Do you think that if three dead bodies are found in a house now any will trouble to inquire how they came to their end? They will be tossed into the plague-cart, and none will make inquiry about them.'

"Hearing voices raised in anger, the old servant ran in. At once the villain drew and ran at him, passing his sword through his body. Then, as if transported at the sight of the blood he had shed, he turned upon his father. It was at this moment that his mother ran to the window and called for help. He dragged her back, and as she fell fainting with horror and fear he again turned upon his father; his passion grew hotter and hotter as the latter, upbraiding him with the deed he had done, refused to sign; and there is no doubt that he would have taken his life had you not luckily ran in at this moment.

"It has truly been a terrible night for them. They have passed it in prayer, and when I went this morning were both calm and composed, though it was easy to see by their faces how they had suffered, and how much the blow has told upon them. They have determined to save their son from any further temptation to enrich himself by their deaths. I fetched a lawyer for them; and when I left Mr. Harvey was giving him instructions for drawing up his will, by which every farthing is left away from him. They request me to go to them this evening with two or three of our friends to witness it, as it is necessary in a time like this that a will should be witnessed by as many as possible, as some may be carried off by the Plague; and should all the witnesses be dead, the will might be disputed as a forgery. So the lawyer will bring his clerks with him, and I shall take four or five of our friends.

"They will return to the country as soon as their servant can be moved. Dr. Hodges came when I was there, and gives hopes that the cure will be a speedy one. We are going to place some men in the house. I have among my poorer friends two men who will be glad to establish themselves there with their wives, seeing that they will pay no rent, and will receive wages as long as Mr. Harvey remains there. There will thus be no fear of any repetition of the attempt. Mr. Harvey, on my advice, will also draw up and sign a paper giving a full account of the occurrence of last evening, and will leave this in the hands of the lawyer.

"This will be a protection to him should his son follow him into the country, as he will then be able to assure him that if he proceeds to violence suspicion will at once fall upon him, and he will be arrested for his murder. But, indeed, the poor gentleman holds but little to his life; and it was only on my representing to him that this document might be the means of averting the commission of the most terrible of all sins from the head of his son, that he agreed to sign it. I gave him your message, and he prays me to say that, deeply grateful as he and his wife are to you, not so much for the saving of their lives, as for preventing their son's soul being stained by the crime, they would indeed rather that you did not call for a time, for they are so sorely shaken that they do not feel equal to seeing you. You will not, I hope, take this amiss."

"By no means," Cyril replied; "it is but a natural feeling; and, in truth, I myself am relieved that such is their decision, for it would be well-nigh as painful to me as to them to see them again, and to talk over the subject."

"By the way, Cyril, Mr. Harvey said that when you saw his son you cried out his name, and that by the manner in which he turned upon you it was clear that he had some cause for hating you. Is this so, or was it merely his fancy?"

"It was no fancy, sir. It is not long since I thwarted his attempt to carry off the daughter of a city merchant, to whom he had represented himself as a nobleman. He was in the act of doing so, with the aid of some friends, when, accompanied by John Wilkes, I came up. There was a fray, in the course of which I ran him through the shoulder. The young lady returned home with us, and has since heartily repented of her folly. I had not seen the man since that time till I met him yesterday; but certainly the house was watched for some time, as I believe, by his associates, who would probably have done me an ill turn had I gone out after nightfall."

"That explains it, Cyril. I will tell Mr. Harvey, whose mind has been much puzzled by your recognition of his son."

CHAPTER XVII.

SMITTEN DOWN.

TWO days later, Cyril started at his usual hour to go to Dr. Hodges'; but he had proceeded but a few yards when a man, who was leaning against the wall, suddenly lurched forward and caught him round the neck. Thinking that the fellow had been drinking, Cyril angrily tried to shake him off. As he did so the man's hat, which had been pressed down over his eyes, fell off, and, to his astonishment, Cyril recognised John Harvey.

"You villain! What are you doing here?" he exclaimed, as he freed himself from the embrace, sending his assailant staggering back against the wall.

The man's face lit up with a look of savage exultation.

"I told you you should hear from me again," he said, "and I have kept my word. I knew the hour you went out, and I have been waiting for you. You are a doomed man. I have the Plague, and I have breathed in your face. Before twenty-four hours have passed you will be, as I am, a dying man. That is a good piece of vengeance. You may be a better swordsman than I am, but you can't fight with the Plague."

Cyril drew back in horror. As he did so, a change came over John Harvey's face, he muttered a few words incoherently, swayed backwards and forwards, and then slid to the ground in a heap. A rush of blood poured from his mouth, and he fell over dead.

Cyril had seen more than one similar death in the streets, but the horrible malignity of this man, and his sudden death, gave him a terrible shock. He felt for the moment completely unmanned, and, conscious that he was too unhinged for work, he turned and went back to the house.

"You look pale, lad," John Wilkes said, as Cyril went upstairs. "What brings you back so soon?"

"I have had rather a shock, John." And he told him of what had happened.

"That was enough to startle you, lad. I should say the best thing you could do would be to take a good strong tumbler of grog, and then lay down."

"That I will do, and will take a dose of the medicine Dr. Hodges makes every one take when the infection first shows itself in a house. As you know, I have never had any fear of the Plague hitherto. I don't say that I am afraid of it now, but I have run a far greater risk of catching it than I have ever done before, for until now I have never been in actual contact with any one with the disease."

After a sleep Cyril rose, and feeling himself again, went to call upon Mr. Wallace.

"I shall not come again for a few days," he said, after telling him what had happened, but without mentioning the name of John Harvey, "but I will send you a note every other day by John Wilkes. If he does not come, you will know that I have taken the malady, and in that case, Mr. Wallace, I know that I shall have your prayers for my recovery. I am sure that I shall be well cared for by John Wilkes."

"Of my prayers you may be sure, Cyril; and, indeed, I have every faith that, should you catch the malady, you will recover from it. You have neither well-nigh frightened yourself to death, nor have you dosed yourself with drugs until nature was exhausted before the struggle began. You will, I am sure, be calm and composed, and above all you have faith in God, and the knowledge that you have done your part to carry out His orders, and to visit the sick and aid those in sorrow."

The next day Cyril was conscious of no change except that he felt a disinclination to exert himself. The next morning he had a feeling of nausea.

"I think that I am in for it, John," he said. "But at any rate it can do no harm to try that remedy you spoke of that is used in the East. First of all, let us fumigate the room. As far as I have seen, the smoke of tobacco is the best preservative against the Plague. Now do you, John, keep a bit of tobacco in your mouth."

"That I mostly do, lad."

"Well, keep a bigger bit than usual, John, and smoke steadily. Still, that will not be enough. Keep the fire burning, and an iron plate heated to redness over it. Bring that into my room from time to time, and burn tobacco on it. Keep the room full of smoke."

"I will do that," John said, "but you must not have too much of it. I am an old hand, and have many times sat in a fo'castle so full of smoke that one could scarce see one's hands, but you are not accustomed to it, and it may like enough make you sick."

"There will be no harm in that, John, so that one does not

push it too far. Now, how are you going to set about this sweating process?"

"While you undress and get into bed I will get a blanket ready. It is to be dipped in boiling water, and then wrung out until it is as dry as we can get it. Then you are wrapped in that, and then rolled in five or six dry blankets to keep in the heat. You will keep in that until you feel almost weak with sweating; then I take you out and sponge you with warmish water, and then wrap you in another dry blanket."

"You had better sponge me with vinegar, John."

Cyril undressed. When he had done so he carefully examined himself, and his eye soon fell on a black spot on the inside of his leg, just above the knee. It was the well-known sign of the Plague.

"I have got it, John," he said, when the latter entered with a pile of blankets.

"Well, then, we have got to fight it, Master Cyril, and we will beat it if it is to be beaten. Now, lad, for the hot blanket."

"Lay it down on the bed, and I will wrap myself in it, and the same with the others. Now I warn you, you are not to come nearer to me than you can help, and above all you are not to lean over me. If you do, I will turn you out of the room and lock the door, and fight it out by myself. Now puff away at that pipe, and the moment you wrap me up get the room full of smoke."

John nodded.

"Don't you bother about me," he growled. "I reckon the Plague ain't going to touch such a tough old bit of seasoned mahogany as I am. Still, I will do as you tell me."

In a few minutes Cyril was in a profuse perspiration, in which even his head, which was above the blankets, shared.

"That is grand," John said complacently.

The cloud of tobacco, with which the room was soon filled, was not long in having the effect that John had predicted, and Cyril was soon violently sick, which had the effect of further increasing the perspiration.

"You must open the window and let the smoke out a bit, John," he gasped. "I can't stand any more of it."

This was done, and for another hour Cyril lay between the blankets.

"I shall faint if I lie here any longer," he said at last. "Now, John, do you go out of the room, and don't come back again until I call you. I see you have put the vinegar handy. It is certain that if this is doing me any good the blankets will be infected. You say you have got a big fire in the kitchen. Well, I shall take them myself, and hang them up in front of it, and you are not to go into the room till they are perfectly dry again. You had better light another fire at once in the parlour, and you can do any cooking there. I will keep the kitchen for my blankets."

John nodded and left the room, and Cyril at once proceeded to unroll the blankets. As he came to the last he was conscious of a strong fetid odour, similar to that he had more than once perceived in houses infected by the Plague.

"I believe it is drawing it out of me," he said to himself. "I will give it another trial presently."

He first sponged himself with vinegar, and felt much refreshed. He then wrapped himself up and lay down for a few minutes, for he felt strangely weak. Then he got up and carried the blankets into the kitchen, where a huge fire had been made up by John. He threw the one that had been next to him into a tub, and poured boiling water on it, and the others he hung on chairs round it. Then he went back to his room, and lay down and slept for half an hour. He returned to the kitchen and rearranged the blankets. When John saw him go back to his room he followed him.

"I have got some strong broth ready," he said. "Do you think that you could take a cupful?"

"Ay, and a good-sized one, John. I feel sure that the sweating has done me good, and I will have another turn at it soon. You must go at once and report that I have got it, or when the examiners come round, and find that the Plague is in the house, you will be fined, or perhaps imprisoned. Before you go there, please leave word at Dr. Hodges' that I am ill, and you might also call at Mr. Wallace's and leave the same message. Tell them, in both cases, that 1 have everything that I want, and trust that I shall make a good recovery."

"Ay, ay, sir; I will be off as soon as I have brought you in your broth, and will be back here in half an hour."

Cyril drank the broth, and then dozed again until John returned. When he heard his step he called out to him to bring the hot iron, and he filled the room with tobacco smoke before allowing him to enter.

"Now, John, the blankets are dry, and can be handled again, and I am ready for another cooking."

Four times that day did Cyril undergo the sweating process. By the evening he was as weak as a child, but his skin was soft and cool, and he was free from all feeling of pain or uneasiness. Dr. Hodges called half an hour after he had taken it for the last time, having only received his message when he returned late from a terrible day's work. Cyril had just turned in for the night.

"Well, lad, how are you feeling? I am so sorry that I did not get your message before."

"I am feeling very well, doctor."

"Your hand is moist and cool," Dr. Hodges said in surprise. "You must have been mistaken. I see no signs whatever of the Plague."

"There was no mistake, doctor; there were the black marks on my thighs, but I think I have pretty well sweated it out of me."

He then described the process he had followed, and said that John Wilkes had told him that it was practised in the Levant.

"Sweating is greatly used here, and I have tried it very repeatedly among my patients, and in some cases, where I had notice of the disease early, have saved them. Some bleed before sweating, but I have not heard of one who did so who recovered.

In many cases the patient, from terror or from weakness of body, cannot get up the heat required, and even if they arrive at it, have not the strength to support it. In your case you lost no time; you had vital heat in plenty, and you had strength to keep up the heat in full force until you washed, as it were, the malady out of you. Henceforth I shall order that treatment with confidence when patients come to me whom I suspect to have the Plague, although it may not have as yet fully declared itself. What have you done with the blankets?"

"I would not suffer John to touch them, but carried them myself into the kitchen. The blankets next to me I throw into a tub and pour boiling water over them; the others I hang up before a huge fire, so as to be dry for the next operation. I take care that John does not enter the kitchen."

"How often have you done this?"

"Four times, and lay each time for an hour in the blankets. I feel very weak, and must have lost very many pounds in weight, but my head is clear, and I suffer no pain whatever. The marks on my legs have not spread, and seem to me less dark in colour than they were."

"Your case is the most hopeful that I have seen," Dr. Hodges said. "The system has had every advantage, and to this it owes its success. In the first place, you began it as soon as you felt unwell. Most people would have gone on for another twelve hours before they paid much attention to the first symptoms, and might not have noticed the Plague marks even when they went to bed. In the second place, you are cool and collected, and voluntarily delivered yourself to the treatment. And in the third place, which is the most important perhaps of all, you were in good health generally. You had not weakened yourself by swallowing every nostrum advertised, or wearing yourself out by vain terrors. Ninety-nine cases out of a hundred would be probably beyond the reach of help before they were conscious of illness, and be too weak to stand so severe a strain on the system as that you have undergone. Another thing is that the remedy could hardly be attempted in a house full of frightened people. There would sure to be carelessness in the matter of the blankets, which, unless treated as you have done, would be a certain means of spreading the infection over the house. At any rate, I would continue the sweating as long as you can possibly stand it. Take nourishment in the shape of broth frequently, but in small quantity. I would do it again at midnight; 'tis well not to let the virus have time to gather strength again. I see you have faith in tobacco."

"Yes, doctor. I never let John Wilkes into the room after I have taken a bath until it is full of tobacco smoke. I have twice made myself ill with it to-day."

"Don't carry it too far, lad; for although I also believe in the virtue of the weed, 'tis a powerful poison, and you do not want to weaken yourself. Well, I see I can do nothing for you. You and your man seem to me to have treated the attack far more successfully than I should have done; for, indeed, this month very few of those attacked have recovered, whatever the treatment has been. I shall come round early to-morrow morning to see how you are going on. At present nothing can be better. Since the first outbreak, I have not seen a single case in which the patient was in so fair a way towards recovery in so short a time after the discovery of the infection."

John Wilkes at this moment came in with a basin of broth.

"This is my good friend, John Wilkes, doctor."

"You ought to be called Dr. John Wilkes," the doctor, who was one of the most famous of his time, said, with a smile, as he shook hands with him. "Your treatment seems to be doing wonders."

"It seems to me he is doing well, doctor, but I am afraid he is carrying it too far; he is so weak he can hardly stand."

"Never mind that," the doctor said; "it will be easy enough to build him up when we have once got the Plague out of him. I have told him to have another turn in the blankets at twelve o'clock to-night; it will not do to let the malady get a fresh hold of him. But don't push it too far, lad. If you begin to feel faint, stop it, even if you have not been a quarter of an hour in the blankets. Do not cover yourself up too warmly when you have done; let nature have a rest. I shall be round between eight and nine, and no doubt you will have had another bath before I come. Do not sleep in the room, Wilkes; he is sure to go off soundly to sleep, and there is no use your running any needless risk. Let his window stand open; indeed, it should always be open, except when he gets out of his blankets, or is fumigating the room. Let him have a chair by the open window, so as to get as much fresh air as possible; but be sure that he is warmly wrapped up with blankets, so as to avoid getting a chill. You might place a hand-bell by the side of his bed to-night, so that he can summons you should he have occasion."

When the doctor came next morning he nodded approvingly as soon as he felt Cyril's hand.

"Nothing could be better," he said; "your pulse is even quieter than last night. Now let me look at those spots."

"They are fainter," Cyril said.

"A great deal," Dr. Hodges said, in a tone of the greatest pleasure. "Thank God, my lad, it is dying out. Not above three or four times since the Plague began have I been able to say so. I shall go about my work with a lighter heart to-day, and shall order your treatment in every case where I see the least chance of its being carried out, but I cannot hope that it will often prove as successful as it has with you. You have had everything in your favour—youth, a good constitution, a tranquil mind, an absence of fear, and a faith in God."

"And a good attendant, doctor—don't forget that."

"No, that goes for a great deal, lad—for a great deal. Not one nurse out of a hundred would carry out my instructions carefully; not one patient in a thousand would be able to see that they were carried out. Of course you will keep on with the treatment, but do not push it to extremes; you have pulled yourself down prodigiously, and must not go too far. Do you perceive any change in the odour when you take off the blankets?"

"Yes, doctor, a great change; I could scarcely distinguish it this morning, and indeed allowed John Wilkes to carry them out, as I don't think I myself could have walked as far as the kitchen, though it is but ten or twelve paces away. I told him to smoke furiously all the time, and to come out of the kitchen as soon as he had hung them up."

Cyril took three more baths in the course of the day, but was only able to sustain them for twenty minutes each, as by the end of that time he nearly fainted. The doctor came in late in the evening.

"The spots are gone, doctor," Cyril said.

"Then I think you may consider yourself cured, lad. Do not take the treatment again to-night; you can take it once in the morning; and then if I find the spots have not reappeared by the time I come, I shall pronounce the cure as complete, and shall begin to build you up again."

The doctor was able to give this opinion in the morning.

"I shall not come again, lad, unless you send for me, for every moment of my time is very precious, and I shall leave you in the hands of Doctor Wilkes. All you want now is nourishment; but take it carefully at first, and not too much at a time; stick to broths for the next two or three days, and when you do begin with solids do so very sparingly."

"There was a gentleman here yesterday asking about you," John Wilkes said, as Cyril, propped up in bed, sipped his broth. "It was Mr. Harvey. He rang at the bell, and I went down to the lower window and talked to him through that, for of course the watchman would not let me go out and speak to him. I had heard you speak of him as one of the gentlemen you met at the minister's, and he seemed muchly interested in you. He said that you had done him a great service, and of course I knew it was by frightening that robber away. I never saw a man more pleased than he was when I told him that the doctor thought you were as good as cured, and he thanked God very piously for the same. After he had done that, he asked me first whether you had said anything to me about him. I said that you had told me you had met him and his wife at the minister's, and that you said you had disturbed a robber you found at his house. He said, quite sharp, 'Nothing more?' 'No, not as I can think of. He is always doing good to somebody,' says I, 'and never a word would he say about it, if it did not get found out somehow. Why, he saved Prince Rupert's ship from being blown up by a fire-vessel, and never should we have known of it if young Lord Oliphant had not written to the Captain telling him all about it, and saying that it was the gallantest feat done in the battle.' Then there were other things, but they were of the nature of private affairs.' 'You can tell me about them, my good man,' he said; 'I am no vain babbler; and as you may well believe, from what he did for me, and for other reasons, I would fain know as much as I can of him.' So then I told him about how you found out about the robbery and saved master from being ruined, and how you prevented Miss Nellie from going off with a rascal who pretended he was an earl."

"Then you did very wrong, John," Cyril said angrily. "I say naught about your speaking about the robbery, for that was told in open Court, but you ought not, on any account, to have said a word about Mistress Nellie's affairs."

"Well, your honour, I doubt not Mistress Nellie herself would have told the gentleman had she been in my place. I am sure he can be trusted not to let it go further. I took care to tell him what good it had done Mistress Nellie, and that good had come out of evil."

"Well, you ought not to have said anything about it, John. It may be that Mistress Nellie out of her goodness of heart might herself have told, but that is no reason why any one else should do so. I charge you in future never to open your lips about that to any one, no matter who. I say not that any harm will come of it in this case, for Mr. Harvey is indeed a sober and God-fearing man, and assuredly asked only because he felt an interest in me, and from no idle curiosity. Still, I would rather that he had not known of a matter touching the honour of Mistress Nellie."

"Mum's the word in future, Master Cyril. I will keep the hatches fast down on my tongue. Now I will push your bed up near the window as the doctor ordered, and then I hope you will get a good long sleep."

The Plague and the process by which it had been expelled had left Cyril so weak that it was some days before he could walk across the room. Every morning he inquired anxiously of John how he felt, and the answer was always satisfactory. John had never been better in his life; therefore, by the time Cyril was able to walk to his easy-chair by the window, he began to hope that John had escaped the infection, which generally declared itself within a day or two, and often within a few hours, of the first outbreak in a house.

A week later the doctor, who paid him a flying visit every two or three days, gave him the welcome news that he had ordered the red cross to be removed from the door, and the watchmen to cease their attendance, as the house might now be considered altogether free from infection.

The Plague continued its ravages with but slight abatement, moving gradually eastward, and Aldgate and the district lying east of the walls were now suffering terribly. It was nearly the end of September before Cyril was strong enough to go out for his first walk. Since the beginning of August some fifty thousand people had been carried off, so that the streets were now almost entirely deserted, and in many places the grass was shooting up thickly in the road. In some streets every house bore the sign of a red cross, and the tolling of the bells of the dead-carts and piteous cries and lamentations were the only sounds that broke the strange silence.

The scene was so disheartening that Cyril did not leave the house again for another fortnight. His first visit was to Mr. Wallace. The sight of a watchman at the door gave him quite a shock, and he was grieved indeed when he heard from the man that the brave minister had died a fortnight before. Then he went to Mr. Harvey's. There was no mark on the door, but his repeated knockings met with no response, and a woman, looking out from a window opposite, called to him that the house had been empty for well-nigh a month, and the people that were in it had gone off in a cart, she supposed into the country.

"There was a gentleman and lady," she said, "who seemed well enough, and their servant, who was carried down and placed in the cart. It could not have been the Plague, though the man looked as if he had been sorely ill."

The next day he called on Dr. Hodges, who had not been near him for the last month. There was no watchman at the door, and his man opened it.

"Can I see the doctor?"

"Ay, you can see him," he said; "he is cured now, and will soon be about again."

"Has he had the Plague, then?"

"That he has, but it is a week now since the watchman left."

Cyril went upstairs. The doctor was sitting, looking pale and thin, by the window.

"I am grieved indeed to hear that you have been ill, doctor," Cyril said; "had I known it I should have come a fortnight since, for I was strong enough to walk this distance then. I did indeed go out, but the streets had so sad an aspect that I shrank from stirring out again."

"Yes, I have had it," the doctor said. "Directly I felt it come on I followed your system exactly, but it had gone further with me than it had with you, and it was a week before I fairly drove the enemy out. I ordered sweating in every case, but, as you know, they seldom sent for me until too late, and it is rare that the system got a fair chance. However, in my case it was a complete success. Two of my servants died; they were taken when I was at my worst. Both were dead before I was told of it. The man you saw was the one who waited on me, and as I adopted all the same precautions you had taken with your man, he did not catch it, and it was only when he went downstairs one day and found the other two servants lying dead in the kitchen that he knew they had been ill."

"Mr. Wallace has gone, you will be sorry to hear, sir."

"I am sorry," the doctor said; "but no one was more fitted to die. He was a brave man and a true Christian, but he ran too many risks, and your news does not surprise me."

"The only other friends I have, Mr. Harvey and his wife, went out of town a month ago, taking with them their servant."

"Yes; I saw them the day before I was taken ill," the doctor said, "and told them that the man was so far out of danger that he might safely be moved. They seemed very interested in you, and were very pleased when I told them that I had now given up attending you, and that you were able to walk across the room, and would, ere long, be yourself again. I hope we are getting to the end of it now, lad. As the Plague travels East it abates in the West, and the returns for the last week show a distinct fall in the rate of mortality. There is no further East for it to go now, and I hope that in another few weeks it will have worn itself out. We are half through October, and may look for cold weather before long."

"I should think that I am strong enough to be useful again now, sir."

"I don't think you are strong enough, and I am sure I shall not give you leave to do so," the doctor said. "I can hardly say how far a first attack is a protection against a second, for the recoveries have been so few that we have scarce means of knowing, but there certainly have been cases where persons have recovered from a first attack and died from a second. Your treatment is too severe to be gone through twice, and it is, therefore, more essential that you should run no risk of infection than it was before. I can see that you are still very far from strong, and your duty now is, in the first place, to regain your health. I should say get on board a hoy and go to

Yarmouth. A week in the bracing air there would do you more good than six months here. But it is useless to give you that advice, because, in the first place, no shipping comes up the river, and, even if you could get down to Yarmouth by road, no one would receive you. Still, that is what I should do myself as soon as I could get away, were it not that, in my case, I have my duties here."

"But, doctor, what you said to me surely applies to yourself also?" Cyril said, with a smile.

"I know that," the doctor said good-humouredly, "and expected it, but it is not for a doctor to choose. He is not free, like other men; he has adopted a vocation in which it is his first duty to go among the sick, whatever their ailment may be, to do all that he can for them, and if, as in the present case, he can do practically nothing else, to set them an example of calmness and fearlessness. Still, for a time, at any rate, I shall be able to go no more into houses where the Plague is raging. 'Tis more than a month since you were cured, yet you are still a mere shadow of what you were. I had a much harder fight with the enemy, and cannot walk across the room yet without William's help. Therefore, it will be a fortnight or three weeks yet before I can see patients, and much longer before I shall have strength to visit them in their houses. By that time I trust that the Plague will have very greatly abated. Thus, you see, I shall not be called upon to stand face to face with it for some time. Those who call upon me here are seldom Plague-stricken. They come for other ailments, or because they feel unwell, and are nervous lest it should be the beginning of an attack; but of late I have had very few come here. My patients are mostly of the middle class, and these have either fled or fallen victims to the Plague, or have shut themselves up in their houses like fortresses, and nothing would tempt them to issue abroad. Therefore, I expect that I shall have naught to do but to gain strength again. Come here when you will, lad, and the oftener the better. Conversation is the best medicine for both of us, and as soon as I can I will visit you. I doubt not that John Wilkes has many a story of the sea that will take our thoughts away from this sad city. Bring him with you sometimes; he is an honest fellow, and the talk of sailors so smacks of the sea that it seems almost to act as a tonic."

Cyril stayed for an hour, and promised to return on the following evening. He said, however, that he was sure John Wilkes would not accompany him.

" He never leaves the house unless I am in it. He considers himself on duty; and although, as I tell him, there is little fear of any one breaking in, seeing how many houses with much more valuable and more portable goods are empty and deserted, he holds to his purpose, saying that, even with the house altogether empty, it would be just as much his duty to remain in charge."

" Well, come yourself, Cyril. If we cannot get this old watch-dog out I must wait until I can go to him."

"I shall be very glad to come, doctor, for time hangs heavily on my hands. John Wilkes spends hours every day in washing and scrubbing decks, as he calls it, and there are but few books in the house."

" As to that, I can furnish you, and will do so gladly. Go across to the shelves there, and choose for yourself."

"Thank you very much indeed, sir. But will you kindly choose for me? I have read but few English books, for of course in France my reading was entirely French."

"Then take Shakespeare. I hold his writings to be the finest in our tongue. I know them nearly by heart, for there is scarce an evening when I do not take him down for an hour, and reading him I forget the worries and cares of my day's work, which would otherwise often keep me from sleep. 'Tis a bulky volume, but do not let that discourage you; it is full of wit and wisdom, and of such romance that you will often find it hard to lay it down. Stay—I have two editions, and can well spare one of them, so take the one on that upper shelf, and keep it when you have read it. There is but little difference between them, but I generally use the other, and have come to look upon it as a friend."

"Nay, sir, I will take it as a loan."

"You will do nothing of the sort. I owe you a fee, and a bumping one."

Henceforth Cyril did not find his time hang heavy on his hands. It seemed to him, as he sat at the window and read, that a new world opened to him. His life had been an eminently practical one. He had studied hard in France, and when he laid his books aside his time had been spent in the open air. It was only since he had been with Captain Dave that he had ever read for amusement, and the Captain's library consisted only of a few books of travels and voyages. He had never so much as dreamt of a book like this, and for the next few days he devoured its pages.

"You are not looking so well, Cyril," Dr. Hodges said to him abruptly one day.

"I am doing nothing but reading Shakespeare, doctor."

"Then you are doing wrong, lad. You will never build yourself up unless you take exercise."

"The streets are so melancholy, doctor, and whenever I go out I return sick at heart and in low spirits."

"That I can understand, lad. But we must think of something," and he sat for a minute or two in silence. Then he said suddenly, "Do you understand the management of a boat?"

"Yes, doctor; it was my greatest pleasure at Dunkirk to be out with the fishermen."

"That will do, then. Go down at once to the riverside. There are hundreds of boats lying idle there, for there are no passengers and no trade, and half of their owners are dead. You are sure to see some men there; having nothing else to do, some will be hanging about. Say you want to hire a boat for a couple of months or to buy one. You will probably get one for a few shillings. Get one with a sail as well as oars. Go out the first thing after breakfast, and go up or down the river as the tide or wind may suit. Take some bread and meat with you, and don't return till supper-time. Then you can spend your evenings with Shakespeare. Maybe I myself will come down and take a sail with you sometimes. That will bring the colour back into your cheeks, and make a new man of you. Would that I had thought of it before!"

Cyril was delighted with the idea, and, going down to Blackfriars, bought a wherry with a sail for a pound. Its owner was dead, but he learned where the widow lived, and effected the bargain without difficulty, for she was almost starving.

"I have bought it," he said, "because it may be that I may get it damaged or sunk; but I only need it for six weeks or two months, and at the end of that time I will give it you back again. As soon as the Plague is over there will be work for boats, and you will be able to let it, or to sell it at a fair price."

John Wilkes was greatly pleased when Cyril came back and told him what he had done.

"That is the very thing for you," he said. "I have been a thick-head not to think of it. I have been worrying for the last week at seeing you sit there and do nothing but read, and yet there seemed nothing else for you to do, for ten minutes out in the streets is enough to give one the heartache. Maybe I will go out for a sail with you myself sometimes, for there is no fear of the house being broken into by daylight."

"Not in the slightest, John. I hope that you will come out with me always. I should soon find it dull by myself, and besides, I don't think that I am strong enough yet to manage a pair of sculls for long, and one must reckon occasionally on having to row against the tide. Even if the worst happened, and any one did break in and carry off a few things, I am sure Captain Dave would not grumble at the loss when he knew that I had wanted you to come out and help me to manage the boat, which I was ordered to use for my health's sake."

"That he wouldn't," John said heartily; "not if they stripped the house and shop of everything there was in them."

CHAPTER XVIII.

A STROKE OF GOOD FORTUNE.

HAVING finally disposed of John Wilkes's scruples as to leaving the house during the daytime, Cyril thenceforth went out with him every day. If the tide was in flood they rowed far up the river, and came down on the ebb. If it was running out they went down as far as it would take them. Whenever the wind was favourable they hoisted the sail; at other times, they rowed. The fresh air, and the exercise, soon did their work. Cyril at first could only take one scull, and that only for a short time, but at the end of a fortnight was able to manage both for a time, or to row with one for hours. The feeling of lassitude which had oppressed him passed away speedily, the colour came back to his cheeks, his muscles strengthened, and he began to put on flesh.

They were now in November, and needed warm garments when on the water, and John insisted on completely muffling him up whenever they hoisted the sail; but the colder weather braced him up, and he was often inclined to shout with pleasure as the wind drove the boat along before it.

It was cheering to know that others were benefiting by the change. In the week ending October 3rd the deaths officially given were 4,328, though at least another thousand must be added to this, for great numbers of deaths from the Plague were put down to other causes, and very many, especially those of infants, were never counted at all. It was said that as many people were infected as ever, but that the virulence of the disease was abated, and that, whereas in August scarce one of those attacked recovered, in October but one out of every three died of the malady.

In the second week of October, the number of deaths by the Plague was but 2,665, and only 1,250 in the third week, though great numbers were still attacked. People, however, grew careless, and ran unnecessary risks, and, in consequence, in the first week of November the number of deaths rose by 400. After this it decreased rapidly, and the people who had fled began to come back again—the more so because it had now spread to other large cities, and it seemed that there was less danger in London, where it had spent its force, than in places where it had but lately broken out. The shops began to open again, and the streets to reassume their former appearance.

Cyril had written several times to Captain Dowsett, telling him how matters were going on, and in November, hearing that they were thinking of returning, he wrote begging them not to do so.

"Many of those who have returned have fallen sick, and died," he said. "It seems to me but a useless risk of life, after taking so much pains to avoid infection, to hurry back before the danger has altogether passed. In your case, Captain Dave, there is the less reason for it, since there is no likelihood of the shipping trade being renewed for the present. All the ports of Europe are closed to our ships, and it is like to be a long time before they lose fear of us. Even the coasting trade is lost for the present. Therefore, my advice is very strongly against your returning for some weeks. All is going on well here. I am getting quite strong again, and, by the orders of the doctor, go out with John daily for a long row, and have gained much benefit from it. John sends his respects. He says that everything is ship-shape above and below, and the craft holding well on her way. He also prays you not to think of returning at present, and says that it would be as bad seamanship, as for a captain who has made a good offing in a gale, and has plenty of sea-room, to run down close to a rocky shore under the lee, before the storm has altogether blown itself out."

Captain Dave took the advice, and only returned with his wife and Nellie a week before Christmas.

"I am glad indeed to be back," he said, after the first greetings were over. "'Twas well enough for the women, who used to help in the dairy, and to feed the fowls, and gather the eggs, and make the butter, but for me there was nothing to do, and it seemed as if the days would never come to an end."

"It was not so bad as that, father," Nellie said. "First of all, you had your pipe to smoke. Then, once a week you used to go over with the market-cart to Gloucester and to look at the shipping there, and talk with the masters and sailors. Then, on a Sunday, of course, there was church. So there were only five days each week to get through; and you know you took a good deal of interest in the horses and cows and pigs."

"I tried to take an interest in them, Nellie; but it was very hard work."

"Well, father, that is just what you were saying you wanted, and I am sure you spent hours every day walking about with the children, or telling them stories."

"Well, perhaps, when I think of it, it was not so very bad after all," Captain Dave admitted. "At any rate, I am heartily glad I am back here again. We will open the shop to-morrow morning, John."

"That we will, master. We sha'n't do much trade at present. Still, a few coasters have come in, and I hope that every day things will get better. Besides, all the vessels that have been lying in the Pool since June will want painting up and getting into trim again before they sail out of the river, so things may not be so slack after all. You will find everything in order in the store. I have had little to do but to polish up brass work and keep the metal from rusting. When do the apprentices come back again?"

"I shall write for them as soon as I find that there is something for them to do. You are not thinking of running away as soon as we come back I hope, Cyril? You said, when you last wrote, that you were fit for sea again."

"I am not thinking of going for some little time, if you

will keep me, Captain Dave. There is no news of the Fleet fitting out at present, and they will not want us on board till they are just ready to start. They say that Albemarle is to command this time instead of the Duke, at which I am right glad, for he has fought the Dutch at sea many times, and although not bred up to the trade, he has shown that he can fight as steadily on sea as on land. All say the Duke showed courage and kept a firm countenance at Lowestoft, but there was certainly great slackness in the pursuit, though this, 'tis said, was not so much his fault as that of those who were over-careful of his safety. Still, as he is the heir to the throne, it is but right that he should be kept out of the fighting."

"It is like to be stern work next time, Cyril, if what I hear be true. Owing partly to all men's minds being occupied by the Plague, and partly to the great sums wasted by the King in his pleasures, nothing whatever has been done for the Fleet. Of course, the squadron at sea has taken great numbers of prizes; but the rest of the Fleet is laid up, and no new ships are being built, while they say that the Dutch are busy in all their ship-yards, and will send out a much stronger fleet this spring than that which fought us at Lowestoft. I suppose you have not heard of any of your grand friends?"

"No. I should have written to Sydney Oliphant, but I knew not whether he was at sea or at home, and, moreover, I read that most folks in the country are afraid of letters from London, thinking that they might carry contagion. Many noblemen have now returned to the West End, and when I hear that the Earl has also come back with his family it will, of course, be my duty to wait upon him, and on Prince Rupert also. But I hope the Prince will not be back yet, for he will be wanting me to go to Court again, and for this, in truth, I have no inclination, and, moreover, it cannot be done without much expense for clothes, and I have no intention to go into expenses on follies or gew-gaws, or to trench upon the store of money that I had from you, Captain Dave."

They had just finished breakfast on the day before Christmas, when one of the apprentices came up from the shop and said that one Master Goldsworthy, a lawyer in the Temple, desired to speak to Sir Cyril Shenstone. Cyril was about to go down when Captain Dave said,—

"Show the gentleman up, Susan. We will leave you here to him, Cyril."

"By no means," Cyril said. "I do not know him, and he can assuredly have no private business with me that you may not hear."

Mrs. Dowsett and her daughter, however, left the room. The lawyer, a grave-looking gentleman of some fifty years of age, glanced at Cyril and the Captain as he entered the room, and then advanced towards the former.

"My name is unknown to you, Sir Cyril," he said, "but it has been said that a bearer of good news needs no introduction, and I come in that capacity. I bring you, sir, a Christmas-box," and he took from a bag he carried a bundle of some size, and a letter. "Before you open it, sir, I will explain the character of its contents, which would take you some time to decipher and understand, while I can explain them in a very few words. I may tell you that I am the legal adviser of Mr. Ebenezer Harvey, of Upmead Court, Norfolk. You are, I presume, familiar with the name?"

Cyril started. Upmead Court was the name of his father's place, but with the name of its present owner he was not familiar. Doubtless, he might sometimes have heard it from his father, but the latter, when he spoke of the present possessor of the Court, generally did so as "that Roundhead dog," or "that canting Puritan."

"The Court I know, sir," he said gravely, "as having once been my father's, but I do not recall the name of its present owner, though it may be that in my childhood my father mentioned it in my hearing."

"Nevertheless, sir, you know the gentleman himself, having met him, as he tells me, frequently at the house of Mr.

Wallace, who was minister of the chapel at which he worshipped, and who came up to London to minister to those sorely afflicted and needing comfort. Not only did you meet with Mr. Harvey and his wife, but you rendered to them very material service."

"I was certainly unaware," Cyril said, "that Mr. Harvey was the possessor of what had been my father's estate, but, had I known it, it would have made no difference in my feeling towards him. I found him a kind and godly gentleman whom, more than others there, was good enough to converse frequently with me, and to whom I was pleased to be of service."

"The service was of a most important nature," the lawyer said, "being nothing less than the saving of his life, and probably that of his wife. He sent for me the next morning, and then drew out his will. By that will he left to you the estates which he had purchased from your father."

Cyril gave a start of surprise, and would have spoken, but Master Goldsworthy held up his hand, and said,—

"Please let me continue my story to the end. This act was not the consequence of the service that you had rendered him. He had previously consulted me on the subject, and stated his intentions to me. He had met you at Mr. Wallace's, and at once recognised your name, and learnt from Mr. Wallace that you were the son of Sir Aubrey Shenstone. He studied your character, had an interview with Dr. Hodges, and learnt how fearlessly you were devoting yourself to the work of aiding those stricken with the Plague. With his own son he had reason for being profoundly dissatisfied. The young man had thrown off his authority, had become a notorious reprobate, and had, he believed, sunk down to become a companion of thieves and highwaymen. He had come up to London solely to make a last effort to save him from his evil courses and to give him a chance of reformation by sending him out to New England.

"Mr. Harvey is possessed of considerable property in addition to the estates purchased of your father, for, previous to that purchase he had been the owner of large tanneries at Norwich, which he has ever since maintained, not so much for the sake of the income he derived from them as because they afforded a livelihood to a large number of workmen. He had, therefore, ample means to leave to his son, should the latter accept his offer and reform his life, without the estates of Upmead. When he saw you, he told me his conscience was moved. He had, of course, a legal right to the estates, but he had purchased them for a sum not exceeeding a fifth of their value, and he considered that in the twenty years he had held them he had drawn from them sums amply sufficient to repay him for the price he had given for them, and had received a large interest on the money in addition. He questioned, therefore, strongly whether he had any right longer to retain them.

"When he consulted me on the subject, he alluded to the fact that, by the laws of the Bible, persons who bought lands were bound to return the land to its former possessors, at the end of seven times seven years. He had already, then, made up his mind to leave that portion of his property to you, when you rendered him that great service, and at the same time it became, alas! but too evident to him that his son was hopelessly bad, and that any money whatever left to him would assuredly be spent in evil courses, and would do evil rather than good. Therefore, when I came in the morning to him he said,—

"'My will must be made immediately. Not one penny is to go to my son. I may be carried off to-morrow by the Plague, or my son may renew his attempt with success. So I must will it away from him at once. For the moment, therefore, make a short will bequeathing the estate of Upmead to Sir Cyril Shenstone, all my other possessions to my wife for her lifetime, and at her death also to Sir Cyril Shenstone.

"'I may alter this later on,' he said, 'but for the present I desire chiefly to place them beyond my son's reach. Please draw up the document at once, for no one can say what half an hour may bring forth to either of us. Get the document in form by this evening, when some friends will be here to witness it. Pray bring your two clerks also!'

"A few days later he called upon me again.

"'I have been making further inquiries about Sir Cyril Shenstone,' he said, 'and have learnt much concerning him from a man who is in the employment of the trader with whom he lives. What I have learnt more than confirms me in my impression of him. He came over from France, three years ago, a boy of scarce fourteen. He was clever at figures, and supported his reprobate father for the last two years of his life by keeping the books of small traders in the City. So much was he esteemed that, at his father's death, Captain Dowsett offered him a home in his house. He rewarded the kindness by making the discovery that the trader was being foully robbed, and brought about the arrest of the thieves, which incidentally led to the breaking-up of one of the worst gangs of robbers in London. Later on he found that his employer's daughter was in communication with a hanger-on of the Court, who told her that he was a nobleman. The young fellow set a watch upon her, came upon her at the moment she was about to elope with this villain, ran him through the shoulder, and took her back to her home, and so far respected her secret that her parents would never have known of it had she not, some time afterwards, confessed it to them. That villain, Mr. Goldsworthy,' he said, 'was my son! Just after that Sir Cyril obtained the good will of the Earl of Wisbech, whose three daughters he saved from being burnt to death at a fire in the Savoy. Thus, you see, this youth is in every way worthy of good fortune, and can be trusted to administer the estate of his fathers worthily and well. I wish you to draw out, at once, a deed conveying to him these estates, and rehearsing that, having obtained them at a small price, and having enjoyed them for a time long enough to return to me the money I paid for them with ample interest thereon, I now return them to him, confident that they will be in good hands, and that their revenues will be worthily spent.'

"In this parcel is the deed in question, duly signed and witnessed, together with the parchments, deeds, and titles of which he became possessed at his purchase of the estate. I may say, Sir Cyril, that I have never carried out a legal transfer with greater pleasure to myself, considering, as I do, that the transaction is alike just and honourable on his part and most creditable to yourself. He begged me to hand the deeds to you myself. They were completed two months since, but he himself suggested that I should bring them to you on Christmas Eve, when it is the custom for many to give to their friends tokens of their regard and good will. I congratulate you heartily, sir, and rejoice that, for once, merit has met with a due reward."

"I do not know, sir," Cyril replied, "how I can express my feelings of deep pleasure and gratitude at the wonderful tidings you have brought me. I had set it before me as the great object of my life, that, some day, should I live to be an old man, I might be enabled to repurchase the estate of my father's. I knew how improbable it was that I should ever be able to do so, and I can scarce credit that what seemed presumptuous even as a hope should have thus been so strangely and unexpectedly realised. I certainly do not feel that it is in any way due to what you are good enough to call my merits, for in all these matters that you have spoken of there has been nothing out of the way, or, so far as I can see, in any way praiseworthy, in what I have done. It would seem, indeed, that in all these matters, and in the saving of my life from the Plague, things have arranged themselves so as to fall out for my benefit."

"That is what Mr. Harvey feels very strongly, Sir Cyril. He has told me, over and over again, that it seemed to him that the finger of God was specially manifest in thus bringing you together, and in placing you in a position to save his life. And now I will take my leave. I may say that in all legal matters connected with the estate I have acted for Mr.

Harvey, and should be naturally glad if you will continue to entrust such matters to me. I have some special facilities in the matter, as Mr. Popham, a lawyer of Norwich, is married to my daughter, and we therefore act together in all business connected with the estate, he performing what may be called the local business, while I am advised by him as to matters requiring attention here in London."

"I shall be glad indeed if you and Mr. Popham will continue to act in the same capacity for me," Cyril said warmly. "I am, as you see, very young, and know nothing of the management of an estate, and shall be grateful if you will, in all matters, act for me until I am of an age to assume the duties of the owner of Upmead."

"I thank you, Sir Cyril, and we shall, I trust, afford you satisfaction. The deed, you will observe, is dated the 29th of September, the day on which it was signed, though there have been other matters to settle. The tenants have already been notified that from that date they are to regard you as their landlord. Now that you authorise us to act for you, my son-in-law will at once proceed to collect the rents for this quarter. I may say that, roughly, they amount to seventeen hundred pounds a year, and as it may be a convenience to you to draw at once, if it so please you I will place, on Monday next, the sum of four hundred pounds to your credit with Messrs. Murchison and Graham, who are my bankers, or with any other firm you may prefer."

"With the bankers you name, by all means," Cyril said; "and I thank you heartily for so doing, for as I shall shortly rejoin the Fleet, a portion, at least, of the money will be very useful to me."

Mr. Goldsworthy took his hat.

"There is one thing further I have forgotten. Mr. Harvey requested me to say that he wished for no thanks in this matter. He regards it as an act of rightful restitution, and, although you will doubtless write to him, he would be pleased if you will abstain altogether from treating it as a gift."

"I will try to obey his wishes," Cyril said, "but it does not seem to me that it will be possible for me to abstain from any expression of gratitude for his noble act."

Cyril accompanied the lawyer to the door, and then returned upstairs.

"Now I can speak," Captain Dowsett said. "I have had hard work to keep a stopper on my tongue all this time, for I have been well nigh bursting to congratulate you. I wish you joy, my lad," and he wrung Cyril's hand heartily, "and a pleasant voyage through life. I am as glad, ay, and a deal more glad than if such a fortune had come in my way, for it would have been of little use to me, seeing I have all that the heart of man could desire."

He ran to the door and shouted loudly for his wife and daughter.

"I have news for you both," he said, as they came in. "What do you think? Cyril, like the King, has come to his own again, and he is now Sir Cyril Shenstone, the owner of the estate of Upmead."

Both broke into exclamations of surprise and pleasure.

"How has the wonder come about?" Nellie asked, after the first congratulations were over. "What good fairy has brought this round?"

"The good fairy was the Mr. Harvey whose name Cyril once mentioned casually, and whose life, as it now appears, he saved, though he has said nothing to us about it. That gentleman was, most strangely, the man who bought the estate from his father. He, it seems, is a wealthy man, and his conscience has for some time been pricked with the thought that he had benefited too largely from the necessities of Sir Aubrey, and that, having received back from the rents all the money he paid, and goodly interest thereon, he ought to restore the estate to its former owner. Possibly he might never have acted on this thought, but he considered the circumstance that he had so strangely met Cyril here at the time of the Plague, and still more strangely that Cyril had saved his life, was a matter of more than chance, and was a direct and manifest interposition of Providence; and he has therefore made restitution, and that parcel on the table contains a deed of gift to Cyril of all his father's estates."

"He has done quite rightly," Mrs. Dowsett said warmly, "though, indeed, it is not every one who would see matters in that light. If men always acted in that spirit it would be a better world."

"Ay, ay, wife. There are not many men who, having got the best of a bargain, voluntarily resign the profits they have made. It is pleasant to come across one who so acts, more especially when one's best friend is the gainer. Ah! Nellie, what a pity some good fairy did not tell you of what was coming! What a chance you have lost, girl! See what might have happened if you had set your cap at Cyril!"

"Indeed, it is terrible to think of," Nellie laughed. "It was hard on me that he was not five or six years older. Then I might have done it, even if my good fairy had not whispered in my ear about this fortune. Never mind. I shall console myself by looking forward to dance at his wedding—that is, if he will send me an invitation."

"Like as not you will be getting past your dancing days by the time that comes off, Nellie. I hope that, years before then, I shall have danced at your wedding—that is to say," he said, imitating her, "if you will send me an invitation."

"What are you going to do next, Cyril?" Captain Dave asked, when the laugh had subsided.

"I don't know, I am sure," Cyril replied. "I have not really woke up to it all yet. It will be some time before I realise that I am not a penniless young baronet, and that I can spend a pound without looking at it a dozen times. I shall have to get accustomed to the thought before I can make any plans. I suppose that one of the first things to do will be to go down to Oxford to see Prince Rupert—who, I suppose, is with the Court, though this I can doubtless learn at the offices of the Admiralty—and to tell him that I am ready to rejoin his ship as soon as he puts to sea again. Then I shall find out where Sydney Oliphant is, and how his family have fared in the Plague. I would fain find out what has become of the Partons, to whom, and especially to Lady Parton, I owe much. I suppose, too, I shall have to go down to Norfolk, but that I shall put off as long as I can, for it will be strange and very unpleasant at first to go down as master to a place I have never seen. I shall have to get you to come down with me, Captain Dave, to keep me in countenance.

"Not I, my lad. You will want a better introducer. I expect that the lawyer who was here will give you a letter to his son-in-law, who will, of course, place himself at your service, establishing you in your house and taking you round to your tenants."

"Oh yes," Nellie said, clapping her hands. "And there will be fine doings, and bonfires, and arches, and all sorts of festivities. I do begin to feel how much I have missed the want of that good fairy."

"It will be all very disagreeable," Cyril said seriously; whereat the others laughed.

Cyril then went downstairs with Captain Dave, and told John Wilkes of the good fortune that had befallen him, at which he was as much delighted as the others had been.

Ten days later Cyril rode to Oxford, and found that Prince Rupert was at present there. The Prince received him with much warmth.

"I have wondered many times what had become of you, Sir Cyril," he said. "From the hour when I saw you leave us in the *Fan Fan* I have lost sight of you altogether. I have not been in London since, for the Plague had set in badly before the ships were laid up, and as I had naught particular to do there I kept away from it. Albemarle has stayed through it, and he and Mr. Pepys were able to do all there was to do, but I have thought of you often and wondered how you fared, and hoped to see you here, seeing that there was, as it seemed to me, nothing to keep you in London after your wounds had healed. I have spoken often to the King of the brave deed by which you saved us all, and he declared that, had it not been that you were already a baronet, he would knight you as soon as you appeared, as many of the captains and others have already received that honour; and he agreed with me that none deserved it better than yourself. Now, what has become of you all this time?"

Cyril related how he had stayed in London, had had the Plague, and had recovered from it.

"I must see about getting you a commission at once in the Navy," the Prince said, "though I fear you will have to wait until we fit out again. There will be no difficulty then, for of course there were many officers killed in the action."

Cyril expressed his thanks, adding,—

"There is no further occasion for me to take a commission, Prince, for, strangely enough, the owner of my father's property has just made it over to me. He is a good man, and, considering that he has already reaped large benefits by his purchase, and has been repaid his money with good interest, his conscience will no longer suffer him to retain it."

"Then he is a Prince of Roundheads," the Prince said, "and I most heartily congratulate you; and I believe that the King will be as pleased as I am. He said but the other day, when I was speaking to him of you, that it grieved him sorely that he was powerless to do anything for so many that had suffered in his cause, and that, after the bravery you had shown, he was determined to do something, and would insist with his ministers that some office should be found for you,— though it is not an easy matter, when each of them has special friends of his own among whom to divide any good things that fall vacant. He holds a Court this evening, and I will take you with me."

The King was most gracious when the Prince again presented Cyril to him and told him of the good fortune that had befallen him.

"By my faith, Sir Cyril, you were born under a lucky star. First of all you saved my Lord of Wisbech's daughters; then, as Prince Rupert tells me, you saved him and all on board his ship from being burned; and now a miracle has well-nigh happened in your favour. I see, too, that you have the use of your arm, which the Prince doubted would ever altogether recover."

"More still, Your Majesty," the Prince said. "He had the Plague in August and recovered from it."

"I shall have to keep you about me, Sir Cyril," the King said, "as a sort of amulet to guard me against ill luck."

"I am going to take him to sea first," Prince Rupert broke in, seeing that Cyril was about to disclaim the idea of coming to Court. "I may want him to save my ship again, and I suppose he will be going down to visit his estate till I want him. You have never seen it, have you, Sir Cyril?"

"No, sir; at least not to have any remembrance of it. I naturally long to see Upmead, of which I have heard much from my father. I should have gone down at once, but I thought it my duty to come hither and report myself to you as being ready to sail again as soon as you put to sea."

"Duty first and pleasure afterwards," the King said. "I am afraid that is a little beyond me—eh, Rupert?"

"Very much so, I should say, Cousin Charles," the Prince replied, with a smile. "However, I have no doubt Sir Cyril will not grudge us a few days before he leaves. There are several of the gentlemen who were his comrades on the *Henrietta* here, and they will be glad to renew their acquaintance with him, knowing, as they all do, that they owe their lives to him."

As Cyril was walking down the High Street, he saw a student coming along whose face seemed familiar to him. He looked hard at him.

"Surely you must be Harry Parton?" he said.

"That is my name, sir; though I cannot recall where I have met you. Yet there seems something familiar in your face, and still more in your voice."

"I am Cyril Shenstone."

"Why, what has become of you, Cyril?" Harry said, shaking him warmly by the hand. "I searched for you a year ago when I was in London, but could obtain no tidings whatever of you, save that you had lost your father. We are alike there, for my father died a few months after yours did."

"I am sorry indeed, Harry. I had not heard of it before. I was not, indeed, in the way of doing so, as I was working in the City and knew nothing of what was passing elsewhere."

"This is my college, Cyril. Come up to my room; there we can talk comfortably, and we have much to tell each other. How is it that you have never been near us?" he went on, when they were seated in front of a blazing fire in his room. "I know that there was some quarrel between our fathers, but when we heard of Sir Aubrey's death, both my father and mother thought that you would come to see us or would have written—for indeed it was not until after my father's death that we paid a visit to London. It was then my mother asked me to search for you; and after great difficulty I found the quarter in which you had lived, and then from the parish register learned where your father had died. Going there, I learned that you had left the lodging directly after his death, but more than that the people could not tell me."

"I should have come to see your mother and Sir John, Harry. I know how deeply I am indebted to them, and as long as I live shall never cease to be grateful for Lady Parton's kindness to me. But I had received so much kindness that I shrank from seeming to wish to presume upon it further. I had, of course, to work for my living, and I wanted, before I recalled myself to them, to be able to say that I had not come as a beggar for further favours, but that I was making my way independently. Sooner or later I should have come, for your father once promised me that if I followed out what you remember was my plan, of entering foreign service, he would give me letters of introduction that would be useful to me. Had I that favour still to ask I could do it without shame. But more than that I would not have asked, even had I wanted bread, which, thank God! was never the case."

"I can understand your feeling, Cyril, but my mother assuredly would always have been pleased to see you. You know you were a favourite of hers."

"Had you been near town, Harry, I should certainly have come to see her and you as soon as I had fairly established myself, but I heard from my father that you had all gone away into the country soon after the unfortunate quarrel he had with Sir John, and therefore delayed taking any step for the time, and indeed did not know in what part of the country your father's estates lay. I know that he recovered them as soon as he returned."

"They had never been forfeited," Harry said. "My father retired from the struggle after Naseby, and as he had influential friends among the Puritans, there was no forfeiture of his estates, and we were therefore able, as you know, to live in comfort at Dunkirk, his steward sending over such monies as were required. And now about yourself. Your brains must have served you rarely somehow, for you are dressed in the latest fashion, and indeed I took you for a Court gallant when you accosted me."

"I have been truly fortunate, Harry, and indeed everything has turned out as if specially designed for my good, and, in a most strange and unlooked-for manner, I have just come into my father's estates again."

"I am glad indeed to hear it, Cyril. Tell me how it has all come about."

Cyril told the story of his life since he had come to London.

"You have, indeed, had strange adventures, Cyril, and, though you say little about it, you must have done something special to have gained Prince Rupert's patronage and introduction to Court; but I shall worm all that out of you some day, or get it from other lips. What a contrast your life has been to mine! Here have you been earning your living bravely, fighting in the great battle against the Dutch, going through that terrible Plague, and winning your way back to fortune, while I have been living the life of a school-boy. Our estates lie in Shropshire, and as soon as we went down there my father placed me at school at Shrewsbury. There I remained till his death, and then, as was his special wish, entered here. I have still a year of my course to complete. I only came up into residence last week. When the summer comes I hope that you will come down to Ardleigh and stay with us; it will give my mother great pleasure to see you again, for I never see her but she speaks of you, and wonders what has become of you, and if you are still alive."

"Assuredly I will come, and that with the greatest pleasure," Cyril said, " providing only that I am not then at sea, which is, I fear, likely, as I rejoin the ship as soon as Prince Rupert takes the sea against the Dutch. However, directly we return I will write to you."

"If you do so, let it be to Ardleigh, near Shrewsbury, Shropshire. Should I be here when your letter arrives, my mother will forward it to me."

CHAPTER XIX.

TAKING POSSESSION.

CYRIL stayed a week at Oxford. He greatly enjoyed the visit; and not only was he most warmly received by his former comrades on board the *Henrietta*, but Prince Rupert spoke so strongly in his favour to other gentlemen to whom he introduced him that he no longer felt a stranger at Court. Much of his spare time he spent with Harry Parton, and in his rooms saw something of college life, which seemed to him a very pleasant and merry one. He had ascertained, as soon as he arrived, that the Earl of Wisbech and his family were down at his estate, near the place from which he took his title, and had at once written to Sydney, from whom he received an answer on the last day of his stay at Oxford. It contained a warm invitation for him to come down to Wisbech.

"You say you will be going to Norwich to take possession of your estate. If you ride direct from Oxford, our place will be but little out of your way, therefore we shall take no excuse for your not coming to see us, and shall look for you within a week or so from the date of this. We were all delighted to get your missive, for although what you say about infection carried by letters is true enough, and, indeed there was no post out of London for months, we had begun to fear that the worst must have befallen you when no letter arrived from you in December. Still, we thought that you might not know where we were, and so hoped that you might be waiting until you could find that out. My father bids me say that he will take no refusal. Since my return he more than ever regards you as being the good genius of the family, and it is certainly passing strange that, after saving my sisters' lives from fire you should, though in so different a way, have saved me from a similar death. So set off as soon as you get this—that is, if you can tear yourself away from the gaieties of Oxford."

Cyril had, indeed, been specially waiting for Sydney's answer, having told him that he should remain at Oxford until he received it, and on the following morning he packed his valise and rode for Wisbech, where he arrived three days later. His welcome at the Earl's was a most cordial one. He spent a week there, at the end of which time Sydney, at his earnest request, started for Norwich with him. The Earl had insisted on Cyril's accepting a splendid horse, and behind him, on his other animal, rode a young fellow, the son of a small tenant on the Earl's estate, whom he had engaged as a servant. He had written, three days before, to Mr. Popham, telling him that he would shortly arrive, and begging him to order the two old servants of his father, whom he had, at his request, engaged to take care of the house, to get two or three chambers in readiness for him, which could doubtless be easily done, as he had learnt from the deed that the furniture and all contents of the house had been included in the gift. After putting up at the inn, he went to the lawyer's. Mr. Popham, he found, had had a room prepared in readiness for him at his house, but Cyril, while thanking him for so doing, said that, as Lord Oliphant was with him, he would stay at the inn for the night.

The next morning they rode over with Mr. Popham to Upmead, which was six miles distant from the town.

"That is the house," the lawyer said, as a fine old mansion came in sight. "There are larger residences in the county, but few more handsome. Indeed, it is almost too large for the estate, but, as perhaps you know, that was at one time a good deal larger than it is at present, for it was diminished by one of your ancestors in the days of Elizabeth."

At the gate where they turned into the Park an arch of evergreens had been erected.

"You don't mean to say you let them know that I was coming home?" Cyril said, in a tone of such alarm that Lord Oliphant laughed and Mr. Popham said apologetically,—

"I certainly wrote to the tenants, sir, when I received your letter, and sent off a message saying that you would be here this morning. Most of them or their fathers were here in the old time, for Mr. Harvey made no changes, and I am sure they would have been very disappointed if they had not had notice that Sir Aubrey's son was coming home."

"Of course it was quite right for you to do so, Mr. Popham, but you see I am quite unaccustomed to such things, and would personally have been much more pleased to have come home quietly. Still, as you say, it is only right that the tenants should have been informed, and at any rate it will be a satisfaction to get it all over at once."

There were indeed quite a large number of men and women assembled in front of the house—all the tenants, with their wives and families, having gathered to greet their young landlord—and loud bursts of cheering arose as he rode up, Sydney and Mr. Popham reining back their horses a little to allow him to precede them. Cyril took off his hat, and bowed repeatedly in reply to the acclamations that greeted him. The tenants crowded round, many of the older men pressing forward to shake him by the hand.

"Welcome back to your own again, Sir Cyril!"

"I fought under your father, sir, and a good landlord he was to us all."

Such were the exclamations that rose around him until he reached the door of the mansion, and, dismounting, took his place at the top of the steps. Then he took off his hat again, and when there was silence he said,—

"I thank you heartily, one and all, good friends, for the welcome that you have given me. Glad indeed I am to come down to my father's home, and to be so greeted by those who knew him, and especially by those who followed him in the field in the evil days which have, we may hope, passed away for ever. You all know, perhaps, that I owe my return here as master to the noble generosity of Mr. Harvey, your late landlord, who restored me the estates, not being bound in any way to do so, but solely because he considered that he had already been repaid the money he gave for them. This may be true, but, nevertheless, there is not one man in a hundred thousand who would so despoil himself of the benefits of a bargain lawfully made, and I beg you therefore to give three cheers, as hearty as those with which you greeted me, for Mr. Harvey."

Three cheers, as long and loud as those that had before risen, responded to the appeal.

"Such a man," Cyril went on, when they subsided, "must have been a just and good landlord to you all, and I shall do my best to give you no cause for regret at the change that has come about."

He paused for a moment to speak to Mr. Popham, who stood beside him, and then went on,—

"WELCOME BACK TO YOUR OWN AGAIN, SIR CYRIL!"

"I did not know whether I could ask you to drink to my health, but I learn from Mr. Popham that the cellars have been left well filled; therefore, my first orders on coming to the house of my fathers will be that a cask of wine shall be speedily broached, and that you shall be enabled to drink my health. While that is being done, Mr. Popham will introduce you to me one by one."

Another loud cheer arose, and then the tenants came forward with their wives and families.

Cyril shook hands with them all, and said a few words to each. The elder men had all ridden by his father in battle, and most of the younger ones said, as he shook hands with them,—

"My father fell, under Sir Aubrey, at Naseby," or "at Worcester," or in other battles.

By the time all had been introduced, a great cask of wine had been broached, and after the tenants had drunk to his health, and he had, in turn, pledged them, Cyril entered the house with Sydney and Mr. Popham, and proceeded to examine it under the guidance of the old man who had been his father's butler, and whose wife had also been a servant in Sir Aubrey's time.

"Everything is just as it was then, Sir Cyril. A few fresh articles of furniture have been added, but Mr. Harvey would have no general change made. The family pictures hang just where they did, and your father himself would scarce notice the changes."

"It is indeed a fine old mansion, Cyril," Lord Oliphant said, when they had made a tour of the house; "and now that I see it and its furniture I am even more inclined than before to admire the man who could voluntarily resign them. I shall have to modify my ideas of the Puritans. They have shown themselves ready to leave the country and cross the ocean to America, and begin life anew for conscience' sake—that is to say, to escape persecution—and they fought very doughtily, and we must own, very successfully, for the same reason, but this is the first time I have ever heard of one of them relinquishing a fine estate for conscience' sake."

"Mr. Harvey is indeed a most worthy gentleman," Mr. Popham said, "and has the esteem and respect of all, even of those who are of wholly different politics. Still, it may be that although he would in any case, I believe, have left this property to Sir Cyril, he might not have handed it over to him in his lifetime, had not he received so great a service at his hands."

"Why, what is this, Cyril?" Sydney said, turning upon him. "You have told us nothing whatever of any services rendered. I never saw such a fellow as you are for helping other people."

"There was nothing worth speaking of," Cyril said, much vexed.

Mr. Popham smiled.

"Most people would think it was a very great service, Lord Oliphant. However, I may not tell you what it was, although I have heard all the details from my father-in-law, Mr. Goldsworthy. They were told in confidence, and in order to enlighten me as to the relations between Mr. Harvey and Sir Cyril, and as they relate to painful family matters I am bound to preserve an absolute silence."

"I will be content to wait, Cyril, till I get you to myself. It is a peculiarity of Sir Cyril Shenstone, Mr. Popham, that he goes through life doing all sorts of services for all sorts of people. You may not know that he saved the lives of my three sisters in a fire at our mansion in the Savoy; he also performed the trifling service of saving Prince Rupert's ship and the lives of all on board, among whom was myself, from a Dutch fire-ship, in the battle of Lowestoft. These are insignificant affairs, that he would not think it worth while to allude to, even if you knew him for twenty years."

"You do not know Lord Oliphant, Mr. Popham," Cyril laughed, "or you would be aware that his custom is to make mountains out of molehills. But let us sit down to dinner.

I suppose it is your forethought, Mr. Popham, that I have to thank for having warned them to make this provision? I had thought that we should be lucky if the resources of the establishment sufficed to furnish us with a meal of bread and cheese."

"I sent on a few things with my messenger yesterday evening, Sir Cyril, but for the hare and those wild ducks methinks you have to thank your tenants, who doubtless guessed that an addition to the larder would be welcome. I have no doubt that, good landlord as Mr. Harvey was, they are really delighted to have you among them again. As you know, these eastern counties were the stronghold of Puritanism, and that feeling is still held by the majority. It is only among the tenants of many gentlemen who, like your father, were devoted Royalists, that there is any very strong feeling the other way. As you heard from their lips, most of your older tenants fought under Sir Aubrey, while the fathers of the younger ones fell under his banner. Consequently, it was galling to them that one of altogether opposite politics should be their landlord, and although in every other respect they had reason to like him, he was, as it were, a symbol of their defeat, and I suppose they viewed him a good deal as the Saxons of old times regarded their Norman lords."

"I can quite understand that, Mr. Popham."

"Another feeling has worked in your favour, Sir Cyril," the lawyer went on. "It may perhaps be a relic of feudalism, but there can be no doubt that there exists, in the minds of English country folks, a feeling of respect and of something like affection for their landlords when men of old family, and that feeling is never transferred to new men who may take their place. Mr. Harvey was, in their eyes, a new man—a wealthy one, no doubt, but owing his wealth to his own exertions—and he would never have excited among them the same feeling as they gave to the family who had, for several hundred years, been owners of the soil."

Cyril remained for a fortnight at Upmead, calling on all

the tenants, and interesting himself in them and their families. The day after his arrival he rode into Norwich, and paid a visit to Mr. Harvey. He had, in compliance to his wishes, written but a short letter of acknowledgment of the restitution of the estate, but he now expressed the deep feeling of gratitude that he entertained.

"I have only done what is right," Mr. Harvey said quietly, "and would rather not be thanked for it; but your feelings are natural, and I have therefore not checked your words. It was assuredly God's doing in so strangely bringing us together, and making you an instrument in saving our lives, and so awakening an uneasy conscience into activity. I have had but small pleasure from Upmead. I have a house here which is more than sufficient for all my wants, and I have, I hope, the respect of my townsfellows, and the affection of my workmen. At Upmead I was always uncomfortable. Such of the county gentlemen who retained their estates looked askance at me. The tenants, I knew, though they doffed their hats as I passed them, regarded me as a usurper. I had no taste for the sports and pleasures of country life, being born and bred a townsman. The ill-doing of my son cast a gloom over my life of late. I have lived chiefly here with the society of friends of my own religious and political feeling. Therefore, I have made no sacrifice in resigning my tenancy of Upmead, and I pray you say no further word of your gratitude. I have heard, from one who was there yesterday, how generously you spoke of me to your tenants, and I thank you for so doing, for it is pleasant for me to stand well in the thoughts of those whose welfare I have had at heart."

"I trust that Mrs. Harvey is in good health?" Cyril said.

"She is far from well, Cyril. The events of that night in London have told heavily upon her, as is not wonderful, for she has suffered much sorrow for years, and this last blow has broken her sorely. She mourns, as David mourned over the death of Absalom, over the wickedness of her son, but she is quite as one with me in the measures that I have taken concerning him, save that, at her earnest prayer, I have made a provision for him which will keep him from absolute want, and will leave him no excuse to urge that he was driven by poverty into crime. Mr. Goldsworthy has not yet discovered means of communicating with him, but when he does so he will notify him that he has my instructions to pay to him fifteen pounds on the first of every month, and that the offer of assistance to pay his passage to America is still open to him, and that on arriving there he will receive for three years the same allowance as here. Then if a favourable report of his conduct is forthcoming from the magistrates and deacons of the town where he takes up his residence, a correspondent of Mr Goldsworthy's will be authorised to expend four thousand pounds on the purchase of an estate for him, and to hand to him another thousand for the due working and maintenance of the same. For these purposes I have already made provisions in my will, with proviso that if, at the end of five years after my death, no news of him shall be obtained, the money set aside for these purposes shall revert to the main provisions of the will. It may be that he died of the Plague. It may be that he has fallen, or will fall, a victim to his own evil courses and evil passions. But I am convinced that, should he be alive, Mr. Goldsworthy will be able to obtain tidings of him long before the five years have expired. And now," he said, abruptly changing the subject, "what are you thinking of doing, Sir Cyril ?"

"In the first place, sir, I am going to sea again with the Fleet very shortly. I entered as a Volunteer for the war, and could not well, even if I wished it, draw back."

"They are a stiff-necked people," Mr. Harvey said. "That the Sovereigns of Europe should have viewed with displeasure the overthrow of the monarchy here was natural enough ; but in Holland, if anywhere, we might have looked for sympathy, seeing that as they had battled for freedom of conscience, so had we done here; and yet they were our worst enemies, and again and again had Blake to sail forth to chastise them. They say that Monk is to command this time?"

"I believe so, sir."

"Monk is the bruised reed that pierced our hand, but he is a good fighter. And after the war is over, Sir Cyril, you will not, I trust, waste your life in the Court of the profligate King?"

"Certainly not," Cyril said earnestly. "As soon as the war is over I shall return to Upmead and take up my residence there. I have lived too hard a life to care for the gaieties of Court, still less of a Court like that of King Charles. I shall travel for a while in Europe if there is a genuine peace. I have lost the opportunity of completing my education, and am too old now to go to either of the Universities. Not too old perhaps; but I have seen too much of the hard side of life to care to pass three years among those who, no older than myself, are still as boys in their feelings. The next best thing, therefore, as it seems to me, would be to travel, and perhaps to spend a year or two in one of the great Universities abroad."

"The matter is worth thinking over," Mr. Harvey said. "You are assuredly young yet to settle down alone at Upmead, and will reap much advantage from speaking French which is everywhere current, and may greatly aid you in making your travels useful to you. I have no fear of your falling into Popish error, Sir Cyril; but if my wishes have any weight with you I would pray you to choose the schools of Leyden or Haarlem, should you enter a foreign University, for they turn out learned men and good divines."

"Certainly your wishes have weight with me, Mr. Harvey, and should events so turn out that I can enter one of the foreign Universities, it shall be one of those you name—that is, should we, after this war is ended, come into peaceful relations with the Dutch."

Before leaving the Earl's, Cyril had promised faithfully that he would return thither with Sydney, and accordingly, at the end of the fortnight, he rode back with him there, and, three weeks later, journeyed up to London with the Earl and his family.

It was the middle of March when they reached London The Court had come up a day or two before, and the Fleet was, as Cyril learnt, being fitted out in great haste. The French had now, after hesitating all through the winter, declared war against us, and it was certain that we should have their fleet as well as that of the Dutch to cope with. Calling upon Prince Rupert on the day he arrived, Cyril learnt that the Fleet would assuredly put to sea in a month's time.

"Would you rather join at once, or wait until I go on board?" the Prince asked.

"I would rather join at once, sir. I have no business to do in London, and it would be of no use for me to take an apartment when I am to leave so soon; therefore, if I can be of any use, I would gladly join at once."

"You would be of no use on board," the Prince said, "but assuredly you could be of use in carrying messages, and letting me know frequently, from your own report, how matters are going on. I heard yesterday that the *Fan Fan* is now fitted out. You shall take the command of her. I will give you a letter to the boatswain, who is at present in charge, saying that I have placed her wholly under your orders. You will, of course, live on board. You will be chiefly at Chatham and Sheerness. If you call early to-morrow I will have a letter prepared for you, addressed to all captains holding commands in the White Squadron, bidding them to acquaint you, whensoever you go on board, with all particulars of how matters have been pushed forward, and to give you a list of all things lacking. Then, twice a week you will sail up to town, and report to me, or, should there be any special news at other times, send it to me by a mounted messenger. Mr. Pepys, the secretary, is a diligent and hardworking man, but he cannot see to everything, and Albemarle so pushes him that I think the White Squadron does not get a fair share of attention; but if I can go to him with your reports in hand, I may succeed in getting what is necessary done."

Bidding farewell to the Earl and his family, and thanking him for his kindness, Cyril stopped that night at Captain Dave's, and told him of all that had happened since they met. The next morning he went early to Prince Rupert's, received the two letters, and rode down to Chatham. Then, sending the horses back by his servant, who was to take them to the Earl's stable, where they would be cared for until his return, Cyril went on board the *Fan Fan*. For the next month he was occupied early and late with his duties. The cabin was small, but very comfortable. The crew was a strong one, for the yacht rowed twelve oars, with which she could make good progress even without her sails. He was waited on by his servant, who returned as soon as he had left the horses in the Earl's stables; his cooking was done for him in the yacht's galley. On occasions, as the tide suited, he either sailed up to London in the afternoon, gave his report to the Prince late in the evening, and was back at Sheerness by daybreak, or he sailed up at night, saw the Prince as soon as he rose, and returned at once.

The Prince highly commended his diligence, and told him that his reports were of great use to him, as, with them in his hand, he could not be put off at the Admiralty with vague assurances. Every day one or more ships went out to join the Fleet that was gathering in the Downs, and on April 20th Cyril sailed in the *Fan Fan*, in company with the last vessel of the White Squadron, and there again took up his quarters on board the *Henrietta*, the *Fan Fan* being anchored hard by in charge of the boatswain.

On the 23rd, the Prince, with the Duke of Albemarle, and a great company of noblemen and gentlemen, arrived at Deal, and came on board the Fleet, which, on May 1st, weighed anchor.

Lord Oliphant was among the volunteers who came down with the Prince, and, as many of the other gentlemen had also been on board during the first voyage, Cyril felt that he was among friends, and had none of the feeling of strangeness and isolation he had before experienced.

The party was indeed a merry one. For upwards of a year the fear of the Plague had weighed on all England. At the time it increased so terribly in London, that all thought it would, like the Black Death, spread over England, and that, once again, half the population of the country might be swept away. Great as the mortality had been, it had been confined almost entirely to London and some of the great towns, and now that it had died away even in these, there was great relief in men's minds, and all felt that they had personally escaped from a terrible and imminent danger. That they were about to face peril even greater than that from which they had escaped did not weigh on the spirits of the gentlemen on board Prince Rupert's ship. To be killed fighting for their country was an honourable death that none feared, while there had been, in the minds of even the bravest, a horror of death by the Plague, with all its ghastly accompaniments. Sailing out to sea to the Downs, then, they felt that the past year's events lay behind them as an evil dream, and laughed and jested and sang with light-hearted mirth.

As yet, the Dutch had not put out from port, and for three weeks the Fleet cruised off their coast. Then, finding that the enemy could not be tempted to come out, they sailed back to the Downs. The day after they arrived there, a messenger came down from London with orders to Prince Rupert to sail at once with the White Squadron to engage the French Fleet, which was reported to be on the point of putting to sea. The Prince had very little belief that the French really intended to fight. Hitherto, although they had been liberal in their promises to the Dutch, they had done nothing whatever to aid them, and the general opinion was that France rejoiced at seeing her rivals damage each other, but had no idea of risking her ships or men in the struggle.

"I believe, gentlemen," Prince Rupert said to his officers, "that this is but a ruse on the part of Louis to aid his Dutch allies by getting part of our fleet out of the way. Still, I have nothing to do but to obey orders, though I fear it is but a fool's errand on which we are sent."

The wind was from the north-east, and was blowing a fresh gale. The Prince prepared to put to sea. While the men were heaving at the anchors a message came to Cyril that Prince Rupert wished to speak to him in his cabin.

"Sir Cyril, I am going to restore you to your command. The wind is so strong and the sea will be so heavy that I would not risk my yacht and the lives of the men by sending her down the Channel. I do not think there is any chance of our meeting the French, and believe that it is here that the battle will be fought, for with this wind the Dutch can be here in a few hours, and I doubt not that as soon as they learn that one of our squadrons has sailed away they will be out. The *Fan Fan* will sail with us, but will run into Dover as we pass. Here is a letter that I have written ordering you to do so, and authorising you to put out and join the Admiral's Fleet, should the Dutch attack before my return. If you like to have young Lord Oliphant with you he can go, but he must go as a Volunteer under you. You are the captain of the *Fan Fan*, and have been so for the last two months; therefore, although your friend is older than you are, he must, if he choose to go, be content to serve under you. Stay, I will put it to him myself."

He touched the bell, and ordered Sydney to be sent for.

"Lord Oliphant," he said, "I know that you and Sir Cyril are great friends. I do not consider that the *Fan Fan*, of which he has for some time been commander, is fit to keep the sea in a gale like this, and I have therefore ordered him to take her into Dover. If the Dutch come out to fight the Admiral, as I think they will, he will join the Fleet, and although the *Fan Fan* can take but small share in the fighting, she may be useful in carrying messages from the

Duke while the battle is going on. It seems to me that, as the *Fan Fan* is more likely to see fighting than my ships, you, as a Volunteer, might prefer to transfer yourself to her until she again joins us. Sir Cyril is younger than you are, but if you go, you must necessarily be under his command seeing that he is captain of the yacht. It is for you to choose whether you will remain here or go with him."

"I should like to go with him, sir. He has had a good deal of experience of the sea, while I have never set foot on board ship till last year. And after what he did at Lowestoft I should say that any gentleman would be glad to serve under him."

"That is the right feeling," Prince Rupert said warmly. "Then get your things transferred to the yacht. If you join Albemarle's Fleet, Sir Cyril, you will of course report yourself to him, and say that I directed you to place yourself under his orders."

Five minutes later Cyril and his friend were on board the *Fan Fan*. Scarcely had they reached her, when a gun was fired from Prince Rupert's ship as a signal, and the ships of the White Squadron shook out their sails, and, with the wind free, raced down towards the South Foreland.

"We are to put into Dover," Cyril said to the boatswain, a weatherbeaten old sailor.

"The Lord be praised for that, sir! She is a tight little craft, but there will be a heavy sea on as soon we are beyond shelter of the sands, and with these two guns on board of her she will make bad weather. Besides, in a wind like this, it ain't pleasant being in a little craft in the middle of a lot of big ones, for if we were not swamped by the sea, we might very well be run down. We had better keep her close to the Point, yer honour, and then run along, under shelter of the cliffs, into Dover. The water will be pretty smooth in there, though we had best carry as little sail as we can, for the gusts will come down from above fit to take the mast out of her."

"I am awfully glad you came with me, Sydney," Cyril said,

as he took his place with his friend near the helmsman, "but I wish the Prince had put you in command. Of course, it is only a nominal thing, for the boatswain is really the captain in everything that concerns making sail and giving orders to the crew. Still, it would have been much nicer the other way."

"I don't see that it would, Cyril," Sydney laughed, "for you know as much more about handling a boat like this than I do, as the boatswain does than yourself. You have been on board her night and day for more than a month, and even if you knew nothing about her at all, Prince Rupert would have been right to choose you as a recognition of your great services last time. Don't think anything about it. We are friends, and it does not matter a fig which is the nominal commander. I was delighted to come, not only to be with you, but because it will be a very great deal pleasanter being our own masters on board this pretty little yacht than being officers on board the *Henrietta* where we would have been only in the way except when we went into action."

As soon as they rounded the Point most of the sail was taken off the *Fan Fan*, but even under the small canvas she carried she lay over until her lee rail was almost under water when the heavy squalls swooped down on her from the cliffs. The rest of the squadron was keeping some distance out, presenting a fine sight as the ships lay over, sending the spray flying high into the air from their bluff bows, and plunging deeply into the waves.

"Yes, it is very distinctly better being where we are," Lord Oliphant said, as he gazed at them. "I was beginning to feel qualmish before we got under shelter of the Point, and by this time, if I had been on board the *Henrietta*, I should have been prostrate, and should have had I know not how long misery before me."

A quarter of an hour later they were snugly moored in Dover Harbour. For twenty-four hours the gale continued; the wind then fell somewhat, but continued to blow strongly from the same quarter. Two days later it veered round to the south-west, and shortly afterwards the English fleet could be seen coming out past the Point. As soon as they did so they headed eastward.

"They are going out to meet the Dutch," Sydney said, as they watched the ships from the cliffs. "The news must have arrived that their fleet has put out to sea."

"Then we may as well be off after them, Sydney; they will sail faster than we shall in this wind, for it is blowing too strongly for us to carry much sail."

They hurried on board. A quarter of an hour later the *Fan Fan* put out from the harbour. The change of wind had caused an ugly cross sea and the yacht made bad weather of it, the waves constantly washing over her decks, but before they were off Calais she had overtaken some of the slower sailers of the Fleet. The sea was less violent as they held on, for they were now, to some extent, sheltered by the coast. In a short time Cyril ran down into the cabin where Sydney was lying ill.

"The Admiral has given the signal to anchor, and the leading ships are already bringing up. We will choose a berth as near the shore as we can; with our light draught we can lie well inside of the others, and shall be in comparatively smooth water."

Before dusk the Fleet was at anchor, with the exception of two or three of the fastest frigates, which were sent on to endeavour to obtain some news of the enemy.

CHAPTER XX.

THE FIGHT OFF DUNKIRK.

AS soon as the *Fan Fan* had been brought to an anchor the boat was lowered, and Cyril was rowed on board the Admiral's ship.

Albemarle was on the poop, and Cyril made his report to him.

"Very well, sir," the Duke said, "I daresay I shall be able to make you of some use. Keep your craft close to us when we sail. I seem to know your face."

"I am Sir Cyril Shenstone, my Lord Duke. I had the honour of meeting you first at the fire in the Savoy, and Prince Rupert afterwards was good enough to present me to you."

"Yes, yes, I remember. And it was you who saved the *Henrietta* from the fire-ship at Lowestoft. You have begun well indeed, young sir, and are like to have further opportunities of showing your bravery."

Cyril bowed, and then, going down the side to his boat, returned to the *Fan Fan*. She was lying in almost smooth water, and Sydney had come up on deck again.

"You heard no news of the Dutch, I suppose, Cyril?"

"No; I asked a young officer as I left the ship, and he said that, so far as he knew, nothing had been heard of them, but news had come in, before the Admiral sailed from the Downs, that everything was ready for sea, and that orders were expected every hour for them to put out."

"It is rather to be hoped that they won't put out for another two days," Sydney said. "That will give the Prince time to rejoin with his squadron. The wind is favourable now for his return, and I should think, as soon as they hear in London that the Dutch are on the point of putting out, and Albemarle has sailed, they will send him orders to join us at once. We have only about sixty sail, while they say that the Dutch have over ninety, which is too heavy odds against us to be pleasant."

"I should think the Duke will not fight till the Prince comes up."

"I don't think he will wait for him if he finds the Dutch near. All say that he is over-confident, and apt to despise the Dutch too much. Anyhow, he is as brave as a lion, and, though he might not attack unless the Dutch begin it, I feel sure he will not run away from them."

The next morning early, the *Bristol* frigate was seen returning from the east. She had to beat her way back in the teeth of the wind, but, when still some miles away, a puff of white smoke was seen to dart out from her side, and presently the boom of a heavy gun was heard. Again and again she fired, and the signal was understood to be a notification that she had seen the Dutch. The signal for the captains of the men-of-war to come on board was at once run up to the mast-head of the flagship, followed by another for the Fleet to be prepared to weigh anchor. Captain Bacon, of the *Bristol*, went on board as soon as his ship came up. In a short time the boats were seen to put off, and as the captains reached their respective ships the signal to weigh anchor was hoisted.

This was hailed with a burst of cheering throughout the Fleet, and all felt that it signified that they would soon meet the Dutch. The *Fan Fan* was under sail long before the men-of-war had got up their heavy anchors, and, sailing out, tacked backwards and forwards until the Fleet were under sail, when Cyril told the boatswain to place her within a few cables' length of the flagship on her weather quarter. After two hours' sail the Dutch Fleet were made out, anchored off Dunkirk. The Blue Squadron, under Sir William Berkley, led the way, the Red Squadron, under the Duke, following.

"I will put a man in the chains with the lead," the boatswain said to Cyril. "There are very bad sands off Dunkirk, and though we might get over them in safety, the big ships would take ground, and if they did so we should be in a bad plight indeed."

"In that case, we had best slack out the sheet a little, and take up our post on the weather bow of the Admiral, so that we can signal to him if we find water failing."

The topsail was hoisted, and the *Fan Fan*, which was a very fast craft in comparatively smooth water, ran past the Admiral's flagship.

"Shall I order him back, your Grace?" the Captain asked angrily.

Albemarle looked at the *Fan Fan* attentively.

"They have got a man sounding," he said. "It is a wise precaution. The young fellow in command knows what he is doing. We ought to have been taking the same care. See! he is taking down his topsail again. Set an officer to watch the yacht, and if they signal, go about at once."

The soundings continued for a short time at six fathoms, when suddenly the man at the lead called out sharply,—

"Three fathoms!"

Cyril ran to the flagstaff, and as the next cry came—"Two fathoms!"—hauled down the flag and stood waving his cap, while the boatswain, who had gone to the tiller, at once pushed it over to starboard, and brought the yacht up into the wind. Cyril heard orders shouted on board the flagship, and saw her stern sweeping round. A moment later her sails were aback, but the men, who already clustered round the guns, were not quick enough in hauling the yards across, and, to his dismay, he saw the main topmast bend, and then go over the side with a crash. All was confusion on board, and for a time it seemed as if the other topmast would also go.

"Run her alongside within hailing distance," Cyril said to the boatswain. "They will want to question us."

As they came alongside the flagship the Duke himself leant over the side.

"What water had you when you came about, sir?"

"We went suddenly from six fathoms to three, your Grace," Cyril shouted, "and a moment after we found but two."

"Very well, sir," the Duke called back. "In that case you have certainly saved our ship. I thought perhaps that you had been over-hasty, and had thus cost us our topmast, but I see it was not so, and thank you. Our pilot assured us there was plenty of water on the course we were taking."

The ships of the Red Squadron had all changed their course on seeing the flagship come about so suddenly, and considerable delay and confusion was caused before they again formed in order, and, in obedience to the Duke's signal, followed in support of the Blue Squadron. This had already dashed into the midst of the Dutch Fleet, who were themselves in some confusion; for, so sudden had been the attack, that they had been forced to cut their cables, having no time to get up their anchors.

The British ships poured in their broadsides as they approached, while the Dutch opened a tremendous cannonade. Besides their great inferiority in numbers, the British were under a serious disadvantage. They had the weather gauge, and the wind was so strong that it heeled them over, so that they were unable to open their lower ports, and were therefore deprived of the use of their heaviest guns.

Four of the ships of the Red Squadron remained by the flag ship, to protect her if attacked, and to keep off fire-ships, while her crew laboured to get up another topmast. More than three hours were occupied in this operation, but so busily did the rest of the Fleet keep the Dutch at work that they were unable to detach sufficient ships to attack her.

As soon as the topmast was in place and the sails hoisted, the flagship and her consorts hastened to join their hard-pressed comrades.

The fight was indeed a desperate one. Sir William Berkley and his ship, the *Swiftsure*, a second-rate, was taken, as was the *Essex*, a third-rate.

The *Henry*, commanded by Sir John Harman, was surrounded by foes. Her sails and rigging were shot to pieces, so she was completely disabled, and the Dutch Admiral, Cornelius Evertz, summoned Sir John Harman to surrender.

"It has not come to that yet," Sir John shouted back, and continued to pour such heavy broadsides into the Dutch that several of their ships were greatly damaged, and Evertz himself killed.

The Dutch captains drew off their vessels, and launched three fire-ships at the *Henry*. The first one, coming up on her starboard quarter, grappled with her. The dense volumes of smoke rising from her prevented the sailors from discovering where the grapnels were fixed, and the flames were spreading to her when her boatswain gallantly leapt on board the fire-ship, and, by the light of its flames, discovered the grapnels and threw them overboard, and succeeded in regaining his ship.

A moment later, the second fire-ship came up on the port side, and so great a body of flames swept across the *Henry* that her chaplain and fifty men sprang overboard. Sir John, however, drew his sword, and threatened to cut down the first man who refused to obey orders, and the rest of the crew, setting manfully to work, succeeded in extinguishing the flames, and in getting free of the fire-ship. The halliards of the main yard, were, however, burnt through, and the spar fell, striking Sir John Harman to the deck and breaking his leg.

The third fire-ship was received with the fire of four cannon loaded with chain shot. These brought her mast down, and she drifted by, clear of the *Henry*, which was brought safely into Harwich.

The fight continued the whole day, and did not terminate until ten o'clock in the evening. The night was spent in repairing damages, and in the morning the English recommenced the battle. It was again obstinately contested. Admiral Van Tromp threw himself into the midst of the British line, and suffered so heavily that he was only saved by the arrival of Admiral de Ruyter. He, in his turn, was in a most perilous position, and his ship disabled, when fresh reinforcements arrived. And so the battle raged, until, in the afternoon, as if by mutual consent, the Fleets drew off from each other, and the battle ceased. The fighting had been extraordinarily obstinate and determined on both sides, many ships had been sunk, several burnt, and some captured. The sea was dotted with wreckage, masts, and spars, fragments of boats and *débris* of all kinds. Both fleets presented a pitiable appearance; the hulls, but forty-eight hours ago so trim and smooth, were splintered and jagged, port-holes were knocked into one, bulwarks carried away, and stern galleries gone. The sails were riddled with shot-holes, many of the ships had lost one or more masts, while the light spars had been, in most cases, carried away, and many of the yards had come down owing to the destruction of the running gear.

In so tremendous a conflict the little *Fan Fan* could bear but a small part. Cyril and Lord Oliphant agreed, at the commencement of the first day's fight, that it would be useless for them to attempt to fire their two little guns, but that their efforts should be entirely directed against the enemy's fire-ships. During each day's battle, then, they hovered round the flagship, getting out of the way whenever she was engaged, as she often was, on both broadsides, and although once or twice struck by stray shots, the *Fan Fan* received no serious damage. In this encounter of giants, the little yacht was entirely overlooked, and none of the great ships wasted a shot upon her. Two or three times each day, when the Admiral's ship had beaten off her foes, a fire-ship directed its course against her. Then came the *Fan Fan's* turn for action. Under the pressure of her twelve oars she sped towards the fire-ship, and on reaching her a grapnel was thrown over the end of the bowsprit, and by the efforts of the rowers her course was changed, so that she swept harmlessly past the flagship.

Twice when the vessels were coming down before the wind at a rate of speed that rendered it evident that the efforts of the men at the oars would be insufficient to turn her course, the *Fan Fan* was steered alongside, grapnels were thrown, and, headed by Lord Oliphant and Cyril, the crew sprang on board, cut down or drove overboard the few men who were in charge of her. Then, taking the helm and trimming the sails, they directed her against one of the Dutch men-of-war, threw the grapnels on board, lighted the train, leapt back into the *Fan Fan*, rowed away, and took up their place near the Admiral, the little craft being greeted with hearty cheers by the whole ship's company.

The afternoon was spent in repairing damages as far as practicable, but even the Duke saw it was impossible to continue the fight. The Dutch had received a reinforcement while the fighting was going on that morning, and although the English had inflicted terrible damage upon the Dutch Fleet, their own loss in ships was greater than that which they had caused their adversaries. A considerable portion of their vessels were not in a condition to renew the battle, and the carpenters had hard work to save them from sinking outright. Albemarle himself embarked on the *Fan Fan*, and sailed from ship to ship, ascertaining the condition of each, and the losses its crew had suffered. As soon as night fell, the vessels most disabled were ordered to sail for England as they best could. The crew of three which were totally dismasted and could hardly be kept afloat, were taken out and divided between the twenty-eight vessels which alone remained in a condition to renew the fight.

These three battered hulks were, early the next morning, set on fire, and the rest of the Fleet, in good order and prepared to give battle, followed their companions that had sailed on the previous evening. The Dutch followed, but at a distance, thinking to repair their damages still farther before they again engaged. In the afternoon the sails of a squadron were seen ahead, and a loud cheer ran from ship to ship, for all knew that this was Prince Rupert coming up with the White Squadron. A serious loss, however, occurred a few minutes afterwards. The *Royal Prince*, the largest and most powerful vessel in the Fleet, which was somewhat in rear of the line, struck on the sands. The tide being with them and the wind light, the rest of the Fleet tried in vain to return to her assistance, and as the Dutch Fleet were fast coming up, and some of the fire-ships making for the *Royal Prince*, they were forced to give up the attempt to succour her, and Sir George Ayscue, her captain, was obliged to haul down his flag and surrender.

As soon as the White Squadron joined the remnant of the Fleet the whole advanced against the Dutch, drums beating

THE FIGHT OFF DUNKIRK. 343

and trumpets sounding, and twice made their way through the enemy's line. But it was now growing dark, and the third day's battle came to an end. The next morning it was seen that the Dutch, although considerably stronger than the English, were almost out of sight. The latter at once hoisted sail and pursued, and, at eight o'clock, came up with them.

The Dutch finding the combat inevitable, the terrible fight was renewed, and raged, without intermission, until seven in the evening. Five times the British passed through the line of the Dutch. On both sides many ships fell out of the fighting line wholly disabled. Several were sunk, and some on both sides forced to surrender, being so battered as to be unable to withdraw from the struggle. Prince Rupert's ship was wholly disabled, and that of Albemarle almost as severely damaged, and the battle, like those of the preceding days, ended without any decided advantage on either side. Both nations claimed the victory, but equally without reason. The Dutch historians compute our loss at sixteen men-of-war, of which ten were sunk and six taken, while we admitted only a loss of nine ships, and claimed that the Dutch lost fifteen men-of-war. Both parties acknowledged that it was the most terrible battle fought in this, or any other modern war.

De Witte, who at that time was at the head of the Dutch Republic, and who was a bitter enemy of the English, owned, some time afterwards, to Sir William Temple, " that the English got more glory to their nation through the invincible courage of their seamen during those engagements than by the two victories of this war, and that he was sure that his own fleet could not have been brought on to fight the fifth day, after the disadvantages of the fourth, and he believed that no other nation was capable of it but the English."

Cyril took no part in the last day's engagement, for Prince Rupert, when the *Fan Fan* came near him on his arrival on the previous evening, returned his salute from the poop, and shouted to him that on no account was he to adventure into the fight with the *Fan Fan*.

On the morning after the battle ended, Lord Oliphant and Cyril rowed on board Prince Rupert's ship, where every unwounded man was hard at work getting up a jury-mast or patching up the holes in the hull.

"Well, Sir Cyril, I see that you have been getting my yacht knocked about," he said, as they came up to him.

"There is not much damage done, sir. She has but two shot-holes in her hull."

"And my new mainsail spoiled. Do you know, sir, that I got a severe rating from the Duke yesterday evening, on your account?"

Cyril looked surprised.

"I trust, sir, that I have not in any way disobeyed orders?"

"No, it was not that. He asked after the *Fan Fan*, and said that he had seen nothing of her during the day's fighting, and I said I had strictly ordered you not to come into the battle. He replied, 'Then you did wrong, Prince, for that little yacht of yours did yeomen's service during the first two days' fighting. I told Sir Cyril to keep her near me, thinking that she would be useful in carrying orders, and during those two days she kept close to us, save when we were surrounded by the enemy. Five times in those three days did she avert fire-ships from us. We were so damaged that we could sail but slowly, and, thinking us altogether unmanageable, the Dutch launched their fire-ships. The *Fan Fan* rowed to meet them. Three of them were diverted from their course by a rope being thrown over the bowsprit, and the crew rowing so as to turn her head. On the second day there was more wind, and the fire-ships could have held on their course in spite of the efforts of the men on board the *Fan Fan*. Twice during the day the little boat was boldly laid alongside them, while the crew boarded and captured them, and then, directing them towards the Dutch ships, grappled and set them on fire. One of the Dutchmen was burned, the other managed to throw off the grapnels. It was all done under our eyes, and five times in the two days did my crew cheer your little yacht as she came alongside. So you see, Prince, by ordering her out of the fight you deprived us of the assistance of as boldly handled a little craft as ever sailed.'

"'I am quite proud of my little yacht, gentlemen, and I thank you for having given her so good a christening under fire.' But I must stay no longer talking. Here is the despatch I have written of my share of the engagement. You, Sir Cyril, will deliver this. You will now row to the Duke's ship, and he will give you his despatches, which you, Lord Oliphant, will deliver. I need not say that you are to make all haste to the Thames. We have no ship to spare except the *Fan Fan*, for we must keep the few that are still able to manœuvre, in case the Dutch should come out again before we have got the crippled ones in a state to make sail."

Taking leave of the Prince, they were at once rowed to the Duke's flagship. They had a short interview with the Admiral, who praised them highly for the service they had rendered.

"You will have to tell the story of the fighting," he said, "for the Prince and myself have written but few lines; we have too many matters on our minds to do scribe's work. They will have heard, ere now, of the first two days' fighting, for some of the ships that were sent back will have arrived at Harwich before this. By to-morrow morning I hope to have the Fleet so far refitted as to be able to follow you."

Five minutes later, the *Fan Fan*, with every stitch of sail set, was on her way to the Thames. As a brisk wind was blowing, they arrived in London twenty-four hours later, and at once proceeded to the Admiralty, the despatches being addressed to the Duke of York. They were immediately ushered in to him. Without a word he seized the despatches, tore them open, and ran his eye down them.

"God be praised!" he exclaimed, when he finished them. "We had feared even worse intelligence, and have been in a terrible state of anxiety since yesterday, when we heard from Harwich that one of the ships had come in with the news that more than half the Fleet was crippled or destroyed, and that twenty-eight only remained capable of continuing the battle. The only hope was that the White Squadron might arrive in time, and it seems that it has done so. The account of our losses is indeed a terrible one, but at least we have suffered no defeat, and as the Dutch have retreated, they must have suffered well-nigh as much as we have done. Come along with me at once, gentlemen; I must go to the King to inform him of this great news, which is vastly beyond what we could have hoped for. The Duke, in his despatch, tells me that the bearers of it, Lord Oliphant and Sir Cyril Shenstone, have done very great service, having, in Prince Rupert's little yacht, saved his flagship no less than five times from the attacks of the Dutch fire-ships."

The Duke had ordered his carriage to be in readiness as soon as he learnt that the bearers of despatches from the Fleet had arrived. It was already at the door, and, taking his seat in it, with Lord Oliphant and Cyril opposite to him, he was driven to the Palace, learning by the way such details as they could give him of the last two days' fighting. He led them at once to the King's dressing-room. Charles was already attired, for he had passed a sleepless night, and had risen early.

"What news, James?" he asked eagerly.

"Good news, brother. After two more days' fighting—and terrible fighting, on both sides—the Dutch Fleet has returned to its ports."

"A victory!" the King exclaimed, in delight.

"A dearly-bought one with the lives of so many brave men, but a victory nevertheless. Here are the despatches from Albemarle and Rupert. They have been brought by these gentlemen, with whom you are already acquainted, in Rupert's yacht. Albemarle speaks very highly of their conduct."

The King took the despatches, and read them eagerly.

"It has indeed been a dearly-bought victory," he said, "but it is marvellous indeed how our captains and men bore

"WHAT NEWS, JAMES?" THE KING ASKED EAGERLY.

themselves. Never have they shown greater courage and endurance. Well may Monk say that, after four days of incessant fighting and four nights spent in the labour of repairing damages, the strength of all has well nigh come to an end, and that he himself can write but a few lines to tell me of what has happened, leaving all details for further occasion. I thank you both, gentlemen, for the speed with which you have brought me this welcome news, and for the services of which the Duke of Albemarle speaks so warmly. This is the second time, Sir Cyril, that my admirals have had occasion to speak of great and honourable service rendered by you. Lord Oliphant, the Earl, your father, will have reason to be proud when he hears you so highly praised. Now, gentlemen, tell me more fully than is done in these despatches as to the incidents of the fighting. I have heard something of what took place in the first two days from an officer who posted up from Harwich yesterday."

Lord Oliphant related the events of the first two days, and then went on.

"Of the last two I can say less, Your Majesty, for we took no part in, having Prince Rupert's orders, given as he came up, that we should not adventure into the fight. Therefore, we were but spectators, though we kept on the edge of the fight and, if opportunity had offered, and we had seen one of our ships too hard pressed, and threatened by fire-ships, we should have ventured so far to transgress orders as to bear in and do what we could on her behalf; but indeed, the smoke was so great that we could see but little.

" It was a strange sight, when, on the Prince's arrival, his ships and those of the Duke's, battered as they were, bore down on the Dutch line; the drums beating, the trumpets sounding, and the crews cheering loudly. We saw them disappear into the Dutch line; then the smoke shut all out from view, and for hours there was but a thick cloud of smoke and a continuous roar of the guns. Sometimes a vessel would come out from the curtain of smoke torn and disabled. Sometimes it was a Dutchman, sometimes one of our own ships. If the latter, we rowed up to them and did our best with planks and nails to stop the yawning holes close to the water-line, while the crew knotted ropes and got up the spars and yards, and then sailed back into the fight.

"The first day's fighting was comparatively slight, for the Dutch seemed to be afraid to close with the Duke's ships, and hung behind at a distance. It was not till the White Squadron came up, and the Duke turned, with Prince Rupert, and fell upon his pursuers like a wounded boar upon the dogs, that the battle commenced in earnest; but the last day it went on for nigh twelve hours without intermission; and when at last the roar of the guns ceased, and the smoke slowly cleared off, it was truly a pitiful sight, so torn and disabled were the ships.

"As the two fleets separated, drifting apart as it would almost seem, so few were the sails now set, we rowed up among them, and for hours were occupied in picking up men clinging to broken spars and wreckage, for but few of the ships had so much as a single boat left. We were fortunate enough to save well-nigh a hundred, of whom more than seventy were our own men, the remainder Dutch. From these last we learnt that the ships of Van Tromp and Ruyter had both been so disabled that they had been forced to fall out of battle, and had been towed away to port. They said that their Admirals Cornelius Evertz and Van der Hulst had both been killed, while on our side we learnt that Admiral Sir Christopher Mings had fallen."

"Did the Dutch Fleet appear to be as much injured as our own?"

"No, Your Majesty. Judging by the sail set when the battle was over, theirs must have been in better condition than ours, which is not surprising, seeing how superior they were in force, and for the most part bigger ships, and carrying more guns."

"Then you will have your hands full, James, or they will

be ready to take to sea again before we are. Next time I hope that we shall meet them with more equal numbers."

"I will do the best I can, brother," the Duke replied. "Though we have so many ships sorely disabled there have been but few lost, and we can supply their places with the vessels that have been building with all haste. If the Dutch will give us but two months' time I warrant that we shall be able to meet them in good force."

As soon as the audience was over, Cyril and his friend returned to the *Fan Fan*, and after giving the crew a few hours for sleep, sailed down to Sheerness, where, shortly afterwards, Prince Rupert arrived with a portion of the Fleet, the rest having been ordered to Harwich, Portsmouth, and other ports, so that they could be more speedily refitted.

Although the work went on almost without intermission day and night, the repairs were not completed before the news arrived that the Dutch Fleet had again put to sea. Two days later they arrived off our coast, where, finding no fleet ready to meet them, they sailed away to France, where they hoped to be joined by their French allies.

Two days later, however, our ships began to assemble at the mouth of the Thames, and on June 24th the whole Fleet was ready to take to sea. It consisted of eighty men-of-war, large and small, and nineteen fire-ships. Prince Rupert was in command of the Red Squadron, and the Duke of Albemarle sailed with him, on board the same ship. Sir Thomas Allen was Admiral of the White, and Sir Jeremiah Smith of the Blue Squadron. Cyril remained on board the *Fan Fan*, Lord Oliphant returning to his duties on board the flagship. Marvels had been effected by the zeal and energy of the crews and dockyard men. But three weeks back, the English ships had, for the most part, been crippled seemingly almost beyond repair, but now, with their holes patched, with new spars, and in the glory of fresh paint and new canvas, they made as brave a show as when they had sailed out from the Downs a month previously.

They were anchored off the Nore when, late in the evening, the news came out from Sheerness that a mounted messenger had just ridden in from Dover, and that the Dutch Fleet had, in the afternoon, passed the town, and had rounded the South Foreland, steering north.

Orders were at once issued that the Fleet should sail at daybreak, and at three o'clock the next morning they were on their way down the river. At ten o'clock the Dutch Fleet was seen off the North Foreland. According to their own accounts they numbered eighty-eight men-of-war, with twenty-five fire-ships, and were also divided into three squadrons, under De Ruyter, John Evertz, and Van Tromp.

The engagement began at noon by an attack by the White Squadron upon that commanded by Evertz. An hour later, Prince Rupert and the Duke, with the Red Squadron, fell upon De Ruyter, while that of Van Tromp, which was at some distance from the others, was engaged by Sir Jeremiah Smith with the Blue Squadron. Sir Thomas Allen completely defeated his opponents, killing Evertz, his vice- and rear-admirals, capturing the vice-admiral of Zeeland, who was with him, and burning a ship of fifty guns.

The Red Squadron was evenly matched by that of De Ruyter, and each vessel laid itself alongside an adversary. Although De Ruyter himself and his vice-admiral, Van Nes, fought obstinately, their ships in general, commanded, for the most part, by men chosen for their family influence rather than for either seamanship or courage, behaved but badly, and all but seven gradually withdrew from the fight, and went off under all sail; and De Ruyter, finding himself thus deserted, was forced also to draw off. During this time, Van Tromp, whose squadron was the strongest of the three Dutch divisions, was so furiously engaged by the Blue Squadron, which was the weakest of the English divisions, that he was unable to come to the assistance of his consorts; when, however, he saw the defeat of the rest of the Dutch Fleet, he, too, was obliged to draw off, lest he should have the whole of the English down upon him, and was able the more easily to do so as darkness was closing in when the battle ended.

The Dutch continued their retreat during the night, followed at a distance by the Red Squadron, which was, next morning, on the point of overtaking them, when the Dutch sought refuge by steering into the shallows, which their light draught enabled them to cross, while the deeper English ships were unable to follow. Great was the wrath and disappointment of the English when they saw themselves thus baulked of reaping the full benefit of the victory. Prince Rupert shouted to Cyril, who, in the *Fan Fan*, had taken but small share in the engagement, as the fire-ships had not played any conspicious part in it.

"Sir Cyril, we can go no farther, but do you pursue De Ruyter and show him in what contempt we hold him."

Cyril lifted his hat to show that he heard and understood the order. Then he ordered his men to get out their oars, for the wind was very light, and, amidst loud cheering, mingled with laughter, from the crews of the vessels that were near enough to hear Prince Rupert's order, the *Fan Fan* rowed out from the English line in pursuit of the Dutch.

CHAPTER XXI.

LONDON IN FLAMES.

THE sailors laughed and joked as they rowed away from the Fleet, but the old boatswain shook his head.

"We shall have to be careful, Sir Cyril," he said. "It is like a small cur barking at the heels of a bull—it is good fun enough for a bit, but when the bull turns, perchance the dog will find himself thrown high in the air."

Cyril nodded. He himself considered Prince Rupert's order to be beyond all reason, and given only in the heat of his anger at De Ruyter having thus escaped him, and felt that it was very likely to cost the lives of all on board the *Fan Fan*. However, there was nothing to do but to carry it out. It seemed to him that the boatswain's simile was a very apt one, and that, although the spectacle of the *Fan Fan* worrying the great Dutch battle-ship might be an amusing one to the English spectators, it was likely to be a very serious adventure for her.

De Ruyter's ship, which was in the rear of all the other Dutch vessels, was but a mile distant when the *Fan Fan* started, and as the wind was so light that it scarce filled her sails, the yacht approached her rapidly.

"We are within half a mile now, your honour," the boatswain said. "I should say we had better go no nearer if we don't want to be blown out of the water."

"Yes; I think we may as well stop rowing now, and get the guns to work. There are only those two cannon in her stern ports which can touch us here. She will scarcely come up in the wind to give us a broadside. She is moving so slowly through the water that it would take her a long time to come round, and De Ruyter would feel ashamed to bring his great flag-ship round to crush such a tiny foe."

The boatswain went forward to the guns, round which the men, after laying in their oars, clustered in great glee.

"Now," he said, "you have got to make those two guns in the stern your mark. Try and send your shots through the portholes. It will be a waste to fire them at the hull, for the balls would not penetrate the thick timber that she is built of. Remember, the straighter you aim the more chance there is that the Dutch won't hit us. Men don't stop to aim very straight when they are expecting a shot among them every second. We will fire alternately, and one gun is not to fire until the other is loaded again. I will lay the first gun myself."

It was a good shot, and the crew cheered as they saw the

splinters fly at the edge of the port-hole. Shot after shot was fired with varying success.

The Dutch made no reply, and seemed to ignore the presence of their tiny foe. The crew were, for the most part, busy aloft repairing damages, and after half an hour's firing, without eliciting a reply, the boatswain went aft to Cyril, and suggested that they should now aim at the spars.

"A lucky shot might do a good deal of damage, sir," he said. "The weather is fine enough at present, but there is no saying when a change may come, and if we could weaken one of the main spars it might be the means of her being blown ashore, should the wind spring up in the right direction."

Cyril assented, and fire was now directed at the masts. A few ropes were cut away, but no serious damage was effected until a shot struck one of the halliard blocks of the spanker, and the sail at once ran down.

"It has taken a big bit out of the mast, too," the boatswain called exultingly to Cyril. "I think that will rouse the Dutchmen up."

A minute later it was evident that the shot had at least had that effect. Two puffs of smoke spirted out from the stern of the Dutch flagship, and, simultaneously with the roar of the guns, came the hum of two heavy shot flying overhead. Delighted at having excited the Dutchmen's wrath at last, the crew of the *Fan Fan* took off their hats and gave a loud cheer, and then, more earnestly than before, settled down to work; their guns aimed now, as at first, at the port-holes. Four or five shots were discharged from each of the little guns before the Dutch were ready again. Then came the thundering reports. The *Fan Fan's* topmast was carried away by one of the shot, but the other went wide. Two or three men were told to cut away the wreckage, and the rest continued their fire. One of the next shots of the enemy was better directed. It struck the deck close to the foot of the mast, committed great havoc in Cyril's cabin, and passed out through the stern below the water-line. Cyril leapt down the companion as he heard the crash, shouting to the boatswain to follow him. The water was coming through the hole in a great jet. Cyril seized a pillow and stuffed it into the shot-hole, being drenched from head to foot in the operation. One of the sailors had followed the boatswain, and Cyril called him to his assistance.

"Get out the oars at once," he said to the boatswain. "Another shot like this and she will go down. Get a piece cut off a spar and make a plug. There is no holding this pillow in its place, and the water comes in fast still."

The sailor took Cyril's post while he ran up on deck and assisted in cutting the plug; this was roughly shaped to the size of the hole, and then driven in. It stopped the rush of the water, but a good deal still leaked through.

By the time this was done the *Fan Fan* had considerably increased her distance from De Ruyter. Four or five more shots were fired from the Dutch ship. The last of these struck the mast ten feet above the deck, bringing it down with a crash. Fortunately, none of the crew were hurt, and, dropping the oars, they hauled the mast alongside, cut the sail from its fastening to the hoops and gaff, and then severed the shrouds and allowed the mast to drift away, while they again settled themselves to the oars. Although every man rowed his hardest, the *Fan Fan* was half full of water before she reached the Fleet, which was two miles astern of them when they first began to row.

"Well done, *Fan Fan*!" Prince Rupert shouted, as the little craft came alongside. "Have you suffered any damage besides your spars? I see you are low in the water."

"We were shot through our stern, sir; we put in a plug, but the water comes in still. Will you send a carpenter on board? For I don't think she will float many minutes longer unless we get the hole better stopped."

The Prince gave some orders to an officer standing by him. The latter called two or three sailors and bade them bring some short lengths of thick hawser, while a strong party were set to reeve tackle to the main yard. As soon as the hawsers, each thirty feet in length, were brought, they were dropped on to the deck of the *Fan Fan*, and the officer told the crew to pass them under her, one near each end, and to knot the hawsers. By the time this was done, two strong tackles were lowered and fixed to the hawsers, and the crew ordered to come up on to the ship. The tackles were then manned and hauled on by strong parties, and the *Fan Fan* was gradually raised. The boatswain went below again and knocked out the plug, and, as the little yacht was hoisted up, the water ran out of it. As soon as the hole was above the water-level, the tackle at the bow was gradually slackened off until she lay with her fore-part in the water, which came some distance up her deck. The carpenter then slung himself over the stern, and nailed, first a piece of tarred canvas, and then a square of plank, over the hole. Then the stern tackle was eased off, and the *Fan Fan* floated on a level keel. Her crew went down to her again, and, in half an hour, pumped her free of water.

By this time, the results of the victory were known. On the English side, the *Resolution* was the only ship lost, she having been burnt by a Dutch fire-ship; three English captains, and about three hundred men were killed. On the other hand, the Dutch lost twenty ships, four admirals, a great many of their captains, and some four thousand men. It was, indeed, the greatest and most complete victory gained throughout the war. Many of the British ships had suffered a good deal, that which carried the Duke's flag most of all, for it had been so battered in the fight with De Ruyter that the Duke and Prince Rupert had been obliged to leave her, and to hoist their flags upon another man-of-war.

The next morning the Fleet sailed to Schonevelt, which was the usual *rendezvous* of the Dutch Fleet, and there remained some time, altogether undisturbed by the enemy. The *Fan Fan* was here thoroughly repaired.

On July 29th they sailed for Ulie, where they arrived on August 7th, the wind being contrary.

Learning that there was a large fleet of merchantmen lying between the islands of Ulie and Schelling, guarded by but two men-of-war, and that there were rich magazines of goods on these islands, it was determined to attack them. Four small frigates, of a slight draught of water, and five fire-ships, were selected for the attack, together with the boats of the Fleet, manned by nine hundred men.

On the evening of the 8th, Cyril was ordered to go, in the *Fan Fan*, to reconnoitre the position of the Dutch. He did not sail until after nightfall, and, on reaching the passage between the islands, he lowered his sails, got out his oars, and drifted with the tide silently down through the Dutch merchant fleet, where no watch seemed to be kept, and in the morning carried the news to Sir Robert Holmes, the commander of the expedition, who had anchored a league from the entrance.

Cyril had sounded the passage as he went through, and it was found that two of the frigates could not enter it. These were left at the anchorage, and, on arriving at the mouth of the harbour, the *Tiger*, Sir Robert Holmes's flagship, was also obliged to anchor, and he came on board the *Fan Fan*, on which he hoisted his flag. The captains of the other ships came on board, and it was arranged that the *Pembroke*, which had but a small draft of water, should enter at once with the five fire-ships.

The attack was completely successful. Two of the fire-ships grappled with the men-of-war and burnt them, while three great merchantmen were destroyed by the others. Then the boats dashed into the fleet, and, with the exception of four or five merchantmen and four privateers, who took refuge in a creek, defended by a battery, the whole of the hundred and seventy merchantmen, the smallest of which was not less than 200 tons burden, and all heavily laden, were burned.

The next day, Sir Robert Holmes landed eleven companies of troops on the Island of Schonevelt and burnt Bandaris, its principal town, with its magazines and store-houses, causing a loss to the Dutch, according to their own admission, of six million guilders. This, and the loss of the great Fleet, inflicted a very heavy blow upon the commerce of Holland. The *Fan Fan* had been hit again by a shot from one of the batteries, and, on her rejoining the Fleet, Prince Rupert determined to send her to England so that she could be thoroughly repaired and fitted out again. Cyril's orders were to take her to Chatham, and to hand her over to the dockyard authorities.

"I do not think the Dutch will come out and fight us again this autumn, Sir Cyril, so you can take your ease in London as it pleases you. We are now halfway through August, and it will probably be at least a month after your arrival before the *Fan Fan* is fit for sea again. It may be a good deal longer than that, for they are busy upon the repairs of the ships sent home after the battle, and will hardly take any hands off these to put on to the *Fan Fan*. In October we shall all be coming home again, so that, until next spring, it is hardly likely that there will be aught doing."

Cyril accordingly returned to London. The wind was contrary, and it was not until the last day of August that he dropped anchor in the Medway. After spending a night at Chatham, he posted up to London the next morning, and, finding convenient chambers in the Savoy, he installed himself there, and then proceeded to the house of the Earl of Wisbech, to whom he was the bearer of a letter from his son. Finding that the Earl and his family were down at his place near Sevenoaks, he went into the City, and spent the evening at Captain Dave's, having ordered his servant to pack a small valise, and bring it with the two horses in the morning. He had gone to bed but an hour when he was awoke by John Wilkes knocking at his door.

"There is a great fire burning not far off, Sir Cyril. A man who ran past told me it was in Pudding Lane, at the top of Fish Street. The Captain is getting up, and is going out to see it; for, with such dry weather as we have been having, there is no saying how far it may go."

Cyril sprang out of his bed and dressed. Captain Dave, accustomed to slip on his clothes in a hurry, was waiting for him, and, with John Wilkes, they sallied out. There was a broad glare of light in the sky, and the bells of many of the churches were ringing out the fire-alarm. As they passed, many people put their heads out from windows and asked where the fire was. In five minutes they approached the scene. A dozen houses were blazing fiercely, while, from those near, the inhabitants were busily removing their valuables. The Fire Companies, with their buckets, were already at work, and lines of men were formed down to the river and were passing along buckets from hand to hand. Well nigh half the water was spilt, however, before it arrived at the fire, and, in the face of such a body of flame, it seemed to make no impression whatever.

"They might as well attempt to pump out a leaky ship with a child's squirt," the Captain said. "The fire will burn itself out, and we must pray heaven that the wind drops altogether; 'tis not strong, but it will suffice to carry the flames across these narrow streets. 'Tis lucky that it is from the east, so there is little fear that it will travel in our direction."

They learnt that the fire had begun in the house of Faryner, the King's baker, though none knew how it had got alight. It was not long before the flames leapt across the lane, five or six houses catching fire almost at the same moment. A cry of dismay broke from the crowd, and the fright of the neighbours increased. Half-clad women hurried from their houses, carrying their babes, and dragging their younger children out. Men staggered along with trunks of clothing and valuables. Many wrung their hands helplessly, while the City Watch guarded the streets leading to Pudding Lane, so as to prevent thieves and vagabonds from taking advantage of the confusion to plunder.

With great rapidity the flames spread from house to house. A portion of Fish Street was already invaded, and the Church of St. Magnus in danger. The fears of the people increased in proportion to the advance of the conflagration. The whole neighbourhood was now alarmed, and, in all the streets round, people were beginning to remove their goods. The river seemed to be regarded by all as the safest place of refuge. The boats from the various landing-places had already come up, and these were doing a thriving trade by taking the frightened people, with what goods they carried, to lighters and ships moored in the river.

The lines of men passing buckets had long since broken up, it being too evident that their efforts were not of the slightest avail. The wind had, in the last two hours, rapidly increased in strength, and was carrying the burning embers far and wide.

Cyril and his companions had, after satisfying their first curiosity, set to work to assist the fugitives, by aiding them to carry down their goods to the waterside. Cyril was now between eighteen and nineteen, and had grown into a powerful, young fellow, having, since he recovered from the Plague, grown fast and widened out greatly. He was able to shoulder heavy trunks, and to carry them down without difficulty.

By six o'clock, however, all were exhausted by their labours, and Captain Dave's proposal, that they should go back and get breakfast and have a wash, was at once agreed to.

At this time the greater part of Fish Street was in flames, the Church of St. Magnus had fallen, and the flames had spread to many of the streets and alleys running west. The houses on the Bridge were blazing.

"Well, father, what is the news?" Nellie exclaimed, as they entered. "What have you been doing? You are all blackened, like the men who carry out the coals from the ships. I never saw such figures."

"We have been helping people to carry their goods down to the water, Nellie. The news is bad. The fire is a terrible one."

"That we can see, father. Mother and I were at the window for hours after you left, and the whole sky seemed ablaze. Do you think that there is any danger of its coming here?"

"The wind is taking the flames the other way, Nellie, but in spite of that I think that there is danger. The heat is so great that the houses catch on this side, and we saw, as we came back, that it had travelled eastwards. Truly, I believe that if the wind keeps on as it is at present, the whole City will be destroyed. However, we will have a wash first and then some breakfast, of which we are sorely in need. Then we can talk over what had best be done."

Little was said during breakfast. The apprentices had already been out, and so excited were they at the scenes they had witnessed that they had difficulty in preserving their usual quiet and submissive demeanour. Captain Dave was wearied with his unwonted exertions. Mrs. Dowsett and Nellie both looked pale and anxious, and Cyril and John Wilkes were oppressed by the terrible scene of destruction and the widespread misery they had witnessed.

When breakfast was over, Captain Dave ordered the apprentices on no account to leave the premises. They were to put up the shutters at once, and then to await orders.

"What do you think we had better do, Cyril?" he said, when the boys had left the room.

"I should say that you had certainly better go on board a ship, Captain Dave. There is time to move now quietly, and to get many things taken on board, but if there were a swift change of wind the flames would come down so suddenly that you would have no time to save anything. Do you know of a captain who would receive you?"

"Certainly; I know of half a dozen."

"Then the first thing is to secure a boat before they are all taken up."

"I will go down to the stairs at once."

"Then I should say, John, you had better go off with Captain Dave, and, as soon as he has arranged with one of the captains, come back to shore. Let the waterman lie off in the stream, for if the flames come this way there will be a rush for boats, and people will not stop to ask to whom they belong. It will be better still to take one of the apprentices with you, leave him at the stairs till you return, and then tie up to a ship till we hail him.

"That will be the best plan," Captain Dave said. "Now, wife, you and Nellie and the maid had best set to work at once packing up all your best clothes and such other things as you may think most valuable. We shall have time, I hope, to make many trips."

"While you are away, I will go along the street and see whether the fire is making any way in this direction," Cyril said. "Of course if it's coming slowly you will have time to take away a great many things. And we may even hope that it may not come here at all."

Taking one of the apprentices, Captain Dave and John at once started for the waterside, while Cyril made his way westward.

Already, people were bringing down their goods from most of the houses. Some acted as if they believed that if they took the goods out of the houses they would be safe, and great piles of articles of all kinds almost blocked the road. Weeping women and frightened children sat on these piles as if to guard them. Some stood at their doors wringing their hands helplessly; others were already starting eastward laden with bundles and boxes, occasionally looking round as if to bid farewell to their homes. Many of the men seemed even more confused and frightened than the women, running hither and thither without purpose, shouting, gesticulating, and seeming almost distraught with fear and grief.

Cyril had not gone far when he saw that the houses on both sides of the street, at the further end, were already in flames. He was obliged to advance with great caution, for many people were recklessly throwing goods of all kinds from the windows, regardless of whom they might fall upon, and without thought of how they were to be carried away. He went on until close to the fire, and stood for a time watching. The noise was bewildering. Mingled with the roar of the flames, the crackling of woodwork, and the heavy crashes that told of the fall of roofs or walls, was the clang of the alarm-bells, shouts, cries, and screams. The fire spread steadily, but with none of the rapidity with which he had seen it fly along from house to house on the other side of the conflagration. The houses, however, were largely composed of wood. The balconies generally caught first, and the fire crept along under the roofs, and sometimes a shower of tiles, and a burst of flames, showed that it had advanced there, while the lower portion of the house was still intact.

"Is it coming, Cyril?" Mrs. Dowsett asked, when he returned.

"It is coming steadily," he said, "and can be stopped by nothing short of a miracle. Can I help you in any way?"

"No," she said; "we have packed as many things as can possibly be carried. It is well that your things are all at your lodging, Cyril, and beyond the risk of this danger."

"It would have mattered little about them," he said. "I could have replaced them easily enough. That is but a question of money. And now, in the first place, I will get the trunks and bundles you have packed downstairs. That will save time."

Assisted by the apprentice and Nellie, Cyril got all the things downstairs.

"How long have we, do you think?" Nellie asked.

"I should say that in three hours the fire will be here," he said, "It may be checked a little at the cross lanes; but I fear that three hours is all we can hope for."

Just as they had finished taking down the trunks, Captain Dave and John Wilkes arrived.

"I have arranged the affair," the former said. "My old friend, Dick Watson, will take us in his ship; she lies but a hundred yards from the stairs. Now, get on your mantle and hood, Nellie, and bring your mother and maid down."

The three women were soon at the foot of the stairs, and Mrs. Dowsett's face showed signs of tears; but, though pale, she was quiet and calm, and the servant, a stout wench, had gained confidence from her mistress's example. As soon as they were ready, the three men each shouldered a trunk. The servant and the apprentice carried one between them. Mrs. Dowsett and her daughter took as many bundles as they could carry. It was but five minutes' walk down to the stairs. The boat was lying twenty yards out in the stream, fastened up to a lighter, with the apprentice and waterman on board. It came at once alongside, and in five minutes they reached the *Good Venture*. As soon as the women had ascended the accommodation ladder, some sailors ran down and helped to carry up the trunks.

"Empty them all out in the cabin," Captain Dave said, to his wife; "we will take them back with us."

As soon as he had seen the ladies into the cabin, Captain Watson called his son Frank, who was his chief mate, and half a dozen of his men. These carried the boxes, as fast as they were emptied, down into the boat.

"We will all go ashore together," he said to Captain Dave. "I was a fool not to think of it before. We will soon make light work of it."

As soon as they reached the house, some of the sailors were sent off with the remaining trunks and bundles, while the others carried upstairs those they had brought, and quickly emptied into them the remaining contents of the drawers and linen press. So quickly and steadily did the work go on, that no less than six trips were made to the *Good Venture* in the next three hours, and at the end of that time almost everything portable had been carried away, including several pieces of valuable furniture, and a large number of objects brought home by Captain Dave from his various voyages. The last journey, indeed, was devoted to saving some of the most valuable contents of the store. Captain Dave, delighted at having saved so much, would not have thought of taking more, but Captain Watson would not hear of this.

"There is time for one more trip, old friend," he said, "and there are many things in your store that are worth more than their weight in silver. I will take my other two hands this time, and, with the eight men and our five selves, we shall be able to bring a good load."

The trunks were therefore this time packed with ship's instruments, and brass fittings of all kinds, to the full weight that could be carried. All hands then set to work, and, in a very short time, a great proportion of the portable goods were carried from the store-house into an arched cellar beneath it. By the time that they were ready to start there were but six houses between them and the fire.

"I wish we had another three hours before us," Captain Watson said. "It goes to one's heart to leave all this new rope and sail cloth, good blocks, and other things, to be burnt."

"There have been better things than that burnt to-day, Watson. Few men have saved as much as I have, thanks to your assistance and that of these stout sailors of yours. Why, the contents of these twelve boxes are worth as much as the whole of the goods remaining."

The sailors' loads were so heavy that they had to help each other to get them upon their shoulders, and the other five were scarcely less weighted; and, short as was the distance, all had to rest several times on the way to the stairs, setting their burdens upon window-sills, or upon boxes scattered in the streets. One of the ship's boats had, after the first trip, taken the place of the light wherry, but even this was weighted down to the gunwale when the men and the goods were all on board. After the first two trips, the contents of the boxes had been emptied on deck, and by the time the last arrived the three women had packed away in the empty cabins all the clothing, linen, and other articles, that had been taken below. Captain Watson ordered a stiff glass of grog to be given to each of the sailors, and then went down with the others into the main cabin, where the steward had already laid the table for a meal, and poured out five tumblers of wine.

"I have not had so tough a job since I was before the mast," he said. "What say you, Captain Dave?"

"It has been a hard morning's work, indeed, Watson, and, in truth, I feel fairly spent. But though weary in body I am cheerful in heart. It seemed to me at breakfast-time that we should save little beyond what we stood in, and now I have rescued well-nigh everything valuable that I have. I should have grieved greatly had I lost all those mementos that it took me nigh thirty years to gather, and those pieces of furniture that belonged to my father I would not have lost for any money. Truly, it has been a noble salvage."

Mrs. Dowsett and Nellie now joined them. They had quite recovered their spirits, and were delighted at the unexpected rescue of so many things precious to them, and Captain Watson was overwhelmed by their thanks for what he had done.

After the meal was over they sat quietly talking for a time, and then Cyril proposed that they should row up the river and see what progress the fire was making above the Bridge. Mrs. Dowsett, however, was too much fatigued by her sleepless night and the troubles and emotions of the morning to care about going. Captain Dave said that he was too stiff to do anything but sit quiet and smoke a pipe, and that he would superintend the getting of their things on deck a little ship-shape. Nellie embraced the offer eagerly, and young Watson, who was a well-built and handsome fellow, with a pleasant face and manner, said that he would go, and would take a couple of hands to row. The tide had just turned to run up when they set out. Cyril asked the first mate to steer, and he sat on one side of him and Nellie on the other.

"You will have to mind your oars, lads," Frank Watson said. "The river is crowded with boats."

They crossed over to the Southwark side, as it would have been dangerous to pass under the arches above which the houses were burning. The flames, however, had not spread right across the bridge, for the houses were built only over the piers, and the openings at the arches had checked the flames, and at these points numbers of men were drawing water in buckets and throwing it over the fronts of the houses, or passing them, by ropes, to other men on the roofs, which were kept deluged with water. Hundreds of willing hands were engaged in the work, for the sight of the tremendous fire on the opposite bank filled people with terror lest the flames should cross the bridge and spread to the south side of the river. The warehouses and wharves on the bank were black with spectators, who looked with astonishment and awe at the terrible scene of destruction.

It was not until they passed under the bridge that the full extent of the conflagration was visible. The fire had made its way some distance along Thames Street, and had spread far up into the City. Gracechurch Street and Lombard Street were in flames, and indeed the fire seemed to have extended a long distance further; but the smoke was so dense that it was difficult to make out the precise point that it had reached. The river was a wonderful sight. It was crowded with boats and lighters, all piled up with goods, while along the quays from Dowgate to the Temple, crowds of people were engaged in placing what goods they had saved on board lighters and other craft. Many of those in the boats seemed altogether helpless and undecided as to what had best be done, and drifted along with the tide, but the best part were making either for the marshes at Lambeth or the fields at Millbank, there to land their goods, the owners of the boats refusing to keep them long on board, as they desired to return by the next tide to fetch away other cargoes, being able to obtain any price they chose to demand for their services.

Among the boats were floating goods and wreckage of all kinds, charred timber that had fallen from the houses on the bridge, and from the warehouses by the quays, bales of goods, articles of furniture, bedding, and other matters. At times, a sudden change of wind drove a dense smoke across the water, flakes of burning embers and papers causing great confusion among the boats, and threatening to set the piles of goods on fire.

At Frank Watson's suggestion, they landed at the Temple, after having been some two hours on the river. Going up into Fleet Street, they found a stream of carts and other vehicles proceeding westward, all piled with furniture and goods, mostly of a valuable kind. The pavements were well-nigh blocked with people, all journeying in the same direction, laden with their belongings. With difficulty they made their way East as far as St. Paul's. The farther end of Cheapside was already in flames, and they learnt that the fire had extended as far as Moorfields. It was said that efforts had been made to pull down houses and so check its progress, but that there was no order or method, and that no benefit was gained by the work.

After looking on at the scene for some time, they returned to Fleet Street. Frank Watson went down with Nellie to the boat, while Cyril went to his lodgings in the Savoy. Here he found his servant anxiously awaiting him.

"I did not bring the horses this morning, sir," he said. "I heard that there was a great fire, and went on foot as far as I could get, but, finding that I could not pass, I thought it best to come back here and await your return."

"Quite right, Reuben; you could not have got the horses to me unless you had ridden round the walls and come in at Aldgate, and they would have been useless had you brought them. The house at which I stayed last night is already burnt to the ground. You had better stay here for the present, I think. There is no fear of the fire extending beyond the City. Should you find that it does so, pack my clothes in the valises, take the horses down to Sevenoaks, and remain at the Earl's until you hear from me."

Having arranged this, Cyril went down to the Savoy stairs, where he found the boat waiting for him, and then they rowed back to London Bridge, where, the force of the tide being now abated, they were able to row through and get to the *Good Venture*.

They had but little sleep that night. Gradually the fire

worked its way eastward until it was abreast of them. The roaring and crackling of the flames was prodigious. Here and there the glare was diversified by columns of a deeper red glow, showing where warehouses, filled with pitch, tar, and oil, were in flames. The heavy crashes of falling buildings were almost incessant. Occasionally they saw a church tower or steeple, that had stood for a time black against the glowing sky, become suddenly wreathed in flames, and, after burning for a time, fall with a crash that could be plainly heard above the general roar.

"Surely such a fire was never seen before!" Captain Dave said.

"Not since Rome was burnt, I should think," Cyril replied.

"How long was that ago, Cyril? I don't remember hearing about it."

"'Tis fifteen hundred years or so since then, Captain Dave; but the greater part of the city was destroyed, and Rome was then many times bigger than London. It burnt for three days."

"Well, this is bad enough," Captain Watson said. "Even here the heat is well-nigh too great to face. Frank, you had better call the crew up and get all the sails off the yards. Were a burning flake to fall on them we might find it difficult to extinguish them. When they have done that, let the men get all the buckets filled with water and ranged on the deck; and it will be as well to get a couple of hands in the boat and let them chuck water against this side. We shall have all the paint blistered off before morning."

So the night passed. Occasionally they went below for a short time, but they found it impossible to sleep, and were soon up again, and felt it a relief when the morning began to break.

CHAPTER XXII.

AFTER THE FIRE.

DAYLIGHT brought little alleviation to the horrors of the scene. The flames were less vivid, but a dense pall of smoke overhung the sky. As soon as they had breakfasted, Captain Watson, his son, Captain Dowsett, Nellie, and Cyril, took their places in the boat, and were rowed up the river. An exclamation burst from them all as they saw how fast the flames had travelled since the previous evening.

"St. Paul's is on fire!" Cyril exclaimed. "See! there are flames bursting through its roof. I think, Captain Watson, if you will put me ashore at the Temple, I will make my way to Whitehall, and report myself there. I may be of use."

"I will do that," Captain Watson said. "Then I will row back to the ship again. We must leave a couple of hands on board, in case some of these burning flakes should set anything alight. We will land with the rest, and do what we can to help these poor women and children."

"I will stay on board and take command, if you like, Watson," Captain Dave said. "You ought to have some one there, and I have not recovered from yesterday's work, and should be of little use ashore."

"Very well, Dowsett. That will certainly be best; but I think it will be prudent, before we leave, to run out a kedge with forty or fifty fathoms of cable towards the middle of the stream, and then veer out the cable on her anchor so as to let her ride thirty fathoms or so farther out. We left six men sluicing her side and deck, but it certainly would be prudent to get her out a bit farther. Even here, the heat is as much as we can stand."

As soon as Cyril had landed, he hurried up into Fleet Street. He had just reached Temple Bar when he saw a party of horsemen making their way through the carts. A hearty cheer greeted them from the crowd, who hoped that the presence of the King—for it was Charles who rode in front—was a sign that vigorous steps were about to be taken to check the progress of the flames. Beside the King rode the Duke of Albemarle, and following were a number of other gentlemen and officers. Cyril made his way through the crowd to the side of the Duke's horse.

"Can I be of any possible use, my Lord Duke?" he asked, doffing his hat.

"Ah, Sir Cyril, it is you, is it? I have not seen you since you bearded De Ruyter in the *Fan Fan*. Yes, you can be of use. We have five hundred sailors and dockyard men behind; they have just arrived from Chatham, and a thousand more have landed below the Bridge to fight the flames on that side. Keep by me now, and, when we decide where to set to work, I will put you under the orders of Captain Warncliffe, who has charge of them."

When they reached the bottom of Fleet Street, the fire was halfway down Ludgate Hill, and it was decided to begin operations along the bottom of the Fleet Valley. The dockyard men and sailors were brought up, and following them were some carts laden with kegs of powder.

"Warncliffe," Lord Albemarle said, as the officer came up at the head of them, "Sir Cyril Shenstone is anxious to help. You know him by repute, and you can trust him in any dangerous business. You had better tell off twenty men under him. You have only to tell him what you want done, and you can rely upon its being done thoroughly."

The sailors were soon at work along the line of the Fleet Ditch. All carried axes, and with these they chopped down the principal beams of the small houses clustered by the Ditch, and so weakened them that a small charge of powder easily brought them down. In many places they met with fierce opposition from the owners, who, still clinging to the faint hope that something might occur to stop the progress of the fire before it reached their abodes, raised vain protestations against the destruction of their houses. All day the men worked unceasingly, but in vain. Driven by the fierce wind, the flames swept down the opposite slope, leapt over the space strewn with rubbish and beams, and began to climb Fleet Street and Holborn Hill and the dense mass of houses between them.

The fight was renewed higher up. Beer, and bread and cheese were obtained from the taverns, and served out to the workmen, and these kept at their task all night. Towards morning the wind had fallen somewhat. The open spaces of the Temple favoured the defenders; the houses to east of it were blown up, and, late in the afternoon, the progress of the flames at this spot was checked. As soon as it was felt that there was no longer any fear of its further advance here, the exhausted men, who had, for twenty-four hours, laboured, half suffocated by the blinding smoke and by the dust made by their own work, threw themselves down on the grass of the Temple Gardens and slept. At midnight they were roused by their officers, and proceeded to assist their comrades, who had been battling with the flames on the other side of Fleet Street. They found that these too had been successful; the flames had swept up to Fetter Lane, but the houses on the west side had been demolished, and although, at one or two points, the fallen beams caught fire, they were speedily extinguished. Halfway up Fetter Lane the houses stood on both sides uninjured, for a large open space round St. Andrew's, Holborn, had aided the defenders in their efforts to check the flames. North of Holborn the fire had spread but little, and that only among the poorer houses in Fleet Valley.

Ascending the hill, they found that, while the flames had overleapt the City wall from Ludgate to Newgate in its progress west, the wall had proved an effective barrier from the sharp corner behind Christchurch up to Aldersgate and thence up to Cripplegate, which was the farthest limit reached by the fire to the north. To the east, the City had fared better. By the river, indeed, the destruction was complete as far as the Tower. Mark Lane, however, stood, and north of this the line of destruction swept westward to Leaden Hall, a massive structure at the entrance to the street that took its name from it, and proved a bulwark against the flames. From this point, the line of devastated ground swept round by the eastern end of Throgmorton Street to the northern end of Basinghall Street.

Cyril remained with the sailors for two days longer, during which time they were kept at work beating out the embers of the fire. In this they were aided by a heavy fall of rain, which put an end to all fear of the flames springing up again.

"There can be no need for you to remain longer with us, Sir Cyril," Captain Warncliffe said, at the end of the second day. "I shall have pleasure in reporting to the Duke of Albemarle the good services that you have rendered. Doubtless we shall remain on duty here for some time, for we may have, for aught I know, to aid in the clearing away of some of the ruins; but, at any rate, there can be no occasion for you to stay longer with us."

Cyril afterwards learnt that the sailors and dockyard men were, on the following day, sent back to Chatham. The fire had rendered so great a number of men homeless and without means of subsistence, that there was an abundant force on hand for the clearing away of ruins. Great numbers were employed by the authorities, while many of the merchants and traders engaged parties to clear away the ruins of their dwellings, in order to get at the cellars below, in which they had, as soon as the danger from fire was perceived, stowed away the main bulk of their goods. As soon as he was released from duty, Cyril made his way to the Tower, and, hiring a boat, was rowed to the *Good Venture*.

The shipping presented a singular appearance, their sides being blistered, and in many places completely stripped of their paint, while in some cases the spars were scorched, and the sails burnt away. There was lively satisfaction at his appearance, as he stepped on to the deck of the *Good Venture*, for, until he did so, he had been unrecognised, so begrimed with smoke and dust was he.

"We have been wondering about you," Captain Dave said, as he shook him by the hand, "but I can scarce say we had become uneasy. We learnt that a large body of seamen and others were at work blowing up houses, and as you had gone to offer your services we doubted not that you were employed with them. Truly you must have been having a rough time of it, for not only are you dirtier than any scavenger, but you look utterly worn out and fatigued."

"It was up-hill work the first twenty-four hours, for we worked unceasingly, and worked hard, too, I can assure you, and that well-nigh smothered with smoke and dust. Since then, our work has been more easy, but no less dirty. In the three days I have not had twelve hours' sleep altogether."

"I will get a tub of hot water placed in your cabin," Captain Watson said, "and should advise you, when you get out from it, to turn into your bunk at once. No one shall go near you in the morning until you wake of your own accord."

Cyril was, however, down to breakfast.

"Now tell us all about the fire," Nellie said, when they had finished the meal.

"I have nothing to tell you, for I know nothing," Cyril replied. "Our work was simply pulling down and blowing up houses. I had scarce time so much as to look at the fire. However, as I have since been working all round its course, I can tell you exactly how far it spread."

When he brought his story to a conclusion he said,—

"And now, Captain Dave, what are you thinking of doing?"

"In the first place, I am going ashore to look at the old house. As soon as I get can men, I shall clear the ground, and begin to rebuild it. I have enough laid by to start me again. I should be like a fish out of water with nothing to see to. I have the most valuable part of my stock still on hand here on deck, and if the cellar has proved staunch my loss in goods will be small indeed, for the anchors and chains in the yard will have suffered no damage. But even if the cellar has caved in, and its contents are destroyed, and if, when I have rebuilt my house, I find I have not enough left to replenish my stock, I am sure that I can get credit from the rope- and sail-makers, and iron-masters with whom I deal."

"Do not trouble yourself about that, Captain Dave," Cyril said. "You came to my help last time, and it will be my turn this time. I am sure that I shall have no difficulty in getting any monies that may be required from Mr. Goldsworthy, and there is nothing that will give me more pleasure than to see you established again in the place that was the first where I ever felt I had a home."

"I hope that it will not be needed, lad," Captain Dave said, shaking his hand warmly, "but if it should, I will not hesitate to accept your offer in the spirit in which it is made, and thus add one more to the obligations that I am under to you."

Cyril went ashore with Captain Dave and John Wilkes. The wall of the yard was, of course, uninjured, but the gate was burnt down. The store-house, which was of wood, had entirely disappeared, and the back wall of the house had fallen over it and the yard. The entrance to the cellar, therefore, could not be seen, and, as yet, the heat from the fallen bricks was too great to attempt to clear them away to get at it.

That night, however, it rained heavily, and in the morning Captain Watson took a party of sailors ashore, and these succeeded in clearing away the rubbish sufficiently to get to the entrance of the cellar. The door was covered by an iron plate, and although the wood behind this was charred it had not caught fire, and on getting it open it was found that the contents of the cellar were uninjured.

In order to prevent marauders from getting at it before preparations could be made for rebuilding, the rubbish was again thrown in so as to completely conceal the entrance. On returning on board there was a consultation on the future, held in the cabin. Captain Dave at once said that he and John, Wilkes must remain in town to make arrangements for the rebuilding and to watch the performance of the work. Cyril warmly pressed Mrs. Dowsett and Nellie to come down with him to Norfolk until the house was ready to receive them, but both were in favour of remaining in London, and it was settled that, next day, they should go down to Stepney, hire a house and store-room there, and remove thither their goods on board the ship, and the contents of the cellar.

There was some little difficulty in getting a house, as so many were seeking for lodgings, but at last they came upon a widow who was willing to let a house, upon the proviso that she was allowed to retain one room for her own occupation. This being settled, Cyril that evening returned to his lodging, and the next day rode down to Norfolk. There he remained until the middle of May, when he received a letter from Captain Dave, saying that his house was finished, and that they should move into it in a fortnight, and that they all earnestly hoped he would be present. As he had already been thinking of going up to London for a time, he decided to accept the invitation.

By this time he had made the acquaintance of all the surrounding gentry, and felt perfectly at home at Upmead. He rode frequently into Norwich, and, whenever he did so, paid a visit to Mr. Harvey, whose wife had died in January, never having completely recovered from the shock that she had received in London. Mr. Harvey himself had aged much; he still took a great interest in the welfare of the tenants of Upmead, and in Cyril's proposals for the improvement of their homes, and was pleased to see how earnestly he had taken up the duties of his new life. He spoke occasionally of his son, of whose death he felt convinced.

"I have never been able to obtain any news of him," he often said, "and assuredly I should have heard of him had he been alive.

"It would ease my mind to know the truth," he said, one day. "It troubles me to think that, if alive, he is assuredly pursuing evil courses, and that he will probably end his days on a gallows. That he will repent, and turn to better courses, I have now no hope whatever. Unless he be living by roguery, he would, long ere this, have written, professing repentance, even if he did not feel it, and begging for assistance. It troubles me much that I can find out nothing for certain of him."

"Would it be a relief to you to know surely that he was dead?" Cyril asked.

"I would rather know that he was dead than feel, as I do, that if alive, he is going on sinning. One can mourn for the dead as David mourned for Absalom, and trust that their sins may be forgiven them; but, uncertain as I am of his death, I cannot so mourn, since it may be that he still lives."

"Then, sir, I am in a position to set your mind at rest. I have known for a long time that he died of the Plague, but I have kept it from you, thinking that it was best you should still think that he might be living. He fell dead beside me on the very day that I sickened of the Plague, and, indeed, it was from him that I took it."

Mr. Harvey remained silent for a minute or two.

"'Tis better so," he said solemnly. "The sins of youth may be forgiven, but, had he lived, his whole course might have been wicked. How know you that it was he who gave you the Plague?"

"I met him in the street. He was tottering in his walk, and, as he came up, he stumbled, and grasped me to save himself. I held him for a moment, and then he slipped from my arms and fell on the pavement, and died."

Mr. Harvey looked keenly at Cyril, and was about to ask a question, but checked himself.

"He is dead," he said. "God rest his soul, and forgive him his sins! Henceforth I shall strive to forget that he ever lived to manhood, and seek to remember him as he was when a child."

Then he held out his hand to Cyril, to signify that he would fain be alone.

On arriving in London, Cyril took up his abode at his former lodgings, and the next day at twelve o'clock, the hour appointed in a letter he found awaiting him on his arrival, he arrived in Tower Street, having ridden through the City. An army of workmen, who had come up from all parts of the country, were engaged in rebuilding the town. In the main thoroughfares many of the houses were already finished, and the shops re-opened. In other parts less progress had been made, as the traders were naturally most anxious to resume their business, and most able to pay for speed.

Captain Dave's was one of the first houses completed in Tower Street, but there were many others far advanced in progress. The front differed materially from that of the old house, in which each story had projected beyond the one below it. Inside, however, there was but little change in its appearance, except that the rooms were somewhat more lofty, and that there were no heavy beams across the ceilings. Captain Dave and his family had moved in that morning.

"It does not look quite like the old place," Mrs. Dowsett said, after the first greetings.

"Not quite," Cyril agreed. "The new furniture, of course, gives it a different appearance as yet; but one will soon get accustomed to that, and you will quickly make it home-like again. I see you have the bits of furniture you saved in their old corners."

"Yes; and it will make a great difference when they get all my curiosities up in their places again," Captain Dave put in. "We pulled them down anyhow, and some of them will want glueing up a bit. And so your fighting is over, Cyril?"

"Yes, it looks like it. The Dutch have evidently had enough of it. They asked for peace, and as both parties consented to the King of Sweden being mediator, and our representatives and those of Holland are now settling affairs at Breda, peace may be considered as finally settled. We have only two small squadrons now afloat; the rest are all snugly laid up. I trust that there is no chance of another war between the two nations for years to come."

"I hope not, Cyril. But De Witte is a crafty knave, and is ever in close alliance with Louis. Were it not for French influence the Prince of Orange would soon oust him from the head of affairs."

"I should think he would not have any power for mischief in the future," Cyril said. "It was he who brought on the last war, and, although it has cost us much, it has cost the Dutch very much more, and the loss of her commerce has well-nigh brought Holland to ruin. Besides, the last victory we won must have lowered their national pride greatly."

"You have not heard the reports that are about, then?"

"No, I have heard no news whatever. It takes a long time for it to travel down to Norwich, and I have seen no one since I came up to town last night."

"Well, there is a report that a Dutch fleet of eighty sail has put to sea. It may be that 'tis but bravado to show that, though they have begged for peace, 'tis not because they are in no condition to fight. I know not how this may be, but it is certain that for the last three days the Naval people have been very busy, and that powder is being sent down to Chatham. As for the Fleet, small as it is, it is doubtful whether it would fight, for the men are in a veritable state of mutiny, having received no pay for many months. Moreover, several ships were but yesterday bought by Government, for what purpose it is not known, but it is conjectured they are meant for fire-ships."

"I cannot but think that it is, as you say, a mere piece of bravado on the part of the Dutch, Captain Dave. They could never be so treacherous as to attack us when peace is well-nigh concluded, but, hurt as their pride must be by the defeat we gave them, it is not unnatural they should wish to show that they can still put a brave fleet on the seas, and are not driven to make peace because they could not, if need be, continue the war."

"And now I have a piece of news for you. We are going to have a wedding here before long."

"I am right glad to hear it," Cyril said heartily. "And who is the happy man, Nellie?" he asked, turning towards where she had been standing the moment before. But Nellie had fled the moment her father had opened his lips.

"It is Frank Watson," her father said. "A right good lad; and her mother and I are well pleased with her choice."

"I thought that he was very attentive the few days we were on board his father's ship," Cyril said. "I am not surprised to hear the news."

"They have been two voyages since then, and while the *Good Venture* was in the Pool, Master Frank spent most of his time down at Stepney, and it was settled a fortnight since. My old friend Watson is as pleased as I am. And the best part of the business is that Frank is going to give up the sea and become my partner. His father owns the *Good Venture*, and, being a careful man, has laid by a round sum, and he settled to give him fifteen hundred pounds, which he will put into the business."

"That is a capital plan, Captain Dave. It will be an excellent thing for you to have so young and active a partner."

"Watson has bought the house down at Stepney that we have been living in, and Frank and Nellie are going to settle there, and Watson will make it his headquarters when his ship is in port, and will, I have no doubt, take up his moorings there, when he gives up the sea. The wedding is to be in a fortnight's time, for Watson has set his heart on seeing them spliced before he sails again, and I see no reason for delay. You must come to the wedding, of course, Cyril. Indeed, I don't think Nellie would consent to be married if you were not there. The girl has often spoken of you lately. You see, now that she really knows what love is, and has a quiet, happy life to look forward to, she feels more than ever the service you did her, and the escape she had. She told the whole story to Frank before she said yes, when he asked her to be his wife, and, of course, he liked her no less for it, though I think it would go hard with that fellow if he ever met him."

"The fellow died of the Plague, Captain Dave. His last action was to try and revenge himself on me by giving me the infection, for, meeting me in the streets, he threw his arms round me and exclaimed, 'I have given you the Plague!'" They were the last words he ever spoke, for he gave a hideous laugh, and then dropped down dead. However, he spoke truly, for that night I sickened of it."

"Then your kindness to Nellie well-nigh cost you your life," Mrs. Dowsett said, laying her hand on his shoulder, while the tears stood in her eyes. "And you never told us this before!"

"There was nothing to tell," Cyril replied. "If I had not caught it from him, I should have, doubtless, taken it from some one else, for I was constantly in the way of it, and could hardly have hoped to escape an attack. Now, Captain Dave, let us go downstairs, and see the store."

"John Wilkes and the two boys are at work there," the Captain said, as he went downstairs, "and we open our doors to-morrow. I have hurried on the house as fast as possible, and as no others in my business have yet opened, I look to do a thriving trade at once. Watson will send all his friends here, and as there is scarce a captain who goes in or out of port but knows Frank, I consider that our new partner will greatly extend the business."

Captain Watson and Frank came in at supper-time, and, after spending a pleasant evening, Cyril returned to his lodgings in the Strand. The next day he was walking near Whitehall when a carriage dashed out at full speed, and, as it came along, he caught sight of the Duke of Albemarle, who looked in a state of strange confusion. His wig was awry, his coat was off, and his face was flushed and excited. As his eye fell on Cyril, he shouted out to the postillions to stop. As they pulled up, he shouted,—

"Jump in, Sir Cyril! Jump in, for your life."

Astonished at this address, Cyril ran to the door, opened it, and jumped in, and the Duke shouted to the postillions to go on.

"What do you think, sir?—what do you think?" roared the Duke. "Those treacherous scoundrels, the Dutch, have appeared with a great Fleet of seventy men-of-war, besides fire-ships, off Sheerness, this morning at daybreak, and have taken the place, and Chatham lies open to them. We have been bamboozled and tricked. While the villains were pretending they were all for peace, they have been secretly fitting out, and there they are at Sheerness. A mounted messenger brought in the news, but ten minutes ago."

"Have they taken Sheerness, sir?"

"Yes; there were but six guns mounted on the fort, and no preparations made. The ships that were there did nothing. The rascals are in mutiny—and small wonder, when they can get no pay, the money voted for them being wasted by the Court. It is enough to drive one wild with vexation, and, had I my will, there are a dozen men, whose names are the foremost in the country, whom I would hang up with my own hands. The wind is from the east, and if they go straight up the Medway they may be there this afternoon, and have the whole of our ships at their mercy. It is enough to make Blake turn in his grave that such an indignity should be offered us, though it be but the outcome of treachery on the part of the Dutch, and of gross negligence on ours. But if they give us a day or two to prepare, we will, at least, give them something to do before they can carry out their design, and, if one could but rely on the sailors, we might even beat them off; but it is doubtful whether the knaves will fight. The forts are unfinished, though the money was voted for them three years since. And all this is not the worst of it, for, after they have taken Chatham, there is naught to prevent their coming up to London. We have had plague and we have had fire, and to be bombarded by the Dutchmen would be the crowning blow, and it would be like to bring about another revolution in England."

They posted down to Chatham as fast as the horses could gallop. The instant the news had arrived, the Duke had sent off a man, on horseback, to order horses to be in readiness to change at each posting station. Not a minute, therefore, was lost. In a little over two hours from the time of leaving Whitehall, they drove into the dockyard.

"Where is Sir Edward Spragge?" the Duke shouted, as he leapt from the carriage.

"He has gone down to the new forts, your Grace," an officer replied.

"Have a gig prepared at once, without the loss of a moment," the Duke said. "What is being done?" he asked another officer, as the first ran off.

"Sir Edward has taken four frigates down to the narrow part of the river, sir, and preparations have been made for placing a great chain there. Several of the ships are being towed out into the river, and are to be sunk in the passage."

"Any news of the Dutch having left Sheerness?"

"No, sir; a shallop rowed up at noon, but was chased back again by one of our pinnaces."

"That is better than I had hoped. Come, come, we shall make a fight for it yet," and he strode away towards the landing.

"Shall I accompany you, sir?" Cyril asked.

"Yes. There is nothing for you to do until we see exactly how things stand. I shall use you as my staff officer—that is, if you are willing, Sir Cyril. I have carried you off without asking whether you consented or no; but, knowing your spirit and quickness, I felt sure you would be of use."

"I am at your service altogether," Cyril said, "and am glad indeed that your Grace encountered me, for I should have been truly sorry to have been idle at such a time."

An eight-oared gig was already at the stairs, and they were rowed rapidly down the river. They stopped at Upnor Castle, and found that Major Scott, who was in command there, was hard at work mounting cannon and putting the place in a posture of defence.

"You will have more men from London by to-morrow night, at the latest," the Duke said, "and powder and shot in abundance was sent off yesterday. We passed a train on our way down, and I told them to push on with all speed. As the Dutch have not moved yet, they cannot be here until the afternoon of to-morrow, and, like enough, will not attack until next day, for they must come slowly, or they will lose some of their ships on the sands. We will try to get up a battery opposite, so as to aid you with a cross fire. I am going down to see Sir Edward Spragge now."

Taking their places in the boat again, they rowed round the horseshoe curve down to Gillingham, and then along to the spot where the frigates were moored. At the sharp bend lower down here the Duke found the Admiral, and they held a long consultation together. It was agreed that the chain should be placed somewhat higher up, where a lightly-armed battery on either side would afford some assistance, that behind the chain the three ships, the *Matthias*, the *Unity*, and the *Charles V.*, all prizes taken from the Dutch, should be moored, and that the *Jonathan* and *Fort of Honinggen*—also a Dutch prize—should be also posted there.

Having arranged this, the Duke was rowed back to Chatham, there to see about getting some of the great ships removed from their moorings off Gillingham, up the river. To his fury, he found that, of all the eighteen hundred men employed in the yard, not more than half a dozen had remained at their work, the rest being, like all the townsmen, occupied in removing their goods in great haste. Even the frigates that were armed had but a third, at most, of their crews on board, so many having deserted owing to the backwardness of their pay.

That night, Sir W. Coventry, Sir W. Penn, Lord Brounker, and other officers and officials of the Admiralty, came down from London. Some of these, especially Lord Brounker, had a hot time of it with the Duke, who rated them roundly for the state of things which prevailed, telling the latter that he was the main cause of all the misfortunes that might occur, owing to his having dismantled and disarmed all the great ships. In spite of the efforts of all these officers, but little could be done, owing to the want of hands, and to the refusal of the dockyard men, and most of the sailors, to do anything. A small battery of sandbags was, however, erected opposite Upnor, and a few guns placed in position there.

Several ships were sunk in the channel above Upnor, and a few of those lying off Gillingham were towed up. Little help was sent down from London, for the efforts of the authorities were directed wholly to the defence of the Thames. The train-bands were all under arms, fire-ships were being fitted out and sent down to Gravesend, and batteries erected there and at Tilbury, while several ships were sunk in the channel.

The Dutch remained at Sheerness from the 7th to the 12th, and had it not been for the misconduct of the men, Chatham could have been put into a good state for defence. As it was, but little could be effected; and when, on the 12th, the Dutch Fleet were seen coming up the river, the chances of successful resistance were small.

The fight commenced by a Dutch frigate, commanded by Captain Brakell, advancing against the chain. Carried up by a strong tide and east wind the ship struck it with such force that it at once gave way. The English frigates, but weakly manned, could offer but slight resistance, and the *Jonathan* was boarded and captured by Brakell. Following his frigate were a host of fire-ships, which at once grappled with the defenders. The *Matthias, Unity, Charles V.*, and *Fort of Honinggen* were speedily in flames. The light batteries on the shore were silenced by the guns of the Fleet, which then anchored. The next day, six of their men-of-war, with five fire-ships, advanced, exchanged broadsides, as they went along, with the *Royal Oak* and presently engaged Upnor. They

AFTER THE FIRE.

were received with so hot a fire from the Castle, and from the battery opposite, where Sir Edward Spragge had stationed himself, that, after a time, they gave up the design of ascending to the dockyard, which at that time occupied a position higher up the river than at present.

The tide was beginning to slacken, and they doubtless feared that a number of fire-barges might be launched at them did they venture higher up. On the way back, they launched a fire-ship at the *Royal Oak*, which was commanded by Captain Douglas. The flames speedily communicated to the ship, and the crew took to the boats and rowed ashore. Captain Douglas refused to leave his vessel, and perished in the flames. The report given by the six men-of-war decided the Dutch not to attempt anything further against Chatham. On the 14th, they set fire to the hulks, the *Loyal London* and the *Great James*, and carried off the hulk of the *Royal Charles*, after the English had twice tried to destroy her by fire. As this was the ship in which the Duke of Albemarle, then General Monk, had brought the King over to England from Holland, her capture was considered a special triumph for the Dutch and a special dishonour to us.

The Duke of Albemarle had left Chatham before the Dutch came up. As the want of crews prevented his being of any use there, and he saw that Sir Edward Spragge would do all that was possible in defence of the place, he posted back to London, where his presence was urgently required, a complete panic reigning. Crowds assembled at Whitehall, and insulted the King and his ministers as the cause of the present misfortunes, while at Deptford and Wapping, the sailors and their wives paraded the streets, shouting that the ill-treatment of our sailors had brought these things about, and so hostile were their manifestations that the officials of the Admiralty scarce dared show themselves in the streets.

Cyril had remained at Chatham, the Duke having recommended him to Sir Edward Spragge, and he, with some other gentlemen and a few sailors, had manned the battery opposite Upnor.

The great proportion of the Dutch ships were still at the Nore, as it would have been dangerous to have hazarded so great a fleet in the narrow water of the Medway. As it was, two of their men-of-war, on the way back from Chatham, ran ashore, and had to be burnt. They had also six fire-ships burnt, and lost over a hundred and fifty men.

Leaving Admiral Van Ness with part of the Fleet in the mouth of the Thames, De Ruyter sailed first for Harwich, where he attempted to land with sixteen hundred men in boats, supported by the guns of the Fleet. The boats, however, failed to effect a landing, being beaten off, with considerable loss, by the county Militia; and Ruyter then sailed for Portsmouth, where he also failed. He then went west to Torbay, where he was likewise repulsed, and then returned to the mouth of the Thames.

On July 23rd, Van Ness, with twenty-five men-of-war, sailed up the Hope, where Sir Edward Spragge had now hoisted his flag on board a squadron of eighteen ships, of whom five were frigates and the rest fire-ships. A sharp engagement ensued, but the wind was very light, and the English, by towing their fire-ships, managed to lay them alongside the Dutch fire-ships, and destroyed twelve of these with a loss of only six English ships. But, the wind then rising, Sir Edward retired from the Hope to Gravesend, where he was protected by the guns at Tilbury.

The next day, being joined by Sir Joseph Jordan, with a few small ships, he took the offensive, and destroyed the last fire-ship that the Dutch had left, and compelled the men-of-war to retire. Sir Edward followed them with his little squadron, and Van Ness, as he retired down the river, was met by five frigates and fourteen fire-ships from Harwich. These boldly attacked him. Two of the Dutch men-of-war narrowly escaped being burnt, another was forced ashore and greatly damaged, and the whole of the Dutch Fleet was compelled to bear away.

While these events had been happening in the Thames, the negotiations at Breda had continued, and, just as the Dutch retreated, the news came that Peace had been signed. The Dutch, on their side, were satisfied with the success with which they had closed the war, while England was, at the moment, unable to continue it, and the King, seeing the intense unpopularity that had been excited against him by the affair at Chatham, was glad to ratify the Peace, especially as we thereby retained possession of several islands we had taken in the West Indies from the Dutch, and it was manifest that Spain was preparing to join the coalition of France and Holland against us.

A Peace concluded under such circumstances was naturally but a short one. When the war was renewed, three years later, the French were in alliance with us, and, after several more desperate battles, in which no great advantages were gained on either side, the Dutch were so exhausted and impoverished by the loss of trade, that a final Peace was arranged on terms far more advantageous to us than those secured by the Treaty of 1667. The De Wittes, the authors of the previous wars, had both been killed in a popular tumult. The Prince of Orange was at the head of the State, and the fact that France and Spain were both hostile to Holland had re-awakened the feeling of England in favour of the Protestant Republic, and the friendship between the two nations has never since been broken.

Cyril took no part in the last war against the Dutch. He, like the majority of the nation, was opposed to it, and, although willing to give his life in defence of his country when attacked, felt it by no means his duty to do so when we were aiding the designs of France in crushing a brave enemy. Such was in fact the result of the war; for although peace was made on even terms, the wars of Holland with England and the ruin caused to her trade thereby, inflicted a blow upon the Republic from which she never recovered. From being the great rival of England, both on the sea and in her foreign commerce, her prosperity and power dwindled until she ceased altogether to be a factor in European affairs.

After the Peace of Breda was signed, Cyril went down to Upmead, where, for the next four years, he devoted himself to the management of his estate. His friendship with Mr. Harvey grew closer and warmer, until the latter came to consider him in really the light of a son; and when he died, in 1681, it was found that his will was unaltered, and that, with the exception of legacies to many of his old employés at his factory, the whole of his property was left to Cyril. The latter received a good offer for the tanyard, and, upon an estate next to his own coming shortly afterwards into the market, he purchased it, and thus the Upmead estates became as extensive as they had been before the time of his ancestor, who had so seriously diminished them during the reign of Elizabeth.

His friendship with the family of the Earl of Wisbech had remained unaltered, and he had every year paid them a visit, either at Wisbech or at Sevenoaks. A year after Mr. Harvey's death, he married Dorothy, who had previously refused several flattering offers.

Captain Dave and his wife lived to a good old age. The business had largely increased, owing to the energy of their son-in-law, who had, with his wife and children, taken up his abode in the next house to theirs, which had been bought to meet the extension of their business. John Wilkes, at the death of Captain Dave, declined Cyril's pressing offer to make his home with him.

"It would never do, Sir Cyril," he said. "I should be miserable out of the sight of ships, and without a place where I could meet seafaring men, and smoke my pipe, and listen to their yarns."

He therefore remained with Frank Watson, nominally in charge of the stores, but doing, in fact, as little as he chose until, long past the allotted age of man, he passed quietly away.

THE END.

BLACKIE & SON'S
BOOKS FOR YOUNG PEOPLE.

BY G. A. HENTY.

Wulf the Saxon: A Story of the Norman Conquest. By G. A. HENTY. With 12 page Illustrations by RALPH PEACOCK. Crown 8vo, cloth elegant, olivine edges, 6s.

The hero is a young thane who wins the favour of Earl Harold and becomes one of his retinue. When Harold becomes King of England, Wulf assists in the Welsh wars, and takes part against the Norsemen at the Battle of Stamford Bridge. When William of Normandy invades England, Wulf is with the English host at Hastings, and stands by his king to the last in the mighty struggle. Altogether this is a noble tale. Wulf himself is a rare example of Saxon vigour, and the spacious background of stormful history lends itself admirably to heroic romance.

When London Burned: A Story of Restoration Times and the Great Fire. By G. A. HENTY. With 12 page Illustrations by J. FINNEMORE. Crown 8vo, cloth elegant, olivine edges, 6s.

The hero of this story was the son of a nobleman who had lost his estates during the troublous times of the Commonwealth. Instead of hanging idly about the court seeking favours, Cyril Shenstone determined to maintain himself by honest work, and, as a scrivener in the city, soon established a reputation for zeal and trustworthiness. He served afterwards as a volunteer in the fleet under Prince Rupert, and highly distinguished himself in the Dutch wars. During the Great Plague and the Great Fire Sir Cyril was prominent among those who brought help to the panic-stricken inhabitants. This tale has rich variety of interest, both national and personal, and in the hero you have an English lad of the noblest type—wise, humane, and unselfish.

Beric the Briton: A Story of the Roman Invasion. By G. A. HENTY. With 12 page Illustrations by W. PARKINSON. Crown 8vo, cloth elegant, olivine edges, 6s.

"We are not aware that any one has given us quite so vigorous a picture of Britain in the days of the Roman conquest. Mr. Henty has done his utmost to make an impressive picture of the haughty Roman character, with its indomitable courage, sternness, and discipline. *Beric* is good all through."—*Spectator.*

A

BY G. A. HENTY.

"Mr. Henty is one of the best of story-tellers for young people."—*Spectator*.

Through the Sikh War: A Tale of the Conquest of the Punjaub. By G. A. HENTY. With 12 page Illustrations by HAL HURST, and a Map. Crown 8vo, cloth elegant, olivine edges, 6s.

"The picture of the Punjaub during its last few years of independence, the description of the battles on the Sutlej, and the portraiture generally of native character, seem admirably true. . . . On the whole, we have never read a more vivid and faithful narrative of military adventure in India."—*The Academy*.

With Wolfe in Canada: Or, The Winning of a Continent. By G. A. HENTY. With 12 page Illustrations by GORDON BROWNE. Crown 8vo, cloth elegant, olivine edges, 6s.

"A model of what a boys' story-book should be. Mr. Henty has a great power of infusing into the dead facts of history new life, and as no pains are spared by him to ensure accuracy in historic details, his books supply useful aids to study as well as amusement."—*School Guardian*.

The Dash for Khartoum: A Tale of the Nile Expedition. By G. A. HENTY. With 10 page Illustrations by J. SCHÖNBERG and J. NASH, and 4 Plans. Crown 8vo, cloth elegant, olivine edges, 6s.

"It is literally true that the narrative never flags a moment; for the incidents which fall to be recorded after the dash for Khartoum has been made and failed are quite as interesting as those which precede it."—*Academy*.

The Lion of St. Mark: A Tale of Venice in the Fourteenth Century. By G. A. HENTY. With 10 page Illustrations by GORDON BROWNE. Crown 8vo, cloth elegant, olivine edges, 6s.

"Every boy should read *The Lion of St. Mark*. Mr. Henty has never produced any story more delightful, more wholesome, or more vivacious. From first to last it will be read with keen enjoyment."—*The Saturday Review*.

By England's Aid: The Freeing of the Netherlands (1585-1604). By G. A. HENTY. With 10 page Illustrations by ALFRED PEARSE, and 4 Maps. Crown 8vo, cloth elegant, olivine edges, 6s.

"The story is told with great animation, and the historical material is most effectively combined with a most excellent plot."—*Saturday Review*.

With Lee in Virginia: A Story of the American Civil War. By G. A. HENTY. With 10 page Illustrations by GORDON BROWNE, and 6 Maps. Crown 8vo, cloth elegant, olivine edges, 6s.

"The story is a capital one and full of variety, and presents us with many picturesque scenes of Southern life. Young Wingfield, who is conscientious, spirited, and 'hard as nails', would have been a man after the very heart of Stonewall Jackson."—*Times*.

By Pike and Dyke: A Tale of the Rise of the Dutch Republic. By G. A. HENTY. With 10 page Illustrations by MAYNARD BROWN, and 4 Maps. Crown 8vo, cloth elegant, olivine edges, 6s.

"The mission of Ned to deliver letters from William the Silent to his adherents at Brussels, the fight of the *Good Venture* with the Spanish man-of-war, the battle on the ice at Amsterdam, the siege of Haarlem, are all told with a vividness and skill which are worthy of Mr. Henty at his best."—*Academy*.

BY G. A. HENTY.

"Surely Mr. Henty should understand boys' tastes better than any man living."
—*The Times.*

Reduced Illustration from "St. Bartholomew's Eve".

St. Bartholomew's Eve: A Tale of the Huguenot Wars. By G. A. Henty. With 12 page Illustrations by H. J. Draper, and a Map. Crown 8vo, cloth elegant, olivine edges, 6s.

"A really noble story, which adult readers will find to the full as satisfying as the boys. Lucky boys! to have such a caterer as Mr. G. A. Henty."—*Black and White.*

With Clive in India: Or, The Beginnings of an Empire. By G. A. Henty. With 12 page Illustrations by Gordon Browne. Crown 8vo, cloth elegant, olivine edges, 6s.

"Among writers of stories of adventure for boys Mr. Henty stands in the very first rank. Those who know something about India will be the most ready to thank Mr. Henty for giving them this instructive volume to place in the hands of their children."—*Academy.*

BY G. A. HENTY.

"Among writers of stories of adventure for boys Mr. Henty stands in the very first rank."—*Academy.*

Under Drake's Flag: A Tale of the Spanish Main. By G. A. HENTY. Illustrated by 12 page Pictures by GORDON BROWNE. Crown 8vo, cloth elegant, olivine edges, 6s.

"There is not a dull chapter, nor, indeed, a dull page in the book; but the author has so carefully worked up his subject that the exciting deeds of his heroes are never incongruous or absurd."—*Observer.*

Bonnie Prince Charlie: A Tale of Fontenoy and Culloden. By G. A. HENTY. With 12 page Illustrations by GORDON BROWNE. Crown 8vo, cloth elegant, olivine edges, 6s.

"Ronald, the hero, is very like the hero of *Quentin Durward*. The lad's journey across France with his faithful attendant Malcolm, and his hairbreadth escapes from the machinations of his father's enemies, make up as good a narrative of the kind as we have ever read. For freshness of treatment and variety of incident, Mr. Henty has here surpassed himself."—*Spectator.*

For the Temple: A Tale of the Fall of Jerusalem. By G. A. HENTY. With 10 page Illustrations by S. J. SOLOMON, and a Coloured Map. Crown 8vo, cloth elegant, olivine edges, 6s.

"Mr. Henty's graphic prose pictures of the hopeless Jewish resistance to Roman sway adds another leaf to his record of the famous wars of the world. The book is one of Mr. Henty's cleverest efforts."—*Graphic.*

True to the Old Flag: A Tale of the American War of Independence. By G. A. HENTY. With 12 page Illustrations by GORDON BROWNE. Crown 8vo, cloth elegant, olivine edges, 6s.

"Does justice to the pluck and determination of the British soldiers. The son of an American loyalist, who remains true to our flag, falls among the hostile redskins in that very Huron country which has been endeared to us by the exploits of Hawkeye and Chingachgook."—*The Times.*

The Lion of the North: A Tale of Gustavus Adolphus and the Wars of Religion. By G. A. HENTY. With 12 page Pictures by J. SCHÖNBERG. Crown 8vo, cloth elegant, olivine edges, 6s.

"A praiseworthy attempt to interest British youth in the great deeds of the Scotch Brigade in the wars of Gustavus Adolphus. Mackay, Hepburn, and Munro live again in Mr. Henty's pages, as those deserve to live whose disciplined bands formed really the germ of the modern British army."—*Athenæum.*

The Young Carthaginian: A Story of the Times of Hannibal. By G. A. HENTY. With 12 page Illustrations by C. J. STANILAND, R.I. Crown 8vo, cloth elegant, olivine edges, 6s.

"The effect of an interesting story, well constructed and vividly told, is enhanced by the picturesque quality of the scenic background. From first to last nothing stays the interest of the narrative. It bears us along as on a stream, whose current varies in direction, but never loses its force."—*Saturday Review.*

BY G. A. HENTY.

"Mr. Henty is the king of story-tellers for boys."—*Sword and Trowel.*

Reduced Illustration from Henty's " Redskin and Cow-boy ".

Redskin and Cow-boy: A Tale of the Western Plains. By G. A. HENTY. With 12 page Illustrations by ALFRED PEARSE. Crown 8vo, cloth elegant, olivine edges, 6s.

"It has a good plot; it abounds in action; the scenes are equally spirited and realistic, and we can only say we have read it with much pleasure from first to last. The pictures of life on a cattle ranche are most graphically painted, as are the manners of the reckless but jovial cow-boys."—*Times.*

In Freedom's Cause: A Story of Wallace and Bruce. By G. A. HENTY. With 12 page Illustrations by GORDON BROWNE. Crown 8vo, cloth elegant, olivine edges, 6s.

"Mr. Henty has broken new ground as an historical novelist. His tale of the days of Wallace and Bruce is full of stirring action, and will commend itself to boys."—*Athenæum.*

BY G. A. HENTY.

"Mr. Henty is one of our most successful writers of historical tales."—*Scotsman.*

By Right of Conquest: Or, With Cortez in Mexico. By G. A. HENTY. With 10 page Illustrations by W. S. STACEY, and 2 Maps. Crown 8vo, cloth elegant, olivine edges, 6s.

"*By Right of Conquest* is the nearest approach to a perfectly successful historical tale that Mr. Henty has yet published."—*Academy.*

In Greek Waters: A Story of the Grecian War of Independence (1821-1827). By G. A. HENTY. With 12 page Illustrations by W. S. STACEY, and a Map. Crown 8vo, cloth elegant, olivine edges, 6s.

"There are adventures of all kinds for the hero and his friends, whose pluck and ingenuity in extricating themselves from awkward fixes are always equal to the occasion. It is an excellent story, and if the proportion of history is smaller than usual, the whole result leaves nothing to be desired."—*Journal of Education.*

Through the Fray: A Story of the Luddite Riots. By G. A. HENTY. With 12 page Illustrations by H. M. PAGET. Crown 8vo, cloth elegant, olivine edges, 6s.

"Mr. Henty inspires a love and admiration for straightforwardness, truth, and courage. This is one of the best of the many good books Mr. Henty has produced, and deserves to be classed with his *Facing Death*."—*Standard.*

Captain Bayley's Heir: A Tale of the Gold Fields of California. By G. A. HENTY. With 12 page Illustrations by H. M. PAGET. Crown 8vo, cloth elegant, olivine edges, 6s.

"A Westminster boy who makes his way in the world by hard work, good temper, and unfailing courage. The descriptions given of life are just what a healthy intelligent lad should delight in."—*St. James's Gazette.*

In the Heart of the Rockies: A Story of Adventure in Colorado. By G. A. HENTY. With 8 page Illustrations by G. C. HINDLEY. Crown 8vo, cloth elegant, olivine edges, 5s.

From first to last this is a story of splendid hazard. The hero, Tom Wade, goes out to his uncle in Colorado, who is a hunter and gold-digger. Going in quest of a gold mine the little band is spied by Indians, chased across the Bad Lands, and overwhelmed by a snow-storm in the mountains, where they camp all winter. They build two canoes and paddle down the terrible gorges of the Rocky Mountains, with many an upset on the way and the instant danger of bloodthirsty Indians shooting from the banks. After many perils they reach Fort Mojarve and safety, and the reader finds that the record of this most daring journey has closed all too soon.

One of the 28th: A Tale of Waterloo. By G. A. HENTY. With 8 page Illustrations by W. H. OVEREND, and 2 Maps. Crown 8vo, cloth elegant, olivine edges, 5s.

"Written with Homeric vigour and heroic inspiration. It is graphic, picturesque, and dramatically effective . . . shows us Mr. Henty at his best and brightest. The adventures will hold a boy of a winter's night enthralled as he rushes through them with breathless interest 'from cover to cover'."—*Observer.*

BY G. A. HENTY.

"No more interesting boys' books are written than Mr. Henty's stories."—
Daily Chronicle.

The Cat of Bubastes: A Story of Ancient Egypt. By G. A. HENTY. With 8 page Illustrations by J. R. WEGUELIN. Crown 8vo, cloth elegant, olivine edges, 5s.

"The story, from the critical moment of the killing of the sacred cat to the perilous exodus into Asia with which it closes, is very skilfully constructed and full of exciting adventures. It is admirably illustrated."—*Saturday Review.*

Maori and Settler: A Story of the New Zealand War. By G. A. HENTY. With 8 page Illustrations by ALFRED PEARSE, and a Map. Crown 8vo, cloth elegant, olivine edges, 5s.

"It is a book which all young people, but especially boys, will read with avidity."—*Athenæum.*

"A first-rate book for boys, brimful of adventure, of humorous and interesting conversation, and of vivid pictures of colonial life."—*Schoolmaster.*

St. George for England: A Tale of Cressy and Poitiers. By G. A. HENTY. With 8 full-page Illustrations by GORDON BROWNE. Crown 8vo, cloth elegant, olivine edges, 5s.

"A story of very great interest for boys. In his own forcible style the author has endeavoured to show that determination and enthusiasm can accomplish marvellous results; and that courage is generally accompanied by magnanimity and gentleness."—*Pall Mall Gazette.*

The Bravest of the Brave: With Peterborough in Spain. By G. A. HENTY. With 8 full-page Pictures by H. M. PAGET. Crown 8vo, cloth elegant, olivine edges, 5s.

"Mr. Henty never loses sight of the moral purpose of his work—to enforce the doctrine of courage and truth, mercy and lovingkindness, as indispensable to the making of an English gentleman. British lads will read *The Bravest of the Brave* with pleasure and profit; of that we are quite sure."—*Daily Telegraph.*

For Name and Fame: Or, Through Afghan Passes. By G. A. HENTY. With 8 full-page Illustrations by GORDON BROWNE. Crown 8vo, cloth elegant, olivine edges, 5s.

"Not only a rousing story, replete with all the varied forms of excitement of a campaign, but, what is still more useful, an account of a territory and its inhabitants which must for a long time possess a supreme interest for Englishmen, as being the key to our Indian Empire."—*Glasgow Herald.*

A Jacobite Exile: Being the Adventures of a Young Englishman in the Service of Charles XII. of Sweden. By G. A. HENTY. With 8 page Illustrations by PAUL HARDY, and a Map. Crown 8vo, cloth elegant, olivine edges, 5s.

"Incident succeeds incident, and adventure is piled upon adventure, and at the end the reader, be he boy or man, will have experienced breathless enjoyment in a romantic story that must have taught him much at its close."—*Army and Navy Gazette.*

BY G. A. HENTY.

"Ask for Henty, and see that you get him."—*Punch.*

Condemned as a Nihilist: A Story of Escape from Siberia.
By G. A. HENTY. With 8 page Illustrations by WALTER PAGET. Crown 8vo, cloth elegant, olivine edges, 5s.

"The best of this year's Henty. His narrative is more interesting than many of the tales with which the public is familiar, of escape from Siberia. Despite their superior claim to authenticity these tales are without doubt no less fictitious than Mr. Henty's, and he beats them hollow in the matter of sensations."—*National Observer.*

Orange and Green: A Tale of the Boyne and Limerick.
By G. A. HENTY. With 8 full-page Illustrations by GORDON BROWNE. Crown 8vo, cloth elegant, olivine edges, 5s.

"The narrative is free from the vice of prejudice, and ripples with life as vivacious as if what is being described were really passing before the eye. . . . Should be in the hands of every young student of Irish history."—*Belfast News.*

Held Fast for England: A Tale of the Siege of Gibraltar.
By G. A. HENTY. With 8 page Illustrations by GORDON BROWNE. Crown 8vo, cloth elegant, olivine edges, 5s.

"Among them we would place first in interest and wholesome educational value the story of the siege of Gibraltar. . . . There is no cessation of exciting incident throughout the story."—*Athenæum.*

In the Reign of Terror: The Adventures of a Westminster Boy.
By G. A. HENTY. With 8 full-page Illustrations by J. SCHÖNBERG. Crown 8vo, cloth elegant, olivine edges, 5s.

"Harry Sandwith, the Westminster boy, may fairly be said to beat Mr. Henty's record. His adventures will delight boys by the audacity and peril they depict. The story is one of Mr. Henty's best."—*Saturday Review.*

By Sheer Pluck: A Tale of the Ashanti War.
By G. A. HENTY. With 8 full-page Pictures by GORDON BROWNE. Crown 8vo, cloth elegant, olivine edges, 5s.

"Morally, the book is everything that could be desired, setting before the boys a bright and bracing ideal of the English gentleman."—*Christian Leader.*

The Dragon and the Raven: Or, The Days of King Alfred.
By G. A. HENTY. With 8 page Illustrations by C. J. STANILAND, R.I. Crown 8vo, cloth elegant, olivine edges, 5s.

"A story that may justly be styled remarkable. Boys, in reading it, will be surprised to find how Alfred persevered, through years of bloodshed and times of peace, to rescue his people from the thraldom of the Danes. We hope the book will soon be widely known in all our schools."—*Schoolmaster.*

A Final Reckoning: A Tale of Bush Life in Australia.
By G. A. HENTY. With 8 page Illustrations by W. B. WOLLEN. Crown 8vo, cloth elegant, olivine edges, 5s.

"All boys will read this story with eager and unflagging interest. The episodes are in Mr. Henty's very best vein—graphic, exciting, realistic; and, as in all Mr. Henty's books, the tendency is to the formation of an honourable, manly, and even heroic character."—*Birmingham Post.*

BY G. A. HENTY.

"Mr. Henty's books are always alive with moving incident."—*Review of Reviews.*

Facing Death: Or, The Hero of the Vaughan Pit. A Tale of the Coal Mines. By G. A. HENTY. With 8 page Pictures by GORDON BROWNE. Crown 8vo, cloth elegant, olivine edges, 5s.

"If any father, godfather, clergyman, or schoolmaster is on the look-out for a good book to give as a present to a boy who is worth his salt, this is the book we would recommend."—*Standard.*

A Chapter of Adventures: Or, Through the Bombardment of Alexandria. By G. A. HENTY. With 6 page Illustrations by W. H. OVEREND. Crown 8vo, cloth elegant, 3s. 6d.

"Jack Robson and his two companions have their fill of excitement, and their chapter of adventures is so brisk and entertaining we could have wished it longer than it is."—*Saturday Review.*

Reduced Illustration from "The Clever Miss Follett"

Two Thousand Years Ago: Or, The Adventures of a Roman Boy. By Professor A. J. CHURCH. With 12 page Illustrations by ADRIEN MARIE. Crown 8vo, cloth elegant, olivine edges, 6s.

"Adventures well worth the telling. The book is extremely entertaining as well as useful, and there is a wonderful freshness in the Roman scenes and characters."—*The Times.*

The Clever Miss Follett. By J. K. H. DENNY. With 12 page Illustrations by GERTRUDE D. HAMMOND. Crown 8vo, cloth elegant, olivine edges, 6s.

"Just the book to give to girls, who will delight both in the letterpress and the illustrations. Miss Hammond has never done better work."—*Review of Reviews.*

BY ROSA MULHOLLAND.

Banshee Castle. By ROSA MULHOLLAND. With 12 page Illustrations by JOHN H. BACON. Crown 8vo, cloth elegant, olivine edges, 6s.

This story deals with the adventures of three girls who, with an old governess, migrate from Kensington to the West of Ireland. Belonging as they do to "the ould family" at the castle, the three girls are made heartily welcome in the cabins of the peasantry, where they learn many weird and curious tales from the folk-lore of the district. There is also an interesting plot running through the narrative, but it is by reason of its happy mingling of Irish humour and pathos that this story holds the reader charmed to the end.

Giannetta: A Girl's Story of Herself. By ROSA MULHOLLAND. With 8 page Illustrations by LOCKHART BOGLE. Crown 8vo, cloth elegant, olivine edges, 5s.

"Giannetta is a true heroine—warm-hearted, self-sacrificing, and, as all good women nowadays are, largely touched with the enthusiasm of humanity. One of the most attractive gift-books of the season."—*The Academy.*

A Fair Claimant: Being a Story for Girls. By FRANCES ARMSTRONG. With 8 page Illustrations by GERTRUDE D. HAMMOND. Crown 8vo, cloth elegant, olivine edges, 5s.

"As a gift-book for big girls it is among the best new books of the kind. The story is interesting and natural, from first to last."—*Westminster Gazette.*

The Heiress of Courtleroy. By ANNE BEALE. With 8 page Illustrations by T. C. H. CASTLE. Crown 8vo, cloth elegant, olivine edges, 5s.

"We can speak highly of the grace with which Miss Beale relates how the young 'Heiress of Courtleroy' had such good influence over her uncle as to win him from his intensely selfish ways."—*Guardian.*

The White Conquerors of Mexico: A Tale of Toltec and Aztec. By KIRK MUNROE. With 8 page Illustrations by W. S. STACEY. Crown 8vo, cloth elegant, olivine edges, 5s.

"Mr. Munroe gives most vivid pictures of the religious and civil polity of the Aztecs, and of everyday life, as he imagines it, in the streets and market-places of the magnificent capital of Montezuma."—*The Times.*

Highways and High Seas: Cyril Harley's Adventures on both. By F. FRANKFORT MOORE. With 8 page Illustrations by ALFRED PEARSE. Crown 8vo, cloth elegant, olivine edges, 5s.

"This is one of the best stories Mr. Moore has written, perhaps the very best. The exciting adventures are sure to attract boys."—*Spectator.*

BY GEORGE MACDONALD.

A Rough Shaking. By GEORGE MACDONALD. With 12 page Illustrations by W. PARKINSON. Crown 8vo, cloth elegant, olivine edges, 6s.

"One of the very best books for boys that has been written. It is full of material peculiarly well adapted for the young, containing in a marked degree the elements of all that is necessary to make up a perfect boys' book."—*Teachers' Aid.*

At the Back of the North Wind. By GEO. MACDONALD. With 75 Illustrations by ARTHUR HUGHES. Crown 8vo, cloth elegant, olivine edges, 5s.

"The story is thoroughly original, full of fancy and pathos. . . . We stand with one foot in fairyland and one on common earth."—*The Times.*

Ranald Bannerman's Boyhood. By GEO. MACDONALD. With 36 Illustrations by ARTHUR HUGHES. Crown 8vo, cloth elegant, olivine edges, 5s.

Reduced Illustration from "A Rough Shaking".

"The sympathy with boy-nature in *Ranald Bannerman's Boyhood* is perfect. It is a beautiful picture of childhood, teaching by its impressions and suggestions all noble things."—*British Quarterly Review.*

The Princess and the Goblin. By GEORGE MACDONALD. With 32 Illustrations. Crown 8vo, cloth extra, 3s. 6d.

"Little of what is written for children has the lightness of touch and play of fancy which are characteristic of George MacDonald's fairy tales. Mr. Arthur Hughes's illustrations are all that illustrations should be."—*Manchester Guardian.*

The Princess and Curdie. By GEORGE MACDONALD. With 8 page Illustrations. Crown 8vo, cloth extra, 3s. 6d.

"There is the finest and rarest genius in this brilliant story. Upgrown people would do wisely occasionally to lay aside their newspapers and magazines to spend an hour with Curdie and the Princess."—*Sheffield Independent.*

BY HARRY COLLINGWOOD.

The Pirate Island: A Story of the South Pacific. By HARRY COLLINGWOOD. With 8 page Pictures by C. J. STANILAND and J. R. WELLS. Crown 8vo, cloth elegant, olivine edges, 5s.

"A capital story of the sea; indeed in our opinion the author is superior in some respects as a marine novelist to the better known Mr. Clark Russell."—*The Times.*

The Log of the "Flying Fish": A Story of Aerial and Submarine Adventure. By HARRY COLLINGWOOD. With 6 page Illustrations by GORDON BROWNE. Crown 8vo, cloth elegant, 3s. 6d.

"The *Flying Fish* actually surpasses all Jules Verne's creations; with incredible speed she flies through the air, skims over the surface of the water, and darts along the ocean bed. We strongly recommend our school-boy friends to possess themselves of her log."—*Athenæum.*

For other Books by Harry Collingwood, see pages 21 and 22.

BY GEORGE MANVILLLE FENN.

"Mr. Fenn stands in the foremost rank of writers in this department."—*Daily News.*

Quicksilver: Or, A Boy with no Skid to his Wheel. By GEORGE MANVILLE FENN. With 10 page Illustrations by FRANK DADD. Crown 8vo, cloth elegant, olivine edges, 6s.

"*Quicksilver* is little short of an inspiration. In it that prince of story-writers for boys—George Manville Fenn—has surpassed himself. It is an ideal book for a boy's library."—*Practical Teacher.*

Dick o' the Fens: A Romance of the Great East Swamp. By G. MANVILLE FENN. With 12 page Illustrations by FRANK DADD. Crown 8vo, cloth elegant, olivine edges, 6s.

"We conscientiously believe that boys will find it capital reading. It is full of incident and mystery, and the mystery is kept up to the last moment. It is rich in effective local colouring; and it has a historical interest."—*Times.*

Devon Boys: A Tale of the North Shore. By G. MANVILLE FENN. With 12 page Illustrations by GORDON BROWNE. Crown 8vo, cloth elegant, olivine edges, 6s.

"An admirable story, as remarkable for the individuality of its young heroes as for the excellent descriptions of coast scenery and life in North Devon. It is one of the best books we have seen this season."—*Athenæum.*

The Golden Magnet: A Tale of the Land of the Incas. By G. MANVILLE FENN. Illustrated by 12 page Pictures by GORDON BROWNE. Crown 8vo, cloth elegant, olivine edges, 6s.

"There could be no more welcome present for a boy. There is not a dull page in the book, and many will be read with breathless interest. 'The Golden Magnet' is, of course, the same one that attracted Raleigh and the heroes of *Westward Ho!*"—*Journal of Education.*

BY GEORGE MANVILLE FENN.

"No one can find his way to the hearts of lads more readily than Mr. Fenn."—*Nottingham Guardian.*

In the King's Name: Or, The Cruise of the *Kestrel*. By G. MANVILLE FENN. Illustrated by 12 page Pictures by GORDON BROWNE. Crown 8vo, cloth elegant, olivine edges, 6s.

"The best of all Mr. Fenn's productions in this field. It has the great quality of always 'moving on', adventure following adventure in constant succession."—*Daily News.*

Nat the Naturalist: A Boy's Adventures in the Eastern Seas. By G. MANVILLE FENN. With 8 page Pictures. Crown 8vo, cloth elegant, olivine edges, 5s.

"This sort of book encourages independence of character, develops resource, and teaches a boy to keep his eyes open."—*Saturday Review.*

Bunyip Land: The Story of a Wild Journey in New Guinea. By G. MANVILLE FENN. With 6 page Illustrations by GORDON BROWNE. Crown 8vo, cloth elegant, 4s.

"Mr. Fenn deserves the thanks of everybody for *Bunyip Land*, and we may venture to promise that a quiet week may be reckoned on whilst the youngsters have such fascinating literature provided for their evenings' amusement."—*Spectator.*

Brownsmith's Boy. By G. MANVILLE FENN. With 6 page Illustrations. Crown 8vo, cloth elegant, 3s. 6d.

"Mr. Fenn's books are among the best, if not altogether the best, of the stories for boys. Mr. Fenn is at his best in *Brownsmith's Boy.*"—*Pictorial World.*

*** For other Books by G. MANVILLE FENN, see pages 21 and 22.

BY ASCOTT R. HOPE.

Young Travellers' Tales. By ASCOTT R. HOPE. With 6 Illustrations by H. J. DRAPER. Crown 8vo, cloth elegant, 3s. 6d.

These lively records of haphazard experience are drawn from various parts of the world. There is a thrilling adventure in the Austrian Tirol, a mischance in Norway, an exciting escapade in Africa, a tale of shooting in India, a cyclist's laughable exploit in France, a runaway experience in Switzerland, an encounter with a Corsican bandit, and other stories of a like entertaining character. All are presented in a crisp and engaging style.

The Seven Wise Scholars. By ASCOTT R. HOPE. With nearly 100 Illustrations by GORDON BROWNE. Cloth elegant, 5s.

"As full of fun as a volume of *Punch*; with illustrations, more laughter-provoking than most we have seen since Leech died."—*Sheffield Independent.*

Stories of Old Renown: Tales of Knights and Heroes. By ASCOTT R. HOPE. With 100 Illustrations by GORDON BROWNE. Crown 8vo, cloth elegant, 3s. 6d.

"A really fascinating book worthy of its telling title. There is, we venture to say, not a dull page in the book, not a story which will not bear a second reading."—*Guardian.*

The Universe: Or The Infinitely Great and the Infinitely Little. A Sketch of Contrasts in Creation, and Marvels revealed and explained by Natural Science. By F. A. POUCHET, M.D. With 272 Engravings on wood, of which 55 are full-page size, and a Coloured Frontispiece. Eleventh Edition, medium 8vo, cloth elegant, gilt edges, 7s. 6d.; also morocco antique, 16s.

"We can honestly commend Professor Pouchet's book, which is admirably, as it is copiously illustrated."—*The Times.*

"Scarcely any book in French or in English is so likely to stimulate in the young an interest in the physical phenomena."—*Fortnightly Review.*

BY ROBERT LEIGHTON.

Olaf the Glorious. By ROBERT LEIGHTON. With 8 page Illustrations by RALPH PEACOCK, and a Map. Crown 8vo, cloth elegant, olivine edges, 5s.

This story of Olaf the Glorious, King of Norway, opens with the incident of his being found by his uncle living as a bond-slave in Esthonia, and it follows him through his romantic youth in the court of King Valdemar of Russia. Then come his adventures as a Viking and his raids upon the coasts of Scotland and England, his victorious battle against the English at Maldon in Essex, and his conversion to Christianity. He then returns to pagan Norway, is accepted as king, and converts his people to the Christian faith. The story closes with the great battle of Svold, when Olaf, defeated, jumps overboard, and is last seen with the sunlight shining on the glittering cross upon his shield.

The Wreck of "The Golden Fleece": The Story of a North Sea Fisher-boy. By ROBERT LEIGHTON. With 8 page Illustrations by FRANK BRANGWYN. Crown 8vo, cloth elegant, olivine edges, 5s.

"This story should add considerably to Mr. Leighton's high reputation. Excellent in every respect, it contains every variety of incident. The plot is very cleverly devised, and the types of the North Sea sailors are capital."—*The Times.*

The Pilots of Pomona: A Story of the Orkney Islands. By ROBERT LEIGHTON. With 8 page Illustrations by JOHN LEIGHTON, and a Map. Crown 8vo, cloth elegant, olivine edges, 5s.

"A story which is quite as good in its way as *Treasure Island*, and is full of adventure of a stirring yet most natural kind. Although it is primarily a boys' book, it is a real godsend to the elderly reader."—*Glasgow Evening Times.*

The Thirsty Sword: A Story of the Norse Invasion of Scotland (1262-63). By ROBERT LEIGHTON. With 8 page Illustrations by ALFRED PEARSE, and a Map. Crown 8vo, cloth elegant, olivine edges, 5s.

"This is one of the most fascinating stories for boys that it has ever been our pleasure to read. From first to last the interest never flags. Boys will worship Kenric, who is a hero in every sense of the word."—*Schoolmaster.*

BY DR. GORDON STABLES.

To Greenland and the Pole. By GORDON STABLES, M.D.
With 8 page Illustrations by G. C. HINDLEY, and a Map. Crown 8vo, cloth elegant, olivine edges, 5s.

The unfailing fascination of Arctic venturing is presented in this story with new vividness. The author is himself an old Arctic voyager, and he is thus enabled to make excellent use of the recent exploits of Nansen in Greenland, and the splendid daring of that explorer's present expedition. The story deals with *skilöbning* in the north of Scotland, deer-hunting in Norway, sealing in the Arctic Seas, bear-stalking on the ice-floes, the hardships of a journey across Greenland, and a successful voyage to the back of the North Pole. This is, indeed, a real sea-yarn by a real sailor, and the tone is as bright and wholesome as the adventures are numerous.

Reduced Illustration from "Grettir the Outlaw".

Westward with Columbus. By GORDON STABLES, M.D., C.M. With 8 page Illustrations by ALFRED PEARSE. Crown 8vo, cloth elegant, olivine edges, 5s.

"We must place *Westward with Columbus* among those books that all boys ought to read."—*The Spectator.*

'Twixt School and College: A Tale of Self-reliance. By GORDON STABLES, C.M., M.D., R.N. With 8 page Illustrations by W. PARKINSON. Crown 8vo, cloth elegant, olivine edges, 5s.

"One of the best of a prolific writer's books for boys, being full of practical instructions as to keeping pets, and inculcates in a way which a little recalls Miss Edgeworth's 'Frank' the virtue of self-reliance."—*Athenæum.*

BY G. NORWAY.

A Prisoner of War: A Story of the Time of Napoleon Bonaparte. By G. NORWAY. With 6 page Illustrations by ROBT. BARNES, A.R.W.S. Crown 8vo, cloth elegant, 3s. 6d.

When Napoleon Bonaparte suddenly broke the treaty of Amiens and declared war against England, many peaceful Englishmen who had ventured to reside upon the Continent were made prisoners. Among these was Captain Wynter, who was arrested at Helvoetsluys in Holland, and from thence carried into France. His family escaped across the Channel, but his son, a young lad, determined to return, trace out his father, and assist him to escape. Disguised as a packman he searched France from fortress to fortress. After many a mischance and many a hair-breadth escape he finds his father, contrives his escape, and brings him safely to England. It is a romantic narrative, with the additional merit of being true.

A True Cornish Maid. By G. NORWAY. With 6 page Illustrations by J. FINNEMORE. Crown 8vo, cloth elegant, 3s. 6d.

"There is some excellent reading. . . . Mrs. Norway brings before the eyes of her readers the good Cornish folk, their speech, their manners, and their ways. A *True Cornish Maid* deserves to be popular."—*Athenæum.*

"Among girls' books the success of the year has fallen, we think, to Mrs. Norway, whose *True Cornish Maid* is really an admirable piece of work. . . . The book is full of vivid and accurate local colour; it contains, too, some very clever character studies."—*Review of Reviews.*

Hussein the Hostage: Or, A Boy's Adventures in Persia. By G. NORWAY. With 8 page Illustrations by JOHN SCHÖNBERG. Crown 8vo, cloth elegant, olivine edges, 5s.

"*Hussein the Hostage* is full of originality and vigour. The characters are lifelike, there is plenty of stirring incident, the interest is sustained throughout, and every boy will enjoy following the fortunes of the hero."—*Journal of Education.*

The Loss of John Humble: What Led to It, and What Came of It. By G. NORWAY. With 8 page Illustrations by JOHN SCHÖNBERG. Crown 8vo, cloth elegant, olivine edges, 5s.

"This story will place the author at once in the front rank. It is full of life and adventure. He is equally at home in his descriptions of life in Sweden and in the more stirring passages of wreck and disaster, and the interest of the story is sustained without a break from first to last."—*Standard.*

Under False Colours: A Story from Two Girls' Lives. By SARAH DOUDNEY. With 6 page Illustrations by G. G. KILBURNE. Crown 8vo, cloth elegant, 4s.

"Sarah Doudney has no superior as a writer of high-toned stories—pure in style, original in conception, and with skilfully wrought-out plots; but we have seen nothing from her pen equal in dramatic energy to this book."—*Christian Leader.*

With the Sea Kings: A Story of the Days of Lord Nelson. By F. H. WINDER. With 6 page Illustrations by W. S. STACEY. Crown 8vo, cloth elegant, 4s.

"Just the book to put into a boy's hands. Every chapter contains boardings, cuttings out, fighting pirates, escapes of thrilling audacity, and captures by corsairs, sufficient to turn the quietest boy's head. The story culminates in a vigorous account of the battle of Trafalgar. Happy boys!"—*The Academy*.

Grettir the Outlaw: A Story of Iceland. By S. BARING-GOULD. With 6 page Illustrations by M. ZENO DIEMER, and a Coloured Map. *New Edition.* Crown 8vo, cloth elegant, 4s.

"Is the boys' book of its year. That is, of course, as much as to say that it will do for men grown as well as juniors. It is told in simple, straightforward English, as all stories should be, and it has a freshness, a freedom, a sense of sun and wind and the open air, which make it irresistible."—*National Observer*.

Gold, Gold, in Cariboo: A Story of Adventure in British Columbia. By CLIVE PHILLIPPS-WOLLEY. With 6 page Illustrations by G. C. HINDLEY. Crown 8vo, cloth extra, 3s. 6d.

"It would be difficult to say too much in favour of *Gold, Gold, in Cariboo*. We have seldom read a more exciting tale of wild mining adventure in a singularly inaccessible country. There is a capital plot, and the interest is sustained to the last page."—*The Times*.

A Champion of the Faith: A Tale of Prince Hal and the Lollards. By J. M. CALLWELL. With 6 page Illustrations by HERBERT J. DRAPER. Crown 8vo, cloth elegant, 4s.

"Will not be less enjoyed than Mr. Henty's books. Sir John Oldcastle's pathetic story, and the history of his brave young squire, will make every boy enjoy this lively story."—*London Quarterly*.

BY ALICE CORKRAN.

Meg's Friend. By ALICE CORKRAN. With 6 page Illustrations by ROBERT FOWLER. Crown 8vo, cloth extra, 3s. 6d.

"One of Miss Corkran's charming books for girls, narrated in that simple and picturesque style which marks the authoress as one of the first amongst writers for young people."—*The Spectator*.

Margery Merton's Girlhood. By ALICE CORKRAN. With 6 page Pictures by GORDON BROWNE. Cr. 8vo, cloth extra, 3s. 6d.

"Another book for girls we can warmly commend. There is a delightful piquancy in the experiences and trials of a young English girl who studies painting in Paris."—*Saturday Review*.

Down the Snow Stairs: Or, From Good-night to Good-morning. By ALICE CORKRAN. With 60 Illustrations by GORDON BROWNE. Crown 8vo, cloth elegant, olivine edges, 3s. 6d.

"A gem of the first water, bearing upon every page the mark of genius. It is indeed a Little Pilgrim's Progress."—*Christian Leader*.

Sou'wester and Sword. By Hugh St. Leger. With 6 page Illustrations by Hal Hurst. Crown 8vo, cloth elegant, 4s.

This is the book for a lad who loves a sea-yarn. The fun no less than the dangers of a sailor's life are faithfully depicted. Shark fishing, mastheading, galley-ranging, mutiny, tropical gales, death at sea, and the final shipwreck, are incidents in a tale which is one continuous adventure. The hero and several of the crew are saved from the wreck, and with the harum-scarum recklessness of seamen they join the English expedition against the Mahdi, taking part in the terrible fighting around Suakim.

BY EDGAR PICKERING.

In Press-Gang Days. By Edgar Pickering. With 6 Illustrations by W. S. Stacey. Crown 8vo, cloth elegant, 3s. 6d.

In this story Harry Waring is caught by the Press-gang and carried on board His Majesty's ship *Sandwich*. He takes part in the mutiny of the Nore, and shares in some hard fighting on board the frigate *Phœnix*. He is with Nelson, also, at the storming of Santa Cruz, and the battle of the Nile. His career is like to end in a French prison, but he, with some companions, manage to escape, seize a French schooner, fight their way out of the harbour, and so return home with a prize.

An Old-Time Yarn: Wherein is set forth divers desperate mischances which befell Anthony Ingram and his shipmates in the West Indies and Mexico with Hawkins and Drake. By Edgar Pickering. Illustrated with 6 page Pictures drawn by Alfred Pearse. Crown 8vo, cloth elegant, 3s. 6d.

"And a very good yarn it is, with not a dull page from first to last. There is a flavour of *Westward Ho!* in this attractive book."—*Educational Review*.

Silas Verney: A Tale of the Time of Charles II. By Edgar Pickering. With 6 page Illustrations by Alfred Pearse. Crown 8vo, cloth elegant, 3s. 6d.

"Wonderful as the adventures of Silas are, it must be admitted that they are very naturally worked out and very plausibly presented. Altogether this is an excellent story for boys."—*Saturday Review*.

BY ANNIE E. ARMSTRONG.

Three Bright Girls: A Story of Chance and Mischance. By Annie E. Armstrong. With 6 page Illustrations by W. Parkinson. Crown 8vo, cloth elegant, 3s. 6d.

"Among many good stories for girls this is undoubtedly one of the very best. The three girls whose portraits are so admirably painted are girls of earnest, practical, and business-like mood. Ever bright and cheerful, they influence other lives, and at last they come out of their trials and difficulties with honour to themselves and benefits to all about them."—*Teachers' Aid*.

A Very Odd Girl: or, Life at the Gabled Farm. By Annie E. Armstrong. With 6 page Illustrations by S. T. Dadd. Crown 8vo, cloth elegant, 3s. 6d.

"The book is one we can heartily recommend, for it is not only bright and interesting, but also pure and healthy in tone and teaching."—*The Lady*.

BY C. J. HYNE.

The Captured Cruiser: or, Two Years from Land. By C. J. HYNE. With 6 page Illustrations by FRANK BRANGWYN. Crown 8vo, cloth elegant, 3s. 6d.

"The two lads and the two skippers are admirably drawn. Mr. Hyne has now secured a position in the first rank of writers of fiction for boys."—*Spectator.*

Afloat at Last: A Sailor Boy's Log of his Life at Sea. By JOHN C. HUTCHESON. With 6 page Illustrations by W. H. OVEREND. Crown 8vo, cloth elegant, 3s. 6d.

"As healthy and breezy a book as one could wish to put into the hands of a boy."—*Academy.*

Picked up at Sea: Or, The Gold Miners of Minturne Creek. By J. C. HUTCHESON. With 6 page Pictures. Cloth extra, 3s. 6d.

"The author's success with this book is so marked that it may well encourage him to further efforts. The description of mining life in the Far West is true and accurate."—*Standard.*

Cousin Geoffrey and I. By CAROLINE AUSTIN. With 6 page Illustrations by W. PARKINSON. Crown 8vo, cloth extra, 3s. 6d.

"Miss Austin's story is bright, clever, and well developed."—*Saturday Review.*

Brother and Sister: Or, The Trials of the Moore Family. By ELIZABETH J. LYSAGHT. With 6 page Illustrations. Crown 8vo, cloth elegant, 3s. 6d.

"A pretty story, and well told. The plot is cleverly constructed, and the moral is excellent."—*Athenæum.*

The Search for the Talisman: A Story of Labrador. By HENRY FRITH. With 6 page Illustrations by J. SCHÖNBERG. Crown 8vo, cloth elegant, 3s. 6d.

"Mr. Frith's volume will be among those most read and highest valued. The adventures among seals, whales, and icebergs in Labrador will delight many a young reader."—*Pall Mall Gazette.*

Reefer and Rifleman: A Tale of the Two Services. By Lieut.-Col. PERCY-GROVES. With 6 page Illustrations by JOHN SCHÖNBERG. Crown 8vo, cloth elegant, 3s. 6d.

"A good, old-fashioned, amphibious story of our fighting with the Frenchmen in the beginning of our century, with a fair sprinkling of fun and frolic."—*Times.*

Dora: Or, A Girl without a Home. By Mrs. R. H. READ. With 6 page Illustrations. Crown 8vo, cloth elegant, 3s. 6d.

"It is no slight thing, in an age of rubbish, to get a story so pure and healthy as this."—*The Academy.*

Life's Daily Ministry: A Story of Everyday Service for Others. By Mrs. E. R. PITMAN. With 4 page Illustrations. Crown 8vo, cloth extra, 3s. 6d.

"Shows exquisite tonches of a master hand. She depicts in graphic outliv the characteristics of the beautiful and the good in life."—*Christian Union.*

Storied Holidays: A Cycle of Red-letter Days. By E. S. BROOKS. With 12 page Illustrations by HOWARD PYLE. Crown 8vo, cloth elegant, 3s. 6d.

"It is a downright good book for a senior boy, and is eminently readable from first to last."—*Schoolmaster.*

Chivalric Days: Stories of Courtesy and Courage in the Olden Times. By E. S. BROOKS. With 20 Illustrations by GORDON BROWNE and other Artists. Crown 8vo, cloth extra, 3s. 6d.

"We have seldom come across a prettier collection of tales. These charming stories of boys and girls of olden days are no mere fictitious or imaginary sketches, but are real and actual records of their sayings and doings."—*Literary World.*

Historic Boys: Their Endeavours, their Achievements, and their Times. By E. S. BROOKS. With 12 page Illustrations by R. B. BIRCH and JOHN SCHÖNBERG. Crown 8vo, cloth extra, 3s. 6d.

"A wholesome book, manly in tone, its character sketches enlivened by brisk dialogue and high-class illustrations; altogether one that should incite boys to further acquaintance with those rulers of men whose careers are narrated. We advise teachers to put it on their list of prizes."—*Knowledge.*

Dr. Jolliffe's Boys: A Tale of Weston School. By LEWIS HOUGH. With 6 page Pictures. Crown 8vo, cloth extra, 3s. 6d.

"Young people who appreciate *Tom Brown's School-days* will find this story a worthy companion to that fascinating book. There is the same manliness of tone, truthfulness of outline, avoidance of exaggeration and caricature, and healthy morality as characterized the masterpiece of Mr. Hughes."—*Newcastle Journal.*

The Bubbling Teapot. A Wonder Story. By Mrs. L. W. CHAMPNEY. With 12 page Pictures by WALTER SATTERLEE. Crown 8vo, cloth extra, 3s. 6d.

"Very literally a 'wonder story', and a wild and fanciful one. Nevertheless it is made realistic enough, and there is a good deal of information to be gained from it."—*The Times.*

BY JENNETT HUMPHREYS.

Laugh and Learn: The Easiest Book of Nursery Lessons and Nursery Games. By JENNETT HUMPHREYS. Profusely Illustrated. Square 8vo, cloth extra, 3s. 6d.

"One of the best books of the kind imaginable, full of practical teaching in word and picture, and helping the little ones pleasantly along a right royal road to learning."—*Graphic.*

Thorndyke Manor: A Tale of Jacobite Times. By MARY C. ROWSELL. With 6 page Illustrations by L. LESLIE BROOKE. Crown 8vo, cloth elegant, 3s. 6d.

"Miss Rowsell has never written a more attractive book than *Thorndyke Manor.*"—*Belfast News-Letter.*

Traitor or Patriot? A Tale of the Rye-House Plot. By MARY C. ROWSELL. With 6 page Pictures by C. O. MURRAY and C. J. STANILAND, R.I. Crown 8vo, cloth elegant, 3s. 6d.

"Here the Rye-House Plot serves as the groundwork for a romantic love episode, whose true characters are lifelike beings."—*Graphic.*

BLACKIE'S NEW THREE-SHILLING SERIES.

Beautifully Illustrated and Handsomely Bound.

NEW VOLUMES.

Under Hatches: or, Ned Woodthorpe's Adventures. By F. FRANKFORT MOORE. With 6 page Illustrations by A. FORESTIER. New Edition. Crown 8vo, cloth elegant, 3s.

"The story as a story is one that will just suit boys all the world over. The characters are well drawn and consistent; Patsy, the Irish steward, will be found especially amusing."—*Schoolmaster.*

The Congo Rovers: A Story of the Slave Squadron. By HARRY COLLINGWOOD. With 6 page Illustrations by J. SCHÖNBERG. New Edition. Crown 8vo, cloth elegant, 3s.

"No better sea story has lately been written than the *Congo Rovers.* It is as original as any boy could desire."—*Morning Post.*

Menhardoc: A Story of Cornish Nets and Mines. By G. MANVILLE FENN. With 6 page Illustrations by C. J. STANILAND, R.I. Crown 8vo, cloth extra, 3s.

"They are real living boys, with their virtues and faults. The Cornish fishermen are drawn from life, and stand out from the pages in their jerseys and sea-boots all sprinkled with silvery pilchard scales."—*Spectator.*

Yussuf the Guide: or, The Mountain Bandits. A Story of Strange Adventure in Asia Minor. By G. MANVILLE FENN. With 6 page Illustrations by J. SCHÖNBERG. Crown 8vo, cloth extra, 3s.

"Told with such real freshness and vigour that the reader feels he is actually one of the party, sharing in the fun and facing the dangers."—*Pall Mall Gazette.*

Robinson Crusoe. With 100 Illustrations by GORDON BROWNE. Crown 8vo, cloth extra, 3s.

"One of the best issues, if not absolutely the best, of Defoe's work which has ever appeared."—*The Standard.*

THREE SHILLING SERIES—Continued.

Gulliver's Travels. With 100 Illustrations by GORDON BROWNE. Crown 8vo, cloth extra, 3s.

"Mr. Gordon Browne is, to my thinking, incomparably the most artistic, spirited, and brilliant of our illustrators of books for boys, and one of the most humorous also, as his illustrations of 'Gulliver' amply testify."—*Truth.*

Patience Wins: or, War in the Works. By GEORGE MANVILLE FENN. With 6 page Illustrations. Cr. 8vo, cloth extra, 3s.

"Mr. Fenn has never hit upon a happier plan than in writing this story of Yorkshire factory life. The whole book is all aglow with life."—*Pall Mall Gazette.*

Mother Carey's Chicken: Her Voyage to the Unknown Isle. By G. MANVILLE FENN. With 6 page Illustrations by A. FORESTIER. Crown 8vo, cloth extra, 3s.

"Undoubtedly one of the best Mr. Fenn has written. The incidents are of thrilling interest, while the characters are drawn with a care and completeness rarely found in a boys' book."—*Literary World.*

The Missing Merchantman. By HARRY COLLINGWOOD. With 6 page Illustrations by W. H. OVEREND. Cloth extra, 3s.

"One of the author's best sea stories. The hero is as heroic as any boy could desire, and the ending is extremely happy."—*British Weekly.*

The Rover's Secret: A Tale of the Pirate Cays and Lagoons of Cuba. By HARRY COLLINGWOOD. With 6 page Illustrations by W. C. SYMONS. Crown 8vo, cloth elegant, 3s.

"*The Rover's Secret* is by far the best sea story we have read for years, and is certain to give unalloyed pleasure to boys."—*Saturday Review.*

The Wigwam and the War-path: Stories of the Red Indians. By ASCOTT R. HOPE. With 6 page Illustrations. Crown 8vo, cloth elegant, 3s.

"Is notably good. It gives a very vivid picture of life among the Indians, which will delight the heart of many a schoolboy."—*Spectator.*

Perseverance Island: or, The Robinson Crusoe of the 19th Century. By DOUGLAS FRAZAR. With 6 page Illustrations. Crown 8vo, cloth extra, 3s.

"This is an interesting story, written with studied simplicity of style, much in Defoe's vein of apparent sincerity and scrupulous veracity; while for practical instruction it is even better than *Robinson Crusoe*."—*Illustrated London News.*

Girl Neighbours: or, The Old Fashion and the New. By SARAH TYTLER. With 6 page Illustrations by C. T. GARLAND. Crown 8vo, cloth elegant, 3s.

"One of the most effective and quietly humorous of Miss Sarah Tytler's stories. It is very healthy, very agreeable, and very well written."—*The Spectator.*

BY BEATRICE HARRADEN.

Things Will Take a Turn. By BEATRICE HARRADEN. A New Edition, with 34 Illustrations by JOHN H. BACON. Crown 8vo, cloth elegant, 2s. 6d.

A happy creation this by the author of "Ships that Pass in the Night". One cannot help loving the sunny-hearted child who assists her grand-dad in his dusty second-hand book-shop, she is so gay, so engaging, so natural. And to love Rosebud is to love all her friends, and enter sympathetically into the good fortune she brought them. The charm of this tale, as of all Miss Harraden's work, is a delicate, wistful sympathy.

The Whispering Winds, and the Tales that they Told. By MARY H. DEBENHAM. With 25 Illustrations by PAUL HARDY. Crown 8vo, cloth elegant, 2s. 6d.

Every wind whispered a story. The South Wind came from Italy and told a bright little fairy tale about Baby Benedetta. The North Wind brought a weird story of the spiteful fairy-folk from a Scottish glen; the laughing West Wind from Devonshire told of the King of the Mist, and the delights of clotted cream; and the East Wind spoke of the brave sea-king's daughter in Norway over the sea. And all the tales were passing good.

BLACKIE'S HALF-CROWN SERIES.

Illustrated by eminent Artists. In crown 8vo, cloth elegant.

Hammond's Hard Lines. By SKELTON KUPPORD. Illustrated by HAROLD COPPING.

Tom Hammond was a pupil at a public school, and, boy-like, was much given to grumbling and discontent with the "powers that be". He wished oh! so many things. At length in a most curious and unexpected way he received the offer of Three Wishes, which he joyfully accepted. The relation of the adventures that ensue forms a graphically diverting narrative of the freshest interest.

Dulcie King: A Story for Girls. By M. CORBET-SEYMOUR. Illustrated by GERTRUDE D. HAMMOND.

A bright, happy-going story in which the heroine is taken from her modest home and adopted by a rich relative. Dulcie King is not dazzled, however, by her new and sumptuous surroundings, and the native goodness of her heart helps her to resist all temptations to dispossess the rightful heir. Dulcie King is a girl whom one cannot help loving.

Hugh Herbert's Inheritance. By CAROLINE AUSTIN. With 4 page Illustrations by C. T. GARLAND. *New Edition*. Crown 8vo, cloth elegant, 2s. 6d.

"Will please by its simplicity, its tenderness, and its healthy interesting motive. It is admirably written."—*Scotsman*.

Nicola: The Career of a Girl Musician. By M. CORBET-SEYMOUR. Illustrated by GERTRUDE D. HAMMOND.

"There is a great deal of quiet force and strength about the story I can thoroughly and heartily recommend *Nicola* as a present for girls."—*Winter's Weekly*.

HALF-CROWN SERIES—Continued.

A Little Handful. By HARRIET J. SCRIPPS.
"A very charming picture of a bright, lovable, mischievous boy, who hails from the New World."—*School Guardian.*

A Golden Age: A Story of Four Merry Children. By ISMAY THORN. Illustrated by GORDON BROWNE.
"Ought to have a place of honour on the nursery shelf."—*The Athenæum.*

A Rough Road: or, How the Boy Made a Man of Himself. By Mrs. G. LINNÆUS BANKS.
"Told with much simple force and that charm which belongs to one who has known herself what a rough road is, and how to traverse it."—*Winter's Weekly.*

The Two Dorothys. By Mrs. HERBERT MARTIN.
"A book that will interest and please all girls."—*The Lady.*

Penelope and the Others. By AMY WALTON.
"This is a charming book for children. Miss Walton proves herself a perfect adept in understanding of school-room joys and sorrows."—*Christian Leader.*

A Cruise in Cloudland. By HENRY FRITH.
"A thoroughly interesting story."—*St. James's Gazette.*

Marian and Dorothy. By ANNIE E. ARMSTRONG.
"This is distinctively a book for girls. A bright wholesome story."—*Academy.*

Stimson's Reef: A Tale of Adventure. By C. J. HYNE.
"It may almost vie with Mr. R. L. Stevenson's *Treasure Island.*"—*Guardian.*

Gladys Anstruther. By LOUISA THOMPSON.
"It is a clever book: novel and striking in the highest degree."—*Schoolmistress.*

The Secret of the Old House. By E. EVERETT-GREEN.
"Tim, the little Jacobite, is a charming creation."—*Academy.*

Hal Hungerford. By J. R. HUTCHINSON, B.A.
"Altogether, Hal Hungerford is a distinct literary success."—*Spectator.*

The Golden Weathercock. By JULIA GODDARD.
"A cleverly conceived quaint story, ingeniously written."—*Saturday Review.*

White Lilac: or, The Queen of the May. By AMY WALTON.
"Every rural parish ought to add *White Lilac* to its library."—*Academy.*

Miriam's Ambition. By EVELYN EVERETT-GREEN.
"Miss Green's children are real British boys and girls."—*Liverpool Mercury.*

The Brig "Audacious". By ALAN COLE.
"Fresh and wholesome as a breath of sea air."—*Court Journal.*

HALF-CROWN SERIES—Continued.

The Saucy May. By Henry Frith.
"Mr. Frith gives a new picture of life on the ocean wave."—*Sheffield Independent.*

Jasper's Conquest. By Elizabeth J. Lysaght.
"One of the best boys' books of the season."—*Schoolmaster.*

Little Lady Clare. By Evelyn Everett-Green.
"Reminds us in its quaintness of Mrs. Ewing's delightful tales."—*Liter. World.*

The Eversley Secrets. By Evelyn Everett-Green.
"Roy Eversley is a very touching picture of high principle."—*Guardian.*

The Hermit Hunter of the Wilds. By G. Stables, R.N.
"Will gladden the heart of many a bright boy."—*Methodist Recorder.*

Sturdy and Strong. By G. A. Henty.
"A hero who stands as a good instance of chivalry in domestic life."—*The Empire.*

Gutta Percha Willie. By George MacDonald.
"Get it for your boys and girls to read for themselves."—*Practical Teacher.*

The War of the Axe: Or, Adventures in South Africa. By J. Percy-Groves.
"The story is well and brilliantly told."—*Literary World.*

The Lads of Little Clayton. By R. Stead.
"A capital book for boys."—*Schoolmaster.*

Ten Boys who lived on the Road from Long Ago to Now. By Jane Andrews. With 20 Illustrations.
"The idea is a very happy one, and admirably carried out."—*Practical Teacher.*

A Waif of the Sea: Or, The Lost Found. By Kate Wood.
"Written with tenderness and grace."—*Morning Advertiser.*

Winnie's Secret. By Kate Wood.
"One of the best story-books we have read."—*Schoolmaster.*

Miss Willowburn's Offer. By Sarah Doudney.
"Patience Willowburn is one of Miss Doudney's best creations."—*Spectator.*

A Garland for Girls. By Louisa M. Alcott.
"These little tales are the beau ideal of girls' stories."—*Christian World.*

Hetty Gray: Or, Nobody's Bairn. By Rosa Mulholland.
"Hetty is a delightful creature—piquant, tender, and true."—*World.*

Brothers in Arms: A Story of the Crusades. By F. Bayford Harrison.
"Sure to prove interesting to young people of both sexes."—*Guardian.*

Miss Fenwick's Failures. By Esmé Stuart.
"A girl true to real life, who will put no nonsense into young heads."—*Graphic.*

Gytha's Message. By Emma Leslie.
"This is the sort of book that all girls like."—*Journal of Education.*

HALF-CROWN SERIES—Continued.

Jack o' Lanthorn: A Tale of Adventure. By HENRY FRITH.
"The narrative is crushed full of stirring incident."—*Christian Leader.*

The Family Failing. By DARLEY DALE.
"A capital lesson on the value of contentedness."—*Aberdeen Journal.*

My Mistress the Queen. By M. A. PAULL.
"The style is pure and graceful, and the story full of interest."—*Scotsman.*

The Stories of Wasa and Menzikoff.

Stories of the Sea in Former Days.

Tales of Captivity and Exile.

Famous Discoveries by Sea and Land.

Stirring Events of History.

Adventures in Field, Flood, and Forest.
"It would be difficult to place in the hands of young people books which combine interest and instruction in a higher degree."—*Manchester Courier.*

BLACKIE'S TWO-SHILLING SERIES.
Illustrated by eminent Artists. In crown 8vo, cloth elegant.

NEW VOLUMES.

The Organist's Baby: A Story for Boys and Girls. By KATHLEEN KNOX. Illustrated by JOHN H. BACON.

School-Days in France. By AN OLD GIRL. Illustrated by W. PARKINSON.

The Ravensworth Scholarship: A High School Story for Girls. By Mrs. HENRY CLARKE, M.A. Illustrated by JOHN H. BACON.

Queen of the Daffodils: A Story of High School Life. By LESLIE LAING.

Raff's Ranche: A Story of Adventure among Cow-boys and Indians. By F. M. HOLMES.

An Unexpected Hero. By ELIZ. J. LYSAGHT.

The Bushranger's Secret. By Mrs. HENRY CLARKE, M.A.

The White Squall. By JOHN C. HUTCHESON.

The Wreck of the "Nancy Bell". By J. C. HUTCHESON.

The Lonely Pyramid. By J. H. YOXALL.

Bab: or, The Triumph of Unselfishness. By ISMAY THORN.

Climbing the Hill, and other Stories. By ANNIE S. SWAN.

TWO-SHILLING SERIES—Continued.

Brave and True, and other Stories. By GREGSON GOW.
The Light Princess. By GEORGE MAC DONALD.
Nutbrown Roger and I. By J. H. YOXALL.
Warner's Chase: Or, The Gentle Heart. By ANNIE S. SWAN.

Reduced Illustration from "The Queen of the Daffodils".

Sam Silvan's Sacrifice. By JESSE COLMAN.
Insect Ways on Summer Days in Garden, Forest, Field, and Stream. By JENNETT HUMPHREYS. With 70 Illustrations.
Susan. By AMY WALTON.
A Pair of Clogs. By AMY WALTON.
The Hawthorns. By AMY WALTON.
Dorothy's Dilemma. By CAROLINE AUSTIN.

TWO-SHILLING SERIES—Continued.

Marie's Home. By CAROLINE AUSTIN.
A Warrior King. By J. EVELYN.
Aboard the "Atalanta". By HENRY FRITH.
The Penang Pirate. By JOHN C. HUTCHESON.
Teddy: The Story of a "Little Pickle". By JOHN C. HUTCHESON.
A Rash Promise. By CECILIA SELBY LOWNDES.
Linda and the Boys. By CECILIA SELBY LOWNDES.
Swiss Stories for Children. From the German of MADAM JOHANNA SPYRI. By LUCY WHEELOCK.
The Squire's Grandson. By J. M. CALLWELL.
Magna Charta Stories. Edited by ARTHUR GILMAN, A.M.
The Wings of Courage; AND THE CLOUD-SPINNER. Translated from the French of GEORGE SAND, by Mrs. CORKRAN.
Chirp and Chatter: Or, LESSONS FROM FIELD AND TREE. By ALICE BANKS. With 54 Illustrations by GORDON BROWNE.
Four Little Mischiefs. By ROSA MULHOLLAND.
New Light through Old Windows. By GREGSON GOW.
Little Tottie, and Two Other Stories. By THOMAS ARCHER.
Naughty Miss Bunny. By CLARA MULHOLLAND.
Adventures of Mrs. Wishing-to-be. By ALICE CORKRAN.
The Joyous Story of Toto. By LAURA E. RICHARDS.
Our Dolly: Her Words and Ways. By MRS. R. H. READ. 2s.
Fairy Fancy: What she Heard and Saw. By MRS. READ. 2s.

BLACKIE'S EIGHTEENPENNY SERIES.

With Illustrations. In crown 8vo, cloth elegant.

NEW VOLUMES.

Olive and Robin: or, A Journey to Nowhere. By the Author of "Two Dorothys".
Mona's Trust: A Story for Girls. By PENELOPE LESLIE.
Little Jimmy: A Story of Adventure. By Rev. D. RICE-JONES, M.A.
Pleasures and Pranks. By ISABELLA PEARSON.
In a Stranger's Garden: A Story for Boys and Girls. By CONSTANCE CUMING.

EIGHTEENPENNY SERIES—Continued.

A Soldier's Son: The Story of a Boy who Succeeded. By ANNETTE LYSTER.

Mischief and Merry-making. By ISABELLA PEARSON.

Littlebourne Lock. By F. BAYFORD HARRISON.

Wild Meg and Wee Dickie. By MARY E. ROPES.

Grannie. By ELIZABETH J. LYSAGHT.

The Seed She Sowed. By EMMA LESLIE.

Unlucky: A Fragment of a Girl's Life. By CAROLINE AUSTIN.

Everybody's Business: or a Friend in Need. By ISMAY THORN.

Tales of Daring and Danger. By G. A. HENTY.

The Seven Golden Keys. By JAMES E. ARNOLD.

The Story of a Queen. By MARY C. ROWSELL.

Edwy: Or, Was he a Coward? By ANNETTE LYSTER.

The Battlefield Treasure. By F. BAYFORD HARRISON.

Joan's Adventures at the North Pole. By ALICE CORKRAN.

Filled with Gold. By J. PERRETT.

Our General: A Story for Girls. By ELIZABETH J. LYSAGHT.

Aunt Hesba's Charge. By ELIZABETH J. LYSAGHT.

Town Mice in the Country. By M. E. FRANCIS.

Phil and his Father. By ISMAY THORN.

Prim's Story. By L. E. TIDDEMAN.

Reduced Specimen of the Illustrations.

By Order of Queen Maude: A Story of Home Life. By LOUISA CROW.

The Late Miss Hollingford. By ROSA MULHOLLAND.

Our Frank. By AMY WALTON.

A Terrible Coward. By G. MANVILLE FENN.

Yarns on the Beach. By G. A. HENTY.

Tom Finch's Monkey. By J. C. HUTCHESON.

Miss Grantley's Girls, and the Stories she told them. By THOS. ARCHER.

The Pedlar and his Dog. By MARY C. ROWSELL.

Down and Up Again. By GREGSON GOW.

Madge's Mistake. By ANNIE E. ARMSTRONG.

The Troubles and Triumphs of Little Tim. By GREGSON GOW.

The Happy Lad: A Story of Peasant Life in Norway. By B. BJÖRNSON.

Into the Haven. By ANNIE S. SWAN.

A Box of Stories. Packed for Young Folk by HORACE HAPPYMAN.

The Patriot Martyr, and other Narratives of Female Heroism.

LIBRARY OF FAMOUS BOOKS FOR BOYS AND GIRLS.

In Crown 8vo. Illustrated. Cloth extra, 1s. 6d. each.

Waterton's Wanderings in S. America.
Anson's Voyage Round the World.
Autobiography of Benjamin Franklin.
Lamb's Tales from Shakspeare.
Southey's Life of Nelson.

Miss Mitford's Our Village.
Dana's Two Years before the Mast.
Marryat's Children of the New Forest.
Scott's The Talisman.
The Basket of Flowers.

[Others in preparation.

THE SHILLING SERIES OF JUVENILES.

Square 16mo, Illustrated, and neatly bound in cloth extra.

NEW VOLUMES.

Only a Shilling. By M. CORBET SEYMOUR.
Sparkles. By HARRIET J. SCRIPPS.
Just Like a Girl. By PENELOPE LESLIE.
Daisy and her Friends. By L. E. TIDDEMAN.

Brave Dorette. By JULIA GODDARD.
Piecrust Promises. By W. L. ROOPER.
Summer Fun and Frolic. By ISABELLA PEARSON.
Little Aunt Dorothy. By JENNIE CHAPPELL.
The Lost Dog. By ASCOTT R. HOPE.
The Rambles of Three Children. By GERALDINE MOCKLER.
A Council of Courtiers. By CORA LANGTON.
A Parliament of Pickles. By CORA LANGTON.
Sharp Tommy. By E. J. LYSAGHT.
Adventures of Nell, Eddie, and Toby. By GERALDINE MOCKLER.
Freda's Folly. By M. S. HAYCRAFT.
Philip Danford: A Story of School Life. By JULIA GODDARD.
The Youngest Princess. By JENNIE CHAPPELL.
Arthur's Temptation. By EMMA LESLIE.

A Change for the Worse. By M. HARRIET M. CAPES.
Our Two Starlings. By C. REDFORD.
Mr. Lipscombe's Apples. By JULIA GODDARD.
Gladys. By E. O'BYRNE.
A Gypsy against Her Will. By EMMA LESLIE.
How the Strike Began. Do
The Castle on the Shore. By ISABEL HORNIBROOK.
An Emigrant Boy's Story. By ASCOTT R. HOPE.
Jock and his Friend. By CORA LANGTON.
John a' Dale. By MARY C. ROWSELL.
In the Summer Holidays. By JENNETT HUMPHREYS.
Tales from the Russian of Madame Kabalensky. By G. JENNER.
Cinderella's Cousin. By PENELOPE.
Their New Home. By A. S. FENN.
Janie's Holiday. By C. REDFORD.
A Boy Musician: or, The Young Days of Mozart.
Hatto's Tower. By M. C. ROWSELL.
Fairy Lovebairn's Favourites.
Alf Jetsam. By Mrs. GEO. CUPPLES.
The Redfords. By Mrs. G. CUPPLES.
Missy. By F. BAYFORD HARRISON.
Hidden Seed. By EMMA LESLIE.
Tom Watkin's Mistake. Do.

SHILLING SERIES—Continued.

Ursula's Aunt. By ANNIE S. FENN.
Jack's Two Sovereigns. By ANNIE S. FENN.
A Little Adventurer. By G. GOW.
Olive Mount. By ANNIE S. FENN.
The Children of Haycombe. Do.
Three Little Ones. By C. LANGTON.
Two Little Brothers. By M. HARRIET M. CAPES.
The New Boy at Merriton. By JULIA GODDARD.
The Cruise of the "Petrel". By F. M. HOLMES.

The Wise Princess. By M. HARRIET M. CAPES.
The Blind Boy of Dresden.
Jon of Iceland.
Stories from Shakespeare.
Every Man in his Place.
Fireside Fairies and Fancies.
To the Sea in Ships.
Jack's Victory: Stories about Dogs.
Story of a King.
Prince Alexis: or, Old Russia.
Little Daniel: A Story of the Rhine.
Sasha the Serf: Stories of Russia.
True Stories of Foreign History.

THE NINEPENNY SERIES FOR CHILDREN.

F'cap 8vo, Illustrated, and neatly bound in cloth extra.

NEW VOLUMES.

Toby. By L. E. TIDDEMAN.
He, She, It. By A. DE V. DAWSON.
The Carved Box. By NORLEY CHESTER.
Darby and Joan. By ETHEL PENROSE.

A Little English Gentleman. By JANE DEAKIN.
The Doctor's Lass. By L. E. TIDDEMAN.
Spark and I. By ANNIE ARMSTRONG.
What Hilda Saw. By PENELOPE LESLIE.
Little Miss Masterful. By L. E. TIDDEMAN.
A Sprig of Honeysuckle. By GEORGINA M. SQUIRE.
An Australian Childhood. By ELLEN CAMPBELL.
Kitty Carroll. By L. E. TIDDEMAN.
A Joke for a Picnic. By W. L. ROOPER.
Cross Purposes, and The Shadows. By GEORGE MAC DONALD.
Patty's Ideas. By L. E. TIDDEMAN.
Daphne. By E. O'BYRNE.
Lily and Rose in One. By CECILIA S. LOWNDES.
Crowded Out. By M. B. MANWELL.
Tom in a Tangle. By T. SPARROW.

Things will Take a Turn. By BEATRICE HARRADEN.
Max or Baby. By ISMAY THORN.
The Lost Thimble. By Mrs. MUSGRAVE.
Jack-a-Dandy. By E. J. LYSAGHT.
A Day of Adventures. By CHARLOTTE WYATT.
The Golden Plums. By F. CLARE.
The Queen of Squats. By ISABEL HORNIBROOK.
Little Troublesome. Do.
Shucks. By EMMA LESLIE.
Sylvia Brooke. By M. H. M. CAPES.
The Little Cousin. By A. S. FENN.
In Cloudland. By Mrs. MUSGRAVE.
Jack and the Gypsies. By KATE WOOD.
Hans the Painter. By MARY C. ROWSELL.
Sepperl the Drummer Boy. Do.
Fisherman Grim. Do.
My Lady May: and One Other Story. By HARRIET BOULTWOOD.
A Little Hero. By Mrs. MUSGRAVE.
Prince Jon's Pilgrimage.
Harold's Ambition: or, A Dream of Fame. By JENNIE PERRETT.
Aboard the Mersey. By Mrs. GEORGE CUPPLES.
A Blind Pupil. By ANNIE S. FENN.
Lost and Found. By Mrs. CARL ROTHER.

SOMETHING FOR THE VERY LITTLE ONES.

Illustrated. 64 pp., cloth. 6d. each.

Tales Easy and Small.
Old Dick Grey and Aunt Kate's Way.
Maud's Doll and Her Walk.
In Holiday Time.
Whisk and Buzz.

Little Tales for Little Folk.
By Miss W. L. ROOPER. 2d. each.
FRED'S RUN.
NORA'S DARK LOOK.
ELLA'S FALL.
PATTY'S WALK.
HONEST DOLLY.
LITTLE QUEEN PET.

THE SIXPENNY SERIES FOR CHILDREN.

Neatly bound in cloth extra. Each contains 64 pages and an Illustration.

NEW VOLUMES.
Nobody's Pet. By A. DE V. DAWSON.
Daisy's Visit to Uncle Jack.
Lady Patience. By F. S. HOLLINGS.
Verta and Jaunette. By Mrs. THORP.

Mrs. Holland's Peaches.
Marjory's White Rat.
Grandmother's Forget-me-nots.
From over the Sea.
The Kitchen Cat. By AMY WALTON.
The Royal Eagle. By L. THOMPSON.
Two Little Mice. By Mrs. GARLICK.
A Little Man of War.
Lady Daisy. By CAROLINE STEWART.
Dew. By H. MARY WILSON.
Chris's Old Violin. By J. LOCKHART.
Mischievous Jack. By A. CORKRAN.
The Twins. By L. E. TIDDEMAN.
Pet's Project. By CORA LANGTON.
The Chosen Treat. By C. WYATT.
Little Neighbours. By A. S. FENN.
Jim: A Story of Child Life.
Little Curiosity. By J. M. CALLWELL.
Sara the Wool-gatherer.

Fairy Stories: told by PENELOPE.
A New Year's Tale. By M. A. CURRIE.
Little Mop. By Mrs. CHARLES BRAY.
The Tree Cake, and other Stories.
Nurse Peggy, and Little Dog Trip.
Fanny's King. By DARLEY DALE.
Wild Marsh Marigolds. By D. DALE.
Kitty's Cousin.
Cleared at Last.
Little Dolly Forbes.
A Year with Nellie. By A. S. FENN.
The Little Brown Bird.
The Maid of Domremy.
Little Eric: a Story of Honesty.
Uncle Ben the Whaler
The Palace of Luxury.
The Charcoal Burner.
Willy Black: A Story of Doing Right.
The Horse and his Ways.
The Shoemaker's Present.
Lights to Walk by.
The Little Merchant.
Nicholina: A Story about an Iceberg.

SERIES OF FOURPENNY REWARD BOOKS.

Each 64 pages. 18mo, Illustrated, in Picture Boards.

A Start in Life. By J. LOCKHART.
Happy Childhood.
Dorothy's Clock.
Toddy. By L. E. TIDDEMAN.
Stories about my Dolls.
Stories about my Cat Timothy.
Della's Boots. By W. L. ROOPER.
Climbing the Hill. By ANNIE S. SWAN.
A Year at Coverley. By Do.
Phil Foster. By J. LOCKHART.

Papa's Birthday. By W. L. ROOPER.
The Charm Fairy. By PENELOPE.
Little Tales for Little Children.
Brave and True. By GREGSON GOW.
Johnnie Tupper's Temptation. Do.
Maudie and Bertie.
The Children and the Water-Lily.
By JULIA GODDARD.
Poor Tom Olliver. Do.
Fritz's Experiment.
Lucy's Christmas-Box.

BLACKIE & SON, LIMITED., LONDON, GLASGOW, AND DUBLIN.